Xenophon's Anabasis Book 4

Greek Text with Facing Vocabulary and Commentary

Geoffrey Steadman

Xenophon's *Anabasis* Book 4
Greek Text with Facing Vocabulary and Commentary

The Greek text for the *Anabasis* Book 4 is taken from the Greek edition by E. C. Marchant published by Oxford University Press in 1904.

ISBN-13: 978-0-9991884-7-7

Published by Geoffrey Steadman
Cover Design: David Steadman

Fonts: Times New Roman, GFS Porson, New Athena Unicode

geoffreysteadman@gmail.com

Table of Contents

Preface to the Series

The aim of this commentary is to make Xenophon's *Anabasis* Book 4 as accessible as possible to intermediate-level Greek readers so that they may experience the joy, insight, and lasting influence that comes from reading some of the greatest works in classical antiquity in the original Greek.

Each page of the commentary includes 9-10 lines of Greek text, exactly one-third of a page from E. C. Marchant's 1904 Oxford Classical Text, with all corresponding vocabulary and grammar notes arranged below. The vocabulary includes all words occurring seven or fewer times, organized alphabetically, while the grammatical notes are arranged according to line numbers.The advantage of this format is that it allows me to include as much information as possible on a single page and yet insure that the numerous commentary entries are distinct and readily accessible to readers.

To complement the vocabulary within the commentary, I have added a list of words occurring 8 or more times at the beginning of this book and recommend that readers review this list before they read each section. An alphabetized form of the core list can be found in the glossary. Together, this book has been designed in such a way that, once readers have mastered the core list, they will be able to rely solely on the Greek text and commentary and not need to turn a page or consult dictionaries as they read.

The grammatical notes are designed to help beginning readers read the text, and so I have passed over detailed literary and philosophical explanations in favor of short and concise entries that focus exclusively on grammar and morphology. The notes are intended to complement, not replace, an advanced-level commentary, and so I recommend that readers consult an advanced-level commentary after each reading from this book. Assuming that readers finish elementary Greek with varying levels of ability, I draw attention to subjunctive and optative constructions, identify unusual aorist and perfect forms, and in general explain aspects of the Greek that they should have encountered in first year study but perhaps forgotten. As a rule, I prefer to offer too much assistance rather than too little.

Better Vocabulary-Building Strategies

One of the virtues of this commentary is that it eliminates time-consuming dictionary work. While there are many occasions where a dictionary is absolutely necessary for developing a nuanced reading of the Greek, in most instances any advantage that may come from looking up a word and exploring alternative meanings is outweighed by the time and effort spent in the process. Many continue to defend this practice, but I am convinced that such work has little pedagogical value for intermediate and advanced students and that the time saved by avoiding such drudgery can be better spent reading more Greek, reviewing morphology, memorizing vocabulary, mastering principal parts of verbs, and reading advanced-level commentaries and secondary literature.

As an alternative to dictionary work, this commentary offers two approaches to building knowledge of vocabulary. First, I isolate the words that occur 8 or more times for immediate drilling and memorization. Second, I include the number of occurrences of each Greek word at the end of each definition entry. I encourage readers who have mastered the core vocabulary list to single out, drill and memorize moderately common words (e.g. 4-7 times) as they encounter them in the reading and devote comparatively little attention to words that occur once or twice. Altogether, I am confident that readers who follow this regimen will learn the vocabulary more efficiently and develop fluency more quickly than with traditional methods.

Geoffrey Steadman Ph.D.
geoffreysteadman@gmail.com
www.geoffreysteadman.com

How to Use this Commentary

Research shows that, as we learn how to read in a second language, a combination of reading and direct vocabulary instruction is statistically superior to reading alone. One of the purposes of this book is to encourage active acquisition of vocabulary.

1. Master the list of words occurring 8 or more times as soon as possible.

A. Develop a daily regimen for memorizing vocabulary before you begin reading. Memorize the words in the running list that occur 8 or more times *before* you read the corresponding pages in Greek. When done, single out and memorize words that occur 4 to 7 times as they appear the the corresponding vocabulary.

B. Research shows that you must review words at least 7-9 times before you can commit them to long term memory, and flashcards are efficient at promoting repetition. If cards are not available, copy and paste a list of vocabulary from this pdf onto a site such as Quizlet or Anki, which will convert the list into flashcards.

2. Read actively and make lots of educated guesses

One of the benefits of traditional dictionary work is that it gives readers an interval between the time they encounter a questionable word or form and the time they find the dictionary entry. That span of time often compels readers to make educated guesses and actively seek out understanding of the Greek.

Despite the benefits of corresponding vocabulary lists there is a risk that without that interval of time you will become complacent in your reading habits and treat the Greek as a puzzle to be decoded rather than a language to be learned. *Your challenge, therefore, is to develop the habit of making an educated guess under your breath each time before you consult the commentary.* If you guess correctly, you will reaffirm your understanding of the Greek. If incorrectly, you will become aware of your weaknesses and more capable of correcting them.

3. Reread a passage immediately after you have completed it.

Repeated readings not only help you commit Greek to memory but also promote your ability to read the Greek as Greek. You learned to read in your first language through repeated readings of the same books. Greek is no different. The more comfortable you are with older passages, the more easily you will read new ones.

4. Reread the most recent passage immediately before you begin a new one.

This additional repetition will strengthen your ability to recognize vocabulary, forms, and syntax quickly, bolster your confidence, and most importantly provide you with much-needed context as you begin the next selection in the text.

5. Consult an advanced-level commentary for a more nuanced interpretation

After your initial reading of a passage and as time permits, consult another commentary. Your initial reading will allow you to better understand the advanced commentary, which in turn will provide a more insightful literary analysis than is possible in this volume.

Xenophon's *Anabasis* IV
Core Vocabulary (8 or more times)

The following is an running list of all words that occur eight or more times in Xenophon's *Anabasis* Book IV. The glossary includes an alphabetized list of these same words. The number preceding each dictionary entry is the page number where the word first occurs. The number at the end of each dictionary entry is the number of occurrences of each word in the commentary.

1 ἀλλά: but, yet, 66
1 ἀνα-βαίνω: to go up, climb, mount, 10
1 ἀφ-ικνέομαι: to come, arrive, 14
1 βασιλεύς, ὁ: a king, chief, 10
1 γίγνομαι: to come to be, become, be born, 48
1 δέ: but, and, on the other hand, 377
1 δή: indeed, surely, really, certainly, just, 34
1 διά: through (+gen) on account of (+ acc), 34
1 Ἕλλην, Ἕλληνος, ὁ: Greek, 37
1 ἐν: in, on, among. (+ dat.), 70
1 ἔνθα: here, there, where, 20
1 ἐπεί: when, after, since, because, 41
1 μετά: with (+ gen.); after (+ acc.), 12
1 μέν: on the one hand, 94
1 ὁ, ἡ, τό: the, 1135
1 ὅσος, -η, -ον: as many as; all who or which 21
1 οὐ, οὐκ, οὐχ: not, 57
1 ποιέω: to do, make, create, compose, 29
1 ποταμός, ὁ: river, stream 35
1 πρός: to (acc.), near, in addition to (dat.), 51
1 στράτευμα, τό: army, expedition, 19
1 σύν: along with, with, together (+ gen.), 15
2 ἀκούω: to hear, listen to, 11
2 ἄκρος, -η, -ον: topmost; heights, highpoints, 17
2 ἅμα: at the same time; as soon as, at, along with (+ dat.), 8
2 ἄν (ἥν): modal adv., 25
2 αὐτός, -ή, -ό: -self; he, she, it; the same, 110
2 βούλομαι: to wish, be willing, desire, 13
2 γάρ: for, since, 55
2 δια-βαίνω: to walk or pass over; cross 27
2 δοκέω: to seem (good), think, imagine, 34
2 εἰ: if, whether, 37
2 εἰμί: to be, exist, 200
2 εἰς (ἐς): into, to, in regard to (+ acc.), 48
2 ἔχω: have, possess; be able; be disposed, 64
2 ἥν: if ever, ἐάν, 10
2 Καρδοῦχοι, οἱ: Carduchians, 17
2 κατα-λαμβάνω: to seize, lay hold of, find, 16

2 λέγω (aor. εἶπον):: to say, speak; gather, 39
2 ὄρος, -εος, τό: a mountain, hill, 39
2 ὅτι: that; because, 38
2 οὕτως: in this way, thus, so, 14
2 πολέμιος, -α, -ον: hostile; *subst.* enemy, 54
2 πρίν: until, before, 9
2 στρατηγός, ὁ: general, 20
2 ὑπέρ: above, on behalf of (gen.); over, beyond (acc.), 10
3 ἀμφί: on both sides, 14
3 ἀν-ίστημι: to make stand up, raise; rise, 10
3 ἀπό: from, away from. (+ gen.), 14
3 ἑαυτοῦ, -ῆς, -οῦ: himself, her-, it-, thems-, 15
3 ἕπομαι: to follow, accompany, escort, 9
3 ἡγέομαι: to lead; consider, believe (dat) 12
3 ἡμέρα, ἡ: day, 36
3 λαμβάνω: to take, receive, catch, grasp, 35
3 νύξ, νυκτος, ἡ: a night, 18
3 Ξενοφῶν, -ῶντος, ὁ: Xenophon, 50
3 ὀπισθο-φύλαξ, -ακος, ὁ: rear-guard, 19
3 ὁπλίτης, -ου ὁ: hoplite, armed soldier, 11
3 πᾶς, πᾶσα, πᾶν: every, all, the whole, 28
3 πεδίον, τό: plain, 12
3 πορεύομαι: to travel, journey, march, 62
3 Χειρίσοφος, ὁ: Cheirisophus, 45
4 ἄνω: up, above, 12
4 ἐκ, ἐξ: out of, from (+ gen.), 30
4 ἐπί: near (gen.), to, toward (acc.); near, at, 49
4 ἐπιτήδειος, -η, -ον: necessities; provisions, 18
4 κώμη, ἡ: town, country town, 27
4 οἰκία, ἡ: house, dwelling, building, 12
4 ὄπισθεν: (from) behind; in the future; (+ gen.), 9
4 οὐδ-είς, οὐδε-μία, οὐδ-έν: no one, nothing, 22
4 παῖς, παιδός, ὁ, ἡ: child, boy, girl; slave, 9
4 πολύς, πολλή, πολύ: much, many, 71
4 τις, τι: anyone, anything, someone, something, 45
4 φεύγω: to flee, escape; defend in court, 17
5 ἄλλος, -η, -ο: other, one...another, 8
5 ἄνθρωπος, ὁ: human being, person, 18
5 ἐθέλω (θέλω): to be willing, wish, desire, 8
5 ἤδη: already, now, at this time, 8
5 κατα-βαίνω: to step, come down, 9
5 ὁδός, ἡ: road, way, path, journey, 26
5 οὐδέ: and not, but not, nor, not even, 13
5 στενός, -ή, -όν: narrow, 8
5 φέρω: to carry, bring, convey; fly, 9

5 χώρα, ἡ: land, region, country, 12
5 ὡς: as, thus, so, that; when, since, 59
6 ἀλλήλος, -α, -ον: one another, 15
6 καίω: to kindle, light, 10
6 λίθος, ὁ: a stone, 12
6 λοχαγός, ὁ: captain, 17
6 ὀλίγος -η, -ον: few, little, small, 10
6 πλείων, -οντος: more, greater, 9
6 πῦρ, πυρός,τό: fire, 10
6 ὑπο-ζύγιον, τό: a yoke-animal, ox, 18
7 δεῖ: it is necessary, must, ought (+ inf.), 13
7 κατα-λείπω: to leave behind, abandon, 8
8 ἤ: or (either...or); than, 27
8 κλέπτω: to steal; do or seize secretly, 9
8 μάχομαι: to fight, contend, quarrel, dispute 10
8 πάλιν: again, once more; back, backwards, 12
8 προσ-έρχομαι: to come or go to, approach, 10
8 χωρίον, τό: place, spot, region, 20
8 ὥστε: so that, that, so as to, 14
9 ἀγαθός, -ή, -όν: good, brave, capable, 9
9 ἄγω: to lead, bring, carry, convey, 17
9 ἀνήρ, ἀνδρός, ὁ: a man, 16
9 ἀπο-θνήσκω: to die off, perish, 9
9 ἐνταῦθα: here, hither, there, thither, then, 28
9 ὅμοιος, -η, -ον: resembling, similar to (dat) 21
9 ὁράω (aor. εἶδον): to see, look, behold, 50
9 παρ-έρχομαι: to go pass, enter, 13
9 ταχύς, -εῖα, -ύ: quick, swift, hastily, 11
10 δύναμαι: to be able, can, be capable, 25
10 δύο: two, 8
10 ἐγώ: I, 14
10 εἷς, μία, ἕν: one, single, alone, 8
10 ἔρχομαι: to come or go, 23
10 εὐθύς: right away, straight, directly, at once 16
10 καλός, -ή, -όν: beautiful, fair, noble, fine, 18
10 ὄρθιος, -α, -ον: steep, straight up, sheer, 13
10 ὅς, ἥ, ὅ: who, which, that, 63
10 οὗτος, αὕτη, τοῦτο: this, these, 121
10 σταθμός, ὁ: stage (~5 parasangs, distance covered in one day's journey), 16
10 σύ: you, 15
10 φημί: to say, claim, assert, 28
10 ὥσπερ: as, just as, as if, 9
11 ἡγεμών, ὁ: leader, commander, guide, 15
11 ὅπως: how, in what way; so that, 14
11 οὖν: and so, then; at all events, 18

11 φανερός, -ά, -όν: visible, manifest, evident, 8
12 ἐρωτάω: to ask, inquire, question, 11
13 πελταστής, ὁ: light troop (with light shield) 11
14 κελεύω: to bid, order, command, exhort, 13
16 ἀπ-έρχομαι: to go away, depart, 15
16 πέτρα, ἡ: a rock, a ledge, 9
17 μένω: to stay, remain, 14
18 ἕκαστος, -η, -ον: each, every one, 13
18 κατά: according to, over (acc); down, against (gen), 25
18 πρῶτος, -η, -ον: first, earliest, 14
19 λόφος, ὁ: hill, 9
19 λόχος, ὁ: company, unit of men, 20
19 ὑπό: by, because of, from (gen) under (dat) 13
22 ὅπλον, τό: a tool, implement; arms, 10
23 ἄρχω: to begin; to rule, be leader of, 12
23 περί: around, about, concerning, 7
25 κωλύω: to hinder or prevent, 14
25 ὁπότε: when, by what time, 9
27 αὖ: again, once more; further, moreover, 8
28 ἱππεύς, ὁ: a horseman, cavalry, 10
28 στάδιον, τό: a stade, (pl. at times στάδιοι), 9
29 τρεῖς, τρία: three, 11
30 μέγας, μεγάλη, μέγα: big, great, important, 8
32 τίς, τί: who? which?, 36
35 ἐπειδή: when, since, after, 15
36 ἐκεῖνος, -η, -ον: that, those, 10
36 θέω: to run, 14
36 στρατιώτης, -ου, ὁ: soldier, 16
39 φάλαξ, φάλαγγος, ὁ: phalanx, 11
40 ἔνθεν: from there, on one side; from where, 8
43 παρασάγγης, ὁ: parasang (5.7 or 5.3 km), 15
44 ἐντεῦθεν: from here, from there, 18
44 ἵππος, ὁ: a horse, 11
46 στρατόπεδον τό: camp, encampment; army 8
46 χιών, -όνος, ἡ: snow, 18
49 δίδωμι: to give, offer, grant, provide, 12
57 κώμ-αρχος, ὁ: leader of a town, 11
64 βοῦς, ὁ, ἡ: ox, bull, cow; cattle, 9

Abbreviations

abs.	absolute	impf.	imperfect	pl.	plural
acc.	accusative	impers.	impersonal	plpf.	pluperfect
act.	active	ind.	indicative	pred.	predicate
adj.	adjective	ind.	indirect	prep.	preposition
adv.	adverb	inf.	infinitive	pres.	present
aor.	aorist	m.	masculine	reflex.	reflexive
dat.	dative	mid.	middle	rel.	relative
dep.	deponent	neut.	neuter	S1517	Smyth §1517
dir.	direct	nom.	nominative	seq.	sequence
disc.	discourse	obj.	object	sg.	singular
f.	feminine	opt.	optative	subj.	subject,
fut.	future	pple.	participle	subj.	subjunctive
gen.	genitive	pass.	passive	superl.	superlative
imper.	imperative	pf.	perfect	voc.	vocative

1s, 2s, 3s denote 1st, 2nd, and 3rd singular.   1p, 2p, 3p denote 1st, 2nd, and 3rd plural.

The English titles found in the headings throughout the text are added for the benefit of the reader and are not found in the original Greek text. I took the titles directly from Goodwin and White's 1896 edition of *The First Four Books of Xenophon's Anabasis.*

To make the ancients speak, we must feed them with our own blood.

-von Wilamowitz-Moellendorff

ΚΥΡΟΥ ΑΝΑΒΑΣΕΩΣ Δ

[ὅσα μὲν δὴ ἐν τῇ ἀναβάσει ἐγένετο μέχρι τῆς μάχης, καὶ ὅσα μετὰ τὴν μάχην ἐν ταῖς σπονδαῖς ἃς βασιλεὺς καὶ οἱ σὺν Κύρῳ ἀναβάντες Ἕλληνες ἐποιήσαντο, καὶ ὅσα παραβάντος τὰς σπονδὰς βασιλέως καὶ Τισσαφέρνους ἐπολεμήθη πρὸς τοὺς Ἕλληνας ἐπακολουθοῦντος τοῦ Περσικοῦ στρατεύματος, ἐν τῷ πρόσθεν λόγῳ δεδήλωται. 2. ἐπεὶ δὲ ἀφίκοντο ἔνθα ὁ μὲν Τίγρης ποταμὸς παντάπασιν ἄπορος ἦν διὰ τὸ βάθος καὶ μέγεθος, πάροδος δὲ οὐκ ἦν, ἀλλὰ τὰ Καρδούχεια

ἀνά-βασις, -εως, ἡ: going up, ascent, 3
ἄ-πορος, -ον: impassable; without means, 1
βάθος, τό: depth, 3
δηλόω: to make clear, show, reveal, 1
ἐπ-ακολουθέω: to follow after, pursue, 1
Καρδούχειος, -α, -ον: Carduchian, 2
Κῦρος, ὁ: Cyrus, 1
λόγος, ὁ: word, speech,a account, argument 2
μάχη, ἡ: battle, fight, combat, 2
μέγεθος, τό: size, magnitude, 1
μέχρι: up to; until, as long as (+ gen.), 5
παντά-πασι: all in all, altogether, entirely, 3
παρα-βαίνω: to go pass; transgress, 1
πάρ-οδος, ὁ: passage, entrance, approach, 4
Περσικός, -ή, -όν: Persian, 4
πολεμέω: wage war, make war, (+ dat.), 2
πρόσθεν: before, 3
σπονδή, ἡ: a drink-offering; truce, treaty, 5
Τίγρης, Τίγρητος, ὁ: Tigris river, 4
Τισσαφέρνης, ὁ: Tissaphernes, 2

1 [...]: The brackets indicate that the editor believes that these lines (sections 1-4) were interpolated (inserted) at a later time and were not Xenophon's own words.
ὅσα...ὅσα...ὅσα: *as many things as...*; the missing neuter pl. antecedent is subject of δεδήλωται in line 6
μὲν δή: *indeed*; 'certainly,' expressing certainty, especially in conclusions or, as here, in a summary (S2900)
ἐγένετο: *occurred, happened*; 3s with neuter pl. subject; aor. γίγνομαι
2 **ἃς...ἐποιήσαντο**: *which...*; relative clause
3 **οἱ σὺν Κύρῳ...Ἕλληνες**: *the Greeks...*; aor. pple. ἀναβαίνω, i.e. those who fought alongside Cyrus against the King in Bk. 1
ὅσα...ἐπολεμήθη: *as many (acts)...*; neuter pl. subject and 3s aor. pass. **Πολεμέω**, 'commit in war'
4 **παραβάντος...βασιλέως καὶ Τισσαφέρνους**: gen. abs., the aor. pple. is sg. but logically modifies both men, who are on the same side of the truce; Τισσαφέρνε-ος is 3rd decl. gen. sg.
5 **πρὸς**: *against...*
ἐπακολουθοῦντος...στρατευματος: gen. abs.
6 **τῷ λόγῳ**: i.e. account or narrative
δεδήλωται: 3s pf. pass., the missing neut. pl. Antecedent of the ὅσα relative clauses above is the subject
ἀφίκοντο: aor. mid. ἀφικνέομαι
ἔνθα: *(to the place) where...*; relative clause
7 **ἦν**: impf. 3s εἰμί
διὰ...: *on account of...*: as often + acc.
πάροδος: i.e. a path alongside the river

ὄρη ἀπότομα ὑπὲρ αὐτοῦ τοῦ ποταμοῦ ἐκρέματο, ἐδόκει δὴ τοῖς στρατηγοῖς διὰ τῶν ὀρέων πορευτέον εἶναι. 3. *ἤκουον γὰρ* 10
τῶν ἁλισκομένων ὅτι εἰ διέλθοιεν τὰ Καρδούχεια ὄρη, ἐν τῇ Ἀρμενίᾳ τὰς πηγὰς τοῦ Τίγρητος ποταμοῦ, ἢν μὲν βούλωνται, διαβήσονται, ἢν δὲ μὴ βούλωνται, περιίασι. καὶ τοῦ Εὐφράτου δὲ τὰς πηγὰς ἐλέγετο οὐ πρόσω τοῦ Τίγρητος εἶναι, καὶ ἔστιν οὕτως ἔχον. 4. *τὴν δ' εἰς τοὺς Καρδούχους ἐμβολὴν* 15
ὧδε ποιοῦνται, ἅμα μὲν λαθεῖν πειρώμενοι, ἅμα δὲ φθάσαι πρὶν τοὺς πολεμίους καταλαβεῖν τὰ ἄκρα.]

ἁλίσκομαι: to be taken, seized, 6
ἀπό-τομος, -ον: cut off; sheer; severe, 2
Ἀρμενία, ἡ: Armenia, 6
δι-έρχομαι: to go through, pass, 7
ἐμ-βολή, ἡ: attack, assault, invasion, 1
Εὐφρήτης, ὁ: Euphrates, 2
Καρδούχειος, -α, -ον: Carduchian, 2
κρεμάννυμι: to hang, suspend, 1
λανθάνω: to escape notice; forget, 5
πειράω: to try, attempt, endeavor, 7
περι-έρχομαι: to go around, go about, 4
πηγή, ἡ: spring (of a river), source, 4
πορευτέος, -ον: to be travelled, 2
πρόσω: forwards into, far from +gen 4
Τίγρης, Τίγρητος, ὁ: Tigris river, 4
φθάνω: to act first, act beforehand, 3
ὧδε: in this way, so, thus, 2

9 **ὄρη**: ὄρε-α, neuter pl. ὄρος
αὐτοῦ: intensive pronoun
ἐκρέματο: impf. mid. κρεμάννυμι, (stem: κρεμ-)
ἐδόκει: *it...*; impersonal
δὴ: *therefore, then*; inferential
10 **ὀρέων**: gen. pl. ὄρος
πορευτέον εἶναι: *that (they) must...*; 'that it is to... (by them)' ind. disc., impersonal verbal adj. + inf. εἰμί expressing necessity; as often, you may translate in the active
11 **τῶν ἁλισκομένων**: *from those...*; gen. of source; pres. mid. pple
ὅτι εἰ διέλθοιεν...διαβήσονται...περιίασι: *that if ...;* .) 3p aor. opt. δι-έρχομαι and fut. ind. διαβαίνω, περιέρχομαι in a fut. more vivid condition (ἐὰν + subj., fut.) where the protasis is in secondary seq. (the opt. replaces ἐὰν δίέλωμεν) and the apodosis remains in primary seq.
12 **ἢν μὲν...ἢν δὲ...**: *if on the one hand...if on the other hand...*; ἐὰν, + pres. subj. βούλομαι; these are two minor protases within the larger fut. more vivid condition
13 **διαβήσονται**: fut. dep. διαβαίνω
περιίασι: 3p fut. περι-έρχομαι
καὶ...δὲ: *and also...*; καί is adverbial
14 **ἐλέγετο**: *it...*; impersonal impf. pass. governing ind. disc. with inf. εἰμί
15 **καὶ ἔστιν οὕτως ἔχον**: *and it is just so*; parenthetical; 'and it is being disposed thus,' neut. pple as pred.; ἔχω ('holds' or 'is disposed') + adv. is often equiv. to 'to be' + adj.
16 **εἰς**: *against...*; or 'into (the land of)...'
ὧδε: i.e. in the following way
ἅμα μὲν...ἅμα δὲ...: *both...and...*; 'at the same time...and the same time...'
λαθεῖν: aor. inf. governed by pple
16 **φθάσαι**: aor. inf. φθάνω also governed by πειρώμενοι
17 **πρὶν**: *before...*; as often with acc. + inf.

5. ἡνίκα δ' ἦν ἀμφὶ τὴν τελευταίαν φυλακὴν καὶ ἐλείπετο τῆς νυκτὸς ὅσον σκοταίους διελθεῖν τὸ πεδίον, τηνικαῦτα ἀναστάντες ἀπὸ παραγγέλσεως πορευόμενοι ἀφικνοῦνται ἅμα 20
τῇ ἡμέρᾳ πρὸς τὸ ὄρος. 6. ἔνθα δὴ Χειρίσοφος μὲν ἡγεῖτο τοῦ στρατεύματος λαβὼν τὸ ἀμφ' αὑτὸν καὶ τοὺς γυμνῆτας πάντας, Ξενοφῶν δὲ σὺν τοῖς ὀπισθοφύλαξιν ὁπλίταις εἵπετο

γυμνήτης, -ου, ὁ: light-armed soldier 6
δι-έρχομαι: to go through, pass, 7
ἡνίκα: at which time, when, since, 1
λείπω: to leave, forsake, abandon, 6
παραγγέλσις -εως ἡ: the giving of orders 1
σκοταῖος, -α, -ον: in the dark; dark, 2
τελευταίος, -α, -ον: last, final, 6
τηνικαῦτα: at that time, then, 2
φυλακή, ἡ: a watch, guard, 4

18 **ἦν**: *it...*; 3s impf. εἰμί
φυλακὴν: *night-watch*; a period of time: the night was divided into three or four periods in which soldiers took turns standing watch of the camp
ἐλείπετο: *there was...*; impf. pass.
(τοσοῦτον) τῆσ νυκτὸς: *(so much) of the night*; partitive gen.; the missing τοσοῦτον is the logical subject of ἐλείπετο
19 **ὅσον...διελθεῖν**: *as much as to...*; i.e. 'enough to...' ὅσος + aor. inf. διέρχομαι
20 **ἀναστάντες**: aor. pple ἀν-ίστημι
ἀπὸ...: i.e. as a result of...; gen. source
ἅμα: + dat.; here as a preposition rather than an adverb
21 **ἔνθα δὴ**: *precisely here, exactly here*; δή is intensive
21 **ἡγεῖτο**: impf. ἡγέομαι, the verb governs a gen. when it means 'to be a leader'
22 **λαβὼν**: aor. pple. λαμβάνω
τὸ ἀμφ(ὶ) (ἑ)αυτὸν (στράτευμα): *that around...*; prepositional phrase with reflexive pronoun (αὑτὸν = ἑαυτὸν) in the attributive position; i.e. those he commands
23 **Ξενοφῶν**: note that Xenophon, the author, talks about himself in the 3rd person
εἵπετο: impf. ἕπομαι

Historical Present

Xenophon frequently employs the present and aorist where English readers expect the simple past and pluperfect. Some readers may wish to preserve the vividness of the Greek, but others will translate present verbs, as γίγνονται above, in the simple past and aorists as pluperfects.

οὐδένα ἔχων γυμνῆτα· οὐδεὶς γὰρ κίνδυνος ἐδόκει εἶναι μή 1
τις ἄνω πορευομένων ἐκ τοῦ ὄπισθεν ἐπίσποιτο. 7. *καὶ ἐπὶ*
μὲν τὸ ἄκρον ἀναβαίνει Χειρίσοφος πρίν τινας αἰσθέσθαι
τῶν πολεμίων· ἔπειτα δ' ὑφηγεῖτο· ἐφείπετο δὲ ἀεὶ τὸ
ὑπερβάλλον τοῦ στρατεύματος εἰς τὰς κώμας τὰς ἐν τοῖς 5
ἄγκεσί τε καὶ μυχοῖς τῶν ὀρέων. 8. *ἔνθα δὴ οἱ μὲν Καρδοῦχοι*
ἐκλιπόντες τὰς οἰκίας ἔχοντες καὶ γυναῖκας καὶ παῖδας ἔφευγον
ἐπὶ τὰ ὄρη. τὰ δὲ ἐπιτήδεια πολλὰ ἦν λαμβάνειν, ἦσαν δὲ
καὶ χαλκώμασι παμπόλλοις κατεσκευασμέναι αἱ οἰκίαι, ὧν 9

ἄγκος, -εος, τό: bend, hollow; glen, 1
ἀεί: always, forever, in every case, 6
αἰσθάνομαι: perceive, feel, learn, realize, 4
γυμνήτης, -ου, ὁ: light-armed soldier 6
γυνή, γυναικός, ἡ: a woman, wife, 7
ἐκ-λείπω: to leave, forsake, abandon, 3
ἔπ-ειτα: then, next, secondly, 4
ἐφ-έπομαι: to follow after, pursue, 4
κατα-σκευάζω: to equip, furnish; prepare, 1
κίνδυνος, ὁ: risk, danger, venture, 2
μύχος, ὁ: recess, nook, corner, 1
παμ-πολύς, -πολλή, -πολύ: very many, 2
ὑπερ-βάλλω: to overshoot, surpass, exceed 5
ὑφ-ηγέομαι: to guide, lead the way, 1
χάλκωμα, -ατος, τό: of bronze, 1

1 **εἶναι**: inf. εἰμί
μή...ἐπίσποιτο: *that...*; or 'lest,' fearing clause following κίνδυνος; opt. replaces subj. in secondary seq.; aor. opt. ἐφ-έπομαι
2 **ἄνω πορευομένων**: *while (they)...*; gen. abs. with a missing gen. noun (i.e. the Greeks); ἄνω indicates movement uphill
τοῦ ὄπισθεν: *the rear*
ἐπὶ: *onto...*
3 **πρὶν...αἰσθέσθαι**: *before...*; + aor. inf.; Cheirisophus and his troops are the object
τινας...τῶν πολεμίων: acc. subject
4 **ἐφείπετο**: impf. mid. ἐφ-έπομαι
ἀεί: *in every case*; i.e. in succession
τὸ ὑπερβάλλον: *the part passing over (the hilltop)*; i.e. each division of the army; neuter pres. pple. as subject
5 **στρατεύματος**: partitive gen.
τὰς ἐν...ὀρέων: all in the attributive position modifying κώμας
6 **ἔνθα δὴ**: *exactly then, just then*; intensive
7 **ἐκλιπόντες**: aor. pple. ἐκλείπω
ἔχοντες: modifies Καρδοῦχοι
καὶ...καὶ: *both...and*
ἔφευγον: *began to...*; inchoative impf.
8 **ὄρη**: ὄρε-α; acc. pl. ὄρος place to which
τὰ...ἐπιτήδεια: *in respect to provisions*; or 'as for...' acc. respect; πολλὰ is not an attributive adj. but neut. pl. obj. of inf.
ἦν: *it was possible*; + inf., 3s impf. εἰμί
7 **ἦσαν...κατεσκευασμέναι**: periphrastic plpf. pass. (impf. εἰμί + pf. pple.. κατασκευάζω)
9 **καὶ**: *also*
χαλκώμασι παμπόλλοις: dat. of means, i.e. bronze vessels
ὧν: gen. pl. relative, the antecedent is χαλκώμασι

οὐδὲν ἔφερον οἱ Ἕλληνες, οὐδὲ τοὺς ἀνθρώπους ἐδίωκον, 10
ὑποφειδόμενοι, εἴ πως ἐθελήσειαν οἱ Καρδοῦχοι διιέναι
αὐτοὺς ὡς διὰ φιλίας τῆς χώρας, ἐπείπερ βασιλεῖ πολέμιοι
ἦσαν· 9. τὰ μέντοι ἐπιτήδεια ὅτῳ τις ἐπιτυγχάνοι ἐλάμβανεν·
ἀνάγκη γὰρ ἦν. οἱ δὲ Καρδοῦχοι οὔτε καλούντων ὑπήκουον
οὔτε ἄλλο φιλικὸν οὐδὲν ἐποίουν. 10. ἐπεὶ δὲ οἱ τελευταῖοι τῶν 15
Ἑλλήνων κατέβαινον εἰς τὰς κώμας ἀπὸ τοῦ ἄκρου ἤδη
σκοταῖοι (διὰ γὰρ τὸ στενὴν εἶναι τὴν ὁδὸν ὅλην τὴν ἡμέραν
ἡ ἀνάβασις αὐτοῖς ἐγένετο καὶ κατάβασις), τότε δὴ συλλε-

ἀνά-βασις, -εως, ἡ: going up, ascent, 3
ἀνάγκη, ἡ: necessity, force, 4
δι-έρχομαι: to go through, pass, 7
διώκω: to pursue, follow; prosecute, 3
ἐπεί-περ: the very time when, when; since, 1
ἐπι-τυγχάνω: to chance upon, encounter, 1
καλέω: to call, summon, invite, 3
κατά-βασις, -εως, ἡ: going down, descent, 3
μέντοι: however, nevertheless; certainly, 6
ὅλος, -η, -ον: whole, entire, complete, 5
ὅστις, ἥτις, ὅ τι: whoever, which-, whatever, 4
οὔ-τε: and not, neither...nor, 6
πως: somehow, in any way, 4
σκοταῖος, -α, -ον: in the dark; dark, 2
συλ-λέγω: to collect, gather, 5
τελευταίος, -α, -ον: last, final, 6
τότε: then, at that time, 7
ὑπ-ακούω: to heed, listen to, hear, 1
ὑπο-φείδομαι: to spare a little, 1
φιλίος, -α, -ον: friendly, allied, 1
φιλικός, -ή, -όν: friendly, 1

11 **ὑποφειδόμενοι**: i.e. showing restraint or being merciful toward the ἀνθρώπους
εἴ πως ἐθελήσειαν: *if...should...*; i.e. 'in the hope that/on the chance that...' 3p aor. opt. expressing the motive of the apodosis (S2354)
12 **αὐτοὺς**: i.e. Greeks; acc. subject of inf.
ὡς δία φιλίας: *as if on account of...*; clause of comparison with acc. pl. of the noun φιλία, 'friendship'
τῆς χώρας: gen. obj. of διιέναι
βασιλεῖ: special dat. with πολέμιοι
13 **ἦσαν**: 3p impf. εἰμί
ὅτῳ: *whatever ...*; neut. dat. sg. ὅστις, dat. of compound verb; the antecedent is the neuter plural ἐπιτήδεια
ἐπιτυγχάνοι: opt. of a general relative clause in secondary seq.
ἐλάμβανεν: add στράτευμα as subject
14 **ἦν**: *it...*; 3s impf. εἰμί
(αὐτῶν) καλούντων: *(them when)...*; pres. pple and gen. of source or with ὑπήκουον
15 **οὐδὲν**: *any*; positive after οὔτε
17 **διὰ**: *on account of...*; + acc.
τὸ...εἶναι: *...being...*; articular inf. εἰμί as object of διὰ; ὁδὸν is acc. subject
ὅλην...ἡμέραν: *over the...*; acc. of duration
18 **ἐγένετο**: aor. γίγνομαι with plural subject
τότε δὴ: *just then, exactly then*; intensive
συλλεγέντες: nom. pl. aor. pass. pple συλλέγω

γέντες τινὲς τῶν Καρδούχων τοῖς τελευταίοις ἐπετίθεντο, καὶ ἀπέκτεινάν τινας καὶ λίθοις καὶ τοξεύμασι κατέτρωσαν, 20 *ὀλίγοι ὄντες· ἐξ ἀπροσδοκήτου γὰρ αὐτοῖς ἐπέπεσε τὸ Ἑλληνικόν.* 11. *εἰ μέντοι τότε πλείους συνελέγησαν, ἐκινδύνευσεν ἂν διαφθαρῆναι πολὺ τοῦ στρατεύματος. καὶ ταύτην μὲν τὴν νύκτα οὕτως ἐν ταῖς κώμαις ηὐλίσθησαν· οἱ δὲ Καρδοῦχοι πυρὰ πολλὰ ἔκαιον κύκλῳ ἐπὶ τῶν ὀρέων καὶ συνεώρων* 25 *ἀλλήλους.* 12. *ἅμα δὲ τῇ ἡμέρᾳ συνελθοῦσι τοῖς στρατηγοῖς καὶ λοχαγοῖς τῶν Ἑλλήνων ἔδοξε τῶν τε ὑποζυγίων τὰ*

ἀπο-κτείνω: to kill, slay, 4
ἀ-προσδοκήτος, -ον: unexpected, unaware, 1
αὐλίζομαι: to bivouac, encamp, lodge, 5
δια-φθείρω: to destroy utterly, kill, ruin, 1
Ἑλληνικός, -ή, -όν: Greek, Hellenic, 3
ἐπι-πίπτω: to fall upon, attack, 3
ἐπι-τίθημι: to put upon; add; set upon, attack 4
κατα-τιτρώσκω: to wound severely, 1
κινδυνεύω: to (run the) risk; is likely 1
κύκλος, ὁ: a circle, round, ring, 4
μέντοι: however, nevertheless; certainly, 6
συν-έρχομαι: come together, meet in battle 3
συν-οράω: see at the same time or together, 1
τελευταίος, -α, -ον: last, final, 6
τόξευμα, -ατος, τό: arrow, 4
τότε: then, at that time, 7

19 **τινὲς**: nom. pl. τις
τελευταίοις: *on…*; i.e. the Greeks; dat. of compound verb
ἐπετίθεντο: impf. mid.
ἀπέκτεινάν: 3p aor.
20 **καὶ...καὶ**: *both...and...*
λίθοις, τοξεύμασι: *with…*; dat. pl. of means
κατέτρωσαν: aor.
21 **ὄντες**: *(although)…*; pple εἰμί is concessive in sense
ἐξ ἀπροσδοκήτου: *on the sudden*; an idiom
αὐτοῖς: *upon…*; dat. of compound
ἐπέπεσε: aor. ἐπι-πίπτω
τὸ Ἑλληνικόν (στράτευμα)
22 **εἰ...συνελέγησαν, ἐκινδύνευσεν ἂν**: *if they had..., would have ...*; contrary-to-fact condition (εἰ aor. ind., ἄν + aor. ind.)
πλείους: πλείο(ν)ες; comparative
23 **διαφθαρῆναι**: aor. pass. inf.
πολὺ: *a majority…*; nom. subject
ταύτην...νύκτα: acc. of duration
24 **ηὐλίσθησαν**: 3p aor. pass. dep., αὐλίζομαι
25 **πυρὰ**: *watch-fires*; neuter acc. pl.
κύκλῳ: *in…*; dat. of manner
συνεώρων: συνεώρά-ον, 3p impf.
26 **συνελθοῦσι**: dat. pl. aor. pple
27 **ἔδοξε**: *it seemed (best)*
τῶν ὑποζυγίων: partitive gen. with the following neut. pl.

ἀναγκαῖα καὶ δυνατώτατα ἔχοντας πορεύεσθαι, καταλιπόντας 1
τἆλλα, καὶ ὅσα ἦν νεωστὶ αἰχμάλωτα ἀνδράποδα ἐν τῇ
στρατιᾷ πάντα ἀφεῖναι. 13. σχολαίαν γὰρ ἐποίουν τὴν πορείαν
πολλὰ ὄντα τὰ ὑποζύγια καὶ τὰ αἰχμάλωτα, πολλοὶ δὲ οἱ ἐπὶ
τούτοις ὄντες ἀπόμαχοι ἦσαν, διπλάσιά τε ἐπιτήδεια ἔδει 5
πορίζεσθαι καὶ φέρεσθαι πολλῶν τῶν ἀνθρώπων ὄντων.
δόξαν δὲ ταῦτα ἐκήρυξαν οὕτω ποιεῖν.

14. ἐπεὶ δὲ ἀριστήσαντες ἐπορεύοντο, ὑποστήσαντες ἐν τῷ
στενῷ οἱ στρατηγοί, εἴ τι εὑρίσκοιεν τῶν εἰρημένων μὴ ἀφει- 9

αἰχμ-άλωτος, -ον: taken by spear, captive, 4
ἀναγκαῖος, -η, -ον: indispensible, necessary 2
ἀνδρά-ποδον, τό: captive, captive-slave, 2
ἀπό-μαχος, -ον: unfit to fight, 1
ἀριστάω: to take breakfast, take a meal, 6
ἀφ-αιρέω: to take away from, remove, 2
ἀφ-ίημι: send away, let go, release; give up, 4
δι-πλάσιος, -α, -ον: two-fold, double, 1
δόξα, ἡ: judgment, decision, opinion, 1
δυνατός, -ή, -όν: capable, strong, possible, 3
εὑρίσκω: to find, discover, devise, invent, 4
κηρύσσω: to proclaim, make public, 1
νεωστί: lately, just now, 1
πορεία, ἡ: march, journey, way, 5
πορίζω: to provide, furnish, carry, 1
στρατία, ἡ: an army, expedition, land force, 4
σχολαῖος, -η, -ον: leisurely, at leisure, 1
ὑφ-ίστημι: to station secretly; make stand, 4

1 **δυνατώτατα**: superlative; neut. pl. because ὑποζυγίων is neut. pl.
καταλιπόντας: aor. pple καταλείπω
2 **τ(ὰ) ἄλλα**: *the rest*; 'other (things)'
ὅσα...: *as many as...*; the antecedent is πάντα
3 **ἦν**: 3s impf. with neuter pl. subject
ἀφεῖναι: aor. inf. still governed by ἔδοξε
4 **ὄντα**: pple εἰμί
οἱ...ὄντες: *those...*; pple as substantive
ἐπὶ τούτοις: *over...*; i.e. in charge of...
ἦσαν: 3p impf. εἰμί
5 **ἔδει**: impersonal impf. δεῖ
6 **φέρεσθαι**: pres. mid. inf.
πολλῶν...ὄντων: (*since*)...; gen. abs. is causal in sense, εἰμί
7 **δόξαν ταῦτα**: *these things seeming (best)*; an acc. abs.; aor. pple δοκέω is neut. sg. modifying, as often, a neut. pl. noun; equiv. to ταῦτα ἔδοξε
8 **ὑποστήσαντες**: *stationing (men) secretly*; or 'making (men) stop secretly,' aor. pple. ὑφ-ίστημι;
9 **εἴ...εὑρίσκοιεν...ἀφῃροῦντο**: *if they found, they..*; past general condition (εἰ opt., impf. ind.); impf. ἀφ-αιρέω; the generals are performing a surprise inspection and removing contraband taken by soldiers
τῶν εἰρημένων: *of the things...*; pf. pass. pple λέγω (ἐρ-)
μὴ ἀφειμενον: *not...*; pf. pass. pple pple ἀφ-ίημι modifying indefinite neut. sg. τι; conditionals govern μή instead of οὐ

μένον, ἀφῃροῦντο, οἱ δ' ἐπείθοντο, πλὴν εἴ τις ἔκλεψεν, οἷον 10
ἢ παιδὸς ἐπιθυμήσας ἢ γυναικὸς τῶν εὐπρεπῶν. καὶ ταύτην
μὲν τὴν ἡμέραν οὕτως ἐπορεύθησαν, τὰ μέν τι μαχόμενοι τὰ
δὲ καὶ ἀναπαυόμενοι. 15. *εἰς δὲ τὴν ὑστεραίαν γίγνεται χειμὼν*
πολύς, ἀναγκαῖον δ' ἦν πορεύεσθαι· οὐ γὰρ ἦν ἱκανὰ τἀπι-
τήδεια. καὶ ἡγεῖτο μὲν Χειρίσοφος, ὠπισθοφυλάκει δὲ 15
Ξενοφῶν. 16. *καὶ οἱ πολέμιοι ἰσχυρῶς ἐπετίθεντο, καὶ στενῶν*
ὄντων τῶν χωρίων ἐγγὺς προσιόντες ἐτόξευον καὶ ἐσφεν-
δόνων· ὥστε ἠναγκάζοντο οἱ Ἕλληνες ἐπιδιώκοντες καὶ πάλιν

ἀνα-παύω: to stop, make cease; *mid.*, rest, 4
ἀναγκάζω: to force, compel, require, 2
ἀναγκαῖος, -η, -ον: indispensible necessary, 2
ἀφ-αιρέω: to take away from, remove, 2
γυνή, γυναικός, ἡ: a woman, wife, 7
ἐγγύς: near (+ gen.); adv. nearby, 7
ἐπι-δίωκω: to pursue after, 2
ἐπι-θυμέω: to desire, long for (gen), 1
ἐπι-τίθημι: to put upon; add; set upon, attack 4
εὐ-πρεπής, -ές: good-looking, decent, 1
ἱκανός, -ή, -όν: enough, sufficient; capable 4
οἷος, -α, -ον: of what sort, as, 5
ὀπισθο-φύλακέω: to guard the rear, 3
πείθω: to persuade, trust; *mid.* obey, 1
πλήν: except, but (+ gen.), 2
σφενδονάω: to use the sling, 4
τοξεύω: to shoot with the bow, 7
ὑστεραῖος, -α, -ον: the next day; later, 5
χειμών, -ῶνος τό: storm, winter, 1

10 **οἱ δ'**: *and they...*; i.e. the soldiers
ἔκλεψει: aor. κλέπτω
οἷον: *for example*; ' in respect to which,' a common acc. of respect
11 **ἢ...ἢ**: *either...or*
παιδὸς...γυναικὸς: i.e. live captives stolen away by individual soldiers; gen. object of the pple but one would logically expect accusatives following ἔκλεψεν
τῶν εὐπρεπῶν: partitive gen.
12 **ταύτην...ἡμέραν**: acc. of duration
ἐπορεύθησαν: 3p aor. dep. pass.: translate as active
τὰ μέν...τὰ μέν: *now...now...*; or 'some times...at other times;' lit. 'in respect to these (circumstances)...in respect to those (circumstances);' acc. of respect emphasizing the μέν...δέ contrast
τι: *some fighting*; inner acc.
13 **εἰς...ὑστεραίαν (ἡμέραν)**: *during...*
14 **ἦν**: *it was*
τ(ὰ) ἐπιτήδεια: a substantive
16 **ἐπετίθεντο**: impf. mid. ἐπιτίθημι
στενῶν...χωρίων: gen. abs., εἰμί
17 **προσιόντες**: pple προσ-έρχομαι
ἐσφενδόνων: 3p impf. α-contract verb
18 **ἠναγκάζοντο**: Assume Xenophon and the rear guard as subject; impf. pass.

ἀναχάζοντες σχολῇ πορεύεσθαι· καὶ θαμινὰ παρήγγελλεν ὁ Ξενοφῶν ὑπομένειν, 17. ὅτε οἱ πολέμιοι ἰσχυρῶς ἐπικέοιντο. 20
ἐνταῦθα ὁ Χειρίσοφος ἄλλοτε μὲν ὅτε παρεγγυῷτο ὑπέμενε, τότε δὲ οὐχ ὑπέμενεν, ἀλλ᾽ ἦγε ταχέως καὶ παρηγγύα ἕπεσθαι, ὥστε δῆλον ἦν ὅτι πρᾶγμά τι εἴη· σχολὴ δ᾽ οὐκ ἦν ἰδεῖν παρελθόντι τὸ αἴτιον τῆς σπουδῆς· ὥστε ἡ πορεία ὁμοία φυγῇ ἐγίγνετο τοῖς ὀπισθοφύλαξι. 18. καὶ ἐνταῦθα ἀποθνῄσκει 25
ἀνὴρ ἀγαθὸς Λακωνικὸς Λεώνυμος τοξευθεὶς διὰ τῆς ἀσπίδος καὶ τῆς σπολάδος εἰς τὰς πλευράς, καὶ Βασίας Ἀρκὰς

αἴτιος, -α, -ον: responsible, blameworthy, 1
ἄλλο-τε: at some time, 1
ἀνα-χάζω: to draw back, recoil, 2
Ἀρκάς, Ἀρκάδος, ὁ: Arcadian, of Arcadia, 5
ἀσπίς, ἀσπίδος, ὁ: a round shield, 6
βασίας, ὁ: Basias (person), 1
δῆλος, -η, -ον: clear, evident, conspicuous, 2
ἐπί-κειμαι: set upon; press upon, attack, 3
θαμινός, -ή, -όν: crowded, close-set, 1
ἰσχυρός, -ά, -όν: strong, powerful; severe, 7
Λακωνικός, -ή, -όν: Laconian, of Laconia, 2
Λεώνυμος, ὁ: Leonymus, 1
ὅτε: when, at some time, 3
παρ-αγγέλλω: to pass word along, order 7
παρ-εγγυάω: to pass on word or command 5
πλευρά, ἡ: a rib, side, 2
πορεία, ἡ: march, journey, way, 5
πρᾶγμα, τό: deed; matter, affair, trouble, 3
σπολάς, σπολάδος, ἡ: leather garment, 1
σπουδή, ἡ: haste, speed, eagerness, 1
σχολή, ἡ: spare time, leisure, rest, 3
τοξεύω: to shoot with the bow, 7
τότε: then, at that time, 7
ὑπο-μένω: to remain, abide, wait up, await, 7
φυγή, ἡ: flight, escape, exile, 3

19 **σχολῇ**: *in a leisurely manner*; i.e. at a slower pace than desired; dat. manner
θαμινὰ: adverbial acc.: translate as an adv.
παρήγγελλεν: *would..., used to..., was accustomed to...*; iterative impf.; i.e. to Chreirisophos
21 **ὅτε...ἐπικέοιντο**: *whenever...*; 3p opt. mid. in a past general temporal clause; the Greeks are the object
ὑπέμενε: iterative impf. (see above)
21 **ὅτε...παρεγγυῷτο**: *whenever...*; 3s pres. pass. opt. (παρεγγυάοιτο) in a past general temporal clause
22 **δὲ**: *but*
ἦγε: impf. ἄγω, not iterative
παρηγγύα: 3s impf. παρεγγυάω
23 **ἦν**: *it was...*
ὅτι...εἴη: *that...*; ind. disc.; opt. often replaces indicative in secondary sequence
πρᾶγμά τι: *some trouble*
ἦν: *there was...*
ἰδεῖν: *to see*; inf. of purpose, aor. inf. ὁράω
24 **παρελθόντι (τινί)**: *for (someone)...*; dat. sg. aor. pple παρέρχομαι modifies a missing dat. of interest
ὁμοία: pred. adj.
25 **φυγῇ**: dat. of special adj. ὁμοία
26 **τοῖς ὀπισθοφύλαξι**: *for...*; 'in the view of...' dat. of reference
Λεώνυμος...βασίας: Xenophon's decision to use personal names reveals an affection for his men: these losses were personal to him and not simply business as usual.
τοξευθείς: nom. sg. aor. pass. pple

διαμπερὲς τὴν κεφαλήν. 19. ἐπεὶ δὲ ἀφίκοντο ἐπὶ σταθμόν, 1
εὐθὺς ὥσπερ εἶχεν ὁ Ξενοφῶν ἐλθὼν πρὸς τὸν Χειρίσοφον
ᾐτιᾶτο αὐτὸν ὅτι οὐχ ὑπέμενεν, ἀλλ' ἠναγκάζοντο φεύγοντες
ἅμα μάχεσθαι. καὶ νῦν δύο καλώ τε καὶ ἀγαθὼ ἄνδρε
τέθνατον καὶ οὔτε ἀνελέσθαι οὔτε θάψαι ἐδυνάμεθα. 20. ἀποκρί- 5
νεται ὁ Χειρίσοφος· 'βλέψον,' ἔφη, 'πρὸς τὰ ὄρη καὶ ἰδὲ ὡς
ἄβατα πάντα ἐστί· μία δ' αὕτη ὁδὸς ἣν ὁρᾷς ὀρθία, καὶ ἐπὶ
ταύτῃ ἀνθρώπων ὁρᾶν ἔξεστί σοι ὄχλον τοσοῦτον, οἳ κατειληφότες φυλάττουσι τὴν ἔκβασιν. 21. ταῦτ' ἐγὼ ἔσπευδον καὶ 9

ἄ-βατος, -ον: untrodden, impassable, 2
αἰτιάομαι: accuse, charge; blame, 1
ἀναγκάζω: to force, compel, require, 2
ἀν-αιρέω: to take up; win, gain, 1
ἀπο-κρίνομαι: to answer, reply, 3
βλέπτω: to look, look at, gaze, 1
διαμπερὲς: clean or right through (acc), 1
ἔκ-βασις, -εως, ἡ: going out, way out, exit, 5
ἔξ-εστί: it is allowed, it is possible, 4
θάπτω: to bury, 1
θνῄσκω: to die, 3
κεφαλή, ἡ: the head, 4
νῦν: now; as it is, 4
οὔ-τε: and not, neither...nor, 6
ὄχλος, ὁ: a crowd, throng, mob, 4
σπεύδω: to be eager, be urgent, 3
τοσοῦτος, -αύτη, -οῦτο: so great, so much, so many, 3
ὑπο-μένω: to remain, abide, wait up, await, 7
φυλάττω: to keep watch, keep guard, 6

1 **σταθμόν**: *the stopping point*; 'station,' Xenophon uses the word to indicate (a) a stopping point or (b) the interval that one must travel between stopping points
2 **εἶχεν**: impf., ἔχω ('holds' or 'is disposed') + adv. is often equiv. to εἰμί + adj.
ἐλθὼν: aor. pple ἔρχομαι
3 **ᾐτιᾶτο**: impf. αἰτιάομαι
ἠναγκάζοντο: impf. pass.
4 **καλώ...ἀγαθὼ ἄνδρε**: dual nominatives; although Xenophon does not name the dead here, his word choice shows his respect for his fellow soldiers.
5 **τέθνατον**: dual 3rd pers. pf. θνῄσκω ; the pf. denotes a state ('be dead') rather than an activity ('have died')
ἀνελέσθαι, θάψαι: aor. inf. mid. and act. ἀναιρέω, θάπτω; add 'the two' as object
6 **βλέψον**: aor. imperative
ἔφη: 3s impf. φημί
πρὸς: often translates as 'at' after βλέπω
ὄρη: ὄρε-α, from ὄρος
ἰδὲ: aor. imperative ὁράω (εἶδον)
ὡς: *how*...
7 **ἐστί**: as often, sg. verb with neut. pl. subject
μία δ' αὕτη ὁδὸς (ἦν): add a linking verb; μία may mean 'only' or 'alone'
ἣν: *which*...; relative clause, ὀρθία, 'steep,' modifies fem. ὁδὸς and is not part of clause
ἐπὶ: *upon*...; dat. of place where
8 **ἀνθρώπων**: partitve gen. with ὄχλον
ὁρᾶν: inf.
οἳ: *who*...
κατειληφότες: pf. pple καταλαμβάνω; ἔκβασιν is the obj. of both verb and pple
9 **ταῦτ(α)**: acc. obj.
ἔσπευδον: 1s impf. + acc.

διὰ τοῦτό σε οὐχ ὑπέμενον, εἴ πως δυναίμην φθάσαι πρὶν 10
κατειλῆφθαι τὴν ὑπερβολήν· οἱ δ' ἡγεμόνες οὓς ἔχομεν οὔ
φασιν εἶναι ἄλλην ὁδόν.' 22. ὁ δὲ Ξενοφῶν λέγει· 'ἀλλ' ἐγὼ ἔχω
δύο ἄνδρας. ἐπεὶ γὰρ ἡμῖν πράγματα παρεῖχον, ἐνηδρεύ-
σαμεν, ὅπερ ἡμᾶς καὶ ἀναπνεῦσαι ἐποίησε, καὶ ἀπεκτείναμέν
τινας αὐτῶν, καὶ ζῶντας προυθυμήθημεν λαβεῖν αὐτοῦ τούτου 15
ἕνεκα ὅπως ἡγεμόσιν εἰδόσι τὴν χώραν χρησαίμεθα.

23. καὶ εὐθὺς ἀγαγόντες τοὺς ἀνθρώπους ἤλεγχον διαλαβόντες
εἴ τινα εἰδεῖεν ἄλλην ὁδὸν ἢ τὴν φανεράν. ὁ μὲν οὖν ἕτερος

ἀνα-πνέω: to breathe (again); recover, 2
ἀπο-κτείνω: to kill, slay, 4
δια-λαμβάνω: to take or receive separately, 1
ἐλέγχω: to question, examine, 1
ἐν-εδρεύω: to set an ambush, lie in wait, 2
ἕνεκα: for the sake of, because of, for (gen.), 2
ἕτερος, -α, -ον: one of two, other, different, 4
ζάω: to live, 1
ἡμεῖς: we, 5
οἶδα: to know, 5
ὅσπερ, ἥπερ, ὅπερ: very one who, which, 4
παρ-έχω: to provide, furnish, supply, 5
πρᾶγμα, τό: deed; matter, affair, trouble, 3
προ-θυμέομαι: to be eager, zealous, ready, 1
πως: somehow, in any way, 4
ὑπερ-βολή, ἡ: crossing, mtn. pass; excess, 6
ὑπο-μένω: to remain, abide, wait up, await, 7
φθάνω: to act first, act beforehand, 3
χράομαι: use, employ, enjoy, indulge (dat) 6

10 **εἴ πως δυναίμην**: *if somehow I should...*; i.e. 'in the hope that/on the chance that...' 1s pres. opt. expressing motive (S2354)
φθάσαι: aor. inf. φθάνω
11 **κατειλῆφθαι**: pf. pass. inf. following πρὶν, ὑπερβολήν is acc. subject
οἱ ἡγεμόνες: *guides*
οὓς: relative
12 **οὔ φασιν**: *say that...not*; or 'deny that...' almost never 'do not say...' 3s φημί
εἶναι: inf. εἰμί
ἀλλὰ: *well, then...*; as often, in response
13 **ἄνδρας**: i.e. as ἡγεμόνες, 'guides'
πράγματα παρεῖχον: *they gave trouble*; a common idiom + dat. indirect object
14 **ὅπερ**: *which very (thing)*; i.e. the ambush, the clause is antecedent; subject of ἐποίησε
ἀναπνεῦσαι: i.e. recover; aor. inf.
ἐποίησε: *made it that...*; or 'brought it about that...' here with acc. + inf.
15 **τινας**: *some*; indefinite
ζῶντας: *(those)...*; acc. pl. pple ζάω
προυθυμήθημεν: 1p aor. dep. pass.
15 **λαβεῖν**: inf. λαμβάνω
αὐτοῦ τούτου: gen. obj. of ἕνεκα; αὐτοῦ is an intensive pronoun
16 **ὅπως...χρησαίμεθα**: *(namely) so that... might...*; purpose clause in apposition to previous phrase; aor. opt. in secondary seq.
ἡγεμόσιν: *guides*; dat. obj. of χρησαίμεθα
εἰδόσι: dat. pl. pple οἶδα governing τὴν χώραν
17 **ἀγαγόντες**: aor. pple ἄγω
ἀνθρώπους: i.e. the prisoners
18 **εἴ...εἰδεῖεν**: *whether...*; ind. question, 3p aor. opt. οἶδα
ἤ: *than...*; following ἄλλην
τὴν φανεράν (ὁδὸν): i.e. the road that is evident and already know
ὁ μὲν...ἕτερος: *one (of the two prisoners)*

οὐκ ἔφη μάλα πολλῶν φόβων προσαγομένων· ἐπεὶ δὲ οὐδὲν ὠφέλιμον ἔλεγεν, ὁρῶντος τοῦ ἑτέρου κατεσφάγη. 24. *ὁ δὲ* 20
λοιπὸς ἔλεξεν ὅτι οὗτος μὲν οὐ φαίη διὰ ταῦτα εἰδέναι, ὅτι αὐτῷ ἐτύγχανε θυγάτηρ ἐκεῖ παρ᾽ ἀνδρὶ ἐκδεδομένη· αὐτὸς δ᾽ ἔφη ἡγήσεσθαι δυνατὴν καὶ ὑποζυγίοις πορεύεσθαι ὁδόν.
25. *ἐρωτώμενος δ᾽ εἰ εἴη τι ἐν αὐτῇ δυσπάριτον χωρίον, ἔφη εἶναι ἄκρον ὃ εἰ μή τις προκαταλήψοιτο, ἀδύνατον ἔσεσθαι* 25

ἀ-δυνατός, -ή, -όν: incapable, impossible, 2
δυνατός, -ή, -όν: capable, strong, possible, 3
δυσ-πάριτος, -όν: hard to pass, 1
ἐκ-δίδωμι, -ον: to give in marriage; give up, 1
ἐκεῖ: there, in that place, 1
ἕτερος, -α, -ον: one of two, other, different, 4
θυγάτηρ, ἡ: a daughter, 2
κατα-σφάζω: to slaughter, murder, slay, 1
λοιπός, ὁ: remaining, the rest, 6
μάλα: very, very much, exceedingly, 4
οἶδα: to know, 5
προ-κατα-λαμβάνω: to seize beforehand, 3
προσ-άγω: to bring up or to, attach, apply, 3
τυγχάνω: chance upon, get; meet; happen, 5
φόβος, ὁ: fear, terror, panic; threat; 1
ὠφέλιμος, -η, -ον: beneficial, helpful, 1

19 **οὐκ ἔφη**: *said 'no'*; i.e. said that he did not know; impf. φημί
μάλα πολλῶν...προσαγομένων: *although...*; gen. abs. concessive in force; φόβων here means 'threats'; pple is pass.
20 **ὁρῶντος τοῦ ἑτέρου**: *(while)...*; gen. abs.; i.e the second of the two men
κατεσφάγη: 3s aor. pass., the subject is the first prisoner, the man who kept silent
ὁ δὲ λοιπὸς: i.e the second prisoner
21 **ἔλεξεν**: aor. λέγω
οὐ φαίη: *said that (he)...not*; 3s opt. φημί in ind. disc. in secondary sequence
εἰδέναι: *that (he)...*; ind. disc.; inf. οἶδα
ὅτι: *(namely) because...*; causal, in apposition to διὰ ταῦτα
22 **αὐτῷ**: *his*; i.e. the first prisoner's; dat. of possession with θυγάτηρ or possibly dat. of agent with the pf. pple: "by him"
ἐτυγχανε ἐκδεδομένη: *happened to...*; as often, τυγχάνω + complementary pple (here, pf. pass. ἐκδίδωμι) is translated as 'happen' + inf. in English
παρ᾽ ἀνδρὶ: *with her husband*: or 'at the house of...' i.e. the first prisoner has a daughter living along this alternative road
αὐτὸς: *he himself*; i.e. the second prisoner
23 **ἡγήσεσθαι**: *that (he)...*; ind. disc. with fut. inf.; supply the missing subject
δυνατὴν: + inf.; modifies fem. sg. ὁδόν
καὶ: *even*; adverbial
ὑποζυγίοις: dat. of means
ὅδόν: *along the road*; acc. extent (S1581)
24 **εἰ εἴη**: *whether...*; ind. question with 3s opt. εἰμί in secondary seq.
ἐν αὐτῇ: *on it*; i.e. fem. ὁδός
ἔφη: impf. φημί; 2nd prisoner is subject
25 **ὃ**: *which*; acc. obj. of προκαταλήψοιτο
εἰ...προκαταλήψοιτο,...ἔσεσθαι: *if they do not..., it will be...*; fut. opt. and fut. inf. εἰμί; an emotional future more vivid (εἰ + ἄν subj., fut. ind.) in which ἄν + subj. in the protasis has been replaced by fut. ind. to express heightened emotion; in ind. disc. in secondary seq. the fut. ind. becomes a fut. opt. and the apodosis an inf.

παρελθεῖν. 26. *ἐνταῦθα δ' ἐδόκει συγκαλέσαντας λοχαγοὺς καὶ* 1
πελταστὰς καὶ τῶν ὁπλιτῶν λέγειν τε τὰ παρόντα καὶ ἐρωτᾶν
εἴ τις αὐτῶν ἔστιν ὅστις ἀνὴρ ἀγαθὸς ἐθέλοι ἂν γενέσθαι καὶ
ὑποστὰς ἐθελοντὴς πορεύεσθαι. 27. *ὑφίσταται τῶν μὲν ὁπλιτῶν*
Ἀριστώνυμος Μεθυδριεὺς [Ἀρκὰς] καὶ Ἀγασίας Στυμφάλιος 5
[Ἀρκάς], ἀντιστασιάζων δὲ αὐτοῖς Καλλίμαχος Παρράσιος
[Ἀρκὰς καὶ οὗτος] ἔφη ἐθέλειν πορεύεσθαι προσλαβὼν
ἐθελοντὰς ἐκ παντὸς τοῦ στρατεύματος· 'ἐγὼ γάρ,' ἔφη,
'οἶδα ὅτι ἕψονται πολλοὶ τῶν νέων ἐμοῦ ἡγουμένου.' 28. *ἐκ* 9

Ἀγασίας, ὁ: Agasias (person), 3
ἀντι-στασιάζω: to form in rivalry, 1
Ἀριστώνυμος, ὁ: Aristonymus (person), 5
Ἀρκάς, Ἀρκάδος, ὁ: Arcadian, of Arcadia, 5
ἐθελοντής, ὁ: volunteer, one willing, 3
Καλλίμαχος, ὁ: Callimachus, 5
Μεθυδριεὺς, ὁ: of Methydrium, 4
νέος, -α, -ον: young; new, novel, strange, 3
οἶδα: to know, 5
ὅστις, ἥτις, ὅ τι: whoever, which-, whatever, 4
πάρ-ειμι: to be near, be present, be at hand, 4
Παρράσιος -α, -ον: of Parrhesia; Parrhesian 2
προσ-λαμβάνω: to take in addition, 1
Στυμφάλιος, -η, -ον: of Stymphalos (city), 4
συγ-καλέω: to call together, assemble, 2
ὑφ-ίστημι: to station secretly; stand up, 4

1 **παρελθεῖν**: aor. inf. παρέρχομαι
2 **καὶ πελταστὰς καὶ τῶν ὁπλιτῶν**: *both... and...*; πελταστὰς is in apposition to λοχαγοὺς and ὁπλιτῶν is a partitive or appositional gen.
τὰ παρόντα: *the matters being at hand*; pple πάρειμι
ἐρωτᾶν: ἐρωτάειν, α-contract inf. ἐρωτάω
3 **ἔι...ἔστιν**: *whether there was...*; ind. question, with historical pres.
ἀνὴρ ἀγαθὸς: predicate of γενέσθαι replaces pres. indicative in secondary seq.
ἐθέλοι ἂν: *would...*; potential pres. opt.
γενέσθαι: aor. inf. γίγνομαι
4 **ὑποστάς**: nom. sg. aor. pple
ἐθελοντής: *as...*
τῶν ὁπλιτῶν: *among...*; partitive gen.
5 **Ἀριστώνυμος...Ἀγασίας**: once again, the use of personal names reveals Xenophon's personal regard for his men; with 3s verb
6 **αὐτοῖς**: *against...*; dat. of compound verb
7 **ἔφη**: impf. εἰμί
ἐθέλειν: *that (he)...*; supply subject
9 **ἕψονται**: fut. ἕπομαι
τῶν νέων: *of the young men*
ἐμοῦ ἡγουμένου: gen. abs.

τούτου ἐρωτῶσιν εἴ τις καὶ τῶν γυμνήτων ταξιάρχων ἐθέλοι συμπορεύεσθαι. ὑφίσταται Ἀριστέας Χῖος, ὃς πολλαχοῦ πολλοῦ ἄξιος τῇ στρατιᾷ εἰς τὰ τοιαῦτα ἐγένετο. 10

1. καὶ ἦν μὲν δείλη, οἱ δ᾽ ἐκέλευον αὐτοὺς ἐμφαγόντας πορεύεσθαι. καὶ τὸν ἡγεμόνα δήσαντες παραδιδόασιν αὐτοῖς, καὶ συντίθενται τὴν μὲν νύκτα, ἢν λάβωσι τὸ ἄκρον, τὸ χωρίον φυλάττειν, ἅμα δὲ τῇ ἡμέρᾳ τῇ σάλπιγγι σημαίνειν· καὶ τοὺς μὲν ἄνω ὄντας ἰέναι ἐπὶ τοὺς κατέχοντας τὴν φανερὰν ἔκβασιν, αὐτοὶ δὲ συμβοηθήσειν ἐκβαίνοντες ὡς ἂν δύνωνται 15

ἄξιος, -η, -ον: worthy of, deserving of (gen) 1
Ἀριστέας, ὁ: Aristeas, 2
γυμνήτης, -ου, ὁ: light-armed soldier 6
δείλη, ἡ: late afternoon, 1
δέω (2): to bind, tie, 3
ἐκ-βαίνω: to step out, disembark; turn out, 7
ἔκ-βασις, -εως, ἡ: going out, way out, exit, 5
ἐν-εσθίω: to eat, consume, 2
κατ-έχω: to hold fast, take possession of, 7
παρα-δίδωμι: to hand over, give over, 4
πολλα-χοῦ: in many places or occasions, 1
σαλπίγξ, -ιγγος, ὁ: war-trumpet, 4
σημαίνω: to show, indicate, give a signal, 3
στρατία, ἡ: an army, expedition, land force, 4
συμ-βοηθέω: to join in helping, 1
συμ-πορεύομαι: to join in traveling, 1
συν-τίθημι: to agree, put together, 3
ταξι-αρχος, ὁ: taxiarch (oversees 128 men), 1
τοιοῦτος, -αύτη, -οῦτο: such, this sort, 3
ὑφ-ίστημι: to station secretly; stand up, 4
φυλάττω: to keep watch, keep guard, 6
Χῖος, -η, -ον: Chian, of Chios, 2

10 **ἐρωτῶσιν**: ἐρωτάουσιν; 3p pres.
εἴ...ἐθέλοι: *whether...*; ind. question with opt. replacing a pres. indicative after a historical pres. (~secondary sequence)
καὶ: *in fact, actually*; adverbial
12 **τῇ στρατιᾷ**: *for the army*; dat. of interest
εἰς τὰ τοιαῦτα: *for...*
ἐγένετο: aor. γίγνομαι
13 **ἦν**: 3s impf. εἰμί
οἱ δ᾽: *and they...*; i.e. Xenophon and Cheirisophus are 3p subject
ἐμφαγόντας: aor. pple ἐμ-εσθίω
14 **τὸν ἡγεμόνα**: i.e. the 2nd prisoner
δήσαντες: aor. pple δέω
αὐτοῖς: i.e. to the volunteers; ind. obj.
15 **συντίθενται**: pres. mid. governing many complementary infinitives
τὴν...νύκτα: *during...*; acc. of duration
ἢν λάβωσι...: *if...*; ἐὰν + aor. subj., protasis in a future more vivid condition
16 **φυλάττειν**: *that (they)...*; ind. disc.
ἅμα...ἡμέρᾳ: *as soon as daybreak*
τῇ σάλπιγγι: dat. of means
17 **τοὺς μὲν ἄνω ὄντας**: *and that those...*; i.e. the volunteers on the hilltop; acc. subj.
ἰέναι: inf. ἔρχομαι, governed by συντίθενται
ἐπὶ: *against...*
τοὺς κατέχοντας: *those...*; i.e. the hostile Carduchians; pres. pple
αὐτοὶ (συντίθενται): i.e. the soldiers with Xenophon and Cheirisophus; intensive
18 **συνβοηθήσειν**: fut. inf. in ind. disc. governed by συντίθενται
ὡς ἂν δύνωνται τάχιστα: *as swiftly as they are able*; ὡς + superlative (here, adv.) often means 'as...as (is) possible,' but is in fact a clause of comparison with the verb missing through ellipsis; in the passage above,the verb is included; ἄν + subj. expresses fut. time, equiv. to protasis of fut. more vivid

τάχιστα. 2. *ταῦτα συνθέμενοι οἱ μὲν ἐπορεύοντο πλῆθος ὡς δισχίλιοι· καὶ ὕδωρ πολὺ ἦν ἐξ οὐρανοῦ· Ξενοφῶν δὲ ἔχων* 20
τοὺς ὀπισθοφύλακας ἡγεῖτο πρὸς τὴν φανερὰν ἔκβασιν, ὅπως ταύτῃ τῇ ὁδῷ οἱ πολέμιοι προσέχοιεν τὸν νοῦν καὶ ὡς μάλιστα λάθοιεν οἱ περιιόντες. 3. *ἐπεὶ δὲ ἦσαν ἐπὶ χαράδρᾳ οἱ ὀπισθοφύλακες ἣν ἔδει διαβάντας πρὸς τὸ ὄρθιον ἐκβαίνειν, τηνικαῦτα ἐκύλινδον οἱ βάρβαροι ὁλοιτρόχους ἁμαξιαίους καὶ* 25

ἁμαξιαῖος, -α, -ον: cart-load, wagon-size, 1
βάρβαρος, -α, -ον: foreigner, barbarian, 7
δισ-χίλιοι, -αι, -α: two thousand, 1
ἐκ-βαίνω: to step out, disembark; turn out, 7
ἔκ-βασις, -εως, ἡ: going out, way out, exit, 5
κυλίνδω: to roll (down) wallow, wander, 5
λανθάνω: to escape notice, forget, 5
μάλιστα: most of all; certainly, especially, 5
νοῦς, ὁ: mind, perception, heart, 1
ὁλοι-τρόχος, ὁ: a rolling or round stone, 1
οὐρανός, ὁ: sky, heaven, 1
περι-έρχομαι: to go around, go about, 4
πλῆθος, ἡ: crowd, multitude; size, 4
προσ-έχω: to offer, provide; direct, 1
συν-τίθημι: to agree (upon), put together, 3
τηνικαῦτα: at that time, then, 2
ὕδωρ, ὕδατος, τό: water, 5
χαράδρα, ἡ: ravine, gully, stream-bed, 1

19 **συνθέμενοι**: aor. mid. pple συντίθημι
οἱ μὲν: *they*...; i.e. the volunteers
πλῆθος: *in*...; acc. of respect
ὡς: *about, nearly*; 'as if,' in approximation (S2995)
20 **ὕδωρ πολὺ**: i.e. rain
ἦν: impf. εἰμί
ὅπως...προσέχοιεν τὸν νοῦν...: *so that... might*...; purpose clause with 3p opt. in secondary sequence; προσέχειν τὸν νοῦν is a common idiom for 'pay attention'
21 **ταύτῃ...ὁδῷ**: *to*...; dat. of compound verb προσέχοιεν
22 **ὡς μάλιστα**: as often, ὡς + superlative is translated 'as...as possible'
23 **λάθοιεν**: *might*...; aor. opt. λανθάνω in the same purpose clause
ἦσαν: 3p impf. εἰμί
ἐπὶ: *near*...; dat. of place where
24 **ἣν**: *which*...; relative obj. of pple
ἔδει: impf. impersonal δεῖ
διαβάντας: aor. pple διαβαίνω
πρὸς τὸ ὄρθιον: *to the ascent*; once they cleared the ravine they had to mount an steep ascent

μείζους καὶ ἐλάττους, οἳ φερόμενοι πρὸς τὰς πέτρας παίοντες 1
διεσφενδονῶντο· καὶ παντάπασιν οὐδὲ πελάσαι οἷόν τ᾽ ἦν τῇ
εἰσόδῳ. 4. ἔνιοι δὲ τῶν λοχαγῶν, εἰ μὴ ταύτῃ δύναιντο, ἄλλῃ
ἐπειρῶντο· καὶ ταῦτα ἐποίουν μέχρι σκότος ἐγένετο· ἐπεὶ δὲ
ᾤοντο ἀφανεῖς εἶναι ἀπιόντες, τότε ἀπῆλθον ἐπὶ τὸ δεῖπνον· 5
ἐτύγχανον δὲ καὶ ἀνάριστοι ὄντες αὐτῶν οἱ ὀπισθοφυλακή-
σαντες. οἱ μέντοι πολέμιοι οὐδὲν ἐπαύσαντο δι᾽ ὅλης τῆς
νυκτὸς κυλίνδοντες τοὺς λίθους· τεκμαίρεσθαι δ᾽ ἦν τῷ ψόφῳ.
5. οἱ δ᾽ ἔχοντες τὸν ἡγεμόνα κύκλῳ περιιόντες καταλαμβάνουσι 9

ἀν-άριστος, -ον: without breakfast, 1
ἀ-φανής, -ές: unseen, unnoticed, 1
δεῖπνον, τό: dinner, meal, 1
δια-σφενδονάω: to scatter (like slingshot), 1
εἴσ-οδος, ἡ: entrance, a way in, 2
ἐλάττων, -ον: smaller, fewer, 2
ἔνιοι, -αι, -α: some, 1
κύκλος, ὁ: a circle, round, ring, 4
κυλίνδω: to roll; wallow, wander, 5
μείζων, -ον (-ονος): greater, larger, 4
μέντοι: however, nevertheless; certainly, 6
μέχρι: up to; until, as long as (+ gen.), 5
οἴομαι: to suppose, think, imagine, 3
οἷος, -α, -ον: of what sort, as, 5
ὅλος, -η, -ον: whole, entire, complete, 5
ὀπισθο-φύλακέω: to guard the rear, 3
παίω: to strike, smite, 2
παντά-πασι: all in all, altogether, entirely, 3
παύω: to stop, make cease, 3
πειράω: to try, attempt, endeavor, 7
πελάζω: to draw near, approach (dat.) 1
περι-έρχομαι: to go around, go about, 4
σκότος, ὁ: darkness, gloom, 2
τεκμαίρομαι: to judge, conjecture, estimate, 1
τότε: then, at that time, 7
τυγχάνω: chance upon, get; meet; happen, 5
ψόφος, ὁ: noise, sound, 1

1 **καὶ...καὶ**: *both... and...*
μείζο(ν)ες, ἐλάττο(ν)ες: comparatives in the acc. pl.
οἳ: relative, the antecedent is ὁλοιτρόχους
φερόμενοι: *flying*; 'bearing along,' mid.
πρὸς...: *against...*; i.e. the rolling rocks hit and set in motion other rocks below
2 **πελάσαι**: aor. inf. πελάζω
οἷόν τε ἦν: *it was possible* + inf.; 'it was the sort to,' οἷος τε + εἰμί is a common idiom for 'to be able' or 'to be possible'
τῇ εἰσόδῳ: dat. object of πελάσαι
3 **εἰ...δύναιντο, ἐπειρῶντο**: *if they were..., would...*; past general condition (εἰ + opt, impf. ind.) iterative impf. mid. πειράω
ταύτῃ, ἄλλῃ: *in this way...in another way*; both dat. of manner
5 **ᾤοντο**: impf. οἴομαι
ἀφανεῖς εἶναι ἀπιόντες: *that those...*; ind. disc. with inf. εἰμί; the pple of ἀπέρχομαι is a substantive and acc subj.
ἀπῆλθον: aor. ἀπέρχομαι
ἐπὶ: *for...*; + acc. expressing purpose
6 **ἐτύγχανον....ὄντες**: *happened to...*; τυγχάνω + complementary pple εἰμί
καὶ: *in fact, actually*; adverbial
αὐτῶν: *among them*; partitive gen.
7 **οὐδὲν**: *not at all*; adverbial acc. (inner acc.: 'made no stop')
ἐπαύσαντο: aor. mid. παύω
8 **ἦν**: *it was possible*; impf. εἰμί
κύκλῳ: *in...*; dat. of manner
9 **περιιόντες**: pple περι-έρχομαι; i.e. those who volunteered

τοὺς φύλακας ἀμφὶ πῦρ καθημένους· καὶ τοὺς μὲν κατα- 10
καίνοντες τοὺς δὲ καταδιώξαντες αὐτοὶ ἐνταῦθ᾽ ἔμενον ὡς τὸ
ἄκρον κατέχοντες. 6. *οἱ δ᾽ οὐ κατεῖχον, ἀλλὰ μαστὸς ἦν ὑπὲρ*
αὐτῶν παρ᾽ ὃν ἦν ἡ στενὴ αὕτη ὁδὸς ἐφ᾽ ᾗ ἐκάθηντο οἱ
φύλακες. ἔφοδος μέντοι αὐτόθεν ἐπὶ τοὺς πολεμίους ἦν
οἳ ἐπὶ τῇ φανερᾷ ὁδῷ ἐκάθηντο. 7. *καὶ τὴν μὲν νύκτα ἐνταῦθα* 15
διήγαγον· ἐπεὶ δ᾽ ἡμέρα ὑπέφαινεν, ἐπορεύοντο σιγῇ συντε-
ταγμένοι ἐπὶ τοὺς πολεμίους· καὶ γὰρ ὁμίχλη ἐγένετο, ὥστ᾽
ἔλαθον ἐγγὺς προσελθόντες. ἐπεὶ δὲ εἶδον ἀλλήλους, ἥ τε

ἀλαλάζω: to raise the war-cry, 1
αὐτό-θεν: from the very spot or moment, 2
δι-άγω: pass, go through; lead across 1
ἐγγύς: near (+ gen.); adv. nearby, 7
ἔφ-οδος, ἡ: an approach, access, 1
ἵημι: to send, throw; let go, release, 4
κάθ-ημαι: to sit, be seated, 4
κατα-διώκω: to pursue or chase closely, 1
κατα-καίνω: to kill, slay, 2
κατ-έχω: to hold fast, take possession of, 7
λανθάνω: to escape notice, forget, 5
μαστός, ὁ: mound, round hill; a breast, 7
μέντοι: however, nevertheless; certainly, 6
ὁμίχλη, ἡ: mist, fog, 1
σάλπιγξ, -ιγγος, ὁ: war-trumpet, 4
σιγῇ: in silence, 1
συν-τάττω: to post/marshall together, order 3
ὑπο-φαίνω: to show oneself, break, 2
φθέγγομαι: utter a sound, cry out, 2
φύλαξ, -ακος, ὁ: guard, sentinal, protector, 4

10 **τοὺς μὲν...τοὺς δὲ**: *some...others*; i.e. the enemy guards; acc. obj. of the participles
κατακαίοντες...καταδιώξαντες: nom. pl. aor. pple
11 **αὐτοὶ**: i.e. the volunteers with the guide; intensive pronoun;
ὡς...κατέχοντες: *on the grounds that...*; or 'since,' ὡς + pple expresses alleged cause, i.e. from the the character's, not narrator's, point of view
12 **οἱ δ᾽**: *but they...*
ἦν: *there was*
13 **παρ(ὰ) ὃν**: *along which*; relative pronoun
ἡ στενὴ αὕτη ὁδὸς: = αὕτη ἡ στενὴ ὁδὸς; unusual word order: according to Smyth, an attributive adj. (here, ἡ στενὴ) may be separated from its noun by a pronoun (here, demonstrative αὕτη) (S1181)
ἐφ᾽ ᾗ: *upon...*; relative
ἐκάθηντο: impf. κάθημαι
14 **ἐπὶ**: *to...*;
15 **οἳ**: *who...*
16 **διήγαγον**: 3p aor.
ὑπέφαινεν: *began to...*; inchoative impf.
σιγῇ: *in...*; dat. of manner
συντεταγμένοι: pf. pass. συντάττω
17 **ἐπὶ**: *against...*
καὶ γὰρ: *and indeed*; γὰρ is adverbial (S2814)
18 **ἔλαθον**: aor. λανθάνω + aor. pple. προσέρχομαι
εἶδον: aor. ὁράω

*σάλπιγξ ἐφθέγξατο καὶ ἀλαλάξαντες ἵεντο ἐπὶ τοὺς ἀνθρώ-
πους· οἱ δὲ οὐκ ἐδέξαντο, ἀλλὰ λιπόντες τὴν ὁδὸν φεύγοντες* 20
ὀλίγοι ἀπέθνῃσκον· εὔζωνοι γὰρ ἦσαν. 8. *οἱ δὲ ἀμφὶ Χειρίσοφον ἀκούσαντες τῆς σάλπιγγος εὐθὺς ἵεντο ἄνω κατὰ τὴν
φανερὰν ὁδόν· ἄλλοι δὲ τῶν στρατηγῶν κατὰ ἀτριβεῖς ὁδοὺς
ἐπορεύοντο ᾗ ἔτυχον ἕκαστοι ὄντες, καὶ ἀναβάντες ὡς ἐδύναντο ἀνίμων ἀλλήλους τοῖς δόρασι.* 9. *καὶ οὗτοι πρῶτοι* 25
συνέμειξαν τοῖς προκαταλαβοῦσι τὸ χωρίον. Ξενοφῶν δὲ

ἀλαλάζω: to raise the war-cry, 1
ἀν-ιμάω: to draw up, pull up, 1
ἀ-τριβής, -ές: unworn, untrodden, pathless, 1
δέχομαι: to receive, accept, 7
δόρυ, δόρατος, τό: spearshaft; pole, stem, 4
εὔ-ζωνος, -ον: well-girdled, nimble, active, 3
ἵημι: to send, throw; let go, release, 4
λείπω: to leave, forsake, abandon, 6
προ-κατα-λαμβάνω: to seize beforehand, 3
σάλπιγξ, -ιγγος, ὁ: war-trumpet, 4
συμ-μίγνυμι: to join together, unite with, 1
τυγχάνω: chance upon, get; meet; happen, 5
φθέγγομαι: utter a sound, cry out, 2

19 **ἵεντο**: *rushed*; 'sent themselves,' impf. mid. ἵημι
ἐπὶ: *against…*
20 **ἐδέξαντο**: aor. δέχομαι i.e. did not fight but instead retreated
λιπόντες: aor. pple λείπω
21 **εὔζωνοι**: i.e. they could move quickly because they were impeded by arms and equipment
γὰρ: explaining why so few enemy died
ἦσαν: 3p impf. εἰμί
οἱ…Χειρίσοφον: i.e. those under Cheirisophus' command
22 **τῆς σάλπιγγος**: gen. of source with pple
ἵεντο: *rushed*; impf. mid. ἵημι
κατὰ: *along…*; or 'over…'
23 **κατὰ ἀτριβεῖς ὁδοὺς**: *along…*; i.e. they made their way up where there were no paths: they made paths where none existed
24 **ᾗ (ὁδῷ)**: *on which (path)*; assume fem. ὁδῷ, dat. of means/manner, different soldiers used different paths
ἔτυχον…ὄντες: *happened to…*; common translation for τυγχάνω + complementary pple; here aor. with the pple εἰμί
ἀναβάντες: aor. pple ἀναβαίνω
ὡς ἐδύναντο: *as…*; i.e. as well as they were able; a clause of comparison
25 **ἀνίμων**: ἀν-ίμαον, 3p impf. α-contract ἀν-ιμάω ; the soldiers held out their spears to their comrades below them to pull them up and help them scale the hill
τοῖς δόρασι: dat. of means
26 **συνέμειξαν**: aor. συν-μίγνυμι
τοῖς προκαταλαβοῦσι: *with…*; dat. of compound verb; dat. pl. aor. pple

ἔχων τῶν ὀπισθοφυλάκων τοὺς ἡμίσεις ἐπορεύετο ᾗπερ οἱ 1
τὸν ἡγεμόνα ἔχοντες· εὐοδωτάτη γὰρ ἦν τοῖς ὑποζυγίοις·
τοὺς δὲ ἡμίσεις ὄπισθεν τῶν ὑποζυγίων ἔταξε. 10. πορευόμενοι
δ᾽ ἐντυγχάνουσι λόφῳ ὑπὲρ τῆς ὁδοῦ κατειλημμένῳ ὑπὸ τῶν
πολεμίων, οὓς ἢ ἀποκόψαι ἦν ἀνάγκη ἢ διεζεῦχθαι ἀπὸ 5
τῶν ἄλλων Ἑλλήνων. καὶ αὐτοὶ μὲν ἂν ἐπορεύθησαν ᾗπερ
οἱ ἄλλοι, τὰ δὲ ὑποζύγια οὐκ ἦν ἄλλῃ ἢ ταύτῃ ἐκβῆναι.
11. ἔνθα δὴ παρακελευσάμενοι ἀλλήλοις προσβάλλουσι πρὸς
τὸν λόφον ὀρθίοις τοῖς λόχοις, οὐ κύκλῳ ἀλλὰ καταλιπόντες 9

ἀνάγκη, ἡ: necessity, force, 4
ἀπο-κόπτω: to cut off, drive off, dislodge, 2
δια-ζεύγνυμι: to separate, disjoin, 1
ἐκ-βαίνω: to step out, disembark; turn out, 7
ἐν-τυγχάνω: to chance upon, encounter, 2
εὔ-οδος, -ον: easy to pass, accessible, 3
ἥμισυς, -εια, -υ: half, 4
κύκλος, ὁ: a circle, round, ring, 4
ὅσπερ, ἥπερ, ὅπερ: very one who, which, 4
παρα-κελεύομαι: to order, urge, encourage, 2
προσ-βάλλω: to attack, strike against, dash 3
τάττω: post, station, arrange, order, 6

1 **τοὺς ἡμίσεις...τοὺς δὲ ἡμίσεις**: *one half... the other half...*
ᾗπερ (ὁδῷ ἐπορεύθησαν): *by the very path...*; or 'just as...' relative clause with missing verb; dat. of manner
2 **εὐοδωτάτη**: superlative
ἦν: impf. εἰμί
τοῖς ὑποζυγίοις: *for..*; dat. of interest
3 **ἔταξε**: aor.
4 **λόφῳ**: dat. of compound verb
καταειλημμένῳ: pf. pass. pple καταλαμβάνω
ὑπὸ: *by...*; + gen. expressing agency
5 **οὓς**: *whom...*
ἢ...ἢ: *either...or*
ἀποκόψαι: aor. act. inf.; supply 'the enemy' as object
διεζεῦχθαι: pf. pass. inf.
ἀπὸ: *from...*; gen. of separation
6 **αὐτοὶ**: *they themselves*; Xenophon's men
ἂν ἐπορεύθησαν: *could have...*; or 'would have...' ἄν + aor. dep. pass. ind. in a contrary to fact (past unrealized potential)
ᾗπερ (ὁδῷ ἐπορεύθησαν): *by the very path...*; or 'just as...' relative clause with missing verb; dat. of manner
7 **τὰ...ὑποζύγια**: *that...*; acc. subj. of the aor. inf. ἐκβαίνω
ἦν: *it was possible*
ἄλλῃ...ταύτῃ: *in another way, in this way*; assume fem. ὁδῷ, dat. of manner
8 **ἔνθα δὴ**: *just then, exactly then*; intensive
παρακελευσάμενοι: aor. mid. pple + dat. of compound verb
προσβάλλουσι: 3p pres.
ὀρθίοις τοῖς λόχοις: *with companies of men in columns*; 'straight units,' manner
9 **κύκλῳ**: *in...*; dat. of manner
καταλιπόντες: aor. pple

ἄφοδον τοῖς πολεμίοις, εἰ βούλοιντο φεύγειν. 12. *καὶ τέως* 10
μὲν αὐτοὺς ἀναβαίνοντας ὅπῃ ἐδύναντο ἕκαστος οἱ βάρβαροι
ἐτόξευον καὶ ἔβαλλον, ἐγγὺς δ' οὐ προσίεντο, ἀλλὰ φυγῇ
λείπουσι τὸ χωρίον. καὶ τοῦτόν τε παρεληλύθεσαν οἱ
Ἕλληνες καὶ ἕτερον ὁρῶσιν ἔμπροσθεν λόφον κατεχόμενον
ἐπὶ τοῦτον αὖθις ἐδόκει πορεύεσθαι. 13. *ἐννοήσας δ' ὁ Ξενοφῶν* 15
μή, εἰ ἔρημον καταλίποι τὸν ἡλωκότα λόφον, [καὶ] πάλιν
λαβόντες οἱ πολέμιοι ἐπιθοῖντο τοῖς ὑποζυγίοις παριοῦσιν
(ἐπὶ πολὺ δ' ἦν τὰ ὑποζύγια ἅτε διὰ στενῆς τῆς ὁδοῦ

ἁλίσκομαι: to be taken, seized, 6
ἅτε: inasmuch as, since, seeing that (+ pple) 3
αὖθις: back, back again, backwards, 2
ἄφ-οδος, ὁ: departure; way of departure, 1
βάλλω: to throw, cast; shoot, 3
βάρβαρος, -α, -ον: foreigner, barbarian, 7
ἐγγύς: near (+ gen.); adv. nearby, 7
ἔμ-προσθεν: in front, before, 5
ἐν-νοέω: to be anxious; consider, reflect, 1
ἐρῆμος, -ον: deserted, desolate, 4
ἕτερος, -α, -ον: one of two, other, different, 4
κατ-έχω: to hold fast, take possession of, 7
λείπω: to leave, forsake, abandon, 6
ὅπῃ: where; in what way, how, 3
πείθω: to persuade, trust; *mid.* obey, 1
προσ-ίημι: to send to; allow; undertake, 4
τέως: for a while, for a time, meanwhile, 1
τοξεύω: shoot with the bow, shoot arrows, 7
φυγή, ἡ: flight, escape, exile, 3

10 **τοῖς πολεμίοις**: *for...*; dat. of interest
εἰ βούλοιντο: pres. opt., protasis with the corresponding apodosis suppressed
ὅπῃ ἐδύναντο: *in what way they...*; the subject are the Greeks, same as αὐτοὺς
11 **ἕκαστος**: *each*; i.e. individually, sg. in apposition to 3p subject of ἐδύναντο
12 **ἔβαλλον**: i.e. other missles than arrows
προσίεντο: *rush forward*; 'send themselves forward,' impf. προσίημι
φυγῇ: *in...*; dat. of manner
13 **καὶ τοῦτόν τε...καὶ**: *and when...then...*; τε...καί here describes actions that are occurring at the same time
τοῦτόν (λόφον): *this one*; i.e. this hill
παρεληλύθεσαν: plpf. act. παρ-έρχομαι
14 **(αὐτοῖς) ὁρῶσιν ἔμπροσθεν**: *to (those Greeks)...*; dat. of reference, dat. pl. pple. ὁράω with ἐδόκει
κατεχόμενον: pres. pass. pple, i.e. by the enemy
15 **ἐπὶ τοῦτον (λόφον)**: *onto...*
16 **μή...ἐπιθοῖντο**: *that...*; or 'lest,' a fearing clause with opt. in secondary sequence; 3p contracted aor. opt. mid. ἐπιτίθημι (θε-)
καταλίποι: aor. opt. καταλείπω
ἡλωκότα: acc. sg. pf. pple ἁλίσκομαι
τοῖς ὑποζυγίοις: *on...*; dat. obj. of compound verb
17 **παριοῦσιν**: dat. pl. pple παρ-έρχομαι
18 **ἐπὶ πολὺ**: *over a great (distance)*; i.e. extended in a long column
ἅτε: *inasmuch as* + pple; or 'since + pple' ὡς + pple indicates alleged cause from the character's point of view, while ἅτε + pple indicates the cause from the speaker's viewpoint (in this case, Xenophon's point of view)

πορευόμενα), καταλείπει ἐπὶ τοῦ λόφου λοχαγοὺς, Κηφισόδωρον Κηφισοφῶντος Ἀθηναῖον καὶ Ἀμφικράτην Ἀμφιδήμου 20 Ἀθηναῖον καὶ Ἀρχαγόραν Ἀργεῖον φυγάδα, αὐτὸς δὲ σὺν τοῖς λοιποῖς ἐπορεύετο ἐπὶ τὸν δεύτερον λόφον, καὶ τῷ αὐτῷ τρόπῳ καὶ τοῦτον αἱροῦσιν. 14. ἔτι δ᾽ αὐτοῖς τρίτος μαστὸς λοιπὸς ἦν πολὺ ὀρθιώτατος ὁ ὑπὲρ τῆς ἐπὶ τῷ πυρὶ καταληφθείσης φυλακῆς τῆς νυκτὸς ὑπὸ τῶν ἐθελοντῶν. 15. ἐπεὶ δ᾽ 25 ἐγγὺς ἐγένοντο οἱ Ἕλληνες, λείπουσιν οἱ βάρβαροι ἀμαχητὶ τὸν μαστόν, ὥστε θαυμαστὸν πᾶσι γενέσθαι καὶ ὑπώπτευον

Ἀθηναῖος, -α, -ον: Athenian, of Athens, 4
αἱρέω: seize, take; *mid.* choose, 3
ἀ-μαχητί: without battle, without a fight, 1
Ἀμφίδημος, ὁ: Amphidemus, 1
Ἀμφικράτης, ὁ: Amphicrates, 2
Ἀργεῖος, -α, -ον: Argive, of Argos, 2
Ἀρχαγόρας, ὁ: Archagoras, 2
βάρβαρος, -α, -ον: foreigner, barbarian, 7
δεύτερος, -η, -ον: second, 1
ἐγγύς: near (+ gen.); adv. nearby, 7
ἐθελοντής, ὁ: volunteer, one willing, 3
ἔτι: still, besides, further, 7
θαυμαστός, -ή, -όν: wonderful, marvelous, strange, 2
Κηφισόδωρος, ὁ: Cephisodorus, 2
Κηφισόφων, ὁ: Cephisophon, 1
λείπω: to leave, forsake, abandon, 6
λοιπός, ὁ: remaining, the rest, 6
μαστός, ὁ: mound, round hill; a breast, 7
τρίτος, -η, -ον: the third, 4
τρόπος, ὁ: a manner, way; turn, direction, 1
ὑπ-οπτεύω: to be suspicuous, suspect, 1
φυγάς, -άδος, ὁ: fugitive, an exile, 1
φυλακή, ἡ: a watch, guard, 4

19 **ἐπι...**: *upon...*
λοχαγοὺς: *captains*; followed by three acc. names in appositio
Κηφισόδωρον Κηφισοφῶτος Ἀθηναῖον: *Cephisodorus (son) of Cephisophon, the Athenian*; Greeks names often included the name of the father in the genitive; this applies for the next name as well.
21 **αὐτὸς**: *he himself*; i.e. Xenophon
22 **ἐπὶ**: *onto...*; acc. place to which
τῷ αὐτῷ τρόπῳ: *in...*; dat. of manner αὐτός means 'same' in the attributive position
τοῦτον: i.e. the λόφον
23 **αὐτοῖς**: *for...*; dat. of interest
24 **πολύ**: *far*; adverbial acc. (acc. of extent in degree)
ὀρθιώτατος: superlative
ὁ...: *the one over...*; i.e. the hill, what folllows is in the attributive position describing ὁ μαστός
ἐπὶ τῷ πυρὶ: *near...*
καταληφθείσης: gen. sg. aor. pass. pple καταλαμβάνω
25 **τῆς νυκτὸς**: *during...*; gen. of time within
ὑπὸ: *by...*; + gen. expressing agency
27 **ὥστε...γενέσθαι**: *so as to...*; result clause
πᾶσι: dat. of reference: in the eyes of all
ὑπώπτευον: 3p impf.

δείσαντας αὐτοὺς μὴ κυκλωθέντες πολιορκοῖντο ἀπολιπεῖν. 1
οἱ δ' ἄρα ἀπὸ τοῦ ἄκρου καθορῶντες τὰ ὄπισθεν γιγνόμενα
πάντες ἐπὶ τοὺς ὀπισθοφύλακας ἐχώρουν. 16. καὶ Ξενοφῶν μὲν
σὺν τοῖς νεωτάτοις ἀνέβαινεν ἐπὶ τὸ ἄκρον, τοὺς δὲ ἄλλους
ἐκέλευσεν ὑπάγειν, ὅπως οἱ τελευταῖοι λόχοι προσμείξειαν, 5
καὶ προελθόντας κατὰ τὴν ὁδὸν ἐν τῷ ὁμαλῷ θέσθαι τὰ ὅπλα
εἶπε. 17. καὶ ἐν τούτῳ τῷ χρόνῳ ἦλθεν Ἀρχαγόρας ὁ Ἀργεῖος
πεφευγὼς καὶ λέγει ὡς ἀπεκόπησαν ἀπὸ τοῦ λόφου καὶ
ὅτι τεθνᾶσι Κηφισόδωρος καὶ Ἀμφικράτης καὶ ἄλλοι ὅσοι

ἄλλος, -η, -ο: other, one...another, 8
Ἀμφικράτης, ὁ: Amphicrates, 2
ἀπο-κόπτω: to cut off, drive off, dislodge, 2
ἀπο-λείπω: to leave behind, abandon, 4
ἄρα: then, therefore, it seems, it turns out, 2
Ἀργεῖος, -α, -ον: Argive, of Argos, 2
Ἀρχαγόρας, ὁ: Archagoras, 2
δείδω: to fear, 5
θνῄσκω: to die, 3
καθ-οράω: to look down, perceive, 7
Κηφισόδωρος, ὁ: Cephisodorus, 2
κυκλόω: to encircle, surround, 1
νέος, -α, -ον: young; new, novel, strange, 3
ὁμαλός, -ή, -όν: level (ground), even, 2
πολιορκέω: to beseige, blockade, 1
προ-έρχομαι: to go forth, advance, 4
προσ-μείγνυμι: to engage/mix/unite with, 1
τελευταίος, -α, -ον: last, final, 6
τίθημι: to put, place; set, establish, 3
ὑπ-άγω: to come up slowly or gradually, 1
χρόνος, ὁ: time, 1
χωρέω: to go, come; have room for, 3

1 **δείσαντας**: pple δείδω modifying αὐτοὺς
αὐτοὺς...ἀπολιπεῖν: *that they*...; i.e. the enemy; ind. disc. with aor. inf.
μὴ...πολιορκοῖντο: *lest*...; fearing clause, pres. pass. opt. in secondary sequence
κυκλωθέντες: aor. pass. pple
2 **οἱ δὲ**: *and they*...; the enemy
ἀπὸ...ἄκρου: i.e. of the latest hill
τὰ ὄπισθεν γιγνόμενα: *the things*...; i.e. Xenophon and the rear guard fighting with the barbarians on the first of the three hills; the enemy left to retake that hill
3 **ἐπὶ**: *onto*...; acc. place to which
ἐχώρουν: *began to*...; inchoative impf.
4 **νεωτάτοις**: superlative, νεός, 'young'
ὅπως...προσμείξειαν: *so that*...; purpose clause with 3p aor. opt. in secondary seq.
προσμείξειαν: i.e. catch up with thim
6 **προελθόντας**: (*those*)...; aor. pple προ-έρχομαι
κατὰ: *along*...
θέσθαι τὰ ὅπλα: *to present arms*; or 'to halt under arms,' an idiom with several related meanings; aor. mid. inf. τίθημι
7 **εἶπε**: i.e. ordered; 3s aor. λέγω (εἶπον)
ἦλθεν: aor. ἔρχομαι
πεφευγὼς: nom. sg. pf. pple φεύγω
8 **ἀπεκόπησαν**: 3p aor. pass.; i.e. the Greeks on the first hill
9 **τεθνᾶσι**: 3p pf. θνῄσκω, the pf. denotes a state, 'are dead,' rather than an activity, 'have died'

μὴ ἁλόμενοι κατὰ τῆς πέτρας πρὸς τοὺς ὀπισθοφύλακας 10
ἀφίκοντο. 18. ταῦτα δὲ διαπραξάμενοι οἱ βάρβαροι ἧκον ἐπ᾽
ἀντίπορον λόφον τῷ μαστῷ· καὶ ὁ Ξενοφῶν διελέγετο αὐτοῖς
δι᾽ ἑρμηνέως περὶ σπονδῶν καὶ τοὺς νεκροὺς ἀπῄτει. 19. οἱ δὲ
ἔφασαν ἀποδώσειν ἐφ᾽ ᾧ μὴ καίειν τὰς οἰκίας. συνωμολόγει
ταῦτα ὁ Ξενοφῶν. ἐν ᾧ δὲ τὸ μὲν ἄλλο στράτευμα παρῄει, 15
οἱ δὲ ταῦτα διελέγοντο, πάντες οἱ ἐκ τούτου τοῦ τόπου
συνερρύησαν· †ἐνταῦθα ἵσταντο οἱ πολέμιοι†. 20. καὶ ἐπεὶ
ἤρξαντο καταβαίνειν ἀπὸ τοῦ μαστοῦ πρὸς τοὺς ἄλλους

p274

ἅλλομαι: to leap, jump, 1
ἀντι-πορος, -ον: opposite, over against +dat 1
ἀπ-αιτέω: to ask back, demand back, 1
ἀπο-δίδωμι: to give back, pay (what is due) 2
βάρβαρος, -α, -ον: foreigner, barbarian, 7
δια-λέγομαι: to converse with, discuss, 5
δια-πράττω: to accomplish, bring about, 2
ἑρμηνεύς, ὁ: an interpreter, 4
ἥκω: to have come, be present, 7
ἵστημι: make stand, set up, stop, establish, 7
μαστός, ὁ: mound, hill; a breast, 7
νεκρός, ὁ: corpse, body, 2
περί: around, about, concerning, 7
σπονδή, ἡ: a drink-offering; truce, treaty, 5
συν-ομο-λογέω: to agree with; concede, 1
συρ-ρέω: to flow together, stream together, 1
τόπος, ὁ: a place, region, 3

10 **μὴ ἁλόμενοι**: *not...*; aor. pple ἅλλομαι conditional in sense, thus μή rather than οὐ
κατὰ: *down from*...; gen. place from which
11 **ἧκον**: 3p impf. ἥκω
τῷ μαστῷ: dat. with special adj.
12 **αὐτοῖς**: *with*...; i.e. the enemy; ind. obj.
περὶ...: *about*...
13 **ἀπῄτει**: impf. ἀπ-αιτέω
14 **οἱ δὲ**: i.e. the Carduchians
ἔφασαν: 3p aor. φημί
ἀποδώσειν: *that (they)*...; ind. disc., add an acc. subject; fut. inf.
ἐφ ᾽ ᾧ: *on the condition that*...; 'on which condition...', ἐπ(ὶ) ᾧ; in the context of forming a pact or treaty (S1689c)
καίειν: *that (they)*...; supply acc. subject μή is used instead of οὐ in wishes and commands
15 **ἐν ᾧ**: *while*...; 'in which (time)'
τὸ ἄλλο στράτευμα: *the rest of the army*
παρῄει: impf. παρ-έρχομαι
16 **οἱ δὲ**: *and they*; Xenophon and the Carduchians
οἱ...τόπου: *those from this place*; i.e the enemy from this particular region distinct from those engaging with Xenophon
17 **συνερρύησαν**: aor. συρ-ρέω
†ἐνταῦθα...πολέμιοι†: A obelus (†) indicates that the word or clause is plainly corrupt but the editor cannot see how to emend it. Omit in translation.
ἵσταντο: impf.
18 **ἤρξαντο**: i.e the Greeks; ἄρχω

ἔνθα τὰ ὅπλα ἔκειντο, ἵεντο δὴ οἱ πολέμιοι πολλῷ πλήθει
καὶ θορύβῳ· καὶ ἐπεὶ ἐγένοντο ἐπὶ τῆς κορυφῆς τοῦ μαστοῦ 20
ἀφ' οὗ Ξενοφῶν κατέβαινεν, ἐκυλίνδουν πέτρους· καὶ ἑνὸς
μὲν κατέαξαν τὸ σκέλος, Ξενοφῶντα δὲ ὁ ὑπασπιστὴς
ἔχων τὴν ἀσπίδα ἀπέλιπεν· 21. Εὐρύλοχος δὲ Λουσιεὺς [Ἀρκὰς]
προσέδραμεν αὐτῷ ὁπλίτης, καὶ πρὸ ἀμφοῖν προβεβλημένος
ἀπεχώρει, καὶ οἱ ἄλλοι πρὸς τοὺς συντεταγμένους ἀπῆλθον. 25
22. ἐκ δὲ τούτου πᾶν ὁμοῦ ἐγένετο τὸ Ἑλληνικόν, καὶ ἐσκήνησαν
αὐτοῦ ἐν πολλαῖς καὶ καλαῖς οἰκίαις καὶ ἐπιτηδείοις δαψιλέσι·

ἄμφω: both, 1
ἀπο-λείπω: to leave behind, abandon, 4
ἀπο-χωρέω: go from, depart, 2
Ἀρκάς, Ἀρκάδος, ὁ: Arcadian, of Arcadia, 5
ἀσπίς, ἀσπίδος, ὁ: a round shield, 6
αὐτοῦ: in that very place, there, 7
δαψιλής, -ές: abundant, plentiful, 2
Ἑλληνικός, -ή, -όν: Greek, Hellenic, 3
Εὐρύλοχος, ὁ: Eurylochus, 3
θόρυβος, ὁ: din, noise, uproar, 3
ἵημι: to send, throw; let go, release, 4
κατ-εάσσω (κατ-άγνυμι): to break, 1
κεῖμαι: to lie, lie down 2
κορυφή, ἡ: top, summit, highest part of, 1
κυλίνδω: to roll (down); wallow, wander, 5
Λουσιεύς, -έως, ὁ: of Lusi, Lusean, 3
μαστός, ὁ: mound, hill; a breast, 7
ὁμοῦ: at the same place, together, 3
πλῆθος, ἡ: crowd, multitude; size, 4
πρό: before, in front; in place of (+ gen.), 3
προσ-βάλλω: to attack, strike against, dash 3
προσ-τρέχω: to run to, run at, 2
σκέλος, -εος, τό: leg, 2
σκηνέω: to encamp, bivouac, set up tents, 5
συν-τάττω: to post/marshall together, order 3
ὑπ-ασπιστής, ὁ: shield-bearer, 1

19 **ἔνθα**: *where...*; relative clause
ἔκειντο: impf. κεῖμαι
ἵεντο: *began to rush*; inchoative impf. mid. ἵημι
δή: *then, now*; temporal
πολλῷ...θορύβῳ: *with...*; dat. of manner
21 **ἀπ(ὸ) οὗ...**: relative clause
ἑνὸς: *of one (man)*; gen. sg. εἷς
22 **κατέαξαν**: 3p aor. κατ-άγνυμι
Ξενοφῶντα: acc. object of ἀπέλιπεν, aor. ἀπολείπω
23 **τὴν ἀσπίδα**: i.e. Xenophon's shield
24 **προσέδραμεν**: aor. προστρέχω
αὐτῷ: *to him*; i.e. to Xenophon, dat. of compound verb
ὁπλίτης: describing Εὐρύλοχος
ἀμφοῖν: dual dat.
προβεβλημένος: *putting (his shield) in front*; pf. mid. προβάλλω, Eurylochus defends Xenophon as they withdraw
25 **συντεταγμένους**: pf. συντάττω
ἀπῆλθον: aor. ἀπ-έρχομαι
26 **Ἑλληνικόν**: add στάτευμα
27 **αὐτοῦ**: *there*; 'in the very place,' adv.
ἐπιτηδείοις: *provisions*

καὶ γὰρ οἶνος πολὺς ἦν, ὥστε ἐν λάκκοις κονιατοῖς εἶχον. 1
23. Ξενοφῶν δὲ καὶ Χειρίσοφος διεπράξαντο ὥστε λαβόντες
τοὺς νεκροὺς ἀπέδοσαν τὸν ἡγεμόνα· καὶ πάντα ἐποίησαν
τοῖς ἀποθανοῦσιν ἐκ τῶν δυνατῶν ὥσπερ νομίζεται ἀνδράσιν
ἀγαθοῖς. 24. τῇ δὲ ὑστεραίᾳ ἄνευ ἡγεμόνος ἐπορεύοντο· μαχό- 5
μενοι δ' οἱ πολέμιοι καὶ ὅπῃ εἴη στενὸν χωρίον προκατα-
λαμβάνοντες ἐκώλυον τὰς παρόδους. 25. ὁπότε μὲν οὖν τοὺς
πρώτους κωλύοιεν, Ξενοφῶν ὄπισθεν ἐκβαίνων πρὸς τὰ ὄρη
ἔλυε τὴν ἀπόφραξιν τῆς ὁδοῦ τοῖς πρώτοις ἀνωτέρω πειρώ-

ἄνευ: without (+ gen.), 4
ἀνωτέρω: upper, higher, 2
ἀπο-δίδωμι: to give back, pay (what is due) 2
ἀπό-φραξις, ἡ: blockade, a blocking up, 2
δια-πράττω: to accomplish, bring about, 2
δυνατός, -ή, -όν: capable, strong, possible, 3
ἐκ-βαίνω: to step out, disembark; turn out, 7
κονιατός, -ή, -όν: plastered, 1
λάκκος, ὁ: reservoir, cistern, 1
λύω: to loosen, free; *mid.* ransom, 4
νεκρός, ὁ: corpse, body, 2
νομίζω: to believe, think; *mid.* is customary 2
οἶνος, ὁ: wine, 5
ὅπῃ: where; in what way, how, 3
πάρ-οδος, ὁ: passage, entrance, approach, 4
πειράω: to try, attempt, endeavor, 7
προ-κατα-λαμβάνω: to seize beforehand, 3
ὑστεραῖος, -α, -ον: the next day; later, 5

1 **καὶ γὰρ**: *for in fact*
ὥστε...εἶχον: *that...*; result clause; impf. ἔχω; add τὸν οἶνον as obj.
2 **διεπράξαντο**: i.e. brought it about through bargaining with the Carduchians; aor. mid.
λαβόντες: aor. pple λαμβάνω
3 **ἀπέδοσαν**: aor. ἀπο-δίδωμι
τὸν ἡγεμόνα: i.e. the non-Greek forced to guide them
4 **τοῖς ἀποθανοῦσιν**: *for (those)...*; dat. of interest; aor. pple ἀποθνῄσκω
ἐκ τῶν δυνατῶν: *as much as possible*; 'from what is possible'
νομίζεται: *it is customary*; impersonal
ἀνδράσιν ἀγαθοῖς: *for...*; dat. interest
5 **τῇ ὑστεραίᾳ (ἡμέρᾳ)**: *on...*; time when
6 **ὅπῃ εἴη...**: *wherever...*; past general relative clause with opt. εἰμί replacing an ἄν + subj. in primary seq.
7 **ἐκώλυον**: *tried to...*; inchoatic impf. or iterative impf. ('kept...')
παρόδους: hindered not several at once but several passages in succession
ὁπότε...κωλύοιεν: *whenever...*; general temporal clause, secondary seq. with opt.
8 **ὄπισθεν**: *from the rear*
ὄρη: ὄρε-α, neuter ὄρος
9 **ἔλυε**: *would break through*; iterative impf., Xenophon did this more than once
τοῖς πρώτοις: *for...*; dat of interest; in contrast to the rear guard

μενος γίγνεσθαι τῶν κωλυόντων, 26. *ὁπότε δὲ τοῖς ὄπισθεν* 10
ἐπιθοῖντο, Χειρίσοφος ἐκβαίνων καὶ πειρώμενος ἀνωτέρω
γίγνεσθαι τῶν κωλυόντων ἔλυε τὴν ἀπόφραξιν τῆς παρόδου
τοῖς ὄπισθεν· καὶ ἀεὶ οὕτως ἐβοήθουν ἀλλήλοις καὶ ἰσχυρῶς
ἀλλήλων ἐπεμέλοντο. 27. *ἦν δὲ καὶ ὁπότε αὐτοῖς τοῖς ἀναβᾶσι*
πολλὰ πράγματα παρεῖχον οἱ βάρβαροι πάλιν καταβαίνουσιν· 15
ἐλαφροὶ γὰρ ἦσαν ὥστε καὶ ἐγγύθεν φεύγοντες ἀποφεύγειν·
οὐδὲν γὰρ εἶχον ἄλλο ἢ τόξα καὶ σφενδόνας. 28. *ἄριστοι δὲ καὶ*
τοξόται ἦσαν· εἶχον δὲ τόξα ἐγγὺς τριπήχη, τὰ δὲ τοξεύ-

ἀεί: always, forever, in every case, 6
ἀνωτέρω: upper, higher, 2
ἀπο-φεύγω: to escape, flee from, 1
ἀπό-φραξις, ἡ: blockade, a blocking up, 2
ἄριστος, -η, -ον: best, most excellent; noble, 2
βάρβαρος, -α, -ον: foreigner, barbarian, 7
βοηθέω: to come to aid, to assist, aid, 2
ἐγγύ-θεν: from nearby, from near, 1
ἐγγύς: near (+ gen.); *adv.* nearby, 7
ἐκ-βαίνω: to step out, disembark; turn out, 7
ἐλαφρός, -ά, -όν: light (in weight), 1
ἐπι-μέλ(ε)ομαι: to care for, look after (gen) 3
ἐπι-τίθημι: to put upon; add; set upon, attack 4
ἰσχυρός, -ά, -όν: strong, powerful; severe, 7
λύω: to loosen, free; *mid.* ransom, 4
παρ-έχω: to provide, furnish, supply, 5
πάρ-οδος, ὁ: passage, entrance, approach, 4
πειράω: to try, attempt, endeavor, 7
πρᾶγμα, τό: deed; matter, affair, trouble, 3
σφενδόνη, ἡ: sling, stone (from a sling), 2
τόξευμα, -ατος, τό: arrow, 4
τόξον, τό: bow, 4
τοξότης, ὁ: an archer, bowman, 4
τρί-πηχυς, -υ: three-cubits long, 1

10 **τῶν κωλυόντων**: *than those...*; i.e. the enemy, gen. of comparison; pres. pple
ὁπότε...ἐπιθοῖντο: *whenever...*; general temporal clause in secondary seq., aor. mid. opt. ἐπιτίθημι
τοῖς ὄπισθεν: *those in the rear (guard)*; dat. of compound verb
12 **τῶν κωλυόντων**: see line 10
ἔλυε: *would break through*; iterative impf.,
13 **τοῖς ὄπισθεν**: *for...*; dat. of interest
ἐβοήθουν: Xenophon and Cheirisophus are the subject
14 **ἦν...ὁπότε**: *sometimes in fact*; 'there was (a time) in fact when,' a common idiom caused by the lack of an antecedent for the relative clause that follows (S2515); καί is adverbial
αὐτοῖς...ἀναβᾶσι: *for those...*; dat. of interest, dat. pl. aor. pple ἀναβαίνω
15 **πολλὰ πράγματα παρεῖχον**: παρέχω πράγματα is a common idiom for 'make trouble'
καταβαίνουσιν: *(while)...*; dat. pl. pres. pple modifies αὐτοῖς
16 **ἦσαν**: 3p impf. εἰμί
ὥστε...: *so as to...*; result clause, ὥστε + inf.
καὶ: *even*
φεύγοντες ἀποφεύγειν: note that φεύγω means 'flee' or 'run away' while ἀποφεύγω means 'escape'
17 **ἤ**: *than...*; as often following ἄλλο
18 **τριπήχη**: τριπήχε-α

ματα πλέον ἢ διπήχη· εἷλκον δὲ τὰς νευρὰς ὁπότε τοξεύοιεν
πρὸς τὸ κάτω τοῦ τόξου τῷ ἀριστερῷ ποδὶ προσβαίνοντες. 20
τὰ δὲ τοξεύματα ἐχώρει διὰ τῶν ἀσπίδων καὶ διὰ τῶν
θωράκων. ἐχρῶντο δὲ αὐτοῖς οἱ Ἕλληνες, ἐπεὶ λάβοιεν,
ἀκοντίοις ἐναγκυλῶντες. ἐν τούτοις τοῖς χωρίοις οἱ Κρῆτες
χρησιμώτατοι ἐγένοντο. ἦρχε δὲ αὐτῶν Στρατοκλῆς Κρής.

1. ταύτην δ' αὖ τὴν ἡμέραν ηὐλίσθησαν ἐν ταῖς κώμαις 25
ταῖς ὑπὲρ τοῦ πεδίου παρὰ τὸν Κεντρίτην ποταμόν, εὖρος ὡς
δίπλεθρον, ὃς ὁρίζει τὴν Ἀρμενίαν καὶ τὴν τῶν Καρδούχων

ἀκόντιον, τό: javelin, 1
ἀριστερός, -ά, -όν: left, on the left, 4
Ἀρμενία, ἡ: Armenia, 6
ἀσπίς, ἀσπίδος, ὁ: a round shield, 6
αὐλίζομαι: to bivouac, encamp, lodge, 5
δι-πήχυς, -εῖα, -υ: of two cubits long, 1
δί-πλεθρος, -όν: of two plethra long, 1
ἕλκω: to draw, drag, 3
ἐν-αγκυλάω: to fit thongs (to javelins), 1
εὖρος, τό: breadth, width, 3
θώραξ, θώρακος, ὁ: breastplace, corset, 2
κάτω: downwards, below, 4
Κεντρίτης, ὁ: Centrites river, 1
Κρής, Κρητός, ὁ: a Cretan, 3
νευρά, ἡ: bow-string, string, 1
ὁρίζω: to divide, define, 3
πούς, ποδός, ὁ: a foot, 7
προσ-βαίνω: to go to, approach, step to, 1
Στρατοκλῆς, ὁ: Stratocles, 1
τόξευμα, -ατος, τό: arrow, 4
τόξον, τό: bow, 4
χράομαι: use, employ, enjoy, indulge (dat) 6
χρήσιμος, -η, -ον: good, useful, serviceable, 1
χωρέω: to go, come; have room for, 3

19 διπήχη: διπήχε-α; neut. pl.
εἷλκον: impf. ἕλκω
ὁπότε τοξεύοιεν: *whenever…*; general temporal clause, pres. opt. in secondary sequence
20 πρὸς τὸ κάτω…προσβαίνοντες: *stepping onto the bottom…*; the bow is placed on the ground and held firm with the foot
τῷ ἀριστερῷ ποδὶ: dat. of means,
21 ἐχώρει: *would go*; customary impf.
ἐχρῶντο: + dat., impf. χράομαι
22 ἐπεὶ λάβοιεν: *whenever…*; general temporal clause, aor. opt. λαμβάνω in secondary seq.
23 ἀκοντίοις: *as javelins…*; following αὐτοῖς in apposition; the arrows were so long they could be thrown by hand as javelins
ἐναγκυλῶντες: a leather loop or thong attached to the javelin was used to sling the javelin farther and more accurately than one otherwise could without the loop
24 χρησιμώτατοι: superlative
ἦρχε: impf. ἄρχω + gen. obj.
25 ταύτην…ἡμέραν: acc. of duration
26 ταῖς…: the prepositional phrases are in the attributive position modifying κώμαις
εὖρος: *in…*; acc. of respect
ὡς: *nearly*; 'as if,' in approximation (S2995)

χώραν. καὶ οἱ Ἕλληνες ἐνταῦθα ἀνέπνευσαν ἄσμενοι ἰδόντες πεδίον· ἀπεῖχε δὲ τῶν ὀρέων ὁ ποταμὸς ἓξ ἢ ἑπτὰ στάδια τῶν Καρδούχων. 2. τότε μὲν οὖν ηὐλίσθησαν μάλα ἡδέως καὶ τἀπιτήδεια ἔχοντες καὶ πολλὰ τῶν παρεληλυθότων πόνων μνημονεύοντες. ἑπτὰ γὰρ ἡμέρας ὅσασπερ ἐπορεύθησαν διὰ τῶν Καρδούχων πάσας μαχόμενοι διετέλεσαν, καὶ ἔπαθον κακὰ ὅσα οὐδὲ τὰ σύμπαντα ὑπὸ βασιλέως καὶ Τισσαφέρνους. ὡς οὖν ἀπηλλαγμένοι τούτων ἡδέως ἐκοιμήθησαν.

3. ἅμα δὲ τῇ ἡμέρᾳ ὁρῶσιν ἱππέας που πέραν τοῦ ποταμοῦ

ἀνα-πνέω: to breathe (again); recover, 2
ἀπ-αλλάττω: set free, deliver; escape, 1
ἀπ-έχω: to be distant, keep away from, 5
ἄσμενος, -η, -ον: well-pleased, glad, 2
αὐλίζομαι: to bivouac, encamp, lodge, 5
δια-τελέω: continue, perservere (to the end) 1
ἕξ: six, 1
ἑπτά: seven, 5
ἡδέως: sweetly, pleasantly, gladly, 2
κακός, -ή, -όν: bad, base, cowardly, evil, 5
κοιμάω: to put to sleep, lull to sleep, 3
μάλα: very, very much, exceedingly, 4
μνημονεύω: to call to mind, recall (gen) 1
πάσχω: to suffer, experience, 3
πέραν: across, beyond, exceeding (gen), 5
πόνος, ὁ: work, toil; trouble, 1
που: anywhere, somewhere; I suppose, 2
σύμπας, -πασα, -παν: all together, 1
Τισσαφέρνης, ὁ: Tissaphernes, 2
τότε: then, at that time, 7

1 **ἄσμενοι**: adjectives in the nom. are often translated as adverbs in English
ἰδόντες: aor. pple ὁράω (εἶδον)
2 **ἀπεῖχε**: impf. ἀπέχω, 'be away from'
τῶν ὀρέων: *from...*; gen. of separation
ἓξ...στάδια: *for...*; acc. of extent
3 **τῶν Καρδούχων**: posssessive gen., modifies ὀρέων
4 **τὰ (ἐ)πιτήδεια**
πολλὰ: *many times*; i.e. often; adverbial acc. with the following pple
παρεληλυθότων: i.e. 'past' or 'previous'; pf. pple παρ-έρχομαι
πόνων: gen obj. of verb of remembering or forgetting
5 **ἑπτὰ...ἡμέρας**: acc. of duration
ὅσασπερ: *for as many (days) as...*; acc. of duration in a relative clause
ἐπορεύθησαν: aor. pass. dep. πορεύομαι
6 **πάσας**: modifes ἡμέρας
ἔπαθον: aor. πάσχω
7 **ὅσα (ἔπαθον)**: *as many as...*; add verb
οὐδὲ: *not even*; adv.
ὑπὸ: *at the hands of...*; 'because of...' gen. of cause or agent; Τισσαφέρνε-ος is gen. sg.
8 **ὡς**: *on the grounds that...*; 'since,' ὡς + pple suggests alleged cause from a character's point of view
ἀπηλλαγμένοι: pf. pass. pple
τούτων: *from...*; gen. of separation
ἐκοιμηθησαν: 3s aor. deponent
9 **που**: *somewhere*
ὁρῶσιν: ὁράουσιν, 3p pres.

ἐξωπλισμένους ὡς κωλύσοντας διαβαίνειν, πεζοὺς δ' ἐπὶ ταῖς 10
ὄχθαις παρατεταγμένους ἄνω τῶν ἱππέων ὡς κωλύσοντας
εἰς τὴν Ἀρμενίαν ἐκβαίνειν. 4. ἦσαν δ' οὗτοι Ὀρόντα καὶ
Ἀρτούχα Ἀρμένιοι καὶ Μάρδοι καὶ Χαλδαῖοι μισθοφόροι.
ἐλέγοντο δὲ οἱ Χαλδαῖοι ἐλεύθεροί τε καὶ ἄλκιμοι εἶναι·
ὅπλα δ' εἶχον γέρρα μακρὰ καὶ λόγχας. 5. αἱ δὲ ὄχθαι αὗται 15
ἐφ' ὧν παρατεταγμένοι οὗτοι ἦσαν τρία ἢ τέτταρα πλέθρα
ἀπὸ τοῦ ποταμοῦ ἀπεῖχον· ὁδὸς δὲ μία ὁρωμένη ἦν ἄγουσα
ἄνω ὥσπερ χειροποίητος· ταύτῃ ἐπειρῶντο διαβαίνειν οἱ

ἄλκιμος, -ον: stout, brave, 2
ἀπ-έχω: to be distant, keep away from, 5
Ἀρμενία, ἡ: Armenia, 6
Ἀρμένιοι, οἱ: Armenian, 3
Ἀρτούχας, -ου (or **-α**) **ὁ**: Artuchas, 1
γέρρον, τό: wicker-work; wicker-shield, 6
ἐκ-βαίνω: to step out, disembark; turn out, 7
ἐλεύθερος, -η, -ον: free, 1
ἐξ-οπλίζομαι: to arm fully, 2
λόγχη, ἡ: spearheard; spear, lance, 4
μακρός, ά, όν: long, far, distant, large, 1
Μάρδοι, οἱ: Mardian, 1
μισθο-φορος, ὁ: mercenary, serving for hire, 2
Ὀρόντας, -ου (or **-α**) **ὁ**: Orontas, 1
ὄχθη, ἡ: bank (of a river), bluff, 4
παρα-τάττω: draw up in battle order, 5
πεζός, ἡ, όν: on foot, 1
πειράω: to try, attempt, endeavor, 7
πλέθρον, τό: a plethron (=100 feet), 3
τέτταρες, -α: four, 6
Χαλδαῖοι, οἱ: Chaldaeans, 2
χειρο-ποίητος, -ον: made by hand, 1

10 **ὡς κωλύσοντας**: *so that...*; ὡς + fut. pple expresses purpose
διαβαίνειν: *from...*; after κωλύσοντας
πεζοὺς: *foot-soldiers*; '(those) on foot'
11 **παρατεταγμένος**: pf. pass. pple
ὡς κωλύσοντας: see above
12 **ἐκβαίνειν**: *from...*; after κωλύσοντας
Ὀρόντα καὶ Ἀρτούχα: *(the troops) of...*; both are Doric genitives (S225, common in non-Greek names with nom. -ας) and predicate following ἦσαν
14 **ἐλέγοντο**: impf. passive λέγω
εἶναι: inf. εἰμί
15 **ὅπλα**: *as arms*; acc. apposition
16 **ἐφ 'ὧν**: *upon which*
παρατεταγμένοι...ἦσαν: periphrastic plpf. pass. (pf. pass. pple + impf. εἰμί)
τρία...πλέθρα: *over...*; acc. of extent
17 **ἀπεῖχον**: *was far away*
ὁρωμένη: *seen*; or 'visible,' this pres. pass. pple is a predicate
ἄγουσα ἄνω: pple modifying fem. ὁδὸς
18 **ταύτῃ**: *in this way*; dat. of manner
ἐπειρῶντο: ἐπειράοντο; impf. πειράω

Ἕλληνες. 6. ἐπεὶ δὲ πειρωμένοις τό τε ὕδωρ ὑπὲρ τῶν μαστῶν ἐφαίνετο, καὶ τραχὺς ἦν ὁ ποταμὸς μεγάλοις λίθοις καὶ 20 *ὀλισθηροῖς, καὶ οὔτ᾽ ἐν τῷ ὕδατι τὰ ὅπλα ἦν ἔχειν· εἰ δὲ μή, ἥρπαζεν ὁ ποταμός· ἐπί τε τῆς κεφαλῆς τὰ ὅπλα εἴ τις φέροι, γυμνοὶ ἐγίγνοντο πρὸς τὰ τοξεύματα καὶ τἆλλα βέλη, ἀνεχώρησαν καὶ αὐτοῦ ἐστρατοπεδεύσαντο παρὰ τὸν ποταμόν. 7. ἔνθα δὲ αὐτοὶ τὴν πρόσθεν νύκτα ἦσαν ἐπὶ τοῦ ὄρους ἑώρων* 25 *τοὺς Καρδούχους πολλοὺς συνειλεγμένους ἐν τοῖς ὅπλοις. ἐνταῦθα δὴ πολλὴ ἀθυμία ἦν τοῖς Ἕλλησιν, ὁρῶσι μὲν τοῦ ποταμοῦ τὴν δυσπορίαν, ὁρῶσι δὲ τοὺς διαβαίνειν κωλύ-*

ἀ-θυμία ἡ: faintheartedness, discouragement 3
ἀνα-χωρέω: to go back, withdraw, 1
ἁρπάζω: seize, carry off, kidnap, 3
αὐτοῦ: in that very place, there, 7
βέλος, -εος, τό: missle, arrow, dart, 2
γυμνός, -ή, -όν: naked, unclad, unarmed, 4
δυσπορία, ἡ: difficulty in passing, 1
κεφαλή, ἡ: the head, 4
μαστός, ὁ: mound, hill; a breast, 7
ὀλισθηρός, -ή, -όν: slippery, 1
οὔ-τε: and not, neither...nor, 6
πειράω: to try, attempt, endeavor, 7
πρόσθεν: before, 3
στρατοπεδεύω: to encamp, take a position, 4
συλ-λέγω: to collect, gather, 5
τόξευμα, -ατος, τό: arrow, 4
τραχύς, -εῖα, -ύ: rough, jagged, 2
ὕδωρ, ὕδατος, τό: water, 5
φαίνω: to show; *mid.* appear, seem, 6

19 **πειρωμένοις**: *for (those)...*; dat. of interest
τε...καὶ: *both...and...*; the two clauses up to ὀλισθηροῖς are in the same ἐπεί clause
ὑπὲρ τῶν μαστῶν: *over their chests*
20 **λίθοις**: *with...*; dat. means
καὶ οὔτ(ε): *also...not*; in this main clause, καί is adverbial and οὔτε is used instead of οὐ to correspond to τε above
21 **ἦν**: *it was possible*
εἰ δὲ μή: *and if not*; not logically correct; we should expect the positive 'and if they held the arms...' from the previous sentence.
22 **ἥρπαζεν**: assume ὅπλα as object
ἐπὶ...: *over...*
εἴ...φέροι...ἐγίγνοντο: *if...carried, they...*; past general condition (εἰ opt., impf. ind.)
23 **πρὸς**: *against..., in regard to...*; i.e. enemies could attack him
τἆλλα βέλα: τὰ ἄλλα βέλε-α
24 **αὐτοῦ**: *there*; 'in the very spot,' adv.
25 **ἔνθα...ἦσαν**: *(at the place) where...*; relative clause with missing antecedent
τὴν...νύκτα: *during...*; acc. of duration
ἐπὶ: *upon...*; + gen. ὄρε-ος
ἑώρων: ἑωράον, 3p impf. ὁράω
26 **συνειλεγμένους**: pf. pass. pple
ἐνταῦθα δὴ: *just then, precisely then*; intensive
27 **τοῖς Ἕλλησιν**: dat. of possession: either (1) 'there were to the Greeks' or (2) 'the Greeks had'
ὁρῶσι μὲν...ὁρῶσι δὲ...: dat. pl. pres. pples in apposition to Ἕλλησιν
28 **διαβαίνειν**: *(them) from...*; as often when an inf. follows κωλύω

σοντας, ὁρῶσι δὲ τοῖς διαβαίνουσιν ἐπικεισομένους τοὺς Καρδούχους ὄπισθεν. 8. ταύτην μὲν οὖν τὴν ἡμέραν καὶ νύκτα ἔμειναν ἐν πολλῇ ἀπορίᾳ ὄντες. Ξενοφῶν δὲ ὄναρ εἶδεν· ἔδοξεν ἐν πέδαις δεδέσθαι, αὗται δὲ αὐτῷ αὐτόμαται περιρρυῆναι, ὥστε λυθῆναι καὶ διαβαίνειν ὁπόσον ἐβούλετο. ἐπεὶ δὲ ὄρθρος ἦν, ἔρχεται πρὸς τὸν Χειρίσοφον καὶ λέγει ὅτι ἐλπίδας ἔχει καλῶς ἔσεσθαι, καὶ διηγεῖται αὐτῷ τὸ ὄναρ. 9. ὁ δὲ ἥδετό τε καὶ ὡς τάχιστα ἕως ὑπέφαινεν ἐθύοντο πάντες παρόντες οἱ στρατηγοί· καὶ τὰ ἱερὰ καλὰ ἦν εὐθὺς ἐπὶ τοῦ

ἀ-πορία, ἡ: difficulty, bewilderment, 1
αὐτό-ματος, -η, -ον: of one's own will, 1
δέω (2): to bind, tie, 3
δι-ηγέομαι: to explain, lead through, 2
ἐλπίς, -ίδος, ἡ: hope, expectation, 1
ἐπί-κειμαι: set upon; press upon, attack, 3
ἕως (ἠός): dawn, 1
ἥδομαι: to enjoy, delight in, 1
θύω: to sacrifice, 3
ἱερόν, τό: (sacrificial) victim, animal, 3
λύω: to loosen, free; *mid.* ransom, 4
ὄναρ, τό: a dream, vision in sleep, 2
ὁπόσος, -α, -ον: as much, many, or great as, 2
ὄρθρος, ὁ: the time just before daybreak, 1
πάρ-ειμι: to be near, be present, be at hand, 4
πέδη, ἡ: fetter, shackles, bindings, 1
περι-ρέω: flow or fall away on all sides, 1
ὑπο-φαίνω: to show oneself, break, 2

1 **ὁρῶσι δὲ**: *and...*; dat. pl. pple
τοῖς διαβαίνουσιν: *upon (those)...*; dat. pl. pple, dat. of compound verb
ἐπικεισομένους: fut. mid. pple
2 **ταύτην...ἡμέραν καὶ νύκτα**: acc. duration
3 **ἔμειναν**: aor. μένω
εἶδεν: aor. ὁράω
4 **ἔδοξεν**: *he seemed...*
δεδέσθαι: pf. pass. inf. δέω
αὗται (πέδαι): *these (fetters)*
περιρρυῆναι (ἔδοξαν): *(seemed) to*; aor. pass. inf., supply 3p ἔδοξαν
5 **ὥστε λυθῆναι...διαβαίνειν**: *so that (he) was...and...*; result clause with aor. pass. inf. and pres. act. inf.
ὁπόσον: *as great (a distance) as...*; or 'as far as,' relative clause with acc. of extent
7 **καλῶς**: *well*; adv.
ἔσεσθαι: *that it...*; ind. disc. with fut. inf. εἰμί in apposition to ἐλπίδας
διηγεῖται: *explains*; Xenophon is subject
αὐτῷ: i.e. to Cheirisophus; dat. ind. obj.
8 **ὁ δὲ**: *and he*; Cheirisophus
ἥδετο: impf. ἥδομαι
ὡς τάχιστα...ὑπέφαινεν: *as soon as...*; 'as quickly as possible' introducing a clause
9 **ἦν**: 3s impf. εἰμί
καλὰ: *auspicious, favorable*; i.e. the gods appear to have approved the sacrifice
ἐπὶ τοῦ πρώτου: *in the case of the first (sacrificial victim)*

πρώτου. καὶ ἀπιόντες ἀπὸ τῶν ἱερῶν οἱ στρατηγοὶ καὶ 10
λοχαγοὶ παρήγγελλον τῇ στρατιᾷ ἀριστοποιεῖσθαι. 10. *καὶ ἀρι-*
στῶντι τῷ Ξενοφῶντι προσέτρεχον δύο νεανίσκω· ᾔδεσαν
γὰρ πάντες ὅτι ἐξείη αὐτῷ καὶ ἀριστῶντι καὶ δειπνοῦντι
προσελθεῖν καί, εἰ καθεύδοι, ἐπεγείραντα εἰπεῖν, εἴ τίς τι
ἔχοι τῶν πρὸς τὸν πόλεμον. 11. *καὶ τότε ἔλεγον ὅτι τυγχά-* 15
νοιεν φρύγανα συλλέγοντες ὡς ἐπὶ πῦρ, κἄπειτα κατίδοιεν
ἐν τῷ πέραν ἐν πέτραις καθηκούσαις ἐπ' αὐτὸν τὸν ποταμὸν
γέροντά τε καὶ γυναῖκα καὶ παιδίσκας ὥσπερ μαρσίπους ἱμα-

ἀριστάω: to take breakfast, take a meal, 6
ἀριστο-ποιέω: to make breakfast, 2
γέρων, -οντος, ὁ: elder, old man, 1
γυνή, γυναικός, ἡ: a woman, wife, 7
δειπνέω: to dine, have dinner, 3
δύο: two, 8
ἔξ-εστί: it is allowed, it is possible, 4
ἐπ-εγείρω: to awaken, rouse up, 1
ἔπ-ειτα: then, next, secondly, 4
ἱερόν, τό: (sacrificial) victim, animal, 3
ἱμάτιον, τό: cloak, mantle, outer garment, 2
καθ-εύδω: to lie down to sleep, sleep, 1
καθ-ηκω: to reach down; it is fitting, 1
καθ-οράω: to look down, perceive, 7
μάρσιπος, ὁ: bag, 1
νεανίσκος, ὁ: a youth, 4
οἶδα: to know, 5
παιδίσκη, ἡ: young girl, maiden, 1
παρ-αγγέλλω: to pass word along, order 7
πέραν: across, beyond, exceeding (gen), 5
πόλεμος, ὁ: battle, fight, war, 2
προσ-τρέχω: to run to, run at, 2
στρατία, ἡ: an army, expedition, land force, 4
συλ-λέγω: to collect, gather, 5
τότε: then, at that time, 7
τυγχάνω: chance upon, get; meet; happen, 5
φρύγανον, τό: firewood, dry sticks, 1

10 **ἀπιόντες**: pple ἀπ-έρχομαι
ἀπὸ τῶν ἱερῶν: *from the sacrifices*
11 **τῇ στρατιᾷ**: dat. of compound verb
Ξενοφῶντι: dat. of compound verb
12 **νεανίσχω**: dual nom. with 3p verb
ᾔδεσαν: 3p plpf. οἶδα, translate in the simple past
13 **ἐξείη**: *it was permitted (for them)*; opt. ἐξεστιν, ind. disc. in secondary sequence
αὐτῷ: *to him*; i.e. Xenophon, dat. of compound προσελθεῖν, ind. obj. of εἰπεῖν
καὶ...καὶ...: *both...and...*
14 **προσελθεῖν... εἰπεῖν**: aor. inf. προσέρχομαι, εἶπον, governed by ἐξείη
εἰ καθεύδοι: *if ever...*; opt. in a past general condition; soldiers could approach him at any time
ἐπεγείραντα: modifies acc. subj. of εἰπεῖν
14 **εἴ τίς...ἔχοι (εἰπεῖν)**: *if someone...were able...*; opt. ἔχω + missing inf. εἰπεῖν; indefinite nom. τις following enclitic τι
τι: *something (important)*
τῶν πρὸς: *of (the things) pertaining to...*; partitive gen. and preposition phrase in the attributive position
15 **τυγχάνοιεν**: *happened to...*; + pple, opt. replacing impf. in ind. disc., secondary seq.
16 **ὡς ἐπὶ πῦρ**: *for a fire*; 'as if for a fire,' ὡς expresses intent of the character (S2996)
κα(ὶ) (ἔ)πειτα
κατίδοιεν: 3p opt. καθοράω parallel to τυγχάνοιεν in ind. disc.
17 **ἐν τῷ πέραν**: *on the side (beyond)*; i.e. the far side of the river
ἐπ(ὶ)...ποταμὸν: *up to the river itself*
18 **ὥσπερ**: *as it were*; or 'it seemed'

τίων κατατιθεμένους ἐν πέτρᾳ ἀντρώδει. 12. ἰδοῦσι δὲ σφίσι
δόξαι ἀσφαλὲς εἶναι διαβῆναι· οὐδὲ γὰρ τοῖς πολεμίοις 20
ἱππεῦσι προσβατὸν εἶναι κατὰ τοῦτο. ἐκδύντες δ' ἔφασαν
ἔχοντες τὰ ἐγχειρίδια γυμνοὶ ὡς νευσόμενοι διαβαίνειν·
πορευόμενοι δὲ πρόσθεν διαβῆναι πρὶν βρέξαι τὰ αἰδοῖα·
καὶ διαβάντες, λαβόντες τὰ ἱμάτια πάλιν ἥκειν. 13. εὐθὺς οὖν
Ξενοφῶν αὐτός τε ἔσπενδε καὶ τοῖς νεανίσκοις ἐγχεῖν ἐκέ- 25
λευε καὶ εὔχεσθαι τοῖς φήνασι θεοῖς τά τε ὀνείρατα καὶ τὸν
πόρον καὶ τὰ λοιπὰ ἀγαθὰ ἐπιτελέσαι. σπείσας δ' εὐθὺς
ἦγε τοὺς νεανίσκους παρὰ τὸν Χειρίσοφον, καὶ διηγοῦνται

αἰδοῖα, τά: the genitals, 1
ἀντρώδης, -ες: cavernous, hollow, 1
ἀ-σφαλής, -ές: safe, secure, not liable to fall 7
βρέχω: be wet, get wet, 2
γυμνός, -ή, -όν: naked, unclad, unarmed, 4
δι-ηγέομαι: to explain, lead through, 2
ἐγχειρίδιος, -α, -ον: hand-dagger, 1
ἐγ-χέω: to pour, pour in; fill a cup, 1
ἐκ-δύνω: to take off, strip; go out, 1
ἐπι-τελέω: to complete, finish, accomplish, 1
εὔχομαι: to pray, offer prayers, vow, 5
ἥκω: to have come, be present, 7
θεός, ὁ: a god, divinity, 3
ἱμάτιον, τό: a cloak or mantle, 2
κατα-τίθημι: to set down, deposit, settle, 1
λοιπός, ὁ: remaining, the rest, 6
νεανίσκος, ὁ: a youth, 4
νέω: to swim, 1
ὄνειρος, ὀνείρατος, τό: dream, 1
πόρος, ὁ: a ford, passage, pathway, 2
προσ-βατός, -ή, -όν: accessible, 2
πρόσθεν: before, earlier, 3
σπένδω: to make a treaty, a drink-offering, 5
σφεῖς: they, 3
φαίνω: to show; *mid.* appear, seem, 6

19 **κατατιθεμένους**: *depositing*
ἰδοῦσι: *(while)…*; dat. pl. pple εἶδον,
σφίσι: dat. pl. σφεῖς, i.e. Greek soldiers
20 **δόξαι**: *it seemed*; aor. inf. in ind. disc.
ἀσφαλὲς: acc. pred. of inf. εἰμί
διαβῆναι: explanatory (epexegetical) aor. inf. διαβαίνω qualifying ἀσφαλὲς
21 **οὐδὲ…τοῖς…ἱππεῦσι**: *not even for…*; dat. of interest; οὐδέ is an adverb here
(δόξαι) εἶναι: *(it seemed) to be*
κατὰ τοῦτο: *at this (point)*; 'over this'
ἐκδύντες: *that (they) taking off their clothes…*; i.e. the soldiers, the pples and adj. modify the missing acc. subject, which is the same as the main subject: therefore, all the modifiers are attracted into the nom.
ἔφασαν…ὡς: *they said that…*; the soldiers talking to Xenophon are the subject
22 **ὡς…νευσόμενοι**: *so that…*; 'so as to…' ὡς + fut. pple. expresses purpose
23 **διαβῆναι**: *that (they)..;* aor. inf. διαβαίνω
πρὶν βρέξαι τὰ αἰδοῖα: *before...*; πρίν governs an inf., here an acc. subj. + aor. inf.
24 **λαβόντες τὰ ἱμάτια**: the soldiers stole the clothes of the man, woman and children, perhaps as proof that the river was fordable
26 **φήνασι…ὀνείρατα...πόρον**: dat. pl. aor. active pple. φαίνω governing two objects
27 **σπείσας**: nom. sg. aor. pple σπένδω
28 **ἦγε**: impf. ἄγω

ταὐτά. ἀκούσας δὲ καὶ ὁ Χειρίσοφος σπονδὰς ἐποίει. 14. σπεί- 1
σαντες δὲ τοῖς μὲν ἄλλοις παρήγγελλον συσκευάζεσθαι,
αὐτοὶ δὲ συγκαλέσαντες τοὺς στρατηγοὺς ἐβουλεύοντο ὅπως
ἂν κάλλιστα διαβαῖεν καὶ τούς τε ἔμπροσθεν νικῷεν καὶ
ὑπὸ τῶν ὄπισθεν μηδὲν πάσχοιεν κακόν. 15. καὶ ἔδοξεν αὐτοῖς 5
Χειρίσοφον μὲν ἡγεῖσθαι καὶ διαβαίνειν ἔχοντα τὸ ἥμισυ
τοῦ στρατεύματος, τὸ δ᾽ ἥμισυ ἔτι ὑπομένειν σὺν Ξενοφῶντι,
τὰ δὲ ὑποζύγια καὶ τὸν ὄχλον ἐν μέσῳ τούτων διαβαίνειν.
ἐπεὶ δὲ ταῦτα καλῶς εἶχεν, ἐπορεύοντο· 16. ἡγοῦντο δ᾽ οἱ νεα-

---

βουλεύω: to deliberate, plan, take counsel, 5
ἔμ-προσθεν: in front, before, 5
ἔτι: still, besides, further, 7
ἥμισυς, -εια, -υ: half, 4
κακός, -ή, -όν: bad, base, cowardly, evil, 5
μέσος, -η, -ον: middle, in the middle of, 5
μηδ-είς, μηδ-εμία, μηδ-έν: no one, nothing, 2
νεανίσκος, ὁ: a youth, 4
νικάω: to conquer, defeat, win, 2
ὄχλος, ὁ: a crowd, throng, mob, 4
παρ-αγγέλλω: to pass word along, order 7
πάσχω: to suffer, experience, 3
σπένδω: to make a treaty, a drink-offering, 5
σπονδή, ἡ: a drink-offering; truce, treaty, 5
συγ-καλέω: to call together, assemble, 2
συσκευάζομαι: to pack up together, prepare, 2
ὑπο-μένω: to remain, abide, wait up, await, 7

1 **τ(ὰ) αὐτά**: αὐτός in the attribute position means 'same'
σπείσαντες: aor. pple σπένδω
2 **αὐτοὶ**: *they themselves*
3 **ὅπως..ἂν...διαβαῖεν...νικῷεν...πάσχοιεν**: *how they might...*; clause of effort (object clause) usually with fut. or, as here, a potential opt. (ἄν + opt.), 3p aor. opt. διαβαίνω and pres. opt. νικάω, πάσχω
4 **κάλλιστα**: superlative adv. καλῶς, 'well'
5 **ὕπο τῶν ὄπισθεν**: *because of those...*; 'at the hands of...' gen. of cause or agent
ἔδοξεν: *it seemed (best)*
Χειρίσοφον...διαβαίνειν...: *that...*; ind. disc.
7 **τὸ δ᾽ἥμισυ...διαβαίνειν**: *and that...*; ind. disc.
9 **καλῶς εἶχεν**: ἔχω ('is disposed' or 'holds') + adv. is often equiv. to εἰμί + adj.; 3s impf. with neuter pl. subject

νίσκοι ἐν ἀριστερᾷ ἔχοντες τὸν ποταμόν· ὁδὸς δὲ ἦν ἐπὶ 10
τὴν διάβασιν ὡς τέτταρες στάδιοι. 17. πορευομένων δ᾽ αὐτῶν
ἀντιπαρῆσαν αἱ τάξεις τῶν ἱππέων. ἐπειδὴ δὲ ἦσαν κατὰ
τὴν διάβασιν καὶ τὰς ὄχθας τοῦ ποταμοῦ, ἔθεντο τὰ ὅπλα,
καὶ αὐτὸς πρῶτος Χειρίσοφος στεφανωσάμενος καὶ ἀποδὺς
ἐλάμβανε τὰ ὅπλα καὶ τοῖς ἄλλοις πᾶσι παρήγγελλε, καὶ 15
τοὺς λοχαγοὺς ἐκέλευεν ἄγειν τοὺς λόχους ὀρθίους, τοὺς μὲν
ἐν ἀριστερᾷ τοὺς δ᾽ ἐν δεξιᾷ ἑαυτοῦ. καὶ οἱ μὲν μάντεις
ἐσφαγιάζοντο εἰς τὸν ποταμόν· 18. οἱ δὲ πολέμιοι ἐτόξευον καὶ

ἀντι-παρ-έρχομαι: to come along opposite, 1
ἀπο-δύω: to strip off, drip off, 1
ἀριστερός, -ά, -όν: left, on the left, 4
δεξιός, -ά, -όν: on the right hand or side, 5
διά-βασις, -εως, ἡ: a crossing, 3
μάντις, ἡ: seer, prophet, 2
ὄχθη, ἡ: bank (of a river), 4
παρ-αγγέλλω: to pass word along, order 7
στεφανόω: to crown, put on a wreath, 1
σφαγιάζομαι: to sacrifice, slay a victim, 3
τάξις, -εως, ἡ: post, order, rank; battle array, 7
τέτταρες, -α: four, 6
τίθημι: to put, place; set, establish, 3
τοξεύω: to shoot with the bow, 7

10 ἐπὶ...: *to...*
11 ὡς: *nearly...*; 'as if' in approximation,
πορευομένων δ᾽αὐτῶν: gen. abs.
12 ἀντιπαρῆσαν: 3p impf., the enemy stood on the opposite side of the river
κατὰ τὴν διάβασιν: *at...*
13 ἔθεντο τὰ ὅπλα: *presented arms*; or 'to halt under arms,' an idiom with several related meanings; aor. mid. inf. τίθημι
14 στεφανωσάμενος: i.e. on himself; mid. [ple; mid. voice is often reflexive in sense
ἀποδὺς: i.e. his cloak; nom. sg. aor. pple ἀποδύω;
16 ὀρθίους: *in columns*; i.e. single file
τοὺς μὲν...τοὺς δ᾽: *some...and others...*
17 ἑαυτοῦ: i.e. of Cheirisophus
18 εἰς: *near..., at...*; 'up to...'

ἐσφενδόνων· ἀλλ᾽ οὔπω ἐξικνοῦντο· 19. ἐπεὶ δὲ καλὰ ἦν τὰ σφάγια, ἐπαιάνιζον πάντες οἱ στρατιῶται καὶ ἀνηλάλαζον, 20 συνωλόλυζον δὲ καὶ αἱ γυναῖκες ἅπασαι. πολλαὶ γὰρ ἦσαν ἑταῖραι ἐν τῷ στρατεύματι. 20. καὶ Χειρίσοφος μὲν ἐνέβαινε καὶ οἱ σὺν ἐκείνῳ· ὁ δὲ Ξενοφῶν τῶν ὀπισθοφυλάκων λαβὼν τοὺς εὐζωνοτάτους ἔθει ἀνὰ κράτος πάλιν ἐπὶ τὸν πόρον τὸν κατὰ τὴν ἔκβασιν τὴν εἰς τὰ τῶν Ἀρμενίων ὄρη, 25 προσποιούμενος ταύτῃ διαβὰς ἀποκλείσειν τοὺς παρὰ τὸν ποταμὸν ἱππέας. 21. οἱ δὲ πολέμιοι ὁρῶντες μὲν τοὺς ἀμφὶ Χειρίσοφον εὐπετῶς τὸ ὕδωρ περῶντας, ὁρῶντες δὲ τοὺς ἀμφὶ Ξενοφῶντα θέοντας εἰς τοὔμπαλιν, δείσαντες μὴ

ἀνα-αλαλάζω: to raise the war-cry, 1
ἅπας, ἅπασα, ἅπαν: every, quite all, 3
ἀπο-κλείω: to cut off, shut off, 1
Ἀρμένιοι, οἱ: Armenian, 3
γυνή, γυναικός, ἡ: a woman, wife, 7
δείδω: to fear, 5
ἔκ-βασις, -εως, ἡ: going out, way out, exit, 5
ἐμ-βαίνω: to step in, walk in, 2
ἔμπαλιν: back, backwards; opposite way 1
ἐξ-ικνέομαι: to arrive at, reach, 3
ἑταῖρα, ἡ: courtesan, female companion, 2
εὔ-ζωνος, -ον: well-girded, nimble, active, 3
εὐ-πετής, -ές: easy, without trouble, 2
κράτος, -εος, τό: strength, power, 3
οὔ-πω: not yet, 1
παιανίζω: to sing a paean, 4
περάω: drive right through, pass, cross, 1
πόρος, ὁ: a ford, passage, pathway, 2
προσ-ποιέομαι: pretend; gain, win over, 2
συν-ολολύζω: to raise a cry together, 1
σφάγιον, τό: omen, offering, victim, 1
σφενδονάω: to use the sling, 4
ὕδωρ, ὕδατος, τό: water, 5

19 **ἐσφενδόνων**: ἐσφενδόναον, impf.
καλὰ: *auspicious, favorable*
22 **ἐνέβαινε**: verb agrees with closest subject
23 **τῶν ὀπισθοφθλάκων**: partitive gen. with the following superlative
24 **εὐζωνοτάτους**: superlative
ἔθει: impf. θέω
24 **ἀνὰ κράτος**: *at full speed*; up to full power
25 **ἐπὶ τὸν πόρον τὴν κατὰ τὴν ἔκβασιν**: *to the ford at the passage out into the mountains of the Armeians*; prepositions in the attributive position modifying πόρον ; i.e. Xenophon heads to the original crossing of the river (IV 3.5-6), where the water reached as high as their chests
ὄρη: ὄρεα, neut. ὄρος
26 **προσποιούμενος**: i.e. he is trying to draw off the enemy from Cheirisophus' crossing
ταύτῃ: *in this way*; dat. of manner
διαβὰς: nom. sg. aor. pple διαβαίνω
παρὰ: *along*...
27 **ὁρῶντες**: pres. pple ὁράω
τοὺς ἀμφὶ Χειρίσοφον...περῶντας: *that those*...; ind. disc. i.e. those under the command of Cheirisophus
28 **τοὺς ἀμφὶ Ξενοφῶντα...θέοντας**: *that those*...; ind. disc.
29 **εἰς τὸ (ἔ)μπαλιν**: i.e. back to the original crossing
δείσαντες: aor. pple δείδω
μὴ: *lest*...; fearing clause

ἀποληφθείησαν φεύγουσιν ἀνὰ κράτος ὡς πρὸς τὴν τοῦ ποταμοῦ 1
ἄνω ἔκβασιν. ἐπεὶ δὲ κατὰ τὴν ὁδὸν ἐγένοντο, ἔτεινον ἄνω
πρὸς τὸ ὄρος. 22. Λύκιος δ' ὁ τὴν τάξιν ἔχων τῶν ἱππέων καὶ
Αἰσχίνης ὁ τὴν τάξιν τῶν πελταστῶν τῶν ἀμφὶ Χειρίσοφον
ἐπεὶ ἑώρων ἀνὰ κράτος φεύγοντας, εἵποντο· οἱ δὲ στρα- 5
τιῶται ἐβόων μὴ ἀπολείπεσθαι, ἀλλὰ συνεκβαίνειν ἐπὶ τὸ
ὄρος. 23. Χειρίσοφος δ' αὖ ἐπεὶ διέβη, τοὺς ἱππέας οὐκ ἐδίωκεν,
εὐθὺς δὲ κατὰ τὰς προσηκούσας ὄχθας ἐπὶ τὸν ποταμὸν
ἐξέβαινεν ἐπὶ τοὺς ἄνω πολεμίους. οἱ δὲ ἄνω, ὁρῶντες μὲν

Αἰσχίνης, ὁ: Aeschines, 2
ἀπο-λαμβάνω: to cut off, intercept, 1
ἀπο-λείπω: to leave behind, abandon, 4
αὖ: again, once more; further, moreover, 8
βοάω: to shout, cry outloud, 5
διώκω: to pursue, follow; prosecute, 3
ἐκ-βαίνω: to step out, disembark; turn out, 7
ἔκ-βασις, -εως, ἡ: going out, way out, exit, 5
κράτος, -εος, τό: strength, power, 3
Λύκιος, ὁ: Lycius, 3
ὄχθη, ἡ: bank (of a river), 4
προσ-ήκω: to come out, be present, 1
συν-εκ-βαίνω: to join in going out, 1
τάξις, -εως, ἡ: unit, squadron; battle array, 7
τείνω: to stretch, extend; exert, hasten 1

1 **ἀποληφθείησαν**: 3p aor. pass. opt. in the fearing clause
ἀνὰ κράτος: *at full speed*; up to full power
ὡς: *as if*; expresses intention and can be translated as 'intending' or 'aiming'
τὴν...ἔκβασιν: *the way out up from the river*; gen. governed by ἔκβασιν
2 **κατὰ**: *over...*
4 **ὁ τὴν τάξιν (ἔχων)**: add pple
5 **ἑώρων**: ἑώραον, 3p impf. ὁράω
ἀνὰ κράτος: see above
εἵποντο: impf. mid. ἕπομαι
6 **ἐβόων**: ἐβόαον; 3p impf. α-contract
μὴ ἀπολείπεσθαι: *that they should not...*; ind. disc. that is a negative command in direct disc.: μή is used instead of οὐ in wishes and commands; pass. inf.
7 **αὖ**: *in turn*; i.e. in response
διέβη: 3s aor. διαβαίνω
ἐδίωκεν: *did not try to pursue*; conative impf.
8 **κατὰ**: *over..., along...*
προσηκούσας: *projecting*
9 **ἐπὶ**: *against...*
οἱ δὲ ἄνω: *those above*
ὁρῶντες: pple

τοὺς ἑαυτῶν ἱππέας φεύγοντας, ὁρῶντες δ' ὁπλίτας σφίσιν 10
ἐπιόντας, ἐκλείπουσι τὰ ὑπὲρ τοῦ ποταμοῦ ἄκρα. 24. Ξενοφῶν
δ' ἐπεὶ τὰ πέραν ἑώρα καλῶς γιγνόμενα, ἀπεχώρει τὴν
ταχίστην πρὸς τὸ διαβαῖνον στράτευμα· καὶ γὰρ οἱ Καρδοῦχοι φανεροὶ ἤδη ἦσαν εἰς τὸ πεδίον καταβαίνοντες ὡς
ἐπιθησόμενοι τοῖς τελευταίοις. 25. καὶ Χειρίσοφος μὲν τὰ ἄνω 15
κατεῖχε, Λύκιος δὲ σὺν ὀλίγοις ἐπιχειρήσας ἐπιδιῶξαι ἔλαβε
τῶν σκευοφόρων τὰ ὑπολειπόμενα καὶ μετὰ τούτων ἐσθῆτά
τε καλὴν καὶ ἐκπώματα. 26. καὶ τὰ σκευοφόρα τῶν Ἑλλήνων

ἀπο-χωρέω: go from, depart, 2
ἐκ-λείπω: to leave, forsake, abandon, 3
ἔκπωμα, -ατος, τό: drinking-cup, 2
ἐπ-έρχομαι: to come upon; attack, 5
ἐπι-δίωκω: to pursue after, 2
ἐπι-τίθημι: to put upon; add; set upon, attack 4
ἐπι-χειρέω: put one's hand on, attempt, try, 1
ἐσθής, ἐστθῆτος, ἡ: clothing, 1
κατ-έχω: to hold fast, take possession of, 7
Λύκιος, ὁ: Lycius, 3
πέραν: across, beyond, exceeding (gen), 5
σκευο-φόρον, τό: baggage train, baggage, 2
σφεῖς: they, 3
τελευταίος, -α, -ον: last, final, 6
ὑπο-λείπω: to leave behind; fail, 2

10 **τοὺς...φεύγοντας**: ind. disc. following ὁρῶντες
ὁπλίτας...ἐπιόντας: see above; pple ἐπ-έρχομαι
σφίσιν: dat. of compound verb; dat. pl. σφεῖς
12 **τὰ πέραν...γιγνόμενα**: *that things across (the river)...*; ind. disc.
ἑώρα: ἑώρα-ε, 3s impf. ὁράω
καλῶς: *well*
τὴν ταχίστην: adverbial acc., translate as a superlative adverb: ταχίστα
διαβαῖνον: neuter sg. pple
13 **καὶ γὰρ**: *for in fact*; καί is adverbial
14 **φανεροὶ...ἦσαν**: *were visibly...*; 'were visible'
ὡς ἐπιθησόμενοι: *so that...*; 'so as to...' ὡς + fut. pple (ἐπιτίθημι) expressing purpose
15 **τοῖς τελευταίοις**: i.e. soldiers; dat of compound verb
τὰ ἄνω: *the heights*; 'things above'
16 **ἐπιδιῶξαι**: aor. act. inf.
ἔλαβε: aor. λαμβάνω
17 **τὰ ὑπολειπόμενα**: *those things...*; i.e the parts of the enemy's baggage train that were trailing behind; pass. pple
ἐσθῆτα...καλὴν: *fine clothing*; pl. in sense

καὶ ὁ ὄχλος ἀκμὴν διέβαινε, Ξενοφῶν δὲ στρέψας πρὸς τοὺς Καρδούχους ἀντία τὰ ὅπλα ἔθετο, καὶ παρήγγειλε τοῖς 20 λοχαγοῖς κατ᾽ ἐνωμοτίας ποιήσασθαι ἕκαστον τὸν ἑαυτοῦ λόχον, παρ᾽ ἀσπίδα παραγαγόντας τὴν ἐνωμοτίαν ἐπὶ φάλαγγος· καὶ τοὺς μὲν λοχαγοὺς καὶ τοὺς ἐνωμοτάρχους πρὸς τῶν Καρδούχων ἰέναι, οὐραγοὺς δὲ καταστήσασθαι πρὸς τοῦ ποταμοῦ. 27. οἱ δὲ Καρδοῦχοι ὡς ἑώρων τοὺς ὀπισθοφύλακας 25 τοῦ ὄχλου ψιλουμένους καὶ ὀλίγους ἤδη φαινομένους, θᾶττον δὴ ἐπῆσαν ᾠδάς τινας ᾄδοντες. ὁ δὲ Χειρίσοφος, ἐπεὶ

ἀείδω: to sing, chant, 2
ἀκμή, ἡ: edge, point, critical moment, 1
ἀντίος, -α, -ον: face to face, facing opposite 1
ἀσπίς, ἀσπίδος, ὁ: a round shield, 6
ἐνωμοτ-άρχης, -ου, ὁ: squadron-leader, 1
ἐνωμοτία, ἡ: squadron, 2
ἐπ-έρχομαι: to come upon; attack, 5
θάττων, θᾶττον: faster, quicker, swifter, 3
καθ-ίστημι: to station, appoint; *intransitive*, stand, 4
οὐραγός, ὁ: leader of the rear guard, 1
ὄχλος, ὁ: a crowd, throng, mob, 4
παρ-αγγέλλω: to pass word along, order 7
παρ-άγω: to lead by, lead alongside, 3
στρέφω: to turn, wheel around, 3
τίθημι: to put, place; set, establish, 3
φαίνω: to show; *mid.* appear, seem, 6
ψιλόω: to strip bear, 1
ᾠδή, ἡ: ode, song, 1

19 **ἀκμὴν διέβαινε**: *just beginning to cross*; 'just at the point of crossing,' ἀκμὴν is adverbial acc. ('just at the point' or 'just') with an inchoative impf.
20 **ἔθετο**: *presented arms*; i.e. stood his ground with shields in front; an idiom with several related meanings; aor. mid. τίθημι
21 **κατὰ ἐνωμοτίας**: *by squadrons*; 'squadron by squadron' κατὰ is distributive in sense
ποιήσασθαι: *that (they) form...*; aor. mid., ἕκαστον ...λόχον is acc. object; the units were in columns when they crossed the river and must now reform into battlelines
22 **παρ(ὰ) ἀσπίδα**: *along the left*; 'along the shield,' i.e. the direction of the shield when held in the left hand
παραγαγόντας: aor. pple modifying the assumed acc. subj. of ποιήσασθαι: λοχαγοὺς
ἐπὶ φάλαγγος: *into line of battle*
πρὸς: *toward...*; or 'on the side facing toward...'
24 **ἰέναι**: inf. ἔρχομαι
καταστήσασθαι: *to station, to cause to stand*; aor. mid. οὐραγοὺς is acc. obj.
πρὸς: *toward...*; or 'on the side facing toward...'
25 **ὡς**: *when, as*
ἑώρων: impf. ὁράω
τοῦ ὄχλου: *of the crowd (of camp-followers)*; gen. of separation
26 **θᾶττον**: comparative adv.
27 **δὴ**: *quite, exceedingly*; strengthening θᾶττον
δὴ: *quite*; intensive
ἐπῆσαν: impf. ἐπέρχομαι
ᾄδοντες: pple ἀείδω

τὰ παρ' αὐτῷ ἀσφαλῶς εἶχε, πέμπει παρὰ Ξενοφῶντα τοὺς 1
πελταστὰς καὶ σφενδονήτας καὶ τοξότας καὶ κελεύει ποιεῖν
ὅ τι ἂν παραγγέλλῃ. 28. ἰδὼν δ' αὐτοὺς διαβαίνοντας Ξενοφῶν
πέμψας ἄγγελον κελεύει αὐτοῦ μεῖναι ἐπὶ τοῦ ποταμοῦ μὴ
διαβάντας· ὅταν δ' ἄρξωνται αὐτοὶ διαβαίνειν, ἐναντίους 5
ἔνθεν καὶ ἔνθεν σφῶν ἐμβαίνειν ὡς διαβησομένους, διηγκυλωμένους τοὺς ἀκοντιστὰς καὶ ἐπιβεβλημένους τοὺς τοξότας·
μὴ πρόσω δὲ τοῦ ποταμοῦ προβαίνειν. 29. τοῖς δὲ παρ' ἑαυτῷ
παρήγγειλεν, ἐπειδὰν σφενδόνη ἐξικνῆται καὶ ἀσπὶς ψοφῇ,

ἄγγελος, ὁ: messenger, envoy 1
ἀκοντιστής, ὁ: javelin-thrower, 1
ἀσπίς, ἀσπίδος, ὁ: a round shield, 6
ἀ-σφαλής, -ές: safe, secure, not liable to fall 7
αὐτοῦ: in that very place, there, 7
δι-αγκυλόω: to crook, bend completely, 1
ἐμ-βαίνω: to step in, walk in, 2
ἐναντίος, -α, -ον: opposite, contrary, 4
ἐξ-ικνέομαι: to arrive at, reach, 3
ἐπειδάν: whenever, 5
ἐπι-βάλλω: to shoot at, cast at, 1
ὅταν: ὅτε ἄν, whenever, 5
παρ-αγγέλλω: to pass word along, order 7
πέμπω: send, conduct, convey, dispatch, 7
προ-βαίνω: to step forward, advance, 1
πρόσω: forwards into, far from +gen 4
σφεῖς: they, 3
σφενδόνη, ἡ: sling, stone (from a sling), 2
σφενδόνήτης, -ου, ὁ: slinger, 1
τοξότης, ὁ: an archer, bowman, 4
ψοφέω: to make a noise, 1

1 **τὰ παρ(ὰ) αὐτῷ**: *matters on his side*; 'things beside him' i.e. Cheirisophus' side
ἀσφαλῶς εἶχε: ἔχω ('is disposed' or 'hold') + adv. is often equiv. to εἰμί + adj.
παρὰ: *to (the side of)...*; place to which
3 **ὅ τι ἂν...**: *whatever..*; general relative clause with ἄν + 3s subj.; neut. acc. ὅστις
ἰδῶν: aor. pple ὁράω
4 **κελεύει**: *orders that they...*; the ind. command lasts to the end of 3.28
αὐτοῦ: *there*; 'in that very place'
μεῖναι: aor. inf. μένω
μὴ διαβάντας: *not crossing*; aor. pple, μὴ instead of οὐ in an ind. command
5 **ὅταν...ἄρξωνται**: *whenever...*; ἄν + aor. subj. in a general temporal clause
αὐτοὶ: *(they) themselves*; intensive
ἐναντίους...ἐμβαίνειν: *to come in opposite*
6 **ἔνθεν καὶ ἔνθεν σφῶν**: *on this side and that side of them*; 'from here and from there'
ὡς διαβησομένους: *as if about to...*; often ὡς + pple expresses purpose, but here it is the pretense of an action; fut. pple
διηγκυλωμένους: *holding...by the thong*; 'bending,' modifies ἀκοντιστὰς
7 **ἐπιβεβλημένος**: *setting (arrow) upon (string)*; i.e. with bow drawn; pf. mid.pple ἐπιβάλλω modifying τοξότας
7 **μὴ...προβαίνειν**: *that they not...*; ind. command; expressing a wish, hence μὴ; the main verb remains κελεύει above
8 **τοῖς παρ(ὰ) ἑαυτῷ**: *those (men) with him*; i.e. under his charge
9 **παρήγγειλεν**: aor. παραγγέλλω
ἐπειδὰν...ἐξικνῆται...ψοφῇ: *whenever...*; 3s pres. subj. in a general temporal clause

παιανίσαντας θεῖν εἰς τοὺς πολεμίους, ἐπειδὰν δ' ἀναστρέ- 10
ψωσιν οἱ πολέμιοι καὶ ἐκ τοῦ ποταμοῦ ὁ σαλπικτὴς σημήνῃ
τὸ πολεμικόν, ἀναστρέψαντας ἐπὶ δόρυ ἡγεῖσθαι μὲν τοὺς
οὐραγούς, θεῖν δὲ πάντας καὶ διαβαίνειν ὅτι τάχιστα ᾗ
ἕκαστος τὴν τάξιν εἶχεν, ὡς μὴ ἐμποδίζειν ἀλλήλους· ὅτι
οὗτος ἄριστος ἔσοιτο ὃς ἂν πρῶτος ἐν τῷ πέραν γένηται. 15
30. *οἱ δὲ* Καρδοῦχοι *ὁρῶντες ὀλίγους ἤδη τοὺς λοιποὺς (πολλοὶ*
γὰρ καὶ τῶν μένειν τεταγμένων ᾤχοντο ἐπιμελόμενοι οἱ μὲν
ὑποζυγίων, οἱ δὲ σκευῶν, οἱ δ' ἑταιρῶν), ἐνταῦθα δὴ ἐπέ-

ἀνα-στρέφω: to turn off (in flight), 2
ἄριστος, -η, -ον: best, most excellent; noble, 2
δόρυ, δόρατος, τό: spearshaft; pole, stem, 4
ἐμ-ποδίζω: to hinder, impede, 1
ἐπειδάν: whenever, 5
ἐπί-κειμαι: set upon; press upon, attack, 3
ἐπι-μέλ(ε)ομαι: to care for, look after (gen) 3
ἑταῖρα, ἡ: courtesan, female companion, 2
λοιπός, ὁ: remaining, the rest, 6
οἴχομαι: to go, go off, depart, 7
οὐραγός, ὁ: leader of the rear guard, 1
παιανίζω: to sing a paean, 4
πέραν: across, beyond, exceeding (gen), 5
πολεμικός, -ή, -όν: (the signal) of war, 1
σαλπικτής, ὁ: trumpeter, 2
σημαίνω: to show, indicate, give a signal, 3
σκευή, ἡ: attire, apparel; equipment, 2
τάξις, -εως, ἡ: unit, squadron; battle array, 7
τάττω: post, station, arrange, order, 6

10 **θεῖν**: inf. θέω
ἐπειδὰν ἀναστρέψωσιν...σημήνῃ: general temporal clause with 3p and 3s aor. subj.
12 **τὸ πολεμικόν**: *the war (charge)*; i.e. in order to deceive the enemy
ἐπὶ δόρυ: *to the right*; 'to the spear,' i.e. the direction of the spear when held in hand; compare παρὰ ἀσπίδα, 'to the left'
ἡγεῖσθαι: *took the lead*; οὐραγούς is subj.
13 **ὅτι τάχιστα**: ὡς or ὅτι + superlative is translated as 'as....as possible'
ᾗ...εἶχεν: *in which way each (soldier) held ranks*; i.e. the soldiers had to maintain ranks; relative clause, dat. of manner
14 **ὡς μὴ...**: *so as not...*; result clause, just as ὥστε, ὡς governs an inf.
ὅτι... ἔσοιτο: *(he said) that...*; ind. disc. with fut. opt. εἰμί; in ind. disc. a fut. opt. replaces fut. ind. in secondary seq.
15 **ἄριστος**: nom. predicate of ἔσοιτο
ὃς ἂν...: *whoever...*; general relative clause with ἄν + aor. subj.
ἐν τῷ πέραν: *on the other side*
17 **καὶ**: *even*
τῶν...τεταγμένων: *of those...*; pf. pass. pple τάττω, partitive gen. with πολλοὶ
ᾤχοντο: impf. οἴχομαι
οἱ μὲν...οἱ δὲ... οἱ δὲ...: *some...others...still others*; the genitives are objects of the pple ἐπιμελόμενοι
18 **ἐνταῦθα δὴ**: *just then, exactly then*
ἐπέκειντο: impf. ἐπίκειμαι

κειντο θρασέως καὶ ἤρχοντο σφενδονᾶν καὶ τοξεύειν. 31. *οἱ δὲ Ἕλληνες παιανίσαντες ὥρμησαν δρόμῳ ἐπ' αὐτούς· οἱ* 20 *δὲ οὐκ ἐδέξαντο· καὶ γὰρ ἦσαν ὡπλισμένοι ὡς μὲν ἐν τοῖς ὄρεσιν ἱκανῶς πρὸς τὸ ἐπιδραμεῖν καὶ φεύγειν, πρὸς δὲ τὸ εἰς χεῖρας δέχεσθαι οὐχ ἱκανῶς.* 32. *ἐν τούτῳ σημαίνει ὁ σαλπικτής· καὶ οἱ μὲν πολέμιοι ἔφευγον πολὺ ἔτι θᾶττον, οἱ δὲ Ἕλληνες τἀναντία στρέψαντες ἔφευγον διὰ τοῦ ποταμοῦ* 25 *ὅτι τάχιστα.* 33. *τῶν δὲ πολεμίων οἱ μέν τινες αἰσθόμενοι πάλιν ἔδραμον ἐπὶ τὸν ποταμὸν καὶ τοξεύοντες ὀλίγους ἔτρωσαν, οἱ δὲ πολλοὶ καὶ πέραν ὄντων τῶν Ἑλλήνων ἔτι*

αἰσθάνομαι: perceive, feel, learn, realize, 4
δέχομαι: to receive, accept, 7
δρόμος, ὁ: run, running, flight; race course, 5
ἐναντίος, -α, -ον: opposite, contrary, 4
ἐπι-τρέχω: to run at, run against, 1
ἔτι: still, besides, further, 7
θάττων, θᾶττον: faster, quicker, swifter, 3
θρασύς, -εῖα, -ύ: bold, spirited, 1
ἱκανός, -ή, -όν: enough, sufficient; capable 4
ὁπλίζω: to make ready, arm, equip, 2
ὁρμάω: to set in motion, set out, begin, 2
παιανίζω: to sing a paean, 4
πέραν: across, beyond, exceeding (gen), 5
σάλπιγξ, -ιγγος, ὁ: war-trumpet, 4
σημαίνω: to show, indicate, give a signal, 3
στρέφω: to turn, wheel around, 3
σφενδονάω: to use the sling, 3
τιτρώσκω: to wound, injure, damage, 2
τοξεύω: to shoot with the bow, 7
τρέχω: to run, 3
χείρ, χειρός, ἡ: hand, 2

19 **σφενδονᾶν**: α-contract inf.
20 **δρόμῳ**: *in a run*; not 'in flight,' dat. of manner
ἐπὶ...: *against...*
οἱ δὲ: *and they*; i.e. the enemies
21 **ἐδέξαντο**: aor. δέχομαι, i.e. they did not stay and fight
καὶ γὰρ: *for in fact*
ἦσαν ὡπλισμένοι: periphrastic plpf. pass. (pf. pple and impf. εἰμί)
ὡς μὲν ἐν τοῖς ὄρεσιν...οὐχ ἱκανῶς: *sufficiently so as to run at and flee in the mountains but not sufficiently so as to engage (the enemy) hand-to-hand*; this is a very ellipical clause of comparison introduced by ὡς; ἱκανῶς modifies ἦσαν ὡλισμένοι; πρός + articular inf. often means 'with regard to' or can be left untranslated
23 **ἐν τούτῳ**: *in this (moment)*; 'meanwhile'
σημαίνει: i.e. gives the signal for charge
24 **πολὺ**: *far*; adverbial acc. (acc. of extent in degree) with comparative adv. θᾶττον
25 **τὰ (ἐ)ναντία**: *the opposite direction*; 'the opposite turn;' inner acc.
26 **ὅτι τάχιστα**: ὡς or ὅτι + superlative is translated as 'as....as possible'
τῶν δὲ πολεμίων: *among...*; partitive gen.
όι μέν...οἱ δὲ πολλοὶ: *some...many others*
αἰσθόμενοι: perceiving that the Greeks were crossing
27 **ἔδραμον**: aor. τρέχω
ἔτρωσαν: aor. τιτρώσκω
28 **καὶ πέραν...Ἑλλήνων**: *even though...*; gen. abs., concessive in sense; καὶ is adverbial, pple εἰμί

φανεροὶ ἦσαν φεύγοντες. 34. οἱ δὲ ὑπαντήσαντες ἀνδριζόμενοι 1
καὶ προσωτέρω τοῦ καιροῦ προϊόντες ὕστερον τῶν μετὰ Ξενοφῶντος διέβησαν πάλιν· καὶ ἐτρώθησάν τινες καὶ τούτων.
1. ἐπεὶ δὲ διέβησαν, συνταξάμενοι ἀμφὶ μέσον ἡμέρας
ἐπορεύθησαν διὰ τῆς Ἀρμενίας πεδίον ἅπαν καὶ λείους γη- 5
λόφους οὐ μεῖον ἢ πέντε παρασάγγας· οὐ γὰρ ἦσαν ἐγγὺς
τοῦ ποταμοῦ κῶμαι διὰ τοὺς πολέμους τοὺς πρὸς τοὺς Καρδούχους. 2. εἰς δὲ ἣν ἀφίκοντο κώμην μεγάλη τε ἦν καὶ
βασίλειον εἶχε τῷ σατράπῃ καὶ ἐπὶ ταῖς πλείσταις οἰκίαις

ἀνδρίζω: to behave as a man, 1
ἅπας, ἅπασα, ἅπαν: every, quite all, 3
Ἀρμενία, ἡ: Armenia, 6
βασίλειον, τό: palace, 2
γηλόφος, ὁ: mound, hill, 1
ἐγγύς: near (+ gen.); adv. nearby, 7
τιτρώσκω: to wound, injure, damage, 2
καιρός, ὁ: time, right moment, due measure, 2
λεῖος, -η, -ον: smooth, level, flat, 1
μείων, μεῖον: smaller, less, of lesser value, 2
μέσος, -η, -ον: middle, in the middle of, 5
πέντε: five, 4
πλεῖστος, -η, -ον: most, very many, 3
πόλεμος, ὁ: battle, fight, war, 2
προ-έρχομαι: to go forth, advance, 4
πρόσω: forwards, far from +gen, 4
σατράπης, ὁ: satrap, 2
συν-τάττω: to post/marshall together, order 3
τιτρώσκω: to wound, injure, damage, 2
ὑπ-αντάω: to come to, meet; reply, 1
ὕστερος, -α, -ον: later, last; coming after, 1

1 **φανεροὶ ἦσαν**: *were visibly*; 'were visible'
οἱ δὲ...: *and those*; i.e. the enemy
2 **προσωτέρω**: comparative adv.
τοῦ καιροῦ: *than due measure*; gen. of comparison
προϊόντες: pple προ-έρχομαι
ὕστερον τῶν μετὰ Ξενοφῶντος: *behind the men accompanying Xenophon*; comparative adv. and gen. of comparison
3 **διέβησαν**: aor. διαβαίνω
ἐτρώθησαν: 3p aor. pass. τιτρώσκω
καὶ: *also*
τούτων: partitive gen.
4 **ἀμφὶ**: an approximation of time, not place
ἡμέρας: partitive gen.
5 **ἐπορεύθησαν**: 3p aor. pass. dep. πορεύομαι; translate actively
πεδίον ἅπαν...γηλόφους: *over...*; acc. of extent (S1581)
6 **μεῖον**: comparative adverb
ἦσαν: *there were*
7 **τοὺς πρὸς...**: *against...*; prepositional phrase in the attributive position modifying πολέμους
8 **εἰς...ἣν...κώμην**: *the town to which...*; 'to which town...', a relative clause with a relative adj; ἡ κώμη the subject of the main verb has been attracted into the acc. case of the relative pronoun
σατράπῃ: *for...*; dat. interest
ἐπὶ: *upon...*; dat. of place where

τύρσεις ἐπῆσαν· 3. *ἐπιτήδεια δ' ἦν δαψιλῆ. ἐντεῦθεν δ' ἐπο-* 10
ρεύθησαν σταθμοὺς δύο παρασάγγας δέκα μέχρι ὑπερῆλθον
τὰς πηγὰς τοῦ Τίγρητος ποταμοῦ. ἐντεῦθεν δ' ἐπορεύθησαν
σταθμοὺς τρεῖς παρασάγγας πεντεκαίδεκα ἐπὶ τὸν Τηλεβόαν
ποταμόν. οὗτος δ' ἦν καλὸς μέν, μέγας δ' οὔ· κῶμαι δὲ
πολλαὶ περὶ τὸν ποταμὸν ἦσαν. 4. *ὁ δὲ τόπος οὗτος Ἀρμενία* 15
ἐκαλεῖτο ἡ πρὸς ἑσπέραν. ὕπαρχος δ' ἦν αὐτῆς Τιρίβαζος,
ὁ καὶ βασιλεῖ φίλος γενόμενος, καὶ ὁπότε παρείη, οὐδεὶς
ἄλλος βασιλέα ἐπὶ τὸν ἵππον ἀνέβαλλεν. 5. *οὗτος προσ-*

Ἀρμενία, ἡ: Armenia, 6
δαψιλής, -ές: abundant, plentiful, 2
δέκα: ten, 7
ἔπ-ειμι: to be upon, be on, 1
ἑσπέρα, ἡ: evening, 2
καλέω: to call, summon, invite, 3
μέχρι: up to; until, as long as (+ gen.), 5
πάρ-ειμι: to be near, be present, be at hand, 4
πεντε-καί-δεκα: fifteen, 5
περί: around, about, concerning, 7
πηγή, ἡ: spring (of a river), 4
προσ-ελαύνω: to drive to, ride to, 1
Τηλεβόας, ὁ: Teleboas river, 1
Τίγρης, Τίγρητος, ὁ: Tigris river, 4
Τιρίβαζος, ὁ: Tiribazus (person), 6
τόπος, ὁ: a place, region, 3
τύρσις, -εως, ἡ: tower, 1
ὕπ-αρχος, ὁ: sub-commander, lieutenant, 1
ὑπερ-έρχομαι: to go past, pass over, 1
φίλος, -α, -ον: friendly, dear; friend, kin, 1

10 **ἐπῆσαν**: impf. ἔπ-ειμι
δαψιλῆ: δαψιλέ-α; neuter pl.
ἐπορεύθησαν: 3p aor. deponent πορέυομαι; translate actively
11 **σταθμοὺς...παρασάγγας**: *for...for...*; acc. of extent; σταθμός refers to a day's travel; παρασάγγας refers to the actual distance
ὑπερῆλθον: aor. ὑπ-έρχομαι
12 **ἐπορεύθησαν**: 3p aor. pass. dep.
13 **σταθμοὺς...παρασάγγας**: *for...for...*; acc. of extent
ἐπὶ: *to...*
16 **ἐκαλεῖτο**: impf. pass. καλέω
Ἀρμενία...ἡ πρὸς ἑσπέραν: *Western Armenia*; 'Armenia toward the evening (sun),' nom. pred.
αὐτῆς: *of this place*
17 **ὁ...γενόμενος**: *a (man)...*; with aor. pple in apposition to Τιρίβαζος
βασιλεῖ: **βασιλέ-ι**, dat. sg. βασιλεύς with the special adj. or noun φίλος
ὁπότε παρείη: *whenever...*; past general temporal clause with 3s opt. πάρειμι
18 **βασιλέα**: acc.
ἀνέβαλλεν: *would help...mount*; 'put upon,' iterative impf

ἤλασεν ἱππέας ἔχων, καὶ προπέμψας ἑρμηνέα εἶπεν ὅτι βούλοιτο διαλεχθῆναι τοῖς ἄρχουσι. τοῖς δὲ στρατηγοῖς ἔδοξεν 20
ἀκοῦσαι· καὶ προσελθόντες εἰς ἐπήκοον ἠρώτων τί θέλει.
6. ὁ δὲ εἶπεν ὅτι σπείσασθαι βούλοιτο ἐφ᾽ ᾧ μήτε αὐτὸς τοὺς
Ἕλληνας ἀδικεῖν μήτε ἐκείνους καίειν τὰς οἰκίας λαμβάνειν
τε τἀπιτήδεια ὅσων δέοιντο. ἔδοξε ταῦτα τοῖς στρατηγοῖς
καὶ ἐσπείσαντο ἐπὶ τούτοις. 25

7. ἐντεῦθεν δ᾽ ἐπορεύθησαν σταθμοὺς τρεῖς διὰ πεδίου
παρασάγγας πεντεκαίδεκα· καὶ Τιρίβαζος παρηκολούθει ἔχων
τὴν ἑαυτοῦ δύναμιν ἀπέχων ὡς δέκα σταδίους· καὶ ἀφίκοντο
εἰς βασίλεια καὶ κώμας πέριξ πολλὰς πολλῶν τῶν ἐπιτηδείων μεστάς. 8. στρατοπεδευομένων δ᾽ αὐτῶν γίγνεται τῆς 30

ἀ-δικέω: to be unjust, do wrong, injure, 1
ἀπ-έχω: to be distant, keep away from, 5
βασίλειον, τό: palace, 2
δέκα: ten, 7
δέομαι: to lack, be in need of (gen.), 2
δια-λέγομαι: to converse with, discuss, 5
δύναμις, -εως, ἡ: power, wealth, strength, 2
ἐπ-ήκοος, -ον: within ear-shot or hearing, 1
ἑρμηνεύς, ὁ: an interpreter, 4
μεστός, -ή, -όν: full, filled, filled full, 1
μή-τε: and not, 2
πεντε-καί-δεκα: fifteen, 5
πέριξ: round about, all round (gen) 1
προ-πέμπω: to send forth, send before, 1
σπένδω: to make a treaty, a drink-offering, 5
στρατοπεδεύω: to encamp, take a position, 4
Τιρίβαζος, ὁ: Tiribazus (person), 6

19 **προσήλασεν**: aor. προσελαύνω (ελα-)
ὅτι βούλοιτο: *that...*; ind. disc. with opt. in secondary seq.
20 **διαλεχθῆναι**: aor. pass. dep. inf.
τοῖς ἄρχουσι: *with the leaders*
ἔδοξεν: *it seemed best*
21 **προσελθόντες**: aor. pple προσέρχομαι
ἠρώτων: ἠρώταον, 3p impf. ἐρωτάω
τί (ἐ)θέλει: ind. question
22 **ὁ δὲ**: *and he*
ὅτι...βούλοιτο: *that...*; opt., secondary seq.
σπείσασθαι: aor. mid. σπένδω
ἐφ᾽ ᾧ: *on the condition that...*; ἐπ(ὶ) ᾧ; in the context of forming a pact or treaty
μήτε...ἀδικεῖν μήτε...καίειν...: *that he himself neither... nor...*; ind. disc.
23 **ἐκείνους**: *nor that...*; i.e. Greeks
24 **λαμβάνειν τε**: *(but) that they take...*; not a prohibition but what is allowed in the pact
τὰ (ἐ)πιτήδεια
δέοιντο: *they needed*; + gen. of separation; pres. opt. mid., past general relative clause
ἔδοξε: *seemed best*; neuter pl. subject
25 **ἐσπείσαντο**: aor. mid. σπένδω
ἐπὶ τούτοις: *on these terms/conditionss*
26 **ἐπορεύθησαν**: aor. pass. dep. πορεύομαι
σταθμοὺς...παρασάγγας...: *for...for...*; acc. of extent
παρηκολούθει: impf.
28 **τὴν ἑαυτοῦ δύναμιν**: *his own force*; i.e. troops under his own command
ὡς: *nearly*; 'as if,' in approximation
29 **εἰς βασίλεια**: neut. pl., but translate as sg.
30 **στρατοπεδευομένων αὐτῶν**: gen. abs.

νυκτὸς χιὼν πολλή· καὶ ἕωθεν ἔδοξε διασκηνῆσαι τὰς τάξεις 1
καὶ τοὺς στρατηγοὺς κατὰ τὰς κώμας· οὐ γὰρ ἑώρων πολέ-
μιον οὐδένα καὶ ἀσφαλὲς ἐδόκει εἶναι διὰ τὸ πλῆθος τῆς
χιόνος. 9. *ἐνταῦθα εἶχον τὰ ἐπιτήδεια ὅσα ἐστὶν ἀγαθά,*
ἱερεῖα, σῖτον, οἴνους παλαιοὺς εὐώδεις, ἀσταφίδας, ὄσπρια 5
παντοδαπά. τῶν δὲ ἀποσκεδαννυμένων τινὲς ἀπὸ τοῦ στρα-
τοπέδου ἔλεγον ὅτι κατίδοιεν νύκτωρ πολλὰ πυρὰ φαίνοντα.
10. *ἐδόκει δὴ τοῖς στρατηγοῖς οὐκ ἀσφαλὲς εἶναι διασκηνοῦν,*
ἀλλὰ συναγαγεῖν τὸ στράτευμα πάλιν. ἐντεῦθεν συνῆλθον·

ἀπο-σκεδαννυμι: to scatter abroad, disperse, 2
ἀσταφίς, -ίδος, ἡ: dried grapes, raisons, 1
δια-σκηνέω: to disperse to quarters/tents, 3
εὐ-ωδής, -ές: sweet-smelling, fragrant, 1
ἕω-θεν: from dawn, in the morning, 1
ἱερεῖον, τό: (sacrificial) victim, animal, 1
καθ-οράω: to look down, perceive, 7
νύκτωρ: at night, 2
οἶνος, ὁ: wine, 5
ὄσπριον, τό: pulse, legume, 2
παλαιός, -ά, -όν: old, aged, ancient, 2
παντο-δαπός, -ή, -όν: of every kind or sort, 1
πλῆθος, ἡ: crowd, multitude; size, 4
πυρά, -ῶν, τά: watch-fire, 6
σῖτος, ὁ: grain, bread, food, 1
συν-άγω: bring together, collect, gather, 2
συν-έρχομαι: come together, meet in battle 3
τάξις, -εως, ἡ: unit, squadron; battle array, 7
φαίνω: to show; *mid.* appear, seem, 6

1 **τῆς νυκτὸς**: *during...*; gen. of time within
ἔδοξε: *it seemed (best)*
διασκηνῆσαι: aor. inf.
2 **κατὰ...**: through...; or 'over...' κατά is distributive in sense
2 **ἑώρων**: 3p impf. ὁράω
3 **εἶναι**: inf. εἰμί
5 **ἱερεῖα...παντοδαπά**: in apposition to τὰ ἐπιτήδεια
6 **τινὲς**: *some*; indefinite
7 **ὅτι κατίδοιεν**: *that they...*; ind. disc. with aor. opt. καθοράω in secondary seq.
πολλὰ πυρὰ φαίνοντα: ind. disc. with pres. pple
8 **δὴ**: *then, accordingly*; inferential
διασκηνοῦν: neuter sg. pple διασκηνέω assume neut. τὸ στράτευμα
9 **συναγαγεῖν**: aor. inf.
συνῆλθον: aor. συνέρχομαι

καὶ γὰρ ἐδόκει διαιθριάζειν. 11. νυκτερευόντων δ' αὐτῶν 10
ἐνταῦθα ἐπιπίπτει χιὼν ἄπλετος, ὥστε ἀπέκρυψε καὶ τὰ
ὅπλα καὶ τοὺς ἀνθρώπους κατακειμένους· καὶ τὰ ὑποζύγια
συνεπόδισεν ἡ χιών· καὶ πολὺς ὄκνος ἦν ἀνίστασθαι· κατακειμένων γὰρ ἀλεεινὸν ἦν ἡ χιὼν ἐπιπεπτωκυῖα ὅτῳ μὴ
παραρρυείη. 12. ἐπεὶ δὲ Ξενοφῶν ἐτόλμησε γυμνὸς ἀναστὰς 15
σχίζειν ξύλα, τάχ' ἀναστάς τις καὶ ἄλλος ἐκείνου ἀφελόμενος ἔσχιζεν. ἐκ δὲ τούτου καὶ ἄλλοι ἀναστάντες πῦρ
ἔκαιον καὶ ἐχρίοντο· 13. πολὺ γὰρ ἐνταῦθα ηὑρίσκετο χρῖμα, ᾧ

ἀλεεινός, -ή, -όν: warm, hot, open to the sun 1
ἄπλετος, -ον: boundless, immense, 1
ἀπο-κρύπτω: to conceal, hide, 1
ἀφ-αιρέω: to take away from, remove, 2
γυμνός, -ή, -όν: naked, unclad, unarmed, 4
δι-αιθριάζω: to be clear (i.e. the weather), 1
ἐπι-πίπτω: to fall upon, attack, 3
εὑρίσκω: to find, discover, devise, invent, 4
κατα-κεῖμαι: to lie down, lie outstretched, 2
νυκτερεύω: to pass the night, 2
ξύλον, τό: wood, timber, firewood, 3
ὄκνος, ὁ: hestitation; reluctance, shrinking, 1
ὅστις, ἥτις, ὅ τι: whoever, which-, whatever, 4
παρα-ρρέω: flow or slip past, fall off, 1
συμ-ποδίζω: to impede, entangle, 1
σχίζω: to split, cleave, 1
τάχα: presently, quickly; perhaps, 2
τολμάω: to dare, venture, undertake, 1
χρῖμα, τό: ointment, oil for anointing, 1
χρίω: to anoint with oil, smear oil, 1

10 καὶ γὰρ: *for in fact*
νυκτερευόντων...αὐτῶν: gen. abs.
11 καὶ...καὶ: *both...and*
13 ἀνίστασθαι: *to stand up*; explanatory (epexegetical) inf. following ὄκνος
κατακειμένων: *(while the men) were lying down*; gen. absolute with missing noun
14 ἀλεεινὸν: *warm*; predicate of ἦν
ἐπιπεπτωκυῖα: fem. sg. pf. pple ἐπιπίπτω
ὅτῳ: *for whomever (the snow)...*; dat. sg. ὅστις; general relative clause with 3s aor. pass. opt.
παραρρέω in secondary seq.; add a subject
15 γυμνὸς: i.e. without his cloak
ἀναστὰς: nom. sg. aor. pple ἀν-ίστημι
16 τις καὶ ἄλλος: *someone else also*
ἐκείνου: *from that one*; i.e. Xenophon, gen. of separation
ἀφελόμενος: supply ξύλα as object, aor. mid. ἀφαιρέω; someone else took over the task from Xenophon
17 ἐκ τούτου: *as a result of this*
καὶ: *else*
18 ἐχρίοντο: mid. voice, as here, is reflexive in sense
ᾧ: *which*; dat. obj. of special verb

ἐχρῶντο ἀντ᾽ ἐλαίου, σύειον καὶ σησάμινον καὶ ἀμυγδάλινον ἐκ τῶν πικρῶν καὶ τερμίνθινον. ἐκ δὲ τῶν αὐτῶν τούτων 20 *καὶ μύρον ηὑρίσκετο.*

14. *μετὰ ταῦτα ἐδόκει πάλιν διασκηνητέον εἶναι [τὰς κώμας] εἰς στέγας. ἔνθα δὴ οἱ στρατιῶται σὺν πολλῇ κραυγῇ καὶ ἡδονῇ ᾖσαν ἐπὶ τὰς στέγας καὶ τὰ ἐπιτήδεια· ὅσοι δὲ*

ἀμυγδάλινος, -η, -ον: of an almond, 1
ἀντί: instead of, in place of (+ gen.), 3
δια-σκηνητέος, -ον: to be dispersed to tents, 1
ἔλαιον, τό: olive oil, 1
εὑρίσκω: to find, discover, devise, invent, 4
ἡδονή, ἡ: pleasure, enjoyment, delight, 1
κραυγή, ἡ: shouting, crying, screaming, 3
μύρον, τό: a fragrant oil; perfume, 1
πικρός, -ά, -όν: sharp, keen, bitter, 1
σησάμινος, -η, -ον: made of sesame, 1
στέγη, ἡ: roof, roofed place, room, shelter, 2
σύειος, -α, -ον: of swine, of a pig, 1
τερμίνθινος, -η, -ον: of the terebinth tree, 1
χράομαι: use, employ, enjoy, indulge (dat) 6

19 **ἐχρῶντο**: impf. χράομαι + dat.
σύειον...τερμίνθινον: supply neuter sg. χρῖμα, 'ointment,' from above
σύειον: i.e. lard
ἀμυγδάλινον ἐκ...πικρῶν: *of the bitter almond*; 'of almonds from the bitter parts'
20 **τῶν αὐτῶν τούτων**: i.e. sesame, etc.; αὐτός in the attributive position means 'same'
μὺρον: *a fragrant oil*; as opposed to an oil just for anointing the skin
22 **διασκηνητέον εἶναι**: *that (they) must...*; 'it is to be...(by them)' impersonal verbal adj. + inf. εἰμί expressing necessity; we often translate this construction in the active voice with the modal verb 'must'
[τὰς κώμας]: The editor suggests that this is interpolated (inserted) and can be omitted from translation.
23 **εἰς στέγας**: *into shelters*
ἔνθα δή: *just then, exactly then*
24 **ᾖσαν**: impf. ἔρχομαι
ἐπὶ: *to...*
ὅσοι δὲ: *as many (soldiers) as...*; the antecedent is missing

ὅτε τὸ πρότερον ἀπῇσαν τὰς οἰκίας ἐνέπρησαν ὑπὸ ἀτασθα- 1
λίας, δίκην ἐδίδοσαν κακῶς σκηνοῦντες. 15. ἐντεῦθεν ἔπεμψαν
νυκτὸς Δημοκράτην Τημνίτην ἄνδρας δόντες ἐπὶ τὰ ὄρη ἔνθα
ἔφασαν οἱ ἀποσκεδαννύμενοι καθορᾶν τὰ πυρά· οὗτος γὰρ
ἐδόκει καὶ πρότερον πολλὰ ἤδη ἀληθεῦσαι τοιαῦτα, τὰ ὄντα τε 5
ὡς ὄντα καὶ τὰ μὴ ὄντα ὡς οὐκ ὄντα. 16. πορευθεὶς δὲ τὰ μὲν
πυρὰ οὐκ ἔφη ἰδεῖν, ἄνδρα δὲ συλλαβὼν ἧκεν ἄγων ἔχοντα
τόξον Περσικὸν καὶ φαρέτραν καὶ σάγαριν οἵανπερ καὶ <αἱ>
Ἀμαζόνες ἔχουσιν. 17. ἐρωτώμενος δὲ ποδαπὸς εἴη, Πέρσης

ἀληθεύω: speak the truth,, speak truthfully, 1
Ἀμαζόνες, αἱ: Amazons, 1
ἀπο-σκεδαννυμι: to scatter abroad, disperse, 2
ἀτασθαλία, ἡ: recklessness, arrogance, 1
Δημοκράτης, ὁ: Democrates, 1
δίκη, ἡ: justice, penalty; lawsuit, trial, 1
ἐμ-πίμπρημι: to burn; kindle, set on fire, 1
ἥκω: to have come, be present, 7
καθ-οράω: to look down, perceive, 7
κακός, -ή, -όν: bad, base, cowardly, evil, 5
οἷοσπερ, -α, -ον: which very sort, 1
ὅτε: when, at some time, 3
πέμπω: send, conduct, convey, dispatch, 7
Πέρσης, -ου, ὁ: a Persian, 1
Περσικός, -ή, -όν: Persian, 4
ποδαπός, -ή, -όν: from what country? 1
πρότερος, -α, -ον: before, in front of; earlier 2
πυρά, -ῶν, τά: watch-fire, 6
σάγαρις, ἡ: axe, single-edged axe, 1
σκηνέω: to encamp, bivouac, set up tents, 5
συλ-λαμβάνω: to catch, gather; help, 1
Τημνίτης, -ου ὁ: of Temnus, 1
τοιοῦτος, -αύτη, -οῦτο: such, this sort, 3
τόξον, τό: bow, 4
φαρέτρα, ἡ: quiver, 1

1 **τὸ πρότερον**: adverbial acc.
ἀπῇσαν: impf. ἀπέρχομαι
ἐνέπρησαν: aor. ἐμ-πίμπρημι
ὑπὸ: *because of*...; gen. of cause
2 **δίκην ἐδίδοσαν**: impf. δίδωμι, this idiom means 'pay the penalty'
κακῶς σκηνοῦντες: *by*...; causal pple explaining the nature of the penalty
3 **νυκτὸς**: *during*...; gen. of time within
δόντες: i.e. to Democrates; aor. pple δίδωμι; he was in charge of a few men
ὄρη: ὄρε-α, neut. pl. ὄρος
ἔνθα: *where*...; relative clause
4 **ἔφασαν**: aor. φημί
καθορᾶν: *that (they)*...; ind. disc. α-contract inf.
οὗτος: i.e. Democrates
5 **καὶ**: *also*; adverb
πρότερον: comparative adverb
ἀληθεῦσαι: aor. inf.
πολλὰ τοιαῦτα: acc. obj. or inner acc.
τὰ ὄντα: *what is the case*; 'things being (the case)' i.e. true, a common translation for εἰμί, all in apposition to τοιαῦτα
6 **ὡς**: *as*
τὰ μὴ ὄντα: *what is*...; see above; μὴ indicates that the pple is conditional: 'thing (if) not being (the case)'
πορευθεὶς: nom. sg. aor. pass. dep. pple πορεύομαι: translate as active
7 **οὐκ ἔφη**: *he said that...not*, or 'he denied' impf. φημί
ἰδεῖν: aor. inf. ὁράω
ἄνδρα: a non-Greek
συλλαβὼν: *catching*; aor. pple
ἄγων: *leading*; i.e. to the camp
9 **ἐρωτώμενος**: pres. passive pple
εἴη: opt. εἰμί in an ind. question

μὲν ἔφη εἶναι, πορεύεσθαι δ' ἀπὸ τοῦ Τιριβάζου στρατο- 10
πέδου, ὅπως ἐπιτήδεια λάβοι. οἱ δὲ ἠρώτων αὐτὸν τὸ
στράτευμα ὁπόσον τε εἴη καὶ ἐπὶ τίνι συνειλεγμένον. 18. *ὁ δὲ*
εἶπεν ὅτι Τιρίβαζος εἴη ἔχων τήν τε ἑαυτοῦ δύναμιν καὶ
μισθοφόρους Χάλυβας καὶ Ταόχους· παρεσκευάσθαι δὲ αὐτὸν
ἔφη ὡς ἐπὶ τῇ ὑπερβολῇ τοῦ ὄρους ἐν τοῖς στενοῖς ᾗπερ 15
μοναχῇ εἴη πορεία, ἐνταῦθα ἐπιθησόμενον τοῖς Ἕλλησιν.
19. *ἀκούσασι τοῖς στρατηγοῖς ταῦτα ἔδοξε τὸ στράτευμα συν-*
αγαγεῖν· καὶ εὐθὺς φύλακας καταλιπόντες καὶ στρατηγὸν ἐπὶ

δύναμις, -εως, ἡ: power, wealth, strength, 2
ἐπι-τίθημι: to put upon; add; set upon, attack 4
μισθο-φορος, ὁ: mercenary, serving for hire, 2
μοναχός, -ή, -όν: alone, single, solitary, 1
ὁπόσος, -α, -ον: as much, many, or great as, 2
ὅσπερ, ἥπερ, ὅπερ: very one who, which, 4
παρασκευάζω: to prepare, get ready, 4
πορεία, ἡ: way, march, journey, 5
στρατοπεδεύω: to encamp, take a position, 4
συλ-λέγω: to collect, gather, 5
συν-άγω: bring together, collect, gather, 2
Τάοχος, -η, -ον: Taochian, 5
Τιρίβαζος, ὁ: Tiribazus (person), 6
ὑπερ-βολή, ἡ: crossing, mtn. pass; excess, 6
φύλαξ, -ακος, ὁ: guard, sentinal, protector, 4
Χάλυψ, -υβος, ὁ: Chalybian, 4

10 **ἔφη εἶναι**: *he claimed to…*; i.e the captive, inf. εἰμί
πορεύεσθαι δ': *and that (he)…*; ind. disc.
11 **ὅπως…λάβοι**: *so that…might…*; purpose, aor. opt. λαμβάνω in secondary seq.
ἠρώτων: ἠρώταον 3p impf. ἐρωτάω
αὐτὸν τὸ στράτευμα: proleptic, treat this acc. as the subject of the following ind. question
12 **ὁπόσον…εἴη**: ind. question with opt. εἰμί replacing indicative in secondary seq.
ἐπὶ τίνι (τὸ στράτευμα εἴη) συνειλεγμένον: *for what (purpose) it had…*; ind. question, with periphrastic plpf. pass. opt. συλλέγω (pf. pass. pple + opt. εἰμί): in secondary seq.: translate as plpf. pass.
13 **ὅτι (τὸ στάτευμα) εἴη**: *that (the army) was…*; ind. disc. with opt. in secondary seq. Τιρίβαζος and the other names are nom. predicate
13 **τήν ἑαυτοῦ δύναμιν**: *his own force*; i.e. military force
14 **παρασκευάσθαι δὲ αὐτὸν**: *that he…;* ind. disc. αὐτὸν (Tiribazus) is acc. subj.
15 **ὡς…ἐπιθησόμενον**: *so that…*; 'so as going to…', ὡς + fut. pple expressing purpose, ἐπιτίθημι
ἐπὶ: *upon…*
ᾗπερ…εἴη πορεία: *by which way…, in which way…*
16 **ἐνταῦθα**: i.e. ἐπὶ τῇ ὑπερβολῇ
τοῖς Ἕλλησιν: *against…, on…*; dat. of compound verb
17 **ἀκούσασι**: dat pl. aor. pple
ταῦτα: object of ἀκούσασι
ἔδοξε: *it seemed best*
καταλιπόντες: aor. pple καταλείπω

τοῖς μένουσι Σοφαίνετον Στυμφάλιον ἐπορεύοντο ἔχοντες ἡγεμόνα τὸν ἁλόντα ἄνθρωπον. 20. ἐπειδὴ δὲ ὑπερέβαλλον τὰ ὄρη, οἱ πελτασταὶ προϊόντες καὶ κατιδόντες τὸ στρατόπεδον οὐκ ἔμειναν τοὺς ὁπλίτας, ἀλλ' ἀνακραγόντες ἔθεον ἐπὶ τὸ στρατόπεδον. 21. οἱ δὲ βάρβαροι ἀκούσαντες τὸν θόρυβον οὐχ ὑπέμειναν, ἀλλ' ἔφευγον· ὅμως δὲ καὶ ἀπέθανόν τινες τῶν βαρβάρων καὶ ἵπποι ἥλωσαν εἰς εἴκοσι καὶ ἡ σκηνὴ ἡ Τιριβάζου ἑάλω καὶ ἐν αὐτῇ κλῖναι ἀργυρόποδες καὶ ἐκπώματα καὶ οἱ ἀρτοκόποι καὶ οἱ οἰνοχόοι φάσκοντες εἶναι. 22. ἐπειδὴ

ἁλίσκομαι: to be taken, seized, 6
ἀνα-κράζω: to cry out, shout, 3
ἀργυρό-πους, -ποδος, ὁ, ἡ: of silver feet, 1
ἀρτο-κόπος, ὁ: baker, 1
βάρβαρος, -α, -ον: foreigner, barbarian, 7
εἴκοσι: twenty, 5
ἔκπωμα, -ατος, τό: drinking-cup, 2
θόρυβος, ὁ: din, noise, uproar, 3
καθ-οράω: to look down, perceive, 7
κλίνη, ἡ: couch; bed, 1
οἰνο-χόος, ὁ: wine-pourer, cupbearer, 1
ὅμως: nevertheless, however, yet, 3
προ-έρχομαι: to go forth, advance, 4
σκηνή, ἡ: tent, 1
Σοφαίνετος, ὁ: Sophaenetus, 1
Στυμφάλιος, -η, -ον: of Stymphalos (city), 4
Τιρίβαζος, ὁ: Tiribazus (person), 6
ὑπερ-βάλλω: to pass over, exceed, 5
ὑπο-μένω: to remain, abide, wait up, await, 7
φάσκω: say, claim, speak, 2

19 **στρατηγὸν ἐπι τοῖς μένουσι...Στυφάλιον**: *Sophaenetus the Stympalian as general over those remaining*; dat. pl. pple μένω
20 **ἡγεμόνα**: *as guide*, acc. apposition
ἁλόντα: acc. sg. aor. pple ἁλίσκομαι
ὑπερέβαλλον: *began to...*; inchoative impf. προ-έρχομαι
21 **προϊόντες**: pple προ-έρχομαι
κατιδόντες: aor. pple καθοράω
22 **ἔμειναν**: aor. μένω
ἀνακραγόντες: aor. pple ἀνακράζω
ἐπὶ: *upon..., against...*; i,.e. the enemy camp
24 **καὶ**: *actually, in fact*; adv.
ἀπέθανον: aor. ἀποθνῄσκω
25 **ἥλωσαν**: 3p aor. ἁλίσκομαι (Ionic 2nd aor. ἥλων, not Attic aor. below)
εἰς: *nearly*; 'up to' in approximation
ἑάλω: 3s aor. ἁλίσκομαι (Attic 2nd aor. ἑάλων, note Ionic aor. above)
26 **ἐν αὐτῇ**: *in it*; i.e. the fem. σκηνή
27 **οἱ...φάσκοντες**: *those claiming...*; with nom. pred.

δὲ ἐπύθοντο ταῦτα οἱ τῶν ὁπλιτῶν στρατηγοί, ἐδόκει αὐτοῖς 1
ἀπιέναι τὴν ταχίστην ἐπὶ τὸ στρατόπεδον, μή τις ἐπίθεσις
γένοιτο τοῖς καταλελειμμένοις. καὶ εὐθὺς ἀνακαλεσάμενοι
τῇ σάλπιγγι ἀπῇσαν, καὶ ἀφίκοντο αὐθημερὸν ἐπὶ τὸ στρατόπεδον. 5

1. τῇ δ' ὑστεραίᾳ ἐδόκει πορευτέον εἶναι ὅπῃ δύναιντο
τάχιστα πρὶν ἢ συλλεγῆναι τὸ στράτευμα πάλιν καὶ καταλαβεῖν τὰ στενά. συσκευασάμενοι δ' εὐθὺς ἐπορεύοντο διὰ
χιόνος πολλῆς ἡγεμόνας ἔχοντες πολλούς· καὶ αὐθημερὸν

ἀνα-καλέω: to call up, call back, 1
αὐθ-ήμερος, -ον: on the same day, 2
ἐπι-θεσις, ἡ: attack, setting upon, 1
ὅπῃ: where; in what way, how, 3
πορευτέος, -ον: to be travelled, 2
πυνθάνομαι: learn (by inquiry or hearsay), 2
σάλπιγξ, -ιγγος, ὁ: war-trumpet, 4
συλ-λέγω: to collect, gather, 5
συσκευάζομαι: to pack up together, prepare, 2
ὑστεραῖος, -α, -ον: the next day; later, 5

1 **ἐπύθοντο**: aor. πυνθάνομαι
2 **ἀπιέναι**: inf. ἀπέρχομαι
τὴν ταχίστην: adverbial acc., superlative
μὴ...γένοιτο: *lest...*; fearing clause with aor. opt. in secondary seq.
3 **τοῖς καταλελειμμένοις**: *for those...*; dat. of interest, pf. pass. pple κατα-λείπω
4 **τῇ σάλπιγγι**: dat. of means
ἀπῇσαν: impf. ἀπέρχομαι
6 **τῇ ὑστεραίᾳ (ἡμέρᾳ)**: *on...*; dat. time when
πορευτέον εἶναι: *that (they) must...*; 'that it is to be...(by them),' impersonal verbal adj. + εἰμί expressing necessity. It is often translated in the active with modal verb 'must.'
ὅπῃ δύναιντο τάχιστα: *in whatever way...*; general relative clause with opt. in secondary sequence
7 **πρὶν ἢ**: *before*; 'earlier than'
συλλεγῆναι...καταλάβειν: *the army (of the enemy)...*; aor. infs. governed by ἐδόκει στράτευμα is acc. subj.
9 **ἡγεμόνας πολλούς**: obj. of ἔχοντες

ὑπερβαλόντες τὸ ἄκρον ἐφ᾽ ᾧ ἔμελλεν ἐπιτίθεσθαι Τιρίβαζος κατεστρατοπεδεύσαντο. 2. ἐντεῦθεν δ᾽ ἐπορεύθησαν σταθμοὺς ἐρήμους τρεῖς παρασάγγας πεντεκαίδεκα ἐπὶ τὸν Εὐφράτην ποταμόν, καὶ διέβαινον αὐτὸν βρεχόμενοι πρὸς τὸν ὀμφαλόν. 3. ἐλέγοντο δ᾽ οὐδὲ πηγαὶ πρόσω εἶναι. ἐντεῦθεν ἐπορεύοντο διὰ χιόνος πολλῆς καὶ πεδίου σταθμοὺς τρεῖς παρασάγγας †πεντεκαίδεκα†. ὁ δὲ τρίτος ἐγένετο χαλεπὸς καὶ ἄνεμος βορρᾶς ἐναντίος ἔπνει παντάπασιν ἀποκαίων πάντα καὶ πηγνὺς τοὺς ἀνθρώπους. 4. ἔνθα δὴ τῶν μάντεών τις εἶπε

ἄνεμος, ὁ: wind, 2
ἀπο-καίω: blast, freeze or burn off, shrival, 1
βορρᾶς (βορέας), ὁ: north (wind), Boreas, 1
βρέχω: be wet, get wet, 2
ἐναντίος, -α, -ον: opposite, contrary, 4
ἐπι-τίθημι: to put upon; add; set upon, attack 4
ἐρῆμος, -ον: deserted, desolate, 4
Εὐφρήτης, ὁ: Euphrates, 2
κατα-στρατοπεδεύω: to encamp, 1
μάντις, ἡ: seer, prophet, 2
μέλλω: to be about to, intend to, 2
ὀμφαλός, ὁ: navel, middle, center, 1
παντά-πασι: all in all, altogether, entirely, 3
πεντε-καί-δεκα: fifteen, 5
πηγή, ἡ: spring, source (of a river), 4
πήγνυμι: to stick, freeze, 1
πνέω: to blow; breathe, 1
πρόσω: forwards into, far from +gen 4
Τιρίβαζος, ὁ: Tiribazus (person), 6
τρίτος, -η, -ον: the third, 4
ὑπερ-βάλλω: to pass over, exceed, 5
χαλεπός, -ά, -όν: difficult, harsh, harmful, 3

10 **ἐφ᾽ᾧ**: *upon which*; ἐπ(ὶ) ᾧ
11 **ἐπορεύθησαν**: aor. pass. dep. πορέυομαι; translate in the active
σταθμοὺς... παρασάγγας: *for...for...*; acc. of extent
14 **οὐδὲ πρόσω**: *also not far away*; predicate after inf. εἰμί; οὐδὲ, 'also not,' is an adv.
16 **†πεντεκαίδεκα†**: A obelus (†) indicates that the word or clause is plainly corrupt but the editor cannot see how to emend it. Omit in translation.
ὁ τρίτος (σταθμός): *the third stage*
17 **ἀποκαίων**: *blasting, freezing off*; used for extreme cold or heat
18 **πηγνὺς**: nom. sg. pres. pple πήγνυμι
ἔνθα δὴ: *just then, exactly then*
εἶπε: *told (them)*; i.e. commanded (them); aor. λέγω; supply an object

σφαγιάσασθαι τῷ ἀνέμῳ, καὶ σφαγιάζεται· καὶ πᾶσι δὴ
περιφανῶς ἔδοξεν λῆξαι τὸ χαλεπὸν τοῦ πνεύματος. ἦν δὲ 20
τῆς χιόνος τὸ βάθος ὀργυιά· ὥστε καὶ τῶν ὑποζυγίων καὶ
τῶν ἀνδραπόδων πολλὰ ἀπώλετο καὶ τῶν στρατιωτῶν ὡς
τριάκοντα. 5. διεγένοντο δὲ τὴν νύκτα πῦρ καίοντες· ξύλα δ'
ἦν ἐν τῷ σταθμῷ πολλά· οἱ δὲ ὀψὲ προσιόντες ξύλα οὐκ
εἶχον. οἱ οὖν πάλαι ἥκοντες καὶ τὸ πῦρ καίοντες οὐ προσ- 25

ἀνδρά-ποδον, τό: captive, captive-slave, 2
ἄνεμος, ὁ: wind, 2
ἀπ-όλλυμι: destroy, lose; *mid.* perish, 2
βάθος, τό: depth, 3
δια-γίγνομαι: to go through, pass, 1
ἥκω: to have come, be present, 7
λήγω: to cease, leave off, abate, 1
ξύλον, τό: wood, timber, firewood, 3
ὀργυιά, ἡ: (length of outstretched arms), 1
ὀψέ: late, 2
πάλαι: long ago, formerly, of old, 2
περι-φανής, -ές: very clear, conspicuous, 1
πνεῦμα, -ατος, τό: wind, blast, breath, 1
προσ-ίημι: to send to; allow; undertake, 4
σφαγιάζομαι: to sacrifice, slay a victim, 3
τριάκοντα: thirty, 4
χαλεπός, -ά, -όν: difficult, harsh, harmful, 3

19 **σφαγιάσασθαι**: equiv. to an ind. command governed by εἶπε
τῷ ἀνέμῷ: *for*...; dat. of interest
σφαγιάζεται: either pres. mid. with the soothesayer as subject or impersonal pass.
πᾶσι: *to*...; dat. pl. of reference πᾶς
δή: *quite, absolutely*; intensive with πᾶσι
20 **λῆξαι**: aor. inf.
τὸ χαλεπὸν: *the harshness*; a substantive and nom. subject
ἦν: impf. εἰμί
21 **καὶ...καὶ**: *both...and...*
ὑποζυγίων...ἀνδραπόδων...στρατιωτῶν: partitive gen. with πολλὰ, the subject
ἀπόλετο: aor. mid. ἀπόλλυμι
ὡς: *nearly*; 'as if' in approximation
23 **τὴν νύκτα**: acc. of duration of time
24 **οἱ...προσιόντες**: *those*...; pple προσέρχομαι
25 **οἱ...ἥκοντες**: *those*...; pple
προσίεσαν: *did allow near*; 3s impf. προσίημι

ἴεσαν πρὸς τὸ πῦρ τοὺς ὀψίζοντας, εἰ μὴ μεταδοῖεν αὐτοῖς πυροὺς ἢ ἄλλο [τι] εἴ τι ἔχοιεν βρωτόν. 6. ἔνθα δὴ μετεδίδοσαν ἀλλήλοις ὧν εἶχον ἕκαστοι. ἔνθα δὲ τὸ πῦρ ἐκαίετο, διατηκομένης τῆς χιόνος βόθροι ἐγένοντο μεγάλοι ἔστε ἐπὶ τὸ δάπεδον· οὗ δὴ παρῆν μετρεῖν τὸ βάθος τῆς χιόνος. 7. ἐντεῦθεν δὲ τὴν ἐπιοῦσαν ἡμέραν ὅλην ἐπορεύοντο διὰ χιόνος, καὶ πολλοὶ τῶν ἀνθρώπων ἐβουλιμίασαν. Ξενοφῶν δ' ὀπισθοφυλακῶν καὶ καταλαμβάνων τοὺς πίπτοντας τῶν ἀνθρώπων ἠγνόει ὅ τι τὸ πάθος εἴη. 8. ἐπειδὴ δὲ εἶπέ τις αὐτῷ

ἀ-γνοέω: be ignorant, not perceive, 1
βάθος, τό: depth, 3
βόθρος, ὁ: hole, 1
βουλιμιάω: to suffer from bulimia, hunger-faintness, suffer extreme hunger, 3
βρωτός, -όν: to be eaten, edible; *neut.* meat, 2
δάπεδον, τό: level surface; floor, ground,1
δια-τήκω: to melt, melt away, thaw, 1
ἐπ-έρχομαι: to come upon; attack, 5
ἔστε (εἰς+τε): up to; until, 2
μετα-δίδωμι: to give a part of or a share of, 2
μετρέω: to measure; pass over, traverse, 1
ὅλος, -η, -ον: whole, entire, complete, 5
ὀπισθο-φύλακέω: to guard the rear, 3
οὗ: where, 2
ὀψίζω: to do late, come late, 1
πάθος τό: suffering, experience, misfortune 1
πάρ-ειμι: to be near, be present, be at hand, 4
πίπτω: to fall, 1
πυρός, ὁ: wheat; a grain of wheat, 2

1 **εἰ μὴ μεταδοῖεν**: *unless they...*; protasis of a past general condition (εἰ + opt., impf.); 3p aor. opt. μεταδίδωμι
αὐτοῖς: dat. ind. object
2 **πυροὺς**: *wheat*
[τι]: omit the bracketed passage
τι...βρωτόν: acc. object
ἔνδα δὴ: *and then, exactly then*
μετεδίδοσαν: impf.
3 **ὧν**: *(of the things) which*; (τοῦτων) ἃ; acc. relative pronoun assumes case of a missing antecedent, a partitive gen. with a verb of sharing
ἔνδα δὲ: *and where...*; relative clause
4 **διατηκομένης...χιόνος**: gen. absolute
ἔστε ἐπὶ: *up to...*; i.e. melts all the way to the ground
5 **οὗ δὴ**: *just where, exactly where*; οὗ, 'where,' is a relative adv.; δή is intensive
παρῆν: *it was possible*; impf. πάρειμι
6 **τὴν...ἡμέραν ὅλην**: acc. of duration
ἐπιοῦσαν: i.e. next day; pple
8 **τοὺς πίπτοντας**: *those...*; i.e. soldiers as they travelled
9 **ὅ τι...εἴη**: *what...*; ind. question with opt. εἰμί in secondary seq. neuter sg. ὅστις
αὐτῷ: i.e. to Xenophon, dat. ind. object

τῶν ἐμπείρων ὅτι σαφῶς βουλιμιῶσι κἄν τι φάγωσιν ἀνα- 10
στήσονται, περιιὼν περὶ τὰ ὑποζύγια, εἴ πού τι ὁρῴη βρωτόν,
διεδίδου καὶ διέπεμπε διδόντας τοὺς δυναμένους περιτρέχειν
τοῖς βουλιμιῶσιν. 9. *ἐπειδὴ δέ τι ἐμφάγοιεν, ἀνίσταντο καὶ*
ἐπορεύοντο. πορευομένων δὲ Χειρίσοφος μὲν ἀμφὶ κνέφας
πρὸς κώμην ἀφικνεῖται, καὶ ὑδροφορούσας ἐκ τῆς κώμης 15
πρὸς τῇ κρήνῃ γυναῖκας καὶ κόρας καταλαμβάνει ἔμπροσθεν
τοῦ ἐρύματος. 10. *αὗται ἠρώτων αὐτοὺς τίνες εἶεν. ὁ δ' ἑρμη-*
νεὺς εἶπε Περσιστὶ ὅτι παρὰ βασιλέως πορεύονται πρὸς τὸν

βουλιμιάω: to suffer from bulimia, hunger-faintness, suffer extreme hunger, 3
βρωτός, -όν: to be eaten; *neut.* meat, 2
γυνή, γυναικός, ἡ: a woman, wife, 7
δια-δίδωμι: to distribute, give out, 1
δια-πέμπω: to send in different ways, 1
ἔμ-πειρος, -ον: experienced, acquainted, 1
ἔμ-προσθεν: in front of, before, 5
ἐν-εσθίω: to eat, consume, 2
ἑρμηνεύς, ὁ: an interpreter, 4
ἔρυμα, ἐρύματος, τό: fence, bulkwark, 2
ἐσθίω: to eat, 3
κνέφας, τό: darkness; dusk, twilight, 1
κόρη, ἡ: girl; daughter, 1
κρήνη, ἡ: spring, fountain, 2
περι-έρχομαι: to go around, go about, 4
περι-τρέχω: to run around, 1
περί: around, about, concerning, 7
Περσιστὶ: in the Persian tongue, 1
που: anywhere, somewhere; I suppose, 2
σαφής, -ές: clear, distinct, definite, 1
ὑδρο-φορέω: to carry water, 1

10 **τῶν ἐμπείρων**: i.e. with knowledge of the symptoms of hunger-faintness
βουλιμιῶσι: βουλιμιάουσι, 3p pres.
κἄν...φάγωσιν: *and if they...*; καὶ ἐὰν, aor. subj. ἐσθίω ; protasis in a fut. more vivid condition (εἰ ἄν + subj., fut. ind.)
ἀναστήσονται: fut. mid. ἀν-ίστημι
11 **περιιὼν**: nom. sg. pple περιέρχομαι, modifying Xenophon
ὁρῴη: ὁραόιη 3s opt. ὁράω in a past general condition (εἰ + opt., impf. ind.)
12 **διεδίδου**: *he would...*; διεδίδοε, 3s iterative impf.
διέπεμπε: *he would...*; iterative impf.
διδόντας: *as givers*; he sent others to help distribute food
τοὺς δυναμένους: i.e. those soldiers with the strength to move
13 **τοῖς βουλιμιῶσιν**: dat. pl. pple, ind. object following διδόντας
ἐμφάγοιεν: 3p aor. opt. ἐμ-εσθίω in a past general temporal clause (equiv. to a past general condition)
ἀνίσταντο: 3p impf. mid. ἀνίστημι
14 **πορευομένων**: *the (men)...;* gen. abs., the noun is missing and must be supplied
16 **ὑδροφορούσας**: modifies γυναῖκας and κόρας
πρὸς: *near...*; dat. place where
17 **αὗται**: *they themselves*; i.e. the females
ἠρώτων: ἠρώταον; 3p impf.
τίνες...εἶεν: ind. question with 3p opt. εἰμί in secondary seq.
18 **παρὰ βασιλέως**: *from the King*

σατράπην. αἱ δὲ ἀπεκρίναντο ὅτι οὐκ ἐνταῦθα εἴη, ἀλλ' ἀπέχει ὅσον παρασάγγην. οἱ δ', ἐπεὶ ὀψὲ ἦν, πρὸς τὸν 20 *κώμαρχον συνεισέρχονται εἰς τὸ ἔρυμα σὺν ταῖς ὑδροφόροις.*

11. *Χειρίσοφος μὲν οὖν καὶ ὅσοι ἐδυνήθησαν τοῦ στρατεύματος ἐνταῦθα ἐστρατοπεδεύσαντο, τῶν δ' ἄλλων στρατιωτῶν οἱ μὴ δυνάμενοι διατελέσαι τὴν ὁδὸν ἐνυκτέρευσαν ἄσιτοι καὶ ἄνευ πυρός· καὶ ἐνταῦθά τινες ἀπώλοντο τῶν στρατιωτῶν.* 25

12. *ἐφείποντο δὲ τῶν πολεμίων συνειλεγμένοι τινὲς καὶ τὰ μὴ δυνάμενα τῶν ὑποζυγίων ἥρπαζον καὶ ἀλλήλοις ἐμάχοντο περὶ αὐτῶν. ἐλείποντο δὲ τῶν στρατιωτῶν οἵ τε διεφθαρ-*

ἄνευ: without (+ gen.), 4
ἀπ-έχω: to be distant, keep away from, 5
ἀπο-κρίνομαι: to answer, reply, 3
ἀπ-όλλυμι: destroy, lose; *mid.* perish, 2
ἁρπάζω: seize, carry off, kidnap, 3
ἄ-σιτος, -ον: without food, fasting, 1
δια-τελέω: continue, perservere (to the end) 1
δια-φθείρω: to destroy utterly, disable, 1
ἔρυμα, ἐρύματος, τό: fence, bulkwark, 2
ἐφ-έπομαι: to follow after, pursue, 4
λείπω: to leave, forsake, abandon, 6
νυκτερεύω: to pass the night, 2
ὀψέ: late, 2
περί: around, about, concerning, 7
σατράπης, ὁ: satrap, 2
στρατοπεδεύω: to encamp, take a position, 4
συλ-λέγω: to collect, gather, 5
συν-εισ-έρχομαι: to go into or enter together 1
ὑδρο-φόρος, -ον: water-carriers, 1

19 **αἱ δὲ**: *and they*
ὅτι...εἴη: *that...*; i.e. the satrap, ind. disc. with 3s pres. opt. εἰμί
20 **ὅσον παρασάγγην**: *as much as...*; acc. of extent
ἐπεὶ: *since...*; causal
ἦν: *it was*; i.e. the time was
22 **οὖν**: *and so*
ὅσοι ἐδυνήθησαν: *(those) as many as...;* the missing antecedent is part of the subject; 3p aor. pass. dep. δύναμαι
τοῦ στρατεύματος: partitive gen.
23 **τῶν...στρατιωτῶν**: *among...*; partitive.
24 **διατελέσαι**: aor. inf.
25 **ἀπώλοντο**: aor. mid. ἀπόλλυμι
26 **ἐφείποντο**: impf. mid.. ἐφ-έπομαι
τῶν πολεμίων: partitive with subject τινὲς
συνειλεγμένοι: pf. pass. pple συλλέγω
τὰ μὴ δυνάμενα: *those not...*; i.e. the weaker animals trailing behind; with partitive ὑποζυγίων; μή instead of οὐ because the participle is conditional in sense: 'those (if) not being...
27 **ἥρπαζον...ἐμάχοντο**: *would...would...*; iterative impf. ἁρπάζω
ἀλλήλοις: *with...*; dat. of association
αὐτῶν: i.e. the animals
28 **ἐλείποντο**: impf. pass. λείπω
τῶν στρατιωτῶν: *among...*; partitive
οἵ διεφθαρμένοι: pf. pass. pple; as often, the pf. denoted a state, 'being Xed,' rather than an activity, 'having been Xed'

μένοι ὑπὸ τῆς χιόνος τοὺς ὀφθαλμοὺς οἵ τε ὑπὸ τοῦ ψύχους 1
τοὺς δακτύλους τῶν ποδῶν ἀποσεσηπότες. 13. *ἦν δὲ τοῖς μὲν*
ὀφθαλμοῖς ἐπικούρημα τῆς χιόνος εἴ τις μέλαν τι ἔχων πρὸ
τῶν ὀφθαλμῶν ἐπορεύετο, τῶν δὲ ποδῶν εἴ τις κινοῖτο καὶ
μηδέποτε ἡσυχίαν ἔχοι καὶ εἰς τὴν νύκτα ὑπολύοιτο· 14. *ὅσοι δὲ* 5
ὑποδεδεμένοι ἐκοιμῶντο, εἰσεδύοντο εἰς τοὺς πόδας οἱ ἱμάντες
καὶ τὰ ὑποδήματα περιεπήγνυντο· καὶ γὰρ ἦσαν, ἐπειδὴ
ἐπέλιπε τὰ ἀρχαῖα ὑποδήματα, καρβάτιναι πεποιημέναι ἐκ
τῶν νεοδάρτων βοῶν. 15. *διὰ τὰς τοιαύτας οὖν ἀνάγκας ὑπελεί-*

ἀνάγκη, ἡ: necessity, force, 4
ἀπο-σήπομαι: to lose by rotting or frostbite 1
ἀρχαῖος, -α, -ον: ancient, old, 1
δάκτυλος, ὁ: finger, 1
εἰσ-δύ(ν)ω: to enter, go into, 1
ἐπι-λείπω: fail, be lacking, be wanting, 2
ἐπίκούρημα, -ατος, τό: protection, 1
ἡσυχία, ἡ: quiet, rest, idleness, silence, 1
ἱμάς, ἱμάντος, ὁ: leather strap, 1
καρβάτιναι, αἱ: shoe (of undressed leather), 1
κινέω: to set in motion, move, 1
κοιμάω: to put to sleep; *mid.* to sleep, 3
μέλας, μέλαινα, μέλαν: black, dark, 2
μηδέ-ποτε: never, 1
νεό-δαρτος, -ον: newly flayed or skinned, 1
ὀφθαλμός, ὁ: the eye, 4
περι-πήγνυμι: to freeze around, fix around, 1
πούς, ποδός, ὁ: a foot, 7
πρό: before, in front; in place of (+ gen.), 3
τοιοῦτος, -αύτη, -οῦτο: such, this sort, 3
ὑπο-δέω: to bind or fasten under (foot), 1
ὑπό-δημα, -ατος, τό: sandal, shoe, 2
ὑπο-λείπω: to leave behind, 2
ὑπο-λύω: to loosen from under, untie, 1
ψῦχος, -εος, τό: the cold, 1

1 **ὑπο**: *because of...*; gen. of cause
τοὺς ὀφθαλμοὺς: *in…*; acc. of respect
οἵ τε: *and those (disabled)*
2 **τοὺς δακτύλους τῶν ποδῶν**: *in…*; acc. of respect and partitive gen.; i.e. toes
ἀποσεσηπότες: pf. pple ἀπο-σήπομαι
ἦν τοῖς ὀφθαλμοῖς: dat. of possession and 3s impf; parallel to gen. τῶν ποδῶν below
εἴ…ἐπορεύετο: *if...*; past general condition (εἰ impf. ind., impf. ind.) where one expects past general with opt.
πρὸ: *in front of…*; i.e. below the eyes on the upper cheeks to deflect the glare
4 **τῶν ποδῶν**: *(there was protection) for the feet*; objective gen., parallel to ὀφθαλμοῖς
εἴ…κινοῖτο…ἔχοι…ὑπολύοιτο: *if...moved*; opt. in past general condition (εἰ + opt., impf. ind.)
5 **ἡσυχίαν ἔχοι**: *kept still*
εἰς: *for…*
ὑπολύοιτο: modified by μηδέποτε
ὅσοι: *(those) as many as*; missing antecedent is subject of main verb
6 **ὑποδεδεμένοι**: pf. pass. pple, conditional in sense
7 **περιεπήγνυντο**: *would…*; iterative impf.
καὶ γὰρ: *for in fact*
ἐπειδὴ: *since*
8 **ἐπέλιπε**: aor.
πεποιημέναι: pf. pass. pple ποιέω
9 **βοῶν**: the word for the hide and the animal are the same
διὰ…ἀνάγκας: i.e. challenges
ὑπελείποντο: iterative impf. passive

ποντό τινες τῶν στρατιωτῶν· καὶ ἰδόντες μέλαν τι χωρίον 10
διὰ τὸ ἐκλελοιπέναι αὐτόθι τὴν χιόνα, εἴκαζον τετηκέναι· καὶ
ἐτετήκει διὰ κρήνην τινὰ ἣ πλησίον ἦν ἀτμίζουσα ἐν νάπῃ.
ἐνταῦθ᾽ ἐκτραπόμενοι ἐκάθηντο καὶ οὐκ ἔφασαν πορεύεσθαι.
16. ὁ δὲ Ξενοφῶν *ἔχων ὀπισθοφύλακας ὡς ᾔσθετο, ἐδεῖτο αὐτῶν*
πάσῃ τέχνῃ καὶ μηχανῇ μὴ ἀπολείπεσθαι, λέγων ὅτι ἕπονται 15
πολλοὶ πολέμιοι συνειλεγμένοι, καὶ τελευτῶν ἐχαλέπαινεν.
οἱ δὲ σφάττειν ἐκέλευον· οὐ γὰρ ἂν δύνασθαι πορευθῆναι.
17. *ἐνταῦθα ἔδοξε κράτιστον εἶναι τοὺς ἑπομένους πολεμίους*

αἰσθάνομαι: perceive, feel, learn, realize, 4
ἀπο-λείπω: to leave behind, abandon, 4
ἀτμίζω: to smoke, steam, 1
αὐτό-θι: on the very spot or moment, 2
δέομαι: to lack, be in need of (gen.), 2
εἰκάζω: to liken, compare; guess, conjecture 1
ἐκ-λείπω: to leave, forsake, abandon, 3
ἐκ-τρέπω: to turn aside, turn off from, 1
ἕπομαι: to follow, accompany, escort, 9
κάθ-ημαι: to sit, be seated, 4
κράτιστος, -η, -ον: best; strongest, 7
κρήνη, ἡ: spring, fountain, 2
μέλας, μέλαινα, μέλαν: black, dark, 2
μηχανή, ἡ: device, contrivance; means, way 1
νάπη, ἡ: glen, wooded vale, 2
πλησίος, -η, -ον: near, close to; neighbors, 5
συλ-λέγω: to collect, gather, 5
σφάττω: to slay, slaughter, 2
τελευτάω: to end, complete, finish; die, 1
τέχνη, ἡ: art, craft, skill, 1
τήκω: to melt, melt away, thaw, 2
χαλεπαίνω: to be angry, be sore with, 2

10 **ἰδόντες**: aor. pple ὁράω (εἶδον)
11 **τὸ ἐκλελοιπέναι**: articular pf. act. inf. ἐκλείπω; τὴν χίονα is subject; in English we often translate the articular inf. as a gerund (-ing) and subject as a possessive
εἴκαζον: 3p impf.
τετηκέναι: pf. inf. τήκω
12 **ἐτετήκει**: plpf. τήκω
ἣ...νάπῃ: *which...*; relative clause
πλησίον: adv.
ἦν: impf. εἰμί
13 **ἐκτραπόμενοι**: aor. mid. ἐκτρέπω
οὐκ ἔφασαν: *refused*; 'said that...not', aor. φημί
14 **ὡς**: *as, when*
ᾔσθετο: aor. αἰσθάνομαι
ἐδεῖτο: *he begged..., he asked...*; impf. mid.. δέομαι
αὐτῶν: *from...*; gen. of source
15 **πάσῃ...μηχανῇ**: *with...*; dat. of manner
ἀπολείπεσθαι: passive. inf.; Xenophon worried that they would not continue with the rest; μή is used instead of οὐ in wishes and commands
16 **συνειλεγμένοι**: pf. pass. συλλέγω
τελευτῶν: *finally*; the pple is very often translated as an adverb
17 **οἱ δὲ**: *they...*; the soldiers who refused to continue
σφάττειν: add Xenophon as acc. subj. and the speakers as acc. object
(ἔφασαν) ἂν δύνασθαι: *(they said that) they would...*; ind. disc. with ἄν + inf. replacing potential opt.; add a main verb
πορευθῆναι: aor. pass. dep. inf.: translate as active
18 **κράτιστον**: *best*

φοβῆσαι, εἴ τις δύναιτο, μὴ ἐπίοιεν τοῖς κάμνουσι. καὶ ἦν μὲν σκότος ἤδη, οἱ δὲ προσῆσαν πολλῷ θορύβῳ ἀμφὶ ὧν 20 εἶχον διαφερόμενοι. 18. ἔνθα δὴ οἱ ὀπισθοφύλακες, ἅτε ὑγιαίνοντες, ἐξαναστάντες ἔδραμον εἰς τοὺς πολεμίους· οἱ δὲ κάμνοντες ἀνακραγόντες ὅσον ἐδύναντο μέγιστον τὰς ἀσπίδας πρὸς τὰ δόρατα ἔκρουσαν. οἱ δὲ πολέμιοι δείσαντες ἧκαν ἑαυτοὺς κατὰ τῆς χιόνος εἰς τὴν νάπην, καὶ οὐδεὶς ἔτι οὐ- 25 δαμοῦ ἐφθέγξατο. 19. καὶ Ξενοφῶν μὲν καὶ οἱ σὺν αὐτῷ εἰπόντες τοῖς ἀσθενοῦσιν ὅτι τῇ ὑστεραίᾳ ἥξουσί τινες ἐπ' αὐτούς, πορευόμενοι πρὶν τέτταρα στάδια διελθεῖν ἐν-

---

ἀνα-κράζω: to cry out, shout, 3
ἀ-σθενεω: to be weak, feeble, sick, 3
ἀσπίς, ἀσπίδος, ὁ: a round shield, 6
ἅτε: inasmuch as, since, seeing that (+ pple) 3
δείδω: to fear, 5
δια-φέρω: to carry over; differ, disagree, 1
δι-έρχομαι: to go through, pass, 7
δόρυ, δόρατος, τό: spearshaft; pole, stem, 4
ἐν-τυγχάνω: to chance upon, encounter, 2
ἐξ-αν-ίστημι: to stand up, rise; raise 1
ἐπ-έρχομαι: to come upon; attack, 5
ἔτι: still, besides, further, 7
ἥκω: to have come, be present, 7
θόρυβος, ὁ: din, noise, uproar, 3
ἵημι: to send, throw; let go, release, 4
κάμνω: to be tired, afflicted, suffering, 2
κρούω: to strike, smite, 1
μέγιστος, -η, -ον: greatest, mightiest, 1
νάπη, ἡ: glen, wooded vale, 2
οὐδαμ-οῦ: nowhere, 2
σκότος, ὁ: darkness, gloom, 2
τέτταρες, -α: four, 6
τρέχω: to run, 3
ὑγιαίνω: to be sound, healthy, 1
ὑστεραῖος, -α, -ον: the next day; later, 5
φθέγγομαι: utter a sound, cry out, 2
φοβέω: to put to flight, terrify, frighten, 1

19 **φοβῆναι**: aor. inf. φοβέω
ἔι τις δύναιτο: *if they could*; 'if anyone could' but refers to the men who refuse to move
μὴ ἐπίοιεν: *lest (the enemy)...*; fearing, with opt. in secondary seq.; 3p opt. ἐπέρχομαι
τοῖς κάμνουσι: *on...*; pres. pple. and dat. of compound verb
ἦν: impf. εἰμί
20 **οἱ δὲ**: *and they*; i.e. the enemy
προσῆσαν: impf. προσέρχομαι
πολλῳ θορύβῳ: *with...*; dat. of manner
ἀμφὶ ὧν...: *about what (loot)...*; relative clause with διαφερόμενοι
21 **ἔνθα δή**: *just then, exactly then*
ἅτε: *inasmuch as..*; 'since...' ἅτε + pple indicates cause from the narrator's view
22 **ἔδραμον**: aor. τρέχω
ἀνακραγόντες: aor. pple
23 **ὅσον ἐδύναντο μέγιστον**: *as loudly as...*
24 **πρὸς**: *against...*; the sick rattled shields and spears together
δείσαντες: *becoming...*; ingressive aor. pple δείδω
ἧκαν: 3p aor. ἵημι
25 **κατὰ...**: *over...*
26 **εἰπόντες**: aor. pple εἶπον (λέγω)
τοῖς ἀσθενοῦσιν: pres. pple., ind. object
27 **τῇ ὑστεραίᾳ (ἡμέρᾳ)**: *on...*; dat. time when
ἥξουσί:; fut. ἥκω
ἐπ(ὶ)...: *for...*; i.e. rescue them
28 **πρὶν...διελθεῖν**: *before...*; πρίν + inf.
τέτταρα στάδια: *for...*; acc. of extent

τυγχάνουσιν ἐν τῇ ὁδῷ ἀναπαυομένοις ἐπὶ τῆς χιόνος τοῖς 1
στρατιώταις ἐγκεκαλυμμένοις, καὶ οὐδὲ φυλακὴ οὐδεμία
καθειστήκει· καὶ ἀνίστασαν αὐτούς. οἱ δ' ἔλεγον ὅτι οἱ
ἔμπροσθεν οὐχ ὑποχωροῖεν. 20. ὁ δὲ παριὼν καὶ παραπέμπων
τῶν πελταστῶν τοὺς ἰσχυροτάτους ἐκέλευε σκέψασθαι τί 5
εἴη τὸ κωλῦον. οἱ δὲ ἀπήγγελλον ὅτι ὅλον οὕτως ἀνα-
παύοιτο τὸ στράτευμα. 21. ἐνταῦθα καὶ οἱ περὶ Ξενοφῶντα
ηὐλίσθησαν αὐτοῦ ἄνευ πυρὸς καὶ ἄδειπνοι, φυλακὰς οἵας
ἐδύναντο καταστησάμενοι. ἐπεὶ δὲ πρὸς ἡμέραν ἦν, ὁ μὲν

ἄ-δειπνος, -ον: without dinner, 1
ἀνα-παύω: to stop, make cease; *mid.*, rest, 4
ἄνευ: without (+ gen.), 4
ἀπ-αγγέλλω: to report (back), announce, 2
αὐλίζομαι: to bivouac, encamp, lodge, 5
αὐτοῦ: in that very place, there, 7
ἐγ-καλύπτω: to cover in, wrap, veil, 1
ἔμ-προσθεν: in front, before, 5
ἐν-τυγχάνω: chance upon, encounter (dat) 2
ἰσχυρός, -ά, -όν: strong, powerful; severe, 7
καθ-ίστημι: to station, appoint; *intransitive*, stand, 4
οἷος, -α, -ον: of what sort, as, 5
ὅλος, -η, -ον: whole, entire, complete, 5
παρα-πέμπω: to send past, send alongside, 1
περί: around, about, concerning, 7
σκέπτομαι: to look for, find out, examine, 2
ὑπο-χωρέω: to go aside, retire, withdraw, 1
φυλακή, ἡ: a watch, guard, 4

1 **ἐντυγχάνουσιν**: historical pres.: translate in the past
τοῖς στρατιώταις: dat. of compound verb, modified by two participles; these soldiers are not the sick, who were left behind, but those whom Xenophon ran ahead to meet
ἐγκεκαλυμμένοις: pf. pass. ἐγκαλύπτω
2 **οὐδὲ οὐδεμία**: *not even...one*; adv.; οὐδεμία is positive after the adv. οὐδὲ, 'not even'
3 **καθειστήκει**: intransitive plpf. act. (note: 'had stood up' can mean 'was standing')
ἀνίστασαν: *(Xenophon and his men) tried to...*; conative and transitive impf. ἀνίστημι
οἱ δ' : *but they...*; those Greeks sitting in the snow
3 **οἱ ἔμπροσθεν**: *those soldiers in front*; i.e. in the baggage train in front of the Greeks now sitting
4 **ὑποχωροῖεν**: i.e. so that those currently sitting can pass them; ind. disc. with opt. in secondary seq.
ὁ δὲ: *and he*....; i.e. Xenophon
παριὼν: pple παρέρχομαι
5 **ἰσχυροτάτους**: superlative adj.
τί εἴη: *what*...; ind. question with opt. εἰμί
6 **τὸ κωλῦον**: *the thing hindering (them)*; substantive, neuter. pres. pple
οἱ δὲ: *and they...*
ὅλον...τὸ στράτευμα: subject
7 **καὶ**: *also*
8 **αὐτοῦ**: *there*; 'in that very place'
9 **καταστησάμενοι**: aor. mid. pple
πρὸς...: *near...*

Ξενοφῶν πέμψας πρὸς τοὺς ἀσθενοῦντας τοὺς νεωτάτους 10
ἀναστήσαντας ἐκέλευεν ἀναγκάζειν προϊέναι. 22. ἐν δὲ τούτῳ
Χειρίσοφος πέμπει τῶν ἐκ τῆς κώμης σκεψομένους πῶς
ἔχοιεν οἱ τελευταῖοι. οἱ δὲ ἄσμενοι ἰδόντες τοὺς μὲν
ἀσθενοῦντας τούτοις παρέδοσαν κομίζειν ἐπὶ τὸ στρατόπεδον, αὐτοὶ δὲ ἐπορεύοντο, καὶ πρὶν εἴκοσι στάδια διεληλυ- 15
θέναι ἦσαν πρὸς τῇ κώμῃ ἔνθα Χειρίσοφος ηὐλίζετο. 23. ἐπεὶ
δὲ συνεγένοντο ἀλλήλοις, ἔδοξε κατὰ τὰς κώμας ἀσφαλὲς
εἶναι τὰς τάξεις σκηνοῦν. καὶ Χειρίσοφος μὲν αὐτοῦ ἔμενεν,

ἀ-σθενεω: to be weak, feeble, sick, 3
ἀ-σφαλής, -ές: safe, secure, not liable to fall 7
ἀναγκάζω: to force, compel, require, 2
ἄσμενος, -η, -ον: well-pleased, glad, 2
αὐτοῦ: in that very place, there, 7
αὐλίζομαι: to bivouac, encamp, lodge, 5
δι-έρχομαι: to go through, pass, 7
εἴκοσι: twenty, 5
κομίζω: to bring, 1
νέος, -α, -ον: young; new, novel, strange, 3
παρα-δίδωμι: to hand over, give over, 4
πέμπω: send, conduct, convey, dispatch, 7
προ-έρχομαι: to go forth, advance, 4
πῶς: how? in what way?, 2
σκέπτομαι: to look for, find out, examine, 2
σκηνόω: to encamp, bivouac; pitch camp, 1
συγ-γίγνομαι: to be with, converse with, 1
τάξις, -εως, ἡ: unit, squadron; battle array, 7
τελευταίος, -α, -ον: last, final, 6

10 **πρὸς...**: i.e. to help those left behind, whom Xenophon promised to rescue
τοὺς νεωτάτους: *the youngest (of Xenophon's soldiers)* with aor. pple πέμψας

11 **ἀναστήσαντας**: *making (the weak) stand up*; modifies τοὺς νεωτάτους
προϊέναι: inf. προέρχομαι
ἐν δὲ τούτῳ: *meanwhile*; 'in this (time)'

12 **(τινὰς) τῶν ἐκ...κώμης**: *(some) of...*; partitive gen.; supply the acc. pronoun
σκεψομένους: *intended to...*; fut. pple expressing purpose or intent
πῶς ἔχοιεν: *how...*; ind. question with 3p opt. in secondary seq.; ἔχω ('is disposed' or 'holds') + adv. is equiv. to εἰμί + adj.

13 **οἱ δὲ...ἰδόντες**: *and those...*; pple ὁράω; Xenophon's troops seeing Cheirisophus' troops
ἄσμενοι: translate nom. adj. as an adv.

14 **τούτοις**: i.e. to Cheirisophus' men; dat. ind. obj.
παρέδοσαν: aor.
κομίζειν: inf. of purpose, supply τοὺς ἀσθενοῦντας, 'the weak' as object

15 **αὐτοὶ**: *they themselves*; Xenophon's men handed off the men they were carrying and continued ahead to the camp.
πρὶν...διεληλυθέναι: *before...*; πρίν + inf. pf. inf. δι-έρχομαι
εἴκοσι στάδια: *for...*; acc. of extent

16 **πρὸς**: *near...*; dat. of place where

17 **ἔδοξε**: *it seemed*
κατὰ τὰς κώμας: *in...throughout...*; κατὰ in the distributive sense

18 **τὰς τάξεις σκηνοῦν**: *to bivouac the units*; inf. o-contract, σκηνόω
αὐτοῦ: *there*; 'in that very place'

οἱ δὲ ἄλλοι διαλαχόντες ἃς ἑώρων κώμας ἐπορεύοντο ἕκαστοι τοὺς ἑαυτῶν ἔχοντες. 24. ἔνθα δὴ Πολυκράτης Ἀθηναῖος λοχα- 20 γὸς ἐκέλευσεν ἀφιέναι ἑαυτόν· καὶ λαβὼν τοὺς εὐζώνους, θέων ἐπὶ τὴν κώμην ἣν εἰλήχει Ξενοφῶν καταλαμβάνει πάντας ἔνδον τοὺς κωμήτας καὶ τὸν κώμαρχον, καὶ πώλους εἰς δασμὸν βασιλεῖ τρεφομένους ἑπτακαίδεκα, καὶ τὴν θυγατέρα τοῦ κωμάρχου ἐνάτην ἡμέραν γεγαμημένην· ὁ δ' 25 ἀνὴρ αὐτῆς λαγῶς ᾤχετο θηράσων καὶ οὐχ ἥλω ἐν τῇ κώμῃ. 25. αἱ δ' οἰκίαι ἦσαν κατάγειοι, τὸ μὲν στόμα ὥσπερ

Ἀθηναῖος, -α, -ον: Athenian, of Athens, 4
ἁλίσκομαι: to be taken, seized, 6
ἀφ-ίημι: send away, let go, release; give up, 4
γαμέω: to marry, wed, 1
δασμός, ὁ: a division (of spoils), tribute, 2
δια-λαγχάνω: to divide or distribute by lot, 1
ἔνατος, -η, -ον: ninth, 1
ἔνδον: within, at home, 2
ἑπτα-καί-δεκα: seventeen, 1
εὔ-ζωνος, -ον: well-girdled, nimble, active, 3
θηράω: to hunt, chase, 1
θυγάτηρ, ἡ: a daughter, 2
κατά-γειος -ον: underground, 1
κωμήτης, ὁ: townsman, villager, 1
λαγχάνω: to obtain by lot, 1
λαγῶς, ὁ: hare, rabbit, 1
οἴχομαι: to go, go off, depart, 7
Πολυκράτης, ὁ: Polycrates, 1
πῶλος, ὁ: foal, young horse, 3
στόμα, -ατος, τό: mouth, opening, 2
τρέφω: to rear, foster, nuture, 3

19 **οἱ ἄλλοι**: i.e. Greek leaders
διαλαχόντες: aor. pple
ἃς...κώμας: *what towns...*; relative adj.
ἑώρων: ἑώραον, 3p impf. ὁράω
20 **τοὺς ἑαυτῶν**: *their own (troops)*
ἔνθα δὴ: *just then, just then*
21 **ἀφιέναι**: *that (they)...*; inf. ἀφ-ίημι, i.e. allow him to move and act freely on behalf of the army
22 **θέων**: pple θέω
ἐπὶ: *to...*
ἣν: *which...*; relative clause
εἰλήχει: plpf. λαγχάνω
24 **εἰς**: *for...*; expressing purpose
βασιλεῖ: *for...*; dat. of interest
25 **ἐνάτην ἡμέραν**: *...ago*; or 'for...' acc. of duration
γεγαμημένην: pf. pass. pple γαμέω
ὁ δ' ἀνὴρ: *and the husband*
26 **λαγῶς**: acc. sg., Attic declension (S237)
ᾤχετο: impf. οἴχομαι
θηράσων: fut. pple expressing purpose
ἥλω: 3s aor. ἁλίσκομαι
27 **ἦσαν**: 3p impf. εἰμί
κατάγειοι: fem. pl. two-ending adjective

φρέατος, κάτω δ' εὐρεῖαι· αἱ δὲ εἴσοδοι τοῖς μὲν ὑποζυγίοις 1
ὀρυκταί, οἱ δὲ ἄνθρωποι κατέβαινον ἐπὶ κλίμακος. ἐν δὲ
ταῖς οἰκίαις ἦσαν αἶγες, οἶες, βόες, ὄρνιθες, καὶ τὰ ἔκγονα
τούτων· τὰ δὲ κτήνη πάντα χιλῷ ἔνδον ἐτρέφοντο. 26. *ἦσαν*
δὲ καὶ πυροὶ καὶ κριθαὶ καὶ ὄσπρια καὶ οἶνος κρίθινος ἐν 5
κρατῆρσιν. ἐνῆσαν δὲ καὶ αὐταὶ αἱ κριθαὶ ἰσοχειλεῖς, καὶ
κάλαμοι ἐνέκειντο, οἱ μὲν μείζους οἱ δὲ ἐλάττους, γόνατα
οὐκ ἔχοντες· 27. *τούτους ἔδει ὁπότε τις διψῴη λαβόντα εἰς τὸ*
στόμα μύζειν. καὶ πάνυ ἄκρατος ἦν, εἰ μή τις ὕδωρ ἐπι-

αἶξ, αἶγος, ὁ, ἡ: goat, 2
ἄ-κρατος, -ον: unmixed, pure, strong, 1
γόνυ, γόνατος, τό: joint; knee, 1
διψάω: to be thirsty, 1
ἔγ-κειμαι: to lie in, 1
εἴσ-οδος, ἡ: entrance, a way in, 2
ἔκ-γονον, τό: offspring, descendent, 1
ἐλάττων, -ον: smaller, fewer, 2
ἔνδον: within, at home, 2
ἐν-ειμί: to be, be in, 1
ἐπι-χέω: to pour over, 1
εὐρύς, -εῖα, -ύ: wide, broad, 1
ἰσο-χειλής, -ές: level with the brim or top, 1
κάλαμος, ὁ: straw, reed, 1
κάτω: downwards, below, 4
κλῖμαξ, κλίμακος, ἡ: ladder, 1
κρατήρ, κρατῆρος, ὁ: mixing vessel, 2
κριθή, ἡ: barley-grain, barley, 2
κριθίνος, -η, -ον: made from barley, 2
κτῆνος, -εος, τό: herd, flock, 3
μείζων, -ον (-ονος): greater, 4
μύζω: to sip, drink with closed lips, 1
οἶνος, ὁ: wine, 5
ὄϊς, ὄϊος, ὁ: ram, 1
ὄρνις, ὄρνιθος, ὁ: bird, 1
ὀρυκτός, -ή, -όν: dug out, dug, 1
ὄσπριον, τό: a pulse, legume, 2
πάνυ: quite, entirely, exceedingly, 3
πυρός, ὁ: wheat; a grain of wheat, 2
στόμα, -ατος, τό: mouth, opening, 2
τρέφω: to rear, foster, nuture, 3
ὕδωρ, ὕδατος, τό: water, 5
φρέαρ, φρέατος, τό: man-made well, cistern 1
χιλός, -όν: forage, fodder (often for cattle), 2

1 **εὐρεῖαι**: modifies fem. pl. οἰκίαι
τοῖς ὑποζυγίοις: *for...*; dat. of interest
ὀρυκτάι (εἰσί): predicate
2 **ἐπὶ**: *on...*
3 **ἦσαν**: impf. εἰμί
4 **χιλῷ**: dat. of means
ἐτρέφοντο: impf. pass.
5 **οἶνος κρίθινος**: *barley-wine*
6 **ἐνῆσαν**: *were in (the drink)*; impf. ἐνειμί
αὐταὶ: *themselves*; intensive
7 **ἐνέκειντο**: impf. ἔγ-κειμαι
οἱ μέν...οἱ δὲ: *some...others*; i.e. κάλαμοι
μείζους, ἐλάττους: μείζο(ν)ες, ἐλάττο(ν)ες nom. pl. comparatives
γόνατα: i.e. sections in the straw, these are drinking straws, as explained below
8 **τούτους**: *these (straws)*; obj. of λάβοντα, aor. pple. of λαμβάνω
ἔδει: impersonal impf. δεῖ
ὁπότε...διψῴη: *whenever...*; διψαοίη, 3s pres. opt. διψάω in a general temporal clause
9 **ἦν**: *would be*; 3s customary impf. εἰμί
εἰ...ἐπιχέοι: *unless...*; 'if not...' pres. opt. in a past general condition (εἰ opt., impf.)

χέοι· καὶ πάνυ ἡδὺ συμμαθόντι τὸ πῶμα ἦν. 28. ὁ δὲ Ξενοφῶν 10
τὸν ἄρχοντα τῆς κώμης ταύτης σύνδειπνον ἐποιήσατο καὶ
θαρρεῖν αὐτὸν ἐκέλευε λέγων ὅτι οὔτε τῶν τέκνων στερήσοιτο τήν τε οἰκίαν αὐτοῦ ἀντεμπλήσαντες τῶν ἐπιτηδείων
ἀπίασιν, ἢν ἀγαθόν τι τῷ στρατεύματι ἐξηγησάμενος φαί-
νηται ἔστ' ἂν ἐν ἄλλῳ ἔθνει γένωνται. 29. ὁ δὲ ταῦτα ὑπισχνεῖτο, 15
καὶ φιλοφρονούμενος οἶνον ἔφρασεν ἔνθα ἦν κατορωρυγμένος.
ταύτην μὲν τὴν νύκτα διασκηνήσαντες οὕτως ἐκοιμήθησαν
ἐν πᾶσιν ἀφθόνοις πάντες οἱ στρατιῶται, ἐν φυλακῇ ἔχοντες

ἀντ-εμ-πίπλημι: fill (acc) of (gen) in reply, 1
ἄ-φθονος, -ον: without envy, plentiful, 1
δια-σκηνέω: to disperse to quarters/tents, 3
ἔθνος, -εος, τό: tribe, people, race, 1
ἐξ-ηγέομαι: to lead out, bring out, 1
ἔστε (εἰς+τε): up to; until, 2
ἡδύς, -εῖα, -ύ: sweet, pleasant, glad, 1
θαρρέω: to be confident, take courage; be bold, 2
κατ-ορύττω: to bury, 1
κοιμάω: to put to sleep, lull to sleep; sleep, 3
οἶνος, ὁ: wine, 5
οὔ-τε: and not, neither...nor, 6
πάνυ: quite, entirely, exceedingly, 3
πῶμα, τό: a drink, 1
στερέω: to deprive from, rob, defraud, 1
συμ-μανθάνω: to learn together with, 1
σύν-δειπνος, ὁ, ἡ: a fellow-dinner, 1
τέκνον, τό: a child, 2
ὑπ-ισχνέομαι: to promise, 1
φαίνω: to show; *mid.* appear, seem, 6
φιλο-φρονέομαι: to treat kindly, greet, 3
φράζω: to point out, tell, indicate, 2
φυλακή, ἡ: a watch, guard, 4

10 **ἡδὺ**: *pleasant*; neuter nom. predicate
συμμαθόντι: *to one accustomed to it*; 'to one knowing it,' aor. pple
11 **τὸν ἄρχοντα**: *the leader*
ἐποιήσατο: *made* (x) (y); governs a double accusative (acc. obj. and acc. pred.)
12 **οὔτε...τε**: *both not...and...*
στερήσοιτο: *he would...*; fut. opt. mid. but pass. in sense; in ind. disc. fut. opt. replaces fut. ind. in secondary seq.
τῶν τέκνων: *from...*; gen. separation
13 **αὐτοῦ**: ie. the leader's
ἀντεμπλήσαντες: aor. pple + gen.
τῶν ἐπιτηδείων: partitive with pple
14 **ἀπίασιν**: 3p fut. ἀπ-έρχομαι; note the lack of parallelism with fut. opt. above
ἢν...φαίνηται: *if he turns out...*; + pple, 'if he appears;' ἐάν + pres. subj. in a fut. more vivid condition with the preceding fut. ind.
τῷ στρατεύματι: *for...*; dat. of interest
15 **ἔστ(ε)...γένωνται**: *until they...*; ἄν + subj. γίγνομαι in a general temporal clause
ὁ δὲ: *and he...*; i.e. the leader
ὑπισχνεῖτο: impf.
οἶνον...ἔνθα: *where the wine...*; 'the wine, where (it)...' proleptic use of οἶνον: make οἶνον the subject within the clause
ἦν κατορωρυγμένος: periphrastic plpf. pass. (pf. pass. pple + impf. εἰμί)
17 **ταύτην...νύκτα**: acc. duration
ἐκοιμήθησαν: 3p aor. pass. dep.
18 **ἐν πᾶσιν ἀφθόνοις**: *among all the abundance*; 'among all the plentiful'
ἐν φυλακῇ: *under guard*

τὸν κώμαρχον καὶ τὰ τέκνα αὐτοῦ ὁμοῦ ἐν ὀφθαλμοῖς. 30. τῇ δ᾽ ἐπιούσῃ ἡμέρᾳ Ξενοφῶν λαβὼν τὸν κώμαρχον πρὸς Χειρί- 20 σοφον ἐπορεύετο· ὅπου δὲ παρίοι κώμην, ἐτρέπετο πρὸς τοὺς ἐν ταῖς κώμαις καὶ κατελάμβανε πανταχοῦ εὐωχουμένους καὶ εὐθυμουμένους, καὶ οὐδαμόθεν ἀφίεσαν πρὶν παραθεῖναι αὐ-τοῖς ἄριστον· 31. οὐκ ἦν δ᾽ ὅπου οὐ παρετίθεσαν ἐπὶ τὴν αὐτὴν τράπεζαν κρέα ἄρνεια, ἐρίφεια, χοίρεια, μόσχεια, ὀρνίθεια, 25 σὺν πολλοῖς ἄρτοις τοῖς μὲν πυρίνοις τοῖς δὲ κριθίνοις. 32. ὁπότε δέ τις φιλοφρονούμενός τῳ βούλοιτο προπιεῖν, εἷλκεν

ἄριστον, τό: breakfast, lunch, 2
ἄρνειος, -α, -ον: of a lamb, 1
ἄρτος, ὁ: bread, loaf, 1
ἀφ-ίημι: send away, let go, release; give up, 4
ἕλκω: to draw, drag, 3
ἐπ-έρχομαι: to come upon; attack, 5
ἐρίφειος, -ον: of a young goat, of a kid, 1
εὐ-θυμέω: be of good spirits, 1
εὐωχέω: to entertain sumptuously, feast, 1
κρέας, τό: meat, piece of meat, 1
κριθίνος, -η, -ον: made from barley, 2
μόσχειος, -ον: of the calf, 1
ὁμοῦ: at the same place, together, 3
ὅπου: where, 5
ὀρνίθειος, -α, -ον: of a bird, 1
οὐδαμό-θεν: nowhere, from nowhere, 1
ὀφθαλμός, ὁ: the eye, 4
παντα-χοῦ: everywhere, in every place, 1
παρα-τίθημι: to place beside, set before, 2
προ-πίνω: to drink on behalf of, 1
πυρίνος, -η, -ον: of wheat, 1
τέκνον, τό: a child, 2
τράπεζα, ἡ: table, 1
τρέπω: to turn; rout, 2
φιλο-φρονέομαι: to treat kindly, greet, 3
χοίρειος, -α, -ον: of a pig, of swine, 1

19 **αὐτοῦ**: *his*
ἐν ὀφθαλμοῖς: i.e. in sight
τῇ...ἡμέρᾳ: *on*...; dat. of time when
20 **ἐπιούσῃ**: i.e. the next...; pres. pple ἐπέρχομαι in dat. of time when
21 **ὅπου...παρίοι**: *wherever*...; 3s pres. opt. παρ-έρχομαι in a general relative clause
ἐτρέπετο: *he would*...; i.e. visit, iterative impf.
πρὸς τοὺς: *to those*...; i.e. the Greeks staying in each village
22 **κατελάμβανε**: *he found (them)*
ἀφίεσαν: *(the troops) would would not let (them) go*; 3p impf. ἀπ-ίημι,
23 **πρὶν...παραθεῖναι**: *before*...; aor. inf. παρατίθημι
αὐτοῖς: *(beside)*...; dat. of compound verb
24 **οὐκ ἦν δ᾽ὅπου**: *and there was not (a place) where*...; impf. εἰμί
αὐτὴν: αὐτός in the attributive position is translated 'same'
25 **ἄρνεια...ὀρνίθεια**: supply κρέα
26 **τοῖς μὲν...τοῖς δὲ**: *some...others..*; in apposition to ἄρτοις
27 **ὁπότε...βούλοιτο**: *whenever*...; opt. in a general temporal clause, secondary seq.
τῳ: *someone*; alternate form for indefinite τινί, dat. of interest or of compound verb
προπιεῖν: aor. inf. προπίνω
εἷλκεν: *he would*...; i.e. escort him, iterative impf. ἕλκω

ἐπὶ τὸν κρατῆρα, ἔνθεν ἐπικύψαντα ἔδει ῥοφοῦντα πίνειν 1
ὥσπερ βοῦν. καὶ τῷ κωμάρχῳ ἐδίδοσαν λαμβάνειν ὅ τι
βούλοιτο. ὁ δὲ ἄλλο μὲν οὐδὲν ἐδέχετο, ὅπου δέ τινα τῶν
συγγενῶν ἴδοι, πρὸς ἑαυτὸν ἀεὶ ἐλάμβανεν. 33. ἐπεὶ δ᾽ ἦλθον
πρὸς Χειρίσοφον, κατελάμβανον κἀκείνους σκηνοῦντας ἐστε- 5
φανωμένους τοῦ ξηροῦ χιλοῦ στεφάνοις, καὶ διακονοῦντας
Ἀρμενίους παῖδας σὺν ταῖς βαρβαρικαῖς στολαῖς· τοῖς παισὶν ἐδείκνυσαν ὥσπερ ἐνεοῖς ὅ τι δέοι ποιεῖν. 34. ἐπεὶ δ᾽ ἀλλήλους ἐφιλοφρονήσαντο Χειρίσοφος καὶ Ξενοφῶν, κοινῇ δὴ

ἀεί: always, forever, in every case, 6
Ἀρμένιοι, οἱ: Armenian, 3
βαρβαρικός, -η, -ον: foreigner, barbarian, 2
δείκνυμι: to show, indicate, 4
δέχομαι: to receive, accept, 7
διακονέω: to serve, render a service, 1
ἐνεός, -α, -ον: dear and dumb, speechless, 1
ἐπι-κύπτω: to bend over, stoop over, 1
κοινός, -ή, -όν: common, ordinary; public, 3
κρατήρ, κρατῆρος, ὁ: mixing vessel, 2
ξηρός, -ά, -όν: dry, 1
ὅπου: where, 5
πίνω: to drink, consume, 1
ῥοφέω: to sip greedily, gulp down, 1
σκηνέω: to encamp, bivouac, set up tents, 5
στέφανος, ὁ: crown, 1
στεφανόω: to crown, put on a wreath, 1
στολή, ἡ: apparel, armament, 2
συγ-γενής, -ές: kinsman, relative, in-born, 1
φιλο-φρονέομαι: to treat kindly, greet, 3
χιλός, -όν: forage, fodder, hay (for cattle), 2

1 ἐπὶ: *to…*; acc. place to which
ἔνθεν: *then*; 'from that point'
ἔδει: impf. δεῖ
2 ὥσπερ: *just as*
τῷ κωμάρχῳ: dat. of indirect object
ἐδίδοσαν: *allowed*; 'granted' + inf.
ὅ τι: *whatever…*, neuter acc. ὅστις with opt. in a general relative clause
3 ὁ δὲ: i.e. the village leader, ὁ κωμάχος
ὅπου δὲ…ἴδοι: *but wherever…*; general relative clause, opt. εἶδον
4 ἐλάμβανεν: *would take (him)*; i.e. welcome him, iterative impf.
ἦλθον: aor. ἔρχομαι
5 κα(ὶ) ἐκείνους: *those also…*
ἐστεφανωμένους: pf. pass./mid. στεφάνω
6 τοῦ ξηροῦ χιλοῦ: gen. of material
διακονοῦντας: supply the Greeks as obj.
7 τοῖς παισὶν: dat. pl. ind. object, παῖς
8 ἔδείκνυσαν: *they pointed out*; i.e. the Greeks used hand gestures and signals
8 ὅ τι δέοι: *whatever…*; neuter acc. ὅστις with opt. δεῖ in a general relative clause
9 ἐφιλφρονήσαντο: i.e. greet each other
κοινῇ: *in common*; dat. in interest

ἀνηρώτων τὸν κώμαρχον διὰ τοῦ Περσίζοντος ἑρμηνέως τίς 10
εἴη ἡ χώρα. ὁ δ' ἔλεγεν ὅτι Ἀρμενία. καὶ πάλιν ἠρώτων
τίνι οἱ ἵπποι τρέφονται. ὁ δ' ἔλεγεν ὅτι βασιλεῖ δασμός·
τὴν δὲ πλησίον χώραν ἔφη εἶναι Χάλυβας, καὶ τὴν ὁδὸν
ἔφραζεν ᾗ εἴη. 35. *καὶ αὐτὸν τότε μὲν ᾤχετο ἄγων ὁ Ξενοφῶν*
πρὸς τοὺς ἑαυτοῦ οἰκέτας, καὶ ἵππον ὃν εἰλήφει παλαίτερον 15
δίδωσι τῷ κωμάρχῳ ἀναθρέψαντι καταθῦσαι, ὅτι ἤκουεν
αὐτὸν ἱερὸν εἶναι τοῦ Ἡλίου, δεδιὼς μὴ ἀποθάνῃ· ἐκεκά-
κωτο γὰρ ὑπὸ τῆς πορείας· αὐτὸς δὲ τῶν πώλων λαμβάνει,

ἀνα-τρέφω: to bring up, nuture, 1
ἀν-ερωτάω: to question, inquire, 1
Ἀρμενία, ἡ: Armenia, 6
δασμός, ὁ: a division (of spoils), tribute, 2
δείδω: to fear, 5
ἑρμηνεύς, ὁ: an interpreter, 4
Ἥλιος, ὁ: Sun, 1
ἱερόν, τό: (sacrificial) victim, animal, 3
κακόω: to harm, injury, maltreat, 1
κατα-θύω: to sacrifice, 1
οἰκέτης, ὁ: of the house, family; slave, 2
οἴχομαι: to go, go off, depart, 7
παλαιός, -ά, -όν: old, aged, ancient, 2
Περσίζω: to speak Persian, 1
πλησίος, -η, -ον: near, close to; neighbors, 5
πορεία, ἡ: march, journey, way, 5
πῶλος, ὁ: foal, young horse, 3
τότε: then, at that time, 7
τρέφω: to rear, foster, nuture, 3
φράζω: to point out, tell, indicate, 2
Χάλυψ, -υβος, ὁ: Chalybian, 4

10 **ἀνηρώτων**: 3p impf. α-contract verb
τίς εἴη: ind. question, with opt. εἰμί in secondary seq.
11 **ὁ δ'**: *and he...*; i.e. village leader
Ἀρμενία (εἴη): supply a verb
ἠρώτων: 3p impf.
12 **τίνι**: *for...*; dat. of interest, τίς and interrogative in an ind. question
ὁ δ': *and he...*; the village leader
βασιλεῖ: dat. possession or interest
δασμός (εἴη): supply a verb
13 **ἔφη**: 3s impf. φημί
εἶναι Χάλυβας: acc. pl. predicate: the name of the people where one expects the name of the country
τὴν ὁδὸν...ᾗ εἴη: *where the road...*; 'the road, where' proleptic uses of ὁδὸν; ind. question with opt. εἰμί; dat. place where
14 **αὐτὸν**: *him*; the village chief
ᾤχετο: impf. οἴχομαι
15 **οἰκέτας**: *family members*
εἰλήφει: plpf. λαμβάνω; Xenophon is subj.
παλαίτερον: comparative adj., 'rather X'
16 **δίδωσι**: the subject is Xenophon
ἀναθρέψαντι: dat. sg. aor. pple ἀνατρέφω
καταθῦσαι: *to...;* aor. inf. of purpose
ὅτι ἤκουεν: *because (Xenophon)...*
17 **αὐτὸν...εἶναι**: *that...*; ind. disc., acc. subj. αὐτὸν refers to the horse
ἱερὸν: substantive
δεδιώς: nom. sg. pf. pple δείδω
μὴ ἀποθάνῃ: *lest...*; or 'that;' fearing clause with 3s aor. subj. ἀποθνῄσκω
ἐκεκάκωτο: plpf. pass. κακόω
18 **ὑπό**: *by...*; 'because of...' gen. of cause
αὐτὸς: i.e. Xenophon; intensive
(τινά) τῶν πώλων: *(one)...*; partitive gen.

καὶ τῶν ἄλλων στρατηγῶν καὶ λοχαγῶν ἔδωκεν ἑκάστῳ πῶλον. 36. ἦσαν δ' οἱ ταύτῃ ἵπποι μείονες μὲν τῶν Περσικῶν, 20
θυμοειδέστεροι δὲ πολύ. ἐνταῦθα δὴ καὶ διδάσκει ὁ κώμαρχος περὶ τοὺς πόδας τῶν ἵππων καὶ τῶν ὑποζυγίων σακία περιειλεῖν, ὅταν διὰ τῆς χιόνος ἄγωσιν· ἄνευ γὰρ τῶν σακίων κατεδύοντο μέχρι τῆς γαστρός.

1. ἐπεὶ δ' ἡμέρα ἦν ὀγδόη, τὸν μὲν ἡγεμόνα παραδίδωσι 25
Χειρισόφῳ, τοὺς δὲ οἰκέτας καταλείπει τῷ κωμάρχῳ, πλὴν τοῦ υἱοῦ τοῦ ἄρτι ἡβάσκοντος· τοῦτον δὲ Πλεισθένει Ἀμφιπολίτῃ δίδωσι φυλάττειν, ὅπως εἰ καλῶς ἡγήσοιτο, ἔχων

Ἀμφιπολίτης, -ου, ὁ: of Amphipolis, 1
ἄνευ: without (+ gen.), 4
ἄρτι: just now, exactly, 1
γαστήρ, γαστρος, ὁ: belly, stomach, 1
διδάσκω: to teach, instruct, tell, 1
ἡβάσκω: to come into puberty, 1
θυμο-ειδής, -ές: high-spirited, courageous, 1
κατα-δύω: to go down, sink, set, 1
μείων, μεῖον: smaller, less, of lesser value, 2
μέχρι: up to; until, as long as (+ gen.), 5
ὄγδοος, -η, -ον: eighth, 1
οἰκέτης, ὁ: of the house, family; slave, 2
ὅταν: ὅτε ἄν, whenever, 5
παρα-δίδωμι: to hand over, give over, 4
περι-είλω: to wrap around, 1
περί: around, about, concerning, 7
Περσικός, -ή, -όν: Persian, 4
Πλεισθένης, ὁ: Pleisthenes, 2
πλήν: except, but (+ gen.), 2
πούς, ποδός, ὁ: a foot, 7
πῶλος, ὁ: foal, young horse, 3
σακίον, τό: small bag, little sack, 2
υἱός, -οῦ, ὁ: a son, 2
φυλάττω: to keep watch, keep guard, 6

19 τῶν...λοχαγῶν: partitive gen.
ἔδωκεν: aor. δίδωμι
20 ταύτῃ: *in this place*; dat. of place where
μείονες: *in* size not in quantity
τῶν Περσικῶν (ἵππων): gen. comparison
21 πολύ: *far*; or 'much,' adverbial acc. (acc. of extent in degree)
ἐνταῦθα δὴ: *in just this place, exactly here*
καί: *also*
διδάσκει: assume people as object
23 ὅταν......ἄγωσιν: *whenever they go*; general temporal clause, pres. subj. ἄγω
24 κατεδύοντο: *would...*; i.e. in the deep snow; iterative impf.
25 τὸν ἡγεμόνα: *(the village chief) as a guide*
26 τοὺς οἰκέτας: *family members*
τῷ κωμάρχῳ: *for...*; dat. of interest or possession
27 τοῦτον: *this one*; i.e. the son
28 φυλάττειν: *to...*; inf. of purpose
ὅπως...ἀπίοι: *so that...*; purpose clause with opt. ἀπέρχομαι in secondary seq,
εἰ...ἡγήσοιτο: *if...*; in ind. disc, fut. opt. replacing fut. ind. in secondary seq.

καὶ τοῦτον ἀπίοι. καὶ εἰς τὴν οἰκίαν αὐτοῦ εἰσεφόρησαν ὡς 1
ἐδύναντο πλεῖστα, καὶ ἀναζεύξαντες ἐπορεύοντο. 2. ἡγεῖτο δ'
αὐτοῖς ὁ κώμαρχος λελυμένος διὰ χιόνος· καὶ ἤδη τε ἦν ἐν
τῷ τρίτῳ σταθμῷ, καὶ Χειρίσοφος αὐτῷ ἐχαλεπάνθη ὅτι οὐκ
εἰς κώμας ἤγαγεν. ὁ δ' ἔλεγεν ὅτι οὐκ εἶεν ἐν τῷ τόπῳ 5
τούτῳ. 3. ὁ δὲ Χειρίσοφος αὐτὸν ἔπαισεν, ἔδησε δ' οὔ. ἐκ
δὲ τούτου ἐκεῖνος τῆς νυκτὸς ἀποδρὰς ᾤχετο καταλιπὼν τὸν
υἱόν. τοῦτό γε δὴ Χειρισόφῳ καὶ Ξενοφῶντι μόνον διάφορον ἐν τῇ πορείᾳ ἐγένετο, ἡ τοῦ ἡγεμόνος κάκωσις καὶ

ἀνα-ζεύγνυμι: break camp, yoke again, 1
ἀπο-διδράσκω: to run away, escape, 1
γε: at least, at any rate; indeed, 3
δέω (2): to bind, tie, 3
διάφορον, τό: difference, disagreement, 1
εἰσ-φοράω: to carry to, bring to, 1
κάκωσις, -εως ἡ: ill-treatment, oppression, 1
λύω: to loosen, free; *mid.* ransom, 4
μόνος, -η, -ον: alone, only, solitary, 2
οἴχομαι: to go, go off, depart, 7
παίω: to strike, smite, 2
πλεῖστος, -η, -ον: most, very many, 3
πορεία, ἡ: march, journey, way, 5
τόπος, ὁ: a place, region, 3
τρίτος, -η, -ον: the third, 4
υἱός, -οῦ, ὁ: a son, 2
χαλεπαίνω: to be sore, be angry with (dat), 2

1 ἔχων καὶ τοῦτον: *having this (son) also*
αὐτοῦ: *his*; the guide's
εἰσεφόρησαν: i.e. the Greeks are subject
ὡς ἐδύναντο πλεῖστα: a*s many things as*...; clause of comparison with a neut. pl. superlative adj.
3 λελυμένος: i.e. not tied up, pf. pass. pple
καὶ ἤδη τε...καὶ: *and now when...then*...; τε...καί 'when...then' is here used for actions suggesting simultaneity (D515, S2975)
4 ἐχαλεπάνθη: *became*...; ingressive aor. 3s pass. dep.
ὅτι: *because*
5 ἤγαγεν: aor. ἄγω
ὁ δ': *and he*...; the guide
ὅτι οὐκ εἶεν (κῶμαι):: *that*...; ind. disc. with 3p opt. εἰμί in secondary seq., supply κῶμαι as subject
6 ἐκ τούτου: *from this (event)*; i.e. as a result
7 ἐκεῖνος: i.e. the guide
τῆς νυκτὸς: *during*...; gen. of time within
ἀποδρὰς: nom. sg. aor. pple
ᾤχετο: impf. οἴχομαι
καταλιπὼν: aor. pple
8 τοῦτό γε δὴ: *this in fact*; or 'this very thing in fact,' γε δή together are strongly emphatic (D245, S2828); neuter subject
Χειρισόφῳ καὶ Ξενοφῶντι: *between*...; 'for... 'dat. of interest
9 ἐγένετο: aor. γίγνομαι

ἀμέλεια. Πλεισθένης δὲ ἠράσθη τοῦ παιδὸς καὶ οἴκαδε 10
κομίσας πιστοτάτῳ ἐχρῆτο. 4. μετὰ τοῦτο ἐπορεύθησαν ἑπτὰ
σταθμοὺς ἀνὰ πέντε παρασάγγας τῆς ἡμέρας παρὰ τὸν Φᾶσιν
ποταμόν, εὖρος πλεθριαῖον. 5. ἐντεῦθεν ἐπορεύθησαν σταθμοὺς δύο παρασάγγας δέκα· ἐπὶ δὲ τῇ εἰς τὸ πεδίον ὑπερβολῇ ἀπήντησαν αὐτοῖς Χάλυβες καὶ Τάοχοι καὶ Φασιανοί. 15
6. Χειρίσοφος δ᾽ ἐπεὶ κατεῖδε τοὺς πολεμίους ἐπὶ τῇ ὑπερβολῇ,
ἐπαύσατο πορευόμενος, ἀπέχων εἰς τριάκοντα σταδίους, ἵνα
μὴ κατὰ κέρας ἄγων πλησιάσῃ τοῖς πολεμίοις· παρήγγειλε

ἀ-μέλεια, ἡ: neglect, carelessness, 1
ἀπ-αντάω: to meet, encounter (dat), 2
ἀπ-έχω: to be distant, keep away from, 5
δέκα: ten, 7
ἑπτά: seven, 5
ἐράω: to love (+ gen.) 1
εὖρος, τό: breadth, width, 3
ἵνα: in order that (+ subj.); where (+ ind.), 4
καθ-οράω: to look down, perceive, 7
κέρας, -ατος, τό: horn, wing (of an army), 2
κομίζω: to bring, 1
οἴκα-δε: homeward, home, 1
παρ-αγγέλλω: to pass word along, order 7
παύω: to stop, make cease, 3
πέντε: five, 4
πιστός, -ή, -όν:: trustworthy, loyal; credible 4
πλεθριαῖος, -α, -ον: broad, of a plethoron, 1
Πλεισθένης, ὁ: Pleisthenes, 2
πλησιάζω: to approach, come near (dat.) 1
Τάοχοι, οἱ: Taochians, 5
τριάκοντα: thirty, 4
ὑπερ-βολή, ἡ: crossing, mtn. pass; excess, 6
Φασιανός, -ά, -όν: Phasian, 1
Φᾶσις, ὁ: Phasis (river), 1
Χάλυψ, -υβος, ὁ: Chalybian, 4
χράομαι: use, employ, enjoy, engage (dat) 6

10 **ἠράσθη**: *fell in love with* + gen.; ingressive aor. 3s pass. deponent ἐράω
11 **πιστοτάτῳ**: *most faithful*; predicative, agreeing with the missing obj. τῷ παιδί
ἐχρῆτο: impf. χράομαι
ἐπορεύθησαν: 3p aor. pass. dep. πορεύομαι: translate in active
12 **σταθμοὺς**: *for…*; acc. of extent
ἀνὰ…: *up to…*
τῆς ἡμέρας: *per day*; 'within a day,' gen. of time within
παρὰ: *to…*; acc. place to which
13 **εὖρος**: *in…*; acc. of respect
ἐπορεύθησαν: see above
14 **ἐπὶ δὲ τῇ…ὑπερβολῇ**: *on…*; place where
16 **κατεῖδε**: aor. καθοράω
ἐπαύσατο: aor. mid. παύω + complementary pple
17 **εἰς**: *nearly*; 'up to', in approximation
τρίακοντα σταδίους: *for…* ; acc. of extent
ἵνα μὴ…πλησιάσῃ: *so that…may…*; neg. purpose clause, 3s aor. subj. πλησιάζω
παρήγγειλε: aor.
18 **κατὰ κέρας ἄγων**: *(while leading) (his men) in wings*; i.e. in columns

δὲ καὶ τοῖς ἄλλοις παράγειν τοὺς λόχους, ὅπως ἐπὶ φάλαγγος γένοιτο τὸ στράτευμα. 7. *ἐπεὶ δὲ ἦλθον οἱ ὀπισθοφύλακες,* 20 *συνεκάλεσε στρατηγοὺς καὶ λοχαγούς, καὶ ἔλεξεν ὧδε. 'οἱ μὲν πολέμιοι, ὡς ὁρᾶτε, κατέχουσι τὰς ὑπερβολὰς τοῦ ὄρους· ὥρα δὲ βουλεύεσθαι ὅπως ὡς κάλλιστα ἀγωνιούμεθα.* 8. *ἐμοὶ μὲν οὖν δοκεῖ παραγγεῖλαι μὲν ἀριστοποιεῖσθαι τοῖς στρατιώταις, ἡμᾶς δὲ βουλεύεσθαι εἴτε τήμερον εἴτε αὔριον δοκεῖ* 25 *ὑπερβάλλειν τὸ ὄρος.'* 9. *'ἐμοὶ δέ γε,' ἔφη ὁ Κλεάνωρ, 'δοκεῖ, ἐπὰν τάχιστα ἀριστήσωμεν, ἐξοπλισαμένους ὡς κράτιστα*

ἀγωνίζομαι: to contend, compete, fight, 3
ἀριστάω: to take breakfast, take a meal, 6
ἀριστο-ποιέω: to make breakfast, 2
αὔριον: tomorrow, 1
βουλεύω: to deliberate, plan, take counsel, 5
γε: at least, at any rate; indeed, 3
εἴτε: either...or; whether...or, 2
ἐξ-οπλίζομαι: to arm fully, 2
ἐπάν (ἐπεί ἄν): when, whenever, 1
ἡμεῖς: we, 5
κατ-έχω: to hold fast, take possession of, 7
Κλεάνωρ, ὁ: Cleanor, 2
κράτιστος, -η, -ον: best; strongest, 7
παρ-αγγέλλω: to pass word along, order 7
παρ-άγω: to lead along, lead alongside, 3
συγ-καλέω: to call together, assemble, 2
τήμερον: today, 2
ὑπερ-βάλλω: to pass over, exceed, 5
ὑπερ-βολή, ἡ: crossing, mtn. pass; excess, 6
ὧδε: in this way, so, thus, 2
ὥρα, ἡ: season, time, period of time, 3

19 **καὶ**: *also*
τοῖς ἄλλοις: i.e. other officers
ὅπως...γένοιτο: *so that...might...*; purpose clause with aor. opt.
ἐπὶ φάλαγγος: *into a phalanx*
20 **ἦλθον**: aor. ἔρχομαι
21 **ἔλεξεν**: aor. λέγω
ὧδε: i.e. in the following way
22 **ὡς**: *as...*; parenthetical
ὁρᾶτε: 2p because he is addressing his men
23 **ὥρα (ἐστί)**: *(it is) time...*; supply verb
ὅπως...ἀγωνιούμεθα: *how...*; clause of effort (object clause) with fut. mid. ind.
ὡς κάλλιστα: *as...as possible*; ὡς + superlative καλῶς, 'well'
24 **δοκεῖ**: *it seems best*
παραγγεῖλαι: aor. inf.
ἡμᾶς δὲ: *and that we...*; ind. disc. governed by δοκεῖ
25 **εἴτε...ὄρος**: *whether...* ; ind. question
26 **ἐμοὶ γε**: *for me at least*; or 'to me for my part,' restrictive
27 **ἐπὰν τάχιστα ἀριστήσωμεν**: *as soon as...*; else 'whenever very quickly...' a general temporal clause with ἄν + aor. subj and superlative adv.
(ἡμᾶς) ἐξοπλισαμένους: *that we...*; supply missing ἡμᾶς as the acc. subject
ὡς κράτιστα: *as...as possible*; ὡς + superlative (here, superlative adv.)

ἰέναι ἐπὶ τοὺς ἄνδρας. εἰ γὰρ διατρίψομεν τὴν τήμερον ἡμέραν, οἵ τε νῦν ἡμᾶς ὁρῶντες πολέμιοι θαρραλεώτεροι ἔσονται καὶ ἄλλους εἰκὸς τούτων θαρρούντων πλείους προσγενέσθαι.' 10. μετὰ τοῦτον Ξενοφῶν εἶπεν· 'ἐγὼ δ' οὕτω γιγνώσκω. εἰ μὲν ἀνάγκη ἐστὶ μάχεσθαι, τοῦτο δεῖ παρασκευάσασθαι, ὅπως ὡς κράτιστα μαχούμεθα· εἰ δὲ βουλόμεθα ὡς ῥᾷστα ὑπερβάλλειν, τοῦτό μοι δοκεῖ σκεπτέον εἶναι, ὅπως ὡς ἐλάχιστα μὲν τραύματα λάβωμεν, ὡς ἐλάχιστα δὲ σώματα ἀνδρῶν ἀποβάλωμεν. 11. τὸ μὲν οὖν ὄρος ἐστὶ τὸ

ἄλλος, -η, -ο: other, one...another, 8
ἀνάγκη, ἡ: necessity, force, 4
ἀπο-βάλλω: to throw off or away, 1
γιγνώσκω: to come to know, learn, realize, 2
δια-τρίβω: to spend time, waste time, 1
εἰκός, ότος, τό: likely, probable, reasonable, 1
ἐλάχιστος, -η, -ον: smallest, least, fewest, 2
ἡμεῖς: we, 5
θαρραλέος, -α, -ον: daring, bold, 1
θαρρέω: to be confident, take courage; be bold, 2
κράτιστος, -η, -ον: best; strongest, 7
νῦν: now; as it is, 4
παρασκευάζω: to prepare, get ready, 4
προσ-γίγνομαι: come to, join oneself to, 1
ῥᾷστος, -η, -ον: easiest, best, 1
σκεπτέος, -ον: to be considered, 1
σῶμα, -ατος, τό: the body, 4
τήμερον: today, 2
τραῦμα, ατος, τό: wound, 1
ὑπερ-βάλλω: to pass over, exceed, 5

1 **ἰέναι**: add ἡμᾶς as subject, inf. ἔρχομαι
ἐπὶ: *against…*; acc. place to which
εἰ…διατρίψομεν…ἔσονται: an emotional fut. more vivid (εἰ ἄν + subj., fut.) is where a fut. replaces ἄν + subj. in the protasis to express heightened emotion
2 **θαρραλεώτεροι**: comperative adj.
3 **ἔσονται**: fut. deponent εἰμί
εἰκὸς (ἔσται): *(it will be) likely...*; a impersonal construction; add a verb
ἄλλους…προσγενέσθαι: *that others...*; acc. subj. + aor. inf.
τούτων θαρρούντων: gen. abs.
πλείο(ν)ες: comparative adj. with ἄλλους
6 **ὅπως…μαχούμεθα**: *(namely) how…*; clause of effort (object clause, ὅπως + fut.) in apposition to τοῦτο,
ὡς κράτιστα: *as….as possible*; ὡς + superlative (adv.)
7 **ὡς ῥᾷστα**: *as….as possible*; ὡς + superlative (adv.)
σκεπτέον εἶναι: *that we must...*; or 'is to be…(by us)' verbal adj. + εἰμί expressing necessity. This construction is often translated in the active voice.
ὅπως…λάβωμεν…ἀποβάλωμεν: *(namely) how…we are to…*; ind. deliberative question in apposition to τοῦτο with 1p aor. subj. λαμβάνω, ἀποβάλλω
8 **ὡς ἐλάχιστα**: *as….as possible*; ὡς + superlative adj.

ὁρώμενον πλέον ἢ ἐφ᾽ ἑξήκοντα στάδια, ἄνδρες δ᾽ οὐδαμοῦ 10
φυλάττοντες ἡμᾶς φανεροί εἰσιν ἀλλ᾽ ἢ κατ᾽ αὐτὴν τὴν ὁδόν·
πολὺ οὖν κρεῖττον τοῦ ἐρήμου ὄρους καὶ κλέψαι τι πειρᾶσθαι
λαθόντας καὶ ἁρπάσαι φθάσαντας, εἰ δυναίμεθα, μᾶλλον ἢ
πρὸς ἰσχυρὰ χωρία καὶ ἀνθρώπους παρεσκευασμένους μάχε-
σθαι. 12. *πολὺ γὰρ ῥᾷον ὄρθιον ἀμαχεὶ ἰέναι ἢ ὁμαλὲς ἔνθεν* 15
καὶ ἔνθεν πολεμίων ὄντων, καὶ νύκτωρ ἀμαχεὶ μᾶλλον ἂν τὰ
πρὸ ποδῶν ὁρῴη τις ἢ μεθ᾽ ἡμέραν μαχόμενος, καὶ ἡ τραχεῖα
τοῖς ποσὶν ἀμαχεὶ ἰοῦσιν εὐμενεστέρα ἢ ἡ ὁμαλὴ τὰς κεφαλὰς

ἀ-μαχεί: without resistance, 3
ἁρπάζω: seize, carry off, kidnap, 3
ἑξήκοντα: sixty, 2
ἐρῆμος, -ον: deserted, desolate, 4
εὐ-μενής, -ές: well-disposed, kindly, 1
ἡμεῖς: we, 5
ἰσχυρός, -ά, -όν: strong, powerful; severe, 7
κεφαλή, ἡ: the head, 4
κρείττων, -ον: better, stronger, superior, 1
λανθάνω: to escape notice, forget, 5
μᾶλλον: more, rather, 4
νύκτωρ: at night, 2
ὁμαλός, -ή, -όν: level (ground), even, 2
οὐδαμ-οῦ: nowhere, 2
παρασκευάζω: to prepare, get ready, 4
πειράω: to try, attempt, endeavor, 7
πούς, ποδός, ὁ: a foot, 7
πρό: before, in front; in place of (+ gen.), 3
ῥᾴων, ῥᾷον: easier, better, 1
τραχύς, -εῖα, -ύ: rough, jagged, 2
φθάνω: to act first, act beforehand, 3
φυλάττω: to keep watch, keep guard, 6

10 **τὸ...ὁρώμενον**: *the part (of the mountain) seen*; in apposition to ὄρος apposition
πλέον: neuter nom. predicate
ἐφ᾽: *over...*; ἐπὶ, acc. of extent
11 **οὐδαμοῦ...ἀλλ(ο) ἢ**: *nowhere other than*; ἄλλο often drops the acute before ἤ
φανεροί εἰσιν: *are visibly*; 'are visible'
κατὰ...ὁδόν: *on...*; 'over' αὐτὴν is an intensive pronoun
12 **πολὺ**: *far, much*; adv. acc. (acc. of extent in degree)
κρεῖττον (ἐστί): *(it is) better...*; a predicate, in an impersonal construction
τοῦ ἐρήμου ὄρους...τι: *some (part)...*; partitive gen. with indefinite τι; ἐρήμου refers to the part unoccupied by the enemy
καὶ...καὶ...: *both...and*
κλέψαι: aor. inf. κλέπτω after πειρᾶσθαι
13 **λαθόντας**: *by...*; causal aor. pple
ἁρπάσαι: aor. inf. ἁρπάζω
φθάσαντας: *by...*; causal aor. pple
εἰ δυνάιμεθα: *if we should...*; pres. opt. in a mixed condition with κρεῖττον (ἐστί)
ἢ: *than*
πρὸς: *against*
15 **πολὺ**: *far*; or 'more'
ῥᾷον (ἐστί): *(it is) easier...*; impersonal
ὄρθιον, ὁμαλὲς: *over....over...*; a variation of acc. of extent
ἰέναι: inf. ἔρχομαι
ἔνθεν καὶ ἔνθεν: *from this side and that side*;
16 **πολεμίων ὄντων**: gen. abs., pple εἰμί
ἂν...ὁρῴη τις: ὁραοίη, 3s potential opt.
τὰ πρὸ ποδῶν: *things before (our) feet*
17 **μετ(ὰ) ἡμέραν**: *after daybreak*
ἡ τραχεῖα (ὁδός): supply fem. sg. 'road'
18 **τοῖς...ἰοῦσιν**: *for (those)...*; dat. pl. of interest, pple ἔρχομαι
ποσὶν: *by...*; dat. pl. of means, πούς
εὐμενεστέρα (ἐστί): comparative, predicate
ἡ ὁμαλὴ (ὁδός): supply fem. sg. 'road'
τὰς κεφαλὰς: *in...*; acc. of respect

βαλλομένοις. 13. *καὶ κλέψαι δ' οὐκ ἀδύνατόν μοι δοκεῖ εἶναι, ἐξὸν μὲν νυκτὸς ἰέναι, ὡς μὴ ὁρᾶσθαι, ἐξὸν δ' ἀπελθεῖν* 20 *τοσοῦτον ὡς μὴ αἴσθησιν παρέχειν. δοκοῦμεν δ' ἄν μοι ταύτῃ προσποιούμενοι προσβάλλειν ἐρημοτέρῳ ἂν τῷ ὄρει χρῆσθαι· μένοιεν γὰρ ἂν αὐτοῦ μᾶλλον ἁθρόοι οἱ πολέμιοι.* 14. *ἀτὰρ τί ἐγὼ περὶ κλοπῆς συμβάλλομαι; ὑμᾶς γὰρ ἔγωγε, ὦ Χειρίσοφε, ἀκούω τοὺς Λακεδαιμονίους ὅσοι ἐστὲ τῶν ὁμοίων* 25 *εὐθὺς ἐκ παίδων κλέπτειν μελετᾶν, καὶ οὐκ αἰσχρὸν εἶναι*

ἀ-δυνατός, -ή, -όν: incapable, impossible, 2
ἁθρόοι, -αι, -α: in a mass, all together, 4
αἴσθησις, ἡ: perception, sense, appearance, 1
αἰσχρός, -ά, -όν: shameful, disgraceful, 1
ἀτάρ: but, nevertheless, 1
αὐτοῦ: in that very place, there, 7
βάλλω: to throw, cast; shoot, 3
ἐγώγε: I for my part, 1
ἔξ-εστί: it is allowed, it is possible, 4
ἐρῆμος, -ον: deserted, desolate, 4
κλοπή, ἡ: theft, 1
Λακεδαιμόνιος, -η, -ον: Lacedaemonian, 1
μᾶλλον: more, rather, 4
μελετάω: to care for, practice, study, 1
παρ-έχω: to provide, furnish, supply, 5
περί: around, about, concerning, 7
προσ-βάλλω: to attack, strike against, dash 3
προσ-ποιέομαι: pretend; gain, win over, 2
συμ-βάλλω: to join (in battle), contribute, 1
τοσοῦτος, -αύτη, -οῦτο: so great, so much, so many, 3
ὑμεῖς: you, 5
χράομαι: use, employ, experience (+ dat) 6
ὦ: O! oh!, 1

19 **βαλλομένοις**: *for (those soldiers)...*; pass. pple βάλλω, 'hit,' in contrast to dat. pple τοῖς ἰοῦσιν pple
κλέψαι: aor. inf. κλέπτω
20 **ἐξὸν...ἰέναι**: *(since)...is possible*; '...being possible;' acc. abs. (common with impers. verbs) which is causal in sense, neut. sg. pple ἔξεστί; inf. ἔρχομαι
νυκτὸς: *during...*; gen. of time within
ὡς μὴ ὁρᾶσθαι: *so as...*; negative result clause with a passive inf.
ἐξὸν...ἀπελθεῖν: *and (since)...is possible*, another acc. abs., inf. ἀπέρχομαι
21 **τοσοῦτον**: *for...*; acc. of extent
ὡς μὴ...: *so as...*; negative result clause
αἴσθησιν παρέχειν: i.e. not to be seen
δόκοῦμεν δ' ἄν...ἂν χρῆσθαι: *it seems to me that we would experience...*; 'we seem... to experience;' ἂν + inf. is equiv. to a potential opt. or apodosis in a fut. less vivid; a duplicated ἄν often emphasizes the intervening words and on other occasions is simply redundant
22 **ταύτῃ προσποιούμενοι προσβάλλειν**: *(if)...;* pple is conditional in sense, equiv. to protasis in a fut. less vivid
ταύτῃ: *in this way*; a dat of manner
23 **μένοιεν ἂν**: *they would...;* 3p pres. potential opt. μενω
αὐτοῦ: *here*; 'in this very spot'
24 **τί**: *why...?*; 'in respect to what?'
συμβάλλομαι (λόγους): *I am contributing (words)*; i.e. why do I make a suggestion
ὑμᾶς...τοὺς λακεδαιμονίους...μελετᾶν: *that you Spartans*; ind. disc.; α-contract inf.
25 **ἐστὲ**: 2p pres. εἰμί
τῶν ὁμοίων: *of equal citizens*; 'of peers' partitive gen. predicate; the Spartans used this term to describe their aristocracy
26 **ἐκ παίδων**: *from childhood*
οὐκ αἰσχρὸν εἶναι: *(that) it is...*; ind. disc. and impersonal

ἀλλὰ καλὸν κλέπτειν ὅσα μὴ κωλύει νόμος. 15. ὅπως δὲ ὡς 1
κράτιστα κλέπτητε καὶ πειρᾶσθε λανθάνειν, νόμιμον ἄρα
ὑμῖν ἐστιν, ἐὰν ληφθῆτε κλέπτοντες, μαστιγοῦσθαι. νῦν
οὖν μάλα σοι καιρός ἐστιν ἐπιδείξασθαι τὴν παιδείαν, καὶ
φυλάξασθαι μὴ ληφθῶμεν κλέπτοντες τοῦ ὄρους, ὡς μὴ 5
πληγὰς λάβωμεν.' 16. 'ἀλλὰ μέντοι,' ἔφη ὁ Χειρίσοφος, 'κἀγὼ
ὑμᾶς τοὺς Ἀθηναίους ἀκούω δεινοὺς εἶναι κλέπτειν τὰ δημόσια, καὶ μάλα ὄντος δεινοῦ κινδύνου τῷ κλέπτοντι, καὶ
τοὺς κρατίστους μέντοι μάλιστα, εἴπερ ὑμῖν οἱ κράτιστοι

Ἀθηναῖος, -α, -ον: Athenian, of Athens, 4
ἄρα: then, therefore, it seems, it turns out, 2
δεινός, -ή, -όν: skillful, clever; terrible, 3
δημόσιος, -α, -ον: of the people, public, 1
ἐάν: εἰ ἄν, if (+ subj.), 2
εἴ-περ: if really, if in fact, 1
ἐπι-δείκνυμι: to indicate, point out, prove, 2
καιρός, ὁ: time, (right) moment, 2
κίνδυνος, ὁ: risk, danger, venture, 2
κράτιστος, -η, -ον: best, mightiest, 7
λανθάνω: to escape notice, forget, 5
μάλα: very, very much, exceedingly, 4
μάλιστα: most of all; certainly, especially, 5
μαστιγόω: whip, flog, 1
μέντοι: however, nevertheless; certainly, 6
νόμιμος, -η, -ον: customary, 1
νόμος, ὁ: law, custom, 1
νῦν: now; as it is, 4
παιδεία, ἡ: education, culture, learning, 2
πειράω: to try, attempt, endeavor, 7
πληγή, ἡ: blow, strike, beating, 1
ὑμεῖς: you, 5
φυλάττω: to keep watch, keep guard, 6

1 **καλόν (εἶναι)**: *but (that it is) noble*
ὅσα: *(all) that...*; '(things) as many as' relative clause with missing antecendent; μὴ is used instead of οὐ in a general relative clause
ὅπως...κλέπτητε...πειρᾶσθε: *so that you may...*; purpose clause, both verbs are pres. subj.; πειρᾶσθε is 2p α-contract subj.
ὡς κράτιστα: *as....as possible*; ὡς + superlative (adv.)
2 **νόμιμον...ἐστιν**: *it is...*; impersonal
3 **ἐὰν ληφθῆτε**: *if ever you...*; 2p aor. pass. subj. λαμβάνω
κλέποντες: *(while)...*; circumstantial pple
μαστιγοῦσθαι: *that (you)...*; pres. pass. inf.
4 **μάλα...καιρός ἐστιν**: *it is...*; + inf.
5 **μὴ...ληφθῶμεν**: *lest...*; fearing clause, 1p aor. pass. subj. λαμβάνω
κλέποντες: *(while)...*; circumstantial pple
τοῦ ὄρους: *(part of) the mountain*; partitive
6 **ὡς μὴ**: *so that we may...*; negative purpose, aor. active subj. λαμβάνω
ἀλλὰ μέντοι: *well, certainly*; both may be adversative but in replies ἀλλὰ often opposes the whole statement (well, but) and μέντοι is affirmative (surely, certainly)
κα(ὶ) (ἐ)γὼ: *I too*
7 **ὑμᾶς τοὺς Ἀθηναίους**: *that you Athenians...* ind. disc., acc. subject
κλέπτειν: *at...*; explanatory (epexegetical) inf. with δεινοὺς: translate as gerund (-ing)
τὰ δημόσια: *public funds*
8 **καὶ μάλα ὄντος δεινοῦ κινδύνου**: *although ...*; gen. abs. is concessive in sense, the adv. καὶ just as καίπερ means 'although'
δεινοῦ: *terrible*; predicate different in sense from its use in the previous clause
9 **τοὺς κρατίστους**: *and moreover the mightest (are) especially (skilled at stealing)*; add δεινοὺς εἶναι κλέπτειν from above
ὑμῖν: obj. of main verb

ἄρχειν ἀξιοῦνται· ὥστε ὥρα καὶ σοὶ ἐπιδείκνυσθαι τὴν παι- 10
δείαν.' 17. 'ἐγὼ μὲν τοίνυν,' ἔφη ὁ Ξενοφῶν, 'ἕτοιμός εἰμι τοὺς
ὀπισθοφύλακας ἔχων, ἐπειδὰν δειπνήσωμεν, ἰέναι καταληψόμενος τὸ ὄρος. ἔχω δὲ καὶ ἡγεμόνας· οἱ γὰρ γυμνῆτες
τῶν ἑπομένων ἡμῖν κλωπῶν ἔλαβόν τινας ἐνεδρεύσαντες·
τούτων καὶ πυνθάνομαι ὅτι οὐκ ἄβατόν ἐστι τὸ ὄρος, ἀλλὰ 15
νέμεται αἰξὶ καὶ βουσίν· ὥστε ἐάνπερ ἅπαξ λάβωμέν τι τοῦ
ὄρους, βατὰ καὶ τοῖς ὑποζυγίοις ἔσται. 18. ἐλπίζω δὲ οὐδὲ τοὺς
πολεμίους μενεῖν ἔτι, ἐπειδὰν ἴδωσιν ἡμᾶς ἐν τῷ ὁμοίῳ ἐπὶ

ἄ-βατος, -ον: untrodden, impassable, 2
αἶξ, αἶγος, ὁ, ἡ: goat, 2
ἀξιόω: deem worthy, think worthy, 1
ἅπαξ: once, once only, once for all, 2
βατός, -ή, -όν: passable, accessible, 1
γυμνήτης, -ου, ὁ: light-armed soldier 6
δειπνέω: to dine, have dinner, 3
ἐάν-περ: if, 1
ἐλπίζω: to hope for, expect, 1
ἐν-εδρεύω: to set an ambush, lie in wait, 2
ἐπειδάν: whenever, 5
ἐπι-δείκνυμι: to indicate, point out, prove, 2
ἔτι: still, besides, further, 7
ἑτοῖμος, -η, -ον: ready, prepared, at hand, 1
ἡμεῖς: we, 5
κλῶψ, κλωπός, ὁ: thief, 1
νέμω: to graze, pasture; distribute, 1
παιδεία, ἡ: education, culture, learning, 2
πυνθάνομαι: learn (by inquiry or hearsay), 2
ὥρα, ἡ: season, time, period of time, 3

10 **ὑμῖν ἄρχειν**: *to rule you*
ὥρα (ἐστί): *it is time*; note the repetition in phrasing from Xenophon's own speech
καὶ σοὶ: *for you also*; καί is adverbial
12 **δειπνήσωμεν**: ἄν + aor. subj. in a general temporal clause
ἰέναι: inf. ἔρχομαι following ἕτοιμος
καταληψόμενος: *intending to...*; fut. pple καταλαμβάνω expressing purpose
13 **καὶ**: *also*
14 **τῶν ἑπομένων...κλωπων**: partitive gen. with τινας; ἕπομαι governs a dat. ind. obj.
ἔλαβον: *captured*; aor. λαμβάνω
τινας: i.e. the enemy
15 **τούτων**: *from these men*; gen. source
καὶ: *also*
16 **νέμεται**: *it...*; impersonal pass.
αἰξὶ καὶ βουσίν: dat. pl. of means
ἐάνπερ...λάβωμεν,...ἔσται: fut. more vivid (εἰ ἄν + subj., fut.), fut. εἰμί
τοῦ ὄρους: partitive gen.
17 **καί**: *also*
τοῖς ὑποζυγίοις: *for...*; dat. of interest
ἔσται: 3s fut. εἰμί with neuter pl. subject
οὐδὲ: *not even*; adv.
18 **μενεῖν**: μενέ-ειν, fut. inf. (μένειν is pres.) in ind. disc.
ἴδωσιν: 3p aor. subj. ὁράω (aor. εἶδον) in a general temporal clause
ἐν τῷ ὁμοίῳ: *on the level (with them);* or 'on par (with them)'
ἐπὶ: *upon...*

τῶν ἄκρων· οὐδὲ γὰρ νῦν ἐθέλουσι καταβαίνειν εἰς τὸ ἴσον ἡμῖν.’ 19. *ὁ δὲ Χειρίσοφος εἶπε· ‘καὶ τί δεῖ σὲ ἰέναι καὶ λιπεῖν* 20 *τὴν ὀπισθοφυλακίαν; ἀλλὰ ἄλλους πέμψον, ἂν μή τινες ἐθέλοντες ἀγαθοὶ φαίνωνται.’* 20. *ἐκ τούτου Ἀριστώνυμος Μεθυδριεὺς ἔρχεται ὁπλίτας ἔχων καὶ Ἀριστέας ὁ Χῖος γυμνῆτας καὶ Νικόμαχος Οἰταῖος γυμνῆτας· καὶ σύνθημα ἐποιήσαντο, ὁπότε ἔχοιεν τὰ ἄκρα, πυρὰ καίειν πολλά.* 21. *ταῦτα συνθέ-* 25 *μενοι ἠρίστων· ἐκ δὲ τοῦ ἀρίστου προήγαγεν ὁ Χειρίσοφος*

ἀριστάω: to take breakfast, take a meal, 6
Ἀριστέας, ὁ: Aristeas, 2
ἄριστον, τό: breakfast, lunch, 2
Ἀριστώνυμος, ὁ: Aristonymus (person), 5
γυμνήτης, -ου, ὁ: light-armed soldier 6
ἐθελοντής, ὁ: volunteer, one willing, 3
ἴσος, -η, -ον: equal to, the same as, like, 1
λείπω: to leave, forsake, abandon, 6
Μεθυδριεύς, ὁ: of Methydrium, 4
Νικόμαχος, ὁ: Nicomachus, 1
νῦν: now; as it is, 4
Οἰταῖος, -α, -ον: of Oeta, Oetaean, 1
ὀπισθο-φύλακία, ἡ: rear-guard, 1
πέμπω: send, conduct, convey, dispatch, 7
προ-άγω: to lead forward, 1
πυρά, -ῶν, τά: watch-fire, 6
σύν-θημα, -ατος, τό: agreement; password 1
συν-τίθημι: to agree, put together, 3
φαίνω: to show; *mid.* appear, seem, 6
Χῖος, -η, -ον: Chian, of Chios, 2

τῶν ἄκρων: *the heights*
19 οὐδὲ γὰρ νῦν: *for...not now*
καταβαίνειν: i.e. from the heights
εἰς τὸ ἴσον ἡμῖν: *on the same level with us*; ‘on the equal to us’
20 τί: *why...?*; ‘in respect to what?’
ἰέναι, λιπεῖν: aor. inf. ἔρχομαι, λείπω
21 ἀλλὰ: *rather...*; or, as often before an imperative, ‘come now’
πέμψον: aor. imperative
ἂν μὴ...φαίνωται: *if...*; contracted ἐὰν + subj., protasis in a pres. general condition
22 ἐθέλοντες: *as volunteers*
ἐκ τούτου: *as a result*; ‘from this’
23 γυμνῆτας (ἔχων): supply the pple
25 ὁπότε ἔχοιεν: *whenever...*; 3p pres. opt. in a past general temporal clause
τὰ ἄκρα: *the heights*
25 πυρὰ καίειν πολλά: *that (they)...*; ind. disc. in apposition to σύνθημα
συνθέμενοι: aor. mid. pple συντίθημι
26 ἠρίστων: ἠρίσταον, 3p impf.

τὸ στράτευμα πᾶν ὡς δέκα σταδίους πρὸς τοὺς πολεμίους, 1
ὅπως ὡς μάλιστα δοκοίη ταύτῃ προσάξειν.

22. ἐπειδὴ δὲ ἐδείπνησαν καὶ νὺξ ἐγένετο, οἱ μὲν ταχθέντες
ᾤχοντο, καὶ καταλαμβάνουσι τὸ ὄρος, οἱ δὲ ἄλλοι αὐτοῦ
ἀνεπαύοντο. οἱ δὲ πολέμιοι ἐπεὶ ᾔσθοντο τὸ ὄρος ἐχόμενον, 5
ἐγρηγόρεσαν καὶ ἔκαιον πυρὰ πολλὰ διὰ νυκτός. 23. ἐπειδὴ δὲ
ἡμέρα ἐγένετο Χειρίσοφος μὲν θυσάμενος ἦγε κατὰ τὴν
ὁδόν, οἱ δὲ τὸ ὄρος καταλαβόντες κατὰ τὰ ἄκρα ἐπῇσαν.
24. τῶν δὲ πολεμίων τὸ μὲν πολὺ ἔμενεν ἐπὶ τῇ ὑπερβολῇ τοῦ

αἰσθάνομαι: perceive, feel, learn, realize, 4
ἀνα-παύω: to stop, make cease; *mid.*, rest, 4
αὐτοῦ: in that very place, there, 7
δειπνέω: to dine, have dinner, 3
δέκα: ten, 7
ἐγείρω: to awaken, rouse, 1
ἐπ-έρχομαι: to come upon; attack, 5
θύω: to sacrifice, 3
μάλιστα: most of all; certainly, especially, 5
οἴχομαι: to go, go off, depart, 7
προσ-άγω: to bring to, attach, apply, 3
πυρά, -ῶν, τά: watch-fire, 6
τάττω: post, station, arrange, order, 6
ὑπερ-βολή, ἡ: crossing, mtn. pass; excess, 6

1 **ὡς**: *nearly*; 'as if,' in approximation
δέκα σταδίους: *for*...; acc. of extent
2 **ὅπως...δοκοίη**: *so that...(the army) might* ...; purpose, 3s opt. in secondary sequence
ὡς μάλιστα: *as...as possible*; ὡς + superlative (adv.) of μάλα, 'much'
ταύτῃ: *in this way*; i.e. in this direction, dat. of manner
3 **οἱ μὲν...οἱ δὲ ἄλλοι**: *some...others*...
ταχθέντες: aor. pass. pple τάττω
ᾤχοντο: impf. οἴχομαι
αὐτοῦ: *here*; 'in this very place'
5 **ᾔσθοντο**: impf. αἴσθομαι
ἐγρηγόρεσαν: plpf. ἐγείρω; the pf. tenses denote a state, e.g. 'were awake,' rather than an activity, e.g. 'had awakened'
7 **ἦγε**: impf. ἄγω
κατὰ: *on*...
οἱ δὲ: *but those*...
8 **κατὰ τὰ ἄκρα**: *on the heights*
ἐπῇσαν: impf. ἐπ-έρχομαι
9 **τὸ πολὺ**: *the majority*; 'a great (part)'

ὄρους, μέρος δ᾽ αὐτῶν ἀπήντα τοῖς κατὰ τὰ ἄκρα. πρὶν δὲ 10
ὁμοῦ εἶναι τοὺς πολλοὺς ἀλλήλοις, συμμιγνύασιν οἱ κατὰ
τὰ ἄκρα, καὶ νικῶσιν οἱ Ἕλληνες καὶ διώκουσιν. 25. ἐν τούτῳ
δὲ καὶ οἱ ἐκ τοῦ πεδίου οἱ μὲν πελτασταὶ τῶν Ἑλλήνων
δρόμῳ ἔθεον πρὸς τοὺς παρατεταγμένους, Χειρίσοφος δὲ
βάδην ταχὺ ἐφείπετο σὺν τοῖς ὁπλίταις. 26. οἱ δὲ πολέμιοι οἱ 15
ἐπὶ τῇ ὁδῷ ἐπειδὴ τὸ ἄνω ἑώρων ἡττώμενον, φεύγουσι· καὶ
ἀπέθανον μὲν οὐ πολλοὶ αὐτῶν, γέρρα δὲ πάμπολλα ἐλήφθη·
ἃ οἱ Ἕλληνες ταῖς μαχαίραις κόπτοντες ἀχρεῖα ἐποίουν.

ἀπ-αντάω: to meet, encounter (dat), 2
ἀχρεῖα, ἡ: rubbish, useless things, 1
βάδην: step by step, gradually, 2
γέρρον, τό: wicker-work; wicker-shield, 6
διώκω: to pursue, follow; prosecute, 3
δρόμος, ὁ: run, running, flight; race course, 5
ἐφ-έπομαι: to follow after, pursue, 4
ἡττάομαι: to be less, be weaker or inferior, 1
κόπτω: to strike, hack, knock, 2
μάχαιρα, ἡ: sabre, curved sword; knife, 1
μέρος, -έος, τό: a part, share; detachment, 1
νικάω: to conquer, defeat, win, 2
ὁμοῦ: at the same place, together (dat) 3
παμ-πολύς, -πολλή, -πολύ: very many, 2
παρα-τάττω: draw up in battle order, 5
συμ-μίγνυμι: to mix together in battle, 1

10 **μέρος αὐτῶν**: i.e. the enemy
ἀπήντα: ἀπήντα-ε; 3s impf.
τοῖς κατὰ τὰ ἄκρα: *those along...*; i.e. the enemy; dat. of compound verb
11 **τοὺς πολλούς**: i.e. the two armies, acc. subject of inf. εἰμί
ὁμοῦ...ἀλλήλοις: predicate of εἶναι
οἱ κατὰ τὰ ἄκρα: *those on the heights*
12 **νικῶσιν**: νικάουσιν; 3p pres.
ἐν τούτῳ: *meanwhile*; 'in this (time)'
13 **οἱ ἐκ τοῦ πεδίου...τῶν Ἑλλήνων**: *those of the Greeks on the plain*
οἱ μὲν πελτασται...Χειρίσοφος δὲ: *the peltasts on the one hand...Cheirisophus on the other hand*; distributive apposition following οἱ ἐκ τοῦ πεδίου
14 **δρόμῳ**: *on...*; dat. of manner
ἔθεον: *began to...*; inchoative impf. θέω
παρατεταγμένους: pf. pass. pple παρατάττω
15 **ταχύ**: adverbial acc. ταχύς
ἐφείπετο: impf. ἐφ-έπομαι
16 **οἱ ἐπὶ τῇ ὁδῷ**: in the attributive position modifying πολέμιοι
τὸ ἄνω (μέρος): *the (unit) above*; i.e. on the mountain, see line 10
ἑώρων: 3p impf. ὁράω
17 **ἀπέθανον**: aor. ἀποθνῄσκω
ἐλήφθη: 3s aor. pass. λαμβάνω with a neuter pl. subject
ταῖς μαχαίραις: dat. of means
18 **ἐποίουν**: *made (x) (y)*; governs a double acc. (obj. and pred.)

27. *ὡς δ' ἀνέβησαν, θύσαντες καὶ τρόπαιον στησάμενοι κατέβησαν εἰς τὸ πεδίον, καὶ εἰς κώμας πολλῶν καὶ ἀγαθῶν* 20
γεμούσας ἦλθον.

1. *ἐκ δὲ τούτων ἐπορεύθησαν εἰς Ταόχους σταθμοὺς πέντε παρασάγγας τριάκοντα· καὶ τὰ ἐπιτήδεια ἐπέλειπε· χωρία γὰρ ᾤκουν ἰσχυρὰ οἱ Τάοχοι, ἐν οἷς καὶ τὰ ἐπιτήδεια ἅπαντα εἶχον ἀνακεκομισμένοι.* 2. *ἐπεὶ δ' ἀφίκοντο πρὸς χωρίον ὃ* 25
πόλιν μὲν οὐκ εἶχεν οὐδ' οἰκίας, συνεληλυθότες δ' ἦσαν αὐτόσε καὶ ἄνδρες καὶ γυναῖκες καὶ κτήνη πολλά, Χειρί-

---

ἀνα-κομίζω: to bring up, bring back, 2
ἅπας, ἅπασα, ἅπαν: every, quite all, 3
αὐτό-σε: to the very spot or moment, 1
γέμω: to be full of, be loaded of, (gen) 1
γυνή, γυναικός, ἡ: a woman, wife, 7
ἐπι-λείπω: fail, be lacking, be wanting, 2
θύω: to sacrifice, 3
ἵστημι: make stand, set up, stop, establish, 7
ἰσχυρός, -ά, -όν: strong, powerful; severe, 7
κτῆνος, -εος, τό: herd, flock, 3
οἰκέω: to inhabit, dwell, live, 5
πέντε: five, 4
πόλις, ἡ: a city, 3
συν-έρχομαι: come together, meet in battle 3
Τάοχοι, οἱ: Taochians, 5
τριάκοντα: thirty, 4
τρόπαιον, τό: monument, trophy, 1

19 **ὡς**: *when*
ἀνέβησαν: 3p aor. ἀναβαίνω
στησάμενοι: aor. mid. ἵστημι is transitive
κατέβησαν: aor. καταβαίνω
20 **πολλῶν καὶ ἀγαθῶν**: neut. pl. partitive gen.
21 **ἦλθον**: aor. ἔρχομαι
22 **ἐπορεύθησαν**: 3p aor. pass. dep. πορεύομαι: translate in active
σταθμοὺς...παρασάγγας: *for...*; acc. of extent
χωρία...ἰσχυρὰ: i.e. strongholds or fortified placed
24 **ᾤκουν**: ᾤκεον, 3p impf. οἰκέω
ἐν οἷς: *in which...*; relative clause
καὶ: *also*
25 **εἶχον ἀνακεκομισμένοι**: periphrastic plpf. mid. (impf. ἔχω + pf. mid. pple), or perhaps separately, equiv. to 'kept Xed'
ἀφίκοντο: aor. ἀφικνέομαι
ὃ: *which*; relative clause
26 **συνεληλυθότες δ' ἦσαν**: periphrastic plpf. act. (pf. pple συνέρχομαι + impf. εἰμί)
27 **κτήμη**: κτήμε-α

σοφος μὲν οὖν πρὸς τοῦτο προσέβαλλεν εὐθὺς ἥκων· ἐπειδὴ 1
δὲ ἡ πρώτη τάξις ἀπέκαμνεν, ἄλλη προσῄει καὶ αὖθις ἄλλη·
οὐ γὰρ ἦν ἀθρόοις περιστῆναι, ἀλλ᾽ ἀπότομον ἦν κύκλῳ.
3. ἐπειδὴ δὲ Ξενοφῶν ἦλθε σὺν τοῖς ὀπισθοφύλαξι καὶ πελτα-
σταῖς καὶ ὁπλίταις, ἐνταῦθα δὴ λέγει Χειρίσοφος· 'εἰς καλὸν 5
ἥκετε· τὸ γὰρ χωρίον αἱρετέον· τῇ γὰρ στρατιᾷ οὐκ ἔστι τὰ
ἐπιτήδεια, εἰ μὴ ληψόμεθα τὸ χωρίον. 4. ἐνταῦθα δὴ κοινῇ ἐβου-
λεύοντο· καὶ τοῦ Ξενοφῶντος ἐρωτῶντος τί τὸ κωλῦον εἴη
εἰσελθεῖν, εἶπεν ὁ Χειρίσοφος· 'μία αὕτη πάροδός ἐστιν ἣν

ἀθρόοι, -αι, -α: in a mass, all together, 4
αἱρετέος, -ον: to be chosen, to be taken, 1
ἀπο-κάμνω: to grow quite weary, tire, 1
ἀπό-τομος, -ον: cut off; sheer; severe, 2
αὖθις: back, back again, backwards, 2
βουλεύω: to deliberate, plan, take counsel, 5
εἰσ-έρχομαι: to go to, approach; enter, 2
ἥκω: to have come, be present, 7
κοινός, -ή, -όν: common, ordinary; public, 3
κύκλος, ὁ: a circle, round, ring, 4
πάρ-οδος, ὁ: passage, entrance, approach, 4
περι-ίστημι: to circle around, encircle, 1
προσ-βάλλω: to attack, strike against, dash 3
στρατία, ἡ: an army, expedition, land force, 4
τάξις, -εως, ἡ: unit, squadron; battle array, 7

1 **πρὸς τοῦτο (χωρίον)**: *against this (stronghold)*; i.e. χωρία ἰσχυρὰ noted above
ἥκων: nom. sg. pple
2 **ἄλλη (τάξις)**: *another unit*
προσῄει: impf. προσέρχομαι
3 **ἦν**: *it was possible*; impf. εἰμί
περιστῆναι: aor. inf. περιίστημι
ἀθρόοις (αὐτοῖς): missing pronoun is dat. pl. obj. of compound verb
κύκλῳ: *on all sides*; 'in a circle'
4 **ἦλθε**: aor. ἔρχομαι
5 **ἐνταῦθα δὴ**: *just then, exactly then*
εἰς καλὸν: *at the right (moment)*; i.e. at the fine moment
6 **αἱρετέον (ἐστί)**: *must…*; 'is to be…' verbal adj. + missing verb εἰμί often expresses obligation or necessity
τῇ…στρατιᾷ…ἔστι: dat. of possession
7 **ληψόμεθα**: fut. mid. λαμβάνω, translate as present with future sense
ἐνταῦθα δὴ: *just then, exactly then*
κοινῇ: *in common*; dat. of manner
8 **τοῦ Ξενοφῶντος ἐρωτῶντος**: gen. abs.
τί…εἴη: *what…*; ind. question with opt. in secondary seq. εἰμί
τὸ κωλῦον: *the thing…*; neut. sg. pple predicate
9 **εἰσελθεῖν**: *from…*; aor. inf. following a verb of hindering
ἐστιν: *there is…*
ἣν: *which…*

ὁρᾷς· ὅταν δέ τις ταύτῃ πειρᾶται παριέναι, κυλίνδουσι λίθους 10
ὑπὲρ ταύτης τῆς ὑπερεχούσης πέτρας· ὃς δ' ἂν καταληφθῇ,
οὕτω διατίθεται.' ἅμα δ' ἔδειξε συντετριμμένους ἀνθρώπους
καὶ σκέλη καὶ πλευράς. 5. 'ἢν δὲ τοὺς λίθους ἀναλώσωσιν,'
ἔφη ὁ Ξενοφῶν, 'ἄλλο τι ἢ οὐδὲν κωλύει παριέναι; οὐ γὰρ
δὴ ἐκ τοῦ ἐναντίου ὁρῶμεν εἰ μὴ ὀλίγους τούτους ἀνθρώπους, 15
καὶ τούτων δύο ἢ τρεῖς ὡπλισμένους. 6. τὸ δὲ χωρίον, ὡς καὶ
σὺ ὁρᾷς, σχεδὸν τρία ἡμίπλεθρά ἐστιν ὃ δεῖ βαλλομένους
διελθεῖν· τούτου δὲ ὅσον πλέθρον δασὺ πίτυσι διαλειπούσαις

ἄλλος, -η, -ο: other, one...another, 8
ἀν-αλίσκω: to use up, to spend, squander, 3
βάλλω: to throw, cast; shoot, 3
δασύς, -εῖα, -ύ: thick; thicket (bush/woods), 5
δείκνυμι: to show, indicate, 4
δια-λείπω: to leave or set at intervals, 3
δια-τίθημι: treat, handle, arrange; dispose, 1
δι-έρχομαι: to go through, pass, 7
ἐναντίος, -α, -ον: opposite, contrary, 4
ἡμί-πλεθρον, τό: half of a plethron (100 ft.), 2
κυλίνδω: to roll; wallow, wander, 5
ὁπλίζω: to make ready, arm, equip, 2
ὅταν: ὅτε ἄν, whenever, 5
πειράω: to try, attempt, endeavor, 7
πίτυς, -υος, ἡ:: pine tree, 1
πλέθρον, τό: a plethron (=100 feet), 3
πλευρά, ἡ: a rib, side, 2
σκέλος, -εος, τό: leg, 2
συν-τρίβω: to crush, shatter, rub together, 1
σχεδόν: nearly, almost, just about, 3
ὑπερ-έχω: to hold over, hold above, 1

10 **ὅταν...πειρᾶται**: general temporal clause, pres. subj. α-contract verb
ταύτῃ: *in this way*; dat. of manner
παριέναι: inf. παρέρχομαι
11 **ὑπερεχούσης**: *overhanging*; i.e. projecting
ὃς...καταληφθῇ: *whoever...*; general relative clause ἄν + 3s aor. pass. subj. καταλαμβάνω; i.e. by the stones
12 **οὕτω**: i.e. in the following way
ἔδειξε: aor. δείκνυμι
συντετριμμένους: pf. pass. pple
13 **καὶ σκέλη καὶ πλευράς**: *both in...and in...*; acc. of respect; σκέλε-α
ἢν...ἀναλώσωσιν: *if...*; ἐάν + 3s aor. subj. ἀναλίσκω
14 **ἄλλο τι ἢ...**: *Nothing prevents (us) from passing, does it?*; '(does anything other than nothing...?' ἄλλο τι ἤ introduces a yes/no question expecting an yes response
παριέναι: inf. παρέρχομαι
15 **ὁρῶμεν**: supply an obj.: 'anything'
ἐκ τοῦ ἐναντίου: i.e. side
εἰ μὴ: *except*
16 **τούτων**: partitive gen.
ὡπλισμένους: pf. pass. pple
τὸ δὲ χωρίον: *the area*; i.e. the distance, not 'stronghold' as earlier in the narrative
ὡς: *as...*; parentehtical
17 **ὃ**: *which...*; χωρίον is antecedent
βαλλομένους: *(while)...*; circumstantial use of pass. pple βάλλω, 'shoot at' or 'pelt'
18 **διελθεῖν**: aor inf. διαέρχομαι, add ἡμᾶς as acc. subject
τούτου (χωρίου): *of this (area/distance)*
ὅσον πλέθρον (ἐστίν) δασὺ: *as much as...*; ὅσον is a relative adj.; add a linking verb
πίτυσι...: dat. of means

μεγάλαις, ἀνθ' ὧν ἑστηκότες ἄνδρες τί ἂν πάσχοιεν ἢ ὑπὸ
τῶν φερομένων λίθων ἢ ὑπὸ τῶν κυλινδομένων; τὸ λοιπὸν 20
οὖν γίγνεται ὡς ἡμίπλεθρον, ὃ δεῖ ὅταν λωφήσωσιν οἱ λίθοι
παραδραμεῖν.' 7. 'ἀλλὰ εὐθύς,' ἔφη ὁ Χειρίσοφος, 'ἐπειδὰν
ἀρξώμεθα εἰς τὸ δασὺ προσιέναι, φέρονται οἱ λίθοι πολλοί.'
'αὐτὸ ἄν,' ἔφη, 'τὸ δέον εἴη· θᾶττον γὰρ ἀναλώσουσι τοὺς
λίθους. ἀλλὰ πορευώμεθα ἔνθεν ἡμῖν μικρόν τι παραδραμεῖν 25
ἔσται, ἢν δυνώμεθα, καὶ ἀπελθεῖν ῥᾴδιον, ἢν βουλώμεθα.'

ἀν-αλίσκω: to use up, to spend, squander, 3
ἀντί: instead of, in place of (+ gen.), 3
δασύς, -εῖα, -ύ: thick; thicket (bush/woods), 5
ἐπειδάν: whenever, 5
ἡμεῖς: we, 5
ἡμί-πλεθρον, τό: half of a plethron (100 ft.), 2
θάττων, θᾶττον: faster, quicker, swifter, 3
ἵστημι: make stand, set up, stop, establish, 7
κυλίνδω: to roll; wallow, wander, 5
λοιπός, ὁ: remaining, the rest, 6
λωφάω: to abate, take rest, recover from, 1
μικρός, -ά, -όν: small, little, 1
ὅταν: ὅτε ἄν, whenever, 5
παρα-τρέχω: to run past, run along, 3
πάσχω: to suffer, experience, 3
ῥᾴδιος, -α, -ον: easy, ready, 3

19 **μεγάλαις**: *tall*
ἀνθ' ὧν: *behind which...*; relative
ἑστηκοτες: pf. pple ἵστημι
τί ἂν πάσχοιεν...: *what would...;* interrogative pronoun; 3p potential opt. ἄνδρες is subject
ὑπὸ: *because of...*; gen. of cause
20 **φερομένων**: *flying*; 'bearing along' mid. pple
21 **ὡς**: *nearly*; 'as if,' in approximation
ὃ: *which...*; relative
ὅταν λωφήσωσιν: *whenever...*; ἄν + aor. subj. in a general temporal clause
22 **παραδραμεῖν**: aor. inf. παρατρέχω
23 **ἀρξώμεθα**: ἄν + aor. subj. in a general temporal clause
προσιέναι: inf. προσέρχομαι
φέρονται: *are flying*; 'are bearing along' likely pres. mid. but possibly pres. passive: 'are carried along;' the emphasis is on the quantity of stones: πολλοί
24 **ἔφη**: *(Xenophon) said*; impf. φημί
ἂν...εἴη: *(this) would...*; potential opt. εἰμί the understood subject is the number of rocks flying in the previous sentence
τὸ δέον: *what is needed*; 'the think lacking' neuter pple,
θᾶττον: comparative adverb
ἀναλώσουσι: fut. ἀναλίσκω
25 **πορευώμεθα**: *Let us...*; hortatory subj.
ἔνθεν: (*to the place) from which*
ἡμῖν: dat. of interest
μικρόν τι: *for...*; acc. of extent
παραδραμεῖν: aor. inf. παρατρέχω
26 **ἔσται**: *it will be possible*; fut. εἰμί
ἢν δυνώμεθα: *if...*; ἐὰν, fut. more vivid condition (εἰ + ἄν + subj., fut.)
ῥᾴδιον (ἔσται): *(it will be)...*; add verb
ἢν: *if...*; ἐὰν + subj., fut. more vivid condition

8. ἐντεῦθεν ἐπορεύοντο Χειρίσοφος καὶ Ξενοφῶν καὶ Καλ- 1
λίμαχος Παρράσιος λοχαγός· τούτου γὰρ ἡ ἡγεμονία ἦν
τῶν ὀπισθοφυλάκων λοχαγῶν ἐκείνῃ τῇ ἡμέρᾳ· οἱ δὲ ἄλλοι
λοχαγοὶ ἔμενον ἐν τῷ ἀσφαλεῖ. μετὰ τοῦτο οὖν ἀπῆλθον
ὑπὸ τὰ δένδρα ἄνθρωποι ὡς ἑβδομήκοντα, οὐχ ἁθρόοι ἀλλὰ 5
καθ' ἕνα, ἕκαστος φυλαττόμενος ὡς ἐδύνατο. 9. Ἀγασίας δὲ
ὁ Στυμφάλιος καὶ Ἀριστώνυμος Μεθυδριεὺς καὶ οὗτοι τῶν
ὀπισθοφυλάκων λοχαγοὶ ὄντες, καὶ ἄλλοι δέ, ἐφέστασαν
ἔξω τῶν δένδρων· οὐ γὰρ ἦν ἀσφαλῶς ἐν τοῖς δένδροις

Ἀγασίας, ὁ: Agasias (person), 3
ἁθρόοι, -αι, -α: in a mass, all together, 4
ἄλλος, -η, -ο: other, one...another, 8
Ἀριστώνυμος, ὁ: Aristonymus (person), 5
ἀ-σφαλής, -ές: safe, secure, not liable to fall 7
δένδρον, τό: tree, 6
ἑβδομήκοντα: seventy, 1
εἷς, μία, ἕν: one, single, alone, 8
ἔξω: out of (+ gen.); adv. outside, 5
ἐφ-ίστημι: set up, place up, 1
ἡγεμονία, ἡ: authority, leadership, 1
Καλλίμαχος, ὁ: Callimachus, 5
Μεθυδριεὺς, ὁ: of Methydrium, 4
Παρράσιος -α, -ον: of Parrhesia; Parrhesian 2
Στυμφάλιος, -η, -ον: of Stymphalos (city), 4
φυλάττω: to keep watch, keep guard, 6

2 **τούτου**: *this one's*; 'of Callimachus' gen. as predicate
ἡγεμονία: i.e. officer of the day; the unit leading the column of soldiers changed daily
3 **ἐκείνῃ τῇ ἡμέρᾳ**: dat. of time when
4 **ἐν τῷ ἀσφαλεῖ**: i.e. place
ἀπῆλθον: aor. ἀπέρχομαι
5 **ὑπὸ**: *beneath*...; the men are behind the trees to avoid the rocks, acc. place to which
ὡς: *nearly*; 'as if,' in approximation
καθ' ἕνα: *one by one*; 'by one(s)' κατά + acc. εἷς; κατά is distributive in sense
6 **ὡς**: *as*...; clause of comparison
8 **ὄντες**: pple εἰμί
ἐφέστασαν: plpf. ἐφίστημι; (note: 'had stood' can mean 'was standing')
9 **ἦν**: *it was possible*; impf. εἰμί
ἀσφαλῶς: adv. modifies the following inf. ἑστάναι

ἑστάναι πλέον ἢ τὸν ἕνα λόχον. 10. ἔνθα δὴ Καλλίμαχος 10
μηχανᾶταί τι· προύτρεχεν ἀπὸ τοῦ δένδρου ὑφ᾽ ᾧ ἦν αὐτὸς
δύο ἢ τρία βήματα· ἐπειδὴ δὲ οἱ λίθοι φέροιντο, ἀνέχαζεν
εὐπετῶς· ἐφ᾽ ἑκάστης δὲ τῆς προδρομῆς πλέον ἢ δέκα ἅμαξαι
πετρῶν ἀνηλίσκοντο. 11. ὁ δὲ Ἀγασίας ὡς ὁρᾷ τὸν Καλλίμαχον ἃ ἐποίει τὸ στράτευμα πᾶν θεώμενον, δείσας μὴ οὐ 15
πρῶτος παραδράμῃ εἰς τὸ χωρίον, οὐδὲ τὸν Ἀριστώνυμον
πλησίον ὄντα παρακαλέσας οὐδὲ Εὐρύλοχον τὸν Λουσιέα,
ἑταίρους ὄντας, οὐδὲ ἄλλον οὐδένα χωρεῖ αὐτός, καὶ παρέρ-

Ἀγασίας, ὁ: Agasias (person), 3
ἅμαξη, ἡ: a wagon, cart, 1
ἀν-αλίσκω: to use up, to spend, squander, 3
ἀνα-χάζω: to draw back, recoil, 2
Ἀριστώνυμος, ὁ: Aristonymus (person), 5
βῆμα, -ατος, τό: step, pace, 1
δείδω: to fear, 5
δέκα: ten, 7
δένδρον, τό: tree, 6
ἑταῖρος, ὁ: comrade, companion, mate, 2
εὐ-πετής, -ές: easy, without trouble, 2
Εὐρύλοχος, ὁ: Eurylochus, 3
θεάομαι: to see, gaze at, watch, 2
ἵστημι: make stand, set up, stop, establish, 7
Καλλίμαχος, ὁ: Callimachus, 5
Λουσιεύς, -έως, ὁ: of Lusi, Lusean, 3
μηχανάομαι: to contrive, devise, 1
παρα-καλέω: to call, summon, 1
παρα-τρέχω: to run beside, run past, 3
πλησίος, -η, -ον: near, close to; neighbors, 5
πρό-δρομή, ἡ: assail, attack, running forth, 1
προ-τρέχω: to run forward, 1
χωρέω: to go, come; have room for, 3

10 **ἑστάναι**: pf. inf. ἵστημι
ἕνα: acc. sg. εἷς
ἔνθα δή: *just then, exactly then*
11 **προύτρεχεν**: προ(έ)τρεχεν, impf.
ὑ(πὸ) ᾧ: under...; relative clause
αὐτὸς: *he himself*; intensive pronoun
δύο...βήματα: *for*...; acc. of extent
12 **ἐπειδὴ φέροιντο**: *whenever...flew*; 'were bearing along;' past general temporal clause with pres. mid. opt.
ἀνέχαλεν: *would*...; iterative impf.
13 **ἐφ᾽**: *in the case of...*
ἅμαξαι: i.e. cart-sized loads
14 **ἀνηλίσκοντο**: iterative impf. pass.
ὡς: *when, as*
τὸν Καλλίμαχον...θεώμενον: *the entire army...*; ind. disc. (acc. + pple), στράτευμα is acc. subj.
τὸν Καλλίμαχον ἃ ἐποίει: obj. of θεώμενον; Callimachus is used proleptically and and should be the subject of ἐποιέι
15 **δείσας**: aor. pple
μὴ οὐ: *that...not*; 'lest not,' neg. fearing clause; μὴ alone introduces a positive clause; 3s aor. subj. παρατρέχω
16 **πρῶτος**: i.e. he be the first to...
οὐδὲ...οὐδὲ...οὐδὲ: *not even...nor...nor*
17 **ὄντα**: acc. sg. pple εἰμί
παρακαλέσας: nom. sg. aor. pple
18 **χωρεῖ**: *moves forward, advances*
αὐτὸς: i.e. by himself, alone; i.e. Agasias

χεται πάντας. 12. ὁ δὲ Καλλίμαχος ὡς ὁρᾷ αὐτὸν παριόντα, ἐπιλαμβάνεται αὐτοῦ τῆς ἴτυος· ἐν δὲ τούτῳ παραθεῖ αὐτοὺς 20 Ἀριστώνυμος Μεθυδριεύς, καὶ μετὰ τοῦτον Εὐρύλοχος Λουσιεύς· πάντες γὰρ οὗτοι ἀντεποιοῦντο ἀρετῆς καὶ διηγωνίζοντο πρὸς ἀλλήλους· καὶ οὕτως ἐρίζοντες αἱροῦσι τὸ χωρίον. ὡς γὰρ ἅπαξ εἰσέδραμον, οὐδεὶς πέτρος ἄνωθεν ἠνέχθη. 13. ἐνταῦθα δὴ δεινὸν ἦν θέαμα. αἱ γὰρ γυναῖκες ῥίπτουσαι 25

αἱρέω: seize, take; *mid.* choose, 3
ἀντι-ποιέω: to do in rivalry for (gen), 1
ἄνω-θεν: from above, from on high, 1
ἅπαξ: once, once only, once for all, 2
ἀρετή, ἡ: excellence, virtue, 1
Ἀριστώνυμος, ὁ: Aristonymus (person), 5
γυνή, γυναικός, ἡ: a woman, wife, 7
δεινός, -ή, -όν: skillful, clever; terrible, 3
δι-αγωνίζομαι: to contend against, 1
εἰσ-τρέχω: to run in, 1
ἐπι-λαμβάνω: to lay hold of, take on, 2
ἐρίζω: to contend, quarrel, wrangle, strive, 1
Εὐρύλοχος, ὁ: Eurylochus, 3
θέαμα, -ατος, τό: sight, spectacle, 1
ἴτυς, -υος, ἡ: rim (of a shield); shield, 1
Καλλίμαχος, ὁ: Callimachus, 5
Λουσιεύς, -έως, ὁ: of Lusi, Lusean, 3
Μεθυδριεὺς, ὁ: of Methydrium, 4
παρα-θέω: to run alongside, run past, 1
ῥίπτω: to throw, cast, hurl, 3

19 ὡς: *as, when*
αὐτὸν: i.e. Agasias
παριόντα: acc. sg. pple παρέρχομαι
20 αὐτοῦ: *his*; possessive, not intensive
τῆς ἴτυος: *by*...; partitive gen. governed by a verb of grabbing
ἐν δὲ τούτῳ: *meanwhile*; 'in this (time)'
22 ἀρετῆς: gen. with main verb
πρὸς: *against*...
23 χωρίον: *stronghold*
24 ὡς: *as, when*
εἰσέδραμον: 3rd pl. aor. εἰστρέχω
ἠνέχθη: *were borne along*; i.e flew, 3s aor. pass. φέρω
25 ἐνταῦθα δὴ: *just then*
ῥίπτουσαι: i.e. off the rock face, fem. nom. pl. pple has τὰ παιδία as object

τὰ παιδία εἶτα ἑαυτὰς ἐπικατερρίπτουν, καὶ οἱ ἄνδρες ὡσαύ- 1
τως. ἐνταῦθα δὴ καὶ Αἰνείας Στυμφάλιος λοχαγὸς ἰδών τινα
θέοντα ὡς ῥίψοντα ἑαυτὸν στολὴν ἔχοντα καλὴν ἐπιλαμβάνεται ὡς κωλύσων· 14. ὁ δὲ αὐτὸν ἐπισπᾶται, καὶ ἀμφότεροι
ᾤχοντο κατὰ τῶν πετρῶν φερόμενοι καὶ ἀπέθανον. ἐντεῦθεν 5
ἄνθρωποι μὲν πάνυ ὀλίγοι ἐλήφθησαν, βόες δὲ καὶ ὄνοι
πολλοὶ καὶ πρόβατα.

15. ἐντεῦθεν ἐπορεύθησαν διὰ Χαλύβων σταθμοὺς ἑπτὰ
παρασάγγας πεντήκοντα. οὗτοι ἦσαν ὧν διῆλθον ἀλκιμώ-

Αἰνείας, ὁ: Aeneas, 1
ἄλκιμος, -ον: stout, brave, 2
ἀμφότερος, -α, -ον: each of two, both, 2
δι-έρχομαι: to go through, pass, 7
εἶτα: then, next, and so, therefore, 6
ἐπι-καταρριπτέω: throw down in addition, 1
ἐπι-λαμβάνω: to lay hold of, take on, 2
ἐπι-σπάω: to drag, draw in, 1
ἑπτά: seven, 5
οἴχομαι: to go, go off, depart, 7
ὄνος, ὁ, ἡ: a mule, 1
παιδίον, τό: a little or young child, child, 1
πάνυ: quite, entirely, exceedingly, 3
πεντήκοντα: fifty, 1
πρό-βατα, τά: sheep, flocks, 1
ῥίπτω: to throw, cast, hurl, 3
στολή, ἡ: apparel, armament, 2
Στυμφάλιος, -η, -ον: of Stymphalos (city), 4
Χάλυψ, -υβος, ὁ: Chalybian, 4
ὡσ-αύτως: in the same manner, just so, 1

1 **ἐπικατερρύπτουν**: 3p impf.
2 **ἐνταῦθα δὴ**: *just then*
ἰδών: nom. sg. aor. pple ὁράω
3 **ὡς ῥίψοντα**: *so that…*; 'so as…' ὡς + fut. pple expresses purpose, ῥίπτω
4 **ὡς κωλύσων**: *so that…*; 'so as…' ὡς + fut. pple again expressing purpose
ὁ δὲ: *and he*; i.e the enemy jumping
αὐτὸν: i.e. Aeneas
5 **ᾤχοντο**: impf. ὄιχομαι
κατὰ: *down from…*
ἀπέθανον: aor. ἀποθνῄσκω
6 **ἐλήφθησαν**: 3p aor. pass. λαμβάνω
8 **ἐπορεύθησαν**: 3p aor. pass. dep. πορεύομαι: translate in active
διὰ Χαλύβων: *through (the land of) the Chalybians*
σταθμοὺς…παρασάγγας: *for…*; acc. of extent
ὧν διῆλθον: (*of those) whom…*; (ἐκείνων) οὕς, relative clause; the acc. pl. pronoun is attractived into the gen. of the missing antecedent (partitive gen.)
ἀλκιμώτατοι: superlative

τατοι, καὶ εἰς χεῖρας ἦσαν. εἶχον δὲ θώρακας λινοῦς μέχρι 10
τοῦ ἤτρου, ἀντὶ δὲ τῶν πτερύγων σπάρτα πυκνὰ ἐστραμμένα.
16. εἶχον δὲ καὶ κνημῖδας καὶ κράνη καὶ παρὰ τὴν ζώνην μαχαίριον
ὅσον ξυήλην Λακωνικήν, ᾧ ἔσφαττον ὧν κρατεῖν δύναιντο,
καὶ ἀποτεμόντες ἂν τὰς κεφαλὰς ἔχοντες ἐπορεύοντο, καὶ
ᾖδον καὶ ἐχόρευον ὁπότε οἱ πολέμιοι αὐτοὺς ὄψεσθαι ἔμελ- 15
λον. εἶχον δὲ καὶ δόρυ ὡς πεντεκαίδεκα πήχεων μίαν
λόγχην ἔχον. 17. οὗτοι ἐνέμενον ἐν τοῖς πολίσμασιν· ἐπεὶ δὲ
παρέλθοιεν οἱ Ἕλληνες, εἵποντο ἀεὶ μαχούμενοι. ᾤκουν

ἀεί: always, forever, in every case, 6
ἀείδω: to sing, chant, 2
ἀντί: instead of, in place of (+ gen.), 3
ἀπο-τέμνω: to cut off, sever, 1
δόρυ, δόρατος, τό: spearshaft; pole, stem, 4
ἐμ-μένω: to remain in, abide in, 1
ζώνη, ἡ: belt, girdle, 1 **ἦτρον, τό**: groin, 1
θώραξ, θώρακος, ὁ: breastplace, corset, 2
κεφαλή, ἡ: the head, 4
κνημίς, -ῖδος, ἡ: greave, leggings, 1
κράνος, -εος, τό: a helmet, 1
κρατέω: to conquer, overpower (gen), 1
Λακωνικός, -ή, -όν: Laconian, of Laconia, 2
λίνεος, , ὁ: linen, 1
λόγχη, ἡ: spearheard; spear, lance, 4
μαχαίριον, τό: knife, (little) dagger) ,1
μέλλω: to be about to, intend to, 2
μέχρι: up to; until, as long as (+ gen.), 5
ξυήλη, ἡ: whittling knife (to make a javelin) 2
οἰκέω: to inhabit, dwell, live, 5
πεντε-καί-δεκα: fifteen, 5
πῆχυς, ὁ: cubit (up to elbow), forearm, 1
πολίσμα, -ατος, τό: city, town, 1
πτέρυξ, -υγος, ὁ: wing, flap, 1
πυκνός, -ή, -όν: thick, close-packed, 2
σπάρτον, τό: cord, rope, 1
στρέφω: to turn, wheel around; twist, 3
σφάττω: to slay, slaughter, 2
χείρ, χειρός, ἡ: hand, 2
χορεύω: to dance, 1

10 **εἰς χεῖρας**: *hand-to-hand*; or 'to blows'
ἦσαν: impf. ἔρχομαι
11 **ἀντὶ...πτερύγων**: *in place of flaps*
ἐστραμμένα: pf. pass. pple στρέφω; i.e. plaited or braided
12 **κράνη**: κράνε-α
παρὰ τὴν ζώνην: *on...*
13 **ὅσον**: *as long as*
ᾧ: *by which...*; relative, dat. of means
ὧν... δύναιντο: *whoever...*; 3p pres. opt. in a general relative clause; gen. obj. of κρατεῖν; the missing antecedent is acc. obj.
14 **ἀποτεμνόντες (καὶ) ἔχοντες**: supply καί
ἂν...ἐπορεύοντο: *they would...*; or 'they used to...' ἄν + ind. here indicates customary past action (S1790)
15 **ᾖδον**: *would...*; customary impf. ἀείδω
ἐχόρευον: *would...*; customary impf.
ὄψεσθαι: fut. dep. inf. ὁράω; μέλλω usually governs a fut. inf.
16 **ὡς**: *nearly*; 'as if,' in approximation
πεντεκαίδεκα πήχεων: *of...*; gen. measure
μίαν λόγχην: *a single spearpoint*; in contrast to Greek spears, which have a sharp spike on the butt-end for counter-balance and planting a spear in the ground
17 **ἔχον**: neuter pple modifies neuter δόρυ
ἐνέμενον: 3p impf. ἐμ-μένω
ἐπεὶ...παρέλθοιεν: *whenever...*; past general temporal clause, aor. opt. παρέρχομαι
18 **εἵποντο**: *would...*; impf. ἕπομαι
μαχούμενοι: μαχεόμενοι, fut. pple
ᾤκουν: ᾤκεον, impf. οἰκέω

δὲ ἐν τοῖς ὀχυροῖς, καὶ τὰ ἐπιτήδεια ἐν τούτοις ἀνακεκομισμένοι ἦσαν· ὥστε μηδὲν λαμβάνειν αὐτόθεν τοὺς Ἕλληνας, 20
ἀλλὰ διετράφησαν τοῖς κτήνεσιν ἃ ἐκ τῶν Ταόχων ἔλαβον.
18. ἐκ τούτων οἱ Ἕλληνες ἀφίκοντο ἐπὶ Ἅρπασον ποταμόν,
εὖρος τεττάρων πλέθρων. ἐντεῦθεν ἐπορεύθησαν διὰ Σκυθηνῶν σταθμοὺς τέτταρας παρασάγγας εἴκοσι διὰ πεδίου
εἰς κώμας· ἐν αἷς ἔμειναν ἡμέρας τρεῖς καὶ ἐπεσιτίσαντο. 25
19. ἐντεῦθεν διῆλθον σταθμοὺς τέτταρας παρασάγγας εἴκοσι

ἀνα-κομίζω: to bring back, store up, 2
Ἅρπασος, ὁ: Harpasus (river), 1
αὐτό-θεν: from the very spot or moment, 2
δια-τρέφω: to nourish, feed continually, 1
δι-έρχομαι: to go through, pass, 7
εἴκοσι: twenty, 5
ἐπι-σιτίζομαι: furnish oneself with food, 1
εὖρος, τό: breadth, width, 3
κτῆνος, -εος, τό: herd, flock, 3
μηδ-είς, μηδ-εμία, μηδ-έν: no one, nothing, 2
ὀχυρός, -ή, -όν: secure, strong, firm, 1
πλέθρον, τό: a plethron (=100 feet), 3
Σκυθηνοί, οἱ: Scythians, 2
Τάοχοι, οἱ: Taochians, 5
τέτταρες, -α: four, 6

19 **ὀχυροῖς**: i.e. positions, 'strongholds'
ἐν τούτοις: ἐν τοῖς ὀχυροῖς
ἀνακεκομισμένοι ἦσαν: periphastic plpf. mid. (pf. mid. pple + impf. εἰμί)
20 **ὥστε...**: *so that...*; result clause, μηδὲν is acc. obj., τοὺς Ἕλληνας is acc. subject
21 **διετράφησαν**: 3p aor. pass. dep.
τοῖς κτήνεσιν: dat. of means
22 **ἀφίκοντο**: aor. ἀφικνέομαι
ἐπὶ: *to...*
23 **εὖρος**: *in...*; acc. of respect
τεττάρων πλέθρων: *of...*; gen. of measure modifying Ἅρπασον ποταμόν
ἐπορεύθησαν: 3p aor. pass. dep. πορεύομαι: translate in the active
24 **σταθμοὺς...παρασάγγας**: *for...*; acc. of extent
25 **ἔμειναν**: aor. μένω
ἡμέρας τρεῖς: acc. of duration of time

πρὸς πόλιν μεγάλην καὶ εὐδαίμονα καὶ οἰκουμένην ἣ ἐκαλεῖτο 1
Γυμνιάς. ἐκ ταύτης †τῆς χώρας† ὁ ἄρχων τοῖς Ἕλλησιν
ἡγεμόνα πέμπει, ὅπως διὰ τῆς ἑαυτῶν πολεμίας χώρας ἄγοι
αὐτούς. 20. ἐλθὼν δ᾽ ἐκεῖνος λέγει ὅτι ἄξει αὐτοὺς πέντε ἡμερῶν
εἰς χωρίον ὅθεν ὄψονται θάλατταν· εἰ δὲ μή, τεθνάναι 5
ἐπηγγείλατο. καὶ ἡγούμενος ἐπειδὴ ἐνέβαλλεν εἰς τὴν
ἑαυτοῦ πολεμίαν, παρεκελεύετο αἴθειν καὶ φθείρειν τὴν
χώραν· ᾧ καὶ δῆλον ἐγένετο ὅτι τούτου ἕνεκα ἔλθοι, οὐ τῆς
τῶν Ἑλλήνων εὐνοίας. 21. καὶ ἀφικνοῦνται ἐπὶ τὸ ὄρος τῇ

αἴθω: to light up, kindle; burn, 1
Γυμνιάς, ὁ: Gymnias (town), 1
δῆλος, -η, -ον: clear, evident, conspicuous, 2
ἐμ-βάλλω: to put in, cast in, 2
ἕνεκα: for the sake of, because of, for (gen.), 2
ἐπ-αγγέλλω: to proclaim; promise, offer, 1
εὐ-δαίμων, -ον: happy, fortunate, blessed, 1
εὔ-νοια, ἡ: goodwill, favor, affection, 1
θάλαττα, ἡ: the sea, 7
θνῄσκω: to die, 3
καλέω: to call, summon, invite, 3
ὅ-θεν: from where, from which, 2
οἰκέω: to inhabit, dwell, live, 5
παρα-κελεύομαι: to order, urge, encourage, 2
πέμπω: send, conduct, convey, dispatch, 7
πέντε: five, 4
πόλις, ἡ: a city, 3
φθείρω: to destroy, ruin, 1

1 οἰκουμένην: *inhabited*
ἐκαλεῖτο: ἐκαλέετο, impf. pass.
2 ὁ ἄρχων: *leader*; i.e. of the town
3 ὅπως...ἄγοι: *so that...*; purpose with opt. in secondary seq.
ἑαυτῶν: *of his own*; the archon's people
4 ἐλθὼν: aor. pple ἔρχομαι
ἐκεῖνος: i.e. the guide
ἄξει: fut. ἄγω
πέντε ἡμερῶν: *within...*; gen. time within
5 ὄψονται: fut. deponent ὁράω
εἰ δὲ μή: ellipsis, assume the entire previous clause
τεθνάναι: pf. inf. θνῄσκω; the guide agrees to die if he does not succeed to lead them to the sea
6 ἐπηγγείλατο: aor.
ἡγούμενος: *guiding*
ἐνέβαλλεν: *he cast (the Greeks) into...*; i.e. led them into
τὴν πολεμίαν (χώραν)
7 ᾧ καὶ: *by this in fact*; 'by which in fact,' dat. of cause; καί is adverbial
8 ὅτι...ἔλθοι: *that...*; ind. disc. with aor. opt. ἔρχομαι in in secondary seq.; i.e. that the guide brought the Greeks on this particular path to destroy the guide' enemies
τῆς...εὐνοίας (ἕνεκα): add the preposition
9 Ἑλλήνων: *for...*; or 'toward,' objective genitive

πέμπτῃ ἡμέρᾳ· ὄνομα δὲ τῷ ὄρει ἦν Θήχης. ἐπεὶ δὲ οἱ 10
πρῶτοι ἐγένοντο ἐπὶ τοῦ ὄρους καὶ κατεῖδον τὴν θάλατταν,
κραυγὴ πολλὴ ἐγένετο. 22. ἀκούσας δὲ ὁ Ξενοφῶν καὶ οἱ
ὀπισθοφύλακες ᾠήθησαν ἔμπροσθεν ἄλλους ἐπιτίθεσθαι πολε-
μίους· εἵποντο γὰρ ὄπισθεν ἐκ τῆς καιομένης χώρας, καὶ
αὐτῶν οἱ ὀπισθοφύλακες ἀπέκτεινάν τέ τινας καὶ ἐζώγρησαν 15
ἐνέδραν ποιησάμενοι, καὶ γέρρα ἔλαβον δασειῶν βοῶν ὠμοβόεια ἀμφὶ τὰ εἴκοσιν. 23. ἐπειδὴ δὲ βοὴ πλείων τε ἐγίγνετο
καὶ ἐγγύτερον καὶ οἱ ἀεὶ ἐπιόντες ἔθεον δρόμῳ ἐπὶ τοὺς ἀεὶ

ἀεί: always, forever, in every case, 6
ἀπο-κτείνω: to kill, slay, 4
βοή, ἡ: shout, cry, 2
γέρρον, τό: wicker-work; wicker-shield, 6
δασύς, -εῖα, -ύ: thick; thicket (bush/woods), 5
δρόμος, ὁ: run, running, flight; race course, 5
ἐγγύ-θεν: from nearby, from near, 1
εἴκοσι: twenty, 5
ἔμ-προσθεν: in front, before, 5
ἐνέδρα, ἡ: a sitting (or lying) in ambush, 1
ἐπ-έρχομαι: to come upon; attack, 5
ἐπι-τίθημι: to put upon; add; set upon, attack 4
ζωγρέω: to take alive, take captive, 1
θάλαττα, ἡ: the sea, 7
Θήχης, ὁ: Theces (mtn.), 1
καθ-οράω: to look down, perceive, 7
κραυγή, ἡ: shouting, crying, screaming, 3
οἴομαι: to suppose, think, imagine, 3
ὄνομα, -ατος, τό: name, 1
πέμπτος, -η, -ον: fifth, 1
ὠμοβόειος, -α, -ον: of raw oxhide, 2

10 **πέμπτῃ ἡμέρᾳ**: dat. of time when
τῷ ὄρε-ι: dat. of possession ὄρος with impf. εἰμί
11 **κατεῖδον**: aor. καθοράω
13 **ᾠήθησαν**: aor. pass. dep. οἴομαι
ἄλλους...ἐπιτίθεσθαι: *that...*; ind. disc. ἄλλους πολεμίους is acc. subject
14 **εἵποντο**: impf. ἕπομαι ; supply 'enemies' as subject
15 **αὐτῶν**: i.e. enemies; partitive with τινας
16 **ἐνέδραν ποιησάμενοι**: *(by)...*; causal pple
ἔλαβον: *they took*
δασειῶν βοῶν: gen. of material
ἀμφὶ: *about...*; in approximation
17 **πλείων**: *louder*; predicate adj.
18 **ἐγγύτερον**: comparative adv.
ἀεὶ: *constantly, continuously*
οἱ...ἐπιόντες: *those coming up...*; i.e. the Greeks who crest the hill and see the sea; ἐπέρχομαι
δρόμῳ: *in a run*; dat. of manner

βοῶντας καὶ πολλῷ μείζων ἐγίγνετο ἡ βοὴ ὅσῳ δὴ πλείους ἐγίγνοντο, 24. *ἐδόκει δὴ μεῖζόν τι εἶναι τῷ Ξενοφῶντι, καὶ* 20 *ἀναβὰς ἐφ' ἵππον καὶ Λύκιον καὶ τοὺς ἱππέας ἀναλαβὼν παρεβοήθει· καὶ τάχα δὴ ἀκούουσι βοώντων τῶν στρατιωτῶν 'θάλαττα θάλαττα' καὶ παρεγγυώντων. ἔνθα δὴ ἔθεον πάντες καὶ οἱ ὀπισθοφύλακες, καὶ τὰ ὑποζύγια ἠλαύνετο καὶ οἱ*

ἀνα-λαμβάνω: to take up, find, resume, 1
βοάω: to shout, cry outloud, 5
βοή, ἡ: shout, cry, 2
ἐλαύνω: to march, ride, drive, 2
θάλαττα, ἡ: the sea, 7
Λύκιος, ὁ: Lycius, 3
μείζων, -ον (-ονος): greater, 4
παρα-βοηθέω: to come to help, 1
παρ-εγγυάω: to pass on word or command 5
τάχα: presently, quickly; perhaps, 2

19 **πολλῷ**: *much*; 'by much,' dat. of degree of difference
μείζων: i.e. louder
ὅσῳ δὴ: *by exactly as much as…*; dat. of degree of difference
πλείο(ν)ες: *more numerous*; pred. nom.
20 **ἐγίγνοντο**: *they…*; i.e. Greek soldiers
δὴ: *then, accordingly*
μεῖζόν τι: *i.e. important*; nom. pred.
τῷ Ξενοφῶντι: dat. of reference (from his viewpoint)
21 **ἀναβὰς**: nom. sg. aor. pple ἀναβαίνω
ἐφ': *upon…*
καὶ…καὶ: *both…and*; both acc. are objects of the following aor. pple
22 **παρεβοήθει**: Xenophon assumes from the shouting that his men are being attacked
τάχα δὴ: *very quickly*; δή is emphatic
βοώντων τῶν στρατιωτῶν: gen. obj. of ἀκούουσι (gen. of source)
23 **ἔνθα δὴ**: *just then*
ἔθεον: *began to…*; inchoative impf.
24 **ἠλαύνετο**: *began to…*; inchoative impf.

ἵπποι. 25. ἐπεὶ δὲ ἀφίκοντο πάντες ἐπὶ τὸ ἄκρον, ἐνταῦθα δὴ 1
περιέβαλλον ἀλλήλους καὶ στρατηγοὺς καὶ λοχαγοὺς δα-
κρύοντες. καὶ ἐξαπίνης ὅτου δὴ παρεγγυήσαντος οἱ στρατιῶται φέρουσι λίθους καὶ ποιοῦσι κολωνὸν μέγαν. 26. ἐνταῦθα
ἀνετίθεσαν δερμάτων πλῆθος ὠμοβοείων καὶ βακτηρίας καὶ 5
τὰ αἰχμάλωτα γέρρα, καὶ ὁ ἡγεμὼν αὐτός τε κατέτεμνε τὰ
γέρρα καὶ τοῖς ἄλλοις διεκελεύετο. 27. μετὰ ταῦτα τὸν ἡγεμόνα
οἱ Ἕλληνες ἀποπέμπουσι δῶρα δόντες ἀπὸ κοινοῦ ἵππον καὶ
φιάλην ἀργυρᾶν καὶ σκευὴν Περσικὴν καὶ δαρεικοὺς δέκα·

αἰχμ-άλωτος, -ον: taken by spear, captive, 4
ἀνα-τίθημι: to set up, dedicate, attribute 1
ἀπο-πέμπω: to send away, dismiss, 1
ἀργυρέος, -α, -ον: of silver, 1
βακτηρία, ἡ: staff, cane; (officer's) wand, 1
γέρρον, τό: wicker-work; wicker-shield, 6
δακρύω: to weep, shed tears, 1
Δαρεικός, ὁ: Daric, gold coin (Persian), 1
δέκα: ten, 7
δέρμα, -ατος, τό: the skin, hide, 2
δια-κελεύω: encourage (one another), urge 2
δῶρον, τό: a gift, present, 1
ἐξαπίνης: suddenly, on the sudden 1
κατα-τέμνω: to cut up, cut in pieces, 1
κοινός, -ή, -όν: common, ordinary; public, 3
κολωνός, ὁ: heap of stones; hilltop, hill, 1
ὅστις, ἥτις, ὅ τι: whoever, which-, whatever, 4
παρ-εγγυάω: to pass on word or command 5
περι-βάλλω: to throw round; embrace, 1
Περσικός, -ή, -όν: Persian, 4
πλῆθος, ἡ: crowd, multitude; size, 4
σκευή, ἡ: attire, apparel; equipment, 2
φιάλη, ἡ: bowl, vessel, 1
ὠμοβόειος, -α, -ον: of raw oxhide, 2

1 ἐνταῦθα δή: *just at that point, just then*
3 ὅτου δὴ παρεγγυήσαντος: *whoever in fact passing word*; =οὗτινος, gen. sg. of ὅστις in a gen. abs.; perhaps an ellipsis for τινός, ὅστις δὴ ἦν, 'someone, whoever in fact it was'
8 δόντες: nom. pl. aor. pple δίδωμι
ἀπὸ κοινοῦ: i.e. from what is held in common; parallel to the gift of rings made by individual soldiers below

ᾔτει δὲ μάλιστα τοὺς δακτυλίους, καὶ ἔλαβε πολλοὺς παρὰ 10
τῶν στρατιωτῶν. κώμην δὲ δείξας αὐτοῖς οὗ σκηνήσουσι
καὶ τὴν ὁδὸν ἣν πορεύσονται εἰς Μάκρωνας, ἐπεὶ ἑσπέρα
ἐγένετο, ᾤχετο τῆς νυκτὸς ἀπιών.

1. ἐντεῦθεν δ᾽ ἐπορεύθησαν οἱ Ἕλληνες διὰ Μακρώνων
σταθμοὺς τρεῖς παρασάγγας δέκα. τῇ πρώτῃ δὲ ἡμέρᾳ 15
ἀφίκοντο ἐπὶ τὸν ποταμὸν ὃς ὥριζε τὴν τῶν Μακρώνων καὶ
τὴν τῶν Σκυθηνῶν. 2. εἶχον δ᾽ ὑπὲρ δεξιῶν χωρίον οἷον
χαλεπώτατον καὶ ἐξ ἀριστερᾶς ἄλλον ποταμόν, εἰς ὃν ἐνέ-

αἰτέω: to ask, ask for, beg, 1
ἀριστερός, -ά, -όν: left, on the left, 4
δακτύλιος, -α, -ον: ring, 1
δείκνυμι: to show, indicate, 4
δέκα: ten, 7
δεξιός, -ά, -όν: on the right hand or side, 5
ἐμ-βάλλω: to put in, cast in, 2
ἑσπέρα, ἡ: evening, 2
Μάκρόνες, οἱ: Macronians, 7
μάλιστα: most of all; certainly, especially, 5
οἷος, -α, -ον: of what sort, as, 5
οἴχομαι: to go, go off, depart, 7
ὁρίζω: to divide, define, 3
οὗ: where, 2
σκηνέω: to encamp, bivouac, set up tents, 5
Σκυθηνοί, οἱ: Scythians, 2
χαλεπός, -ά, -όν: difficult, hard, harmful, 3

10 **ᾔτει**: 3s impf. αἰτέω; the guide is subject
παρὰ: *from*...; gen. of source
11 **δείξας**: aor. pple
οὗ: *where*...; relative adv.
12 **ἣν**: *along which*
13 **ᾤχετο**: impf. οἴχομαι
τῆς νυκτὸς: *during*...; gen. of time within
ἀπιών: pple ἀπέρχομαι
14 **ἐπορεύθησαν**: 3p aor. pass. dep. πορεύομαι: translate in active
15 **σταθμοὺς... παρασάγγας**: *for*...; acc. of extent
τῇ...ἡμέρᾳ: dat. of time when
16 **ἀφίκοντο**: aor. ἀφικνέομαι
τὴν (χώραν): *the land*
17 **ὑπὲρ δεξιῶν**: *over on the right*; 'above the right'
οἷον χαλεπώτατον: *as...as possible*; 'which sort (was) very harsh,' an idiom similar to ὡς, ὅτι + superlative
18 **ἐξ ἀριστερᾶς**: *on the left*; 'from the left'
εἰς ὃν: *into which*; acc. place to which
ἐνέβαλλεν: i.e. flows into

βαλλεν ὁ ὁρίζων, δι' οὗ ἔδει διαβῆναι. ἦν δὲ οὗτος δασὺς δένδρεσι παχέσι μὲν οὔ, πυκνοῖς δέ. ταῦτ' ἐπεὶ προσῆλθον 20 οἱ Ἕλληνες ἔκοπτον, σπεύδοντες ἐκ τοῦ χωρίου ὡς τάχιστα ἐξελθεῖν. 3. οἱ δὲ Μάκρωνες ἔχοντες γέρρα καὶ λόγχας καὶ τριχίνους χιτῶνας κατ' ἀντιπέραν τῆς διαβάσεως παρατεταγμένοι ἦσαν καὶ ἀλλήλοις διεκελεύοντο καὶ λίθους εἰς τὸν ποταμὸν ἔρριπτον· ἐξικνοῦντο γὰρ οὒ οὐδ' ἔβλαπτον οὐδέν. 25

4. ἔνθα δὴ προσέρχεται Ξενοφῶντι τῶν πελταστῶν ἀνὴρ

ἀντι-πέρα, ἡ: opposite shore, other side, 1
βλάπτω: to harm, hurt, damage, 1
γέρρον, τό: wicker-work; wicker-shield, 6
δασύς, -εῖα, -ύ: thick; thicket (bush/woods), 5
δένδρ(ε)ον, τό: tree, 6
διά-βασις, -εως, ἡ: a crossing, 3
δια-κελεύω: encourage (on another), urge 2
ἐξ-έρχομαι: to go out, come out, 1
ἐξ-ικνέομαι: to arrive at, reach, 3
κόπτω: to strike, hack, knock, 2
λόγχη, ἡ: spearheard; spear, lance, 4
Μάκρόνες, οἱ: Macronians, 7
ὁρίζω: to divide, define, 3
παρα-τάττω: draw up in battle order, 5
παχύς, -εῖα, -ύ: massive, 1
πυκνός, -ή, -όν: thick, close-packed, 2
ῥίπτω: to throw, cast, hurl, 3
σπεύδω: to be eager, be urgent, 3
τριχίνους, -η, -ον: of hair, of fur, 1
χιτών, -ῶνος, ἡ: tunic, 1

19 **ὁ ὁρίζων (ποταμός)**: *the dividing river*; i.e. the boundary river in line 16
δι(ὰ) οὗ: *over...*
διαβῆναι: aor. inf.
20 **δένδρεσι παχέσι μὲν οὔ, πυκνοῖς δέ**: *with...*; dat pl. of means;
ταῦτ(α): *these (trees)*; obj. of ἔκοπτον
21 **ὡς τάχιστα**: *as...as possible*; ὡς + superlative (here, superlative adv.)
22 **ἐξελθεῖν**: aor. inf. ἐξέρχομαι
23 **κατ(ὰ) ἀντιπέραν**: *on the opposite shore*
παρατεταγμένοι ἦσαν: periphrastic plpf. pass. (pf. pass. pple + impf. εἰμί)
25 **ἔρριπτον**: impf. ῥίπτω
ἐξικνοῦντο...οὒ: the λίθοι are subject
οὐδὲ...οὐδέν: *nor...anything*
26 **ἔνθα δὴ**: *just then*
Ξενοφῶντι: *to...*; dat. of compound verb

Ἀθήνησι φάσκων δεδουλευκέναι, λέγων ὅτι γιγνώσκοι τὴν 1
φωνὴν τῶν ἀνθρώπων. 'καὶ οἶμαι,' ἔφη, 'ἐμὴν ταύτην πατρίδα
εἶναι· καὶ εἰ μή τι κωλύει, ἐθέλω αὐτοῖς διαλεχθῆναι.'
5. 'ἀλλ' οὐδὲν κωλύει,' ἔφη, 'ἀλλὰ διαλέγου καὶ μάθε πρῶτον
τίνες εἰσίν.' οἱ δ' εἶπον ἐρωτήσαντος ὅτι 'Μάκρωνες.' 'ἐρώτα 5
τοίνυν,' ἔφη, 'αὐτοὺς τί ἀντιτετάχαται καὶ χρῄζουσιν ἡμῖν
πολέμιοι εἶναι.' 6. οἱ δ' ἀπεκρίναντο ὅτι 'καὶ ὑμεῖς ἐπὶ τὴν
ἡμετέραν χώραν ἔρχεσθε.' λέγειν ἐκέλευον οἱ στρατηγοὶ
ὅτι 'οὐ κακῶς γε ποιήσοντες, ἀλλὰ βασιλεῖ πολεμήσαντες

Ἀθῆναι, αἱ: Athens, 1
ἀντι-τάττω: to marshall or set opposite, 1
ἀπο-κρίνομαι: to answer, reply, 3
γε: at least, at any rate; indeed, in fact, 3
γιγνώσκω: to come to know, learn, realize, 2
δια-λέγομαι: to converse with, discuss, 5
δουλεύω: to be a slave, 1
ἐμός, -ή, -όν: my, mine, 1
ἡμεῖς: we, 5
ἡμέτερος, -α, -ον: our, 1
κακός, -ή, -όν: bad, base, cowardly, evil, 5
Μάκρόνες, οἱ: Macronians, 7
μανθάνω: to learn, understand, 1
οἴομαι: to suppose, think, imagine, 3
πατρίς, -ίδος: fatherland, native land, 1
πολεμέω: wage war, make war, (+ dat.), 2
τοί-νυν: well then; therefore, accordingly, 2
ὑμεῖς: you, 5
φάσκω: say, claim, speak, 2
φωνή, ἡ: speech, voice; dialect, 1
χρῄζω: to need, lack; want, ask for, 1

1 **Ἀθήνησι**: locative, the city Athens is plural
δεδουλευκέναι: *that he had…*; pf. act. inf. in secondary seq.
ὅτι γιγνώσκοι: *that…*; ind. disc. with opt. replacing indicative in secondary seq.; the Greek recognized the language of the Macronians as his native tongue
2 **οἶμαι**: οἴομαι
καὶ: *actually, in fact*; adv.
ἔφη: i.e. the former slave; impf. φημί
ταύτην…εἶναι: *that…*; ind. disc. with acc. subject; ἐμὴν πατρίδα is acc. predicate
3 **κωλύει**: add 'me' as object
διαλεχθῆναι: aor. pass. dep.
4 **κωλύει**: add 'you' as object; Xenophon is now talking
διαλέγου: διαλεγε(σ)ο, pres. mid. imper.
μάθε: aor. imper.
πρῶτον: adverbial acc.
5 **τίνες εἰσίν**: ind. question with 3p εἰμί
οἱ δ': *and they…*; i.e the Macronians approached by the former slave
εἶπον: aor. λέγω
(αὐτοῦ) ἐρωτήσαντος: gen. abs., the missing noun αὐτοῦ, 'him,' refers to the former slave
ὅτι Μάκρωνες (εἶεν): *that…*; add linking verb
ἐρώτα: ἐρώταε, pres. imperative
6 **ἔφη**: Xenophon is talking to the former slave, who is acting as interpreter; φιμί
τί: *why…*; ind. question, 'in respect to what?'
ἀντιτετάχαται: pf. mind.
7 **οἱ δ'**: *and they…*; again, the Macronians,
καὶ: *actually, in fact*; adverbial
8 **ἐκέλευον**: supply "the former slave"
9 **κακῶς γε ποιήσοντες**: *not intending…*; ; a fut. pple expressing purpose; the idiom κακῶς ποιεῖν means 'to treat poorly;' γε emphasizes the preceding wor
βασιλεῖ: *with…*; dat. of association

ἀπερχόμεθα εἰς τὴν Ἑλλάδα, καὶ ἐπὶ θάλατταν βουλόμεθα 10
ἀφικέσθαι.’ 7. *ἠρώτων ἐκεῖνοι εἰ δοῖεν ἂν τούτων τὰ πιστά.*
οἱ δ’ ἔφασαν καὶ δοῦναι καὶ λαβεῖν ἐθέλειν. ἐντεῦθεν
διδόασιν οἱ Μάκρωνες βαρβαρικὴν λόγχην τοῖς Ἕλλησιν,
οἱ δὲ Ἕλληνες ἐκείνοις Ἑλληνικήν· ταῦτα γὰρ ἔφασαν
πιστὰ εἶναι· θεοὺς δ’ ἐπεμαρτύραντο ἀμφότεροι. 15

8. *μετὰ δὲ τὰ πιστὰ εὐθὺς οἱ Μάκρωνες τὰ δένδρα συνεξέ-*
κοπτον τήν τε ὁδὸν ὡδοποίουν ὡς διαβιβάσοντες ἐν μέσοις
ἀναμεμιγμένοι τοῖς Ἕλλησι, καὶ ἀγορὰν οἵαν ἐδύναντο

ἀγορά, ἡ: marketplace, exchange; assembly 2
ἀμφότερος, -α, -ον: each of two, both, 2
ἀνα-μίσγω: to mingle with, mix with, 1
βαρβαρικός, -η, -ον: foreigner, barbarian, 2
δένδρον, τό: tree, 6
δια-βιβάζω: to carry across, transport, 1
Ἑλλάς, -άδος, ἡ : Greece, 1
Ἑλληνικός, -ή, -όν: Greek, Hellenic, 3
ἐπι-μαρτύρομαι: appeal to, call as witness, 1
θάλαττα, ἡ: the sea, 7
θεός, ὁ: a god, divinity, 3
λόγχη, ἡ: spearheard; spear, lance, 4
Μάκρόνες, οἱ: Macronians, 7
μέσος, -η, -ον: middle, in the middle of, 5
ὁδο-ποιέω: to make (a road), 1
οἷος, -α, -ον: of what sort, as, 5
πιστός, -ή, -όν:: trustworthy, loyal; credible 4
συν-εκ-κόπτω: to help in cutting, 1

11 **ἠρώτων**: ἐρώταον, 3p impf. ἐρωτάω
ἐκεῖνοι: the Macronians
εἰ δοῖεν ἂν: *whether they would…*; ind. question, 3p aor. potential opt. δίδωμι
τὰ πιστά: *pledges*
12 **ἔφασαν**: aor. φημί; the Greeks are subject
καὶ...καὶ... ἐθέλειν: *that they...both...and...* ind. disc., assume the subject of the main clause as acc. subject
δοῦναι: aor. inf. δίδωμι
13 **διδόασιν**: 3p pres.
τοῖς Ἕλλησιν: dat. ind. obj.
14 **Ἑλληνικήν (λόγχην διδόασιν)**
15 **πιστὰ**: *pledges*
16 **τὰ πιστὰ**: *pledges*
17 **ὡς διαβιβάσοντες**: *so that…*; ‘so as’ ὡς + fut. pple expresses purpose; add the Greeks the object
ἐν μέσοις... τοῖς Ἕλλησι: a single construction divided by a pple
18 **ἀναμεμιγμένοι**: pf. mid. pple; i.e. engage or interact with
οἷαν ἐδύναντο (παρέχειν): *such as…*; relative clause

παρεῖχον, καὶ παρήγαγον ἐν τρισὶν ἡμέραις ἕως ἐπὶ τὰ Κόλχων ὅρια κατέστησαν τοὺς Ἕλληνας. 9. *ἐνταῦθα ἦν ὄρος* 20 *μέγα, προσβατὸν δέ· καὶ ἐπὶ τούτου οἱ Κόλχοι παρατεταγμένοι ἦσαν. καὶ τὸ μὲν πρῶτον οἱ Ἕλληνες ἀντιπαρετάξαντο φάλαγγα, ὡς οὕτως ἄξοντες πρὸς τὸ ὄρος· ἔπειτα δὲ ἔδοξε τοῖς στρατηγοῖς βουλεύσασθαι συλλεγεῖσιν ὅπως ὡς κάλλιστα ἀγωνιοῦνται.* 10. *ἔλεξεν οὖν Ξενοφῶν ὅτι δοκοίη* 25 *παύσαντας τὴν φάλαγγα λόχους ὀρθίους ποιῆσαι· 'ἡ μὲν γὰρ*

ἀγωνίζομαι: to contend, compete, fight, 3
ἀντι-παρα-τάττομαι: to draw up against, 1
βουλεύω: to deliberate, plan, take counsel, 5
ἔπ-ειτα: then, next, secondly, 4
ἕως: until, as long as, 1
καθ-ίστημι: to station, appoint; *intransitive*, stand, 4
Καλλίμαχος, ὁ: Callimachus, 5
Κόλχοι, οἱ: Colchians, 5
μέγας, μεγάλη, μέγα: big, great, important, 8
ὅριον, τό: boundary, border, limit, 1
παρ-άγω: to lead along, go alongside, 3
παρα-τάττω: draw up in battle order, 5
παρ-έχω: to provide, furnish, supply, 5
παύω: to stop, make cease, 3
προσ-βατός, -ή, -όν: accessible, 2
συλ-λέγω: to collect, gather, 5

19 **παρεῖχον**: impf. παρέχω
παρήγαγον: aor.; Marconians guided the Greeks through the territory
τρίσιν: dat. pl. τρεῖς
20 **κατέστησαν**: *set*; aor. the Marconians are subject
ἦν: impf. εἰμί
21 **ἐπὶ...**: *upon...*
παρατεταγμένοι ἦσαν: periphrastic plpf. pass. (pf. pass. pple + impf. εἰμί)
22 **τὸ πρῶτον**: *at first, first*; adverbial acc.
ὡς...ἄξοντες: *so that...*; 'so as...' ὡς + fut. pple. expressing purpose
οὕτως: i.e. in formation
24 **ἔδοξε**: *it seemed best*
24 **συλλεγεῖσιν**: *with those...*; dat. pl. aor. pass. pple
ὅπως...ἀγωνιοῦνται: *how...*; ind. question with fut. mid.
ὡς κάλλιστα: *as...as possible*; ὡς + superlative adv. καλῶς, 'well'
25 **ὅτι δοκοίη**: ind. disc. with 3s opt. δοκέω, 'seem best,' in secondary sequence
26 **παύσαντας**: transitive with φάλαγγα
ὀρθίους: *in columns*; i.e. single file
ποιῆσαι: *make (x) (y)*; inf.governs a double acc. (acc. obj. and acc. pred.)
ἡ μὲν γὰρ...: in the middle of ind. disc., Xenophon slips into direct disc. (note the punctuation) with 1p verbs

φάλαγξ διασπασθήσεται εὐθύς· τῇ μὲν γὰρ ἄνοδον τῇ δὲ 1
εὔοδον εὑρήσομεν τὸ ὄρος· καὶ εὐθὺς τοῦτο ἀθυμίαν ποιήσει
ὅταν τεταγμένοι εἰς φάλαγγα ταύτην διεσπασμένην ὁρῶσιν.
11. ἔπειτα ἢν μὲν ἐπὶ πολλῶν τεταγμένοι προσάγωμεν, περιτ-
τεύσουσιν ἡμῶν οἱ πολέμιοι καὶ τοῖς περιττοῖς χρήσονται 5
ὅ τι ἂν βούλωνται· ἐὰν δὲ ἐπ᾽ ὀλίγων τεταγμένοι ὦμεν,
οὐδὲν ἂν εἴη θαυμαστὸν εἰ διακοπείη ἡμῶν ἡ φάλαγξ ὑπὸ
ἀθρόων καὶ βελῶν καὶ ἀνθρώπων πολλῶν ἐμπεσόντων· εἰ δέ
πῃ τοῦτο ἔσται, τῇ ὅλῃ φάλαγγι κακὸν ἔσται. 12. ἀλλά μοι δοκεῖ

ἀθρόοι, -αι, -α: in a mass, all together, 4
ἀ-θυμία ἡ: faintheartedness, discouragement 3
ἄν-οδος, -ον: hard to pass, inaccessible, 1
βέλος, -εος, τό: missle, arrow, dart, 2
δια-κόπτω: to cut through, break in two, 2
δια-σπάω: to pull apart, separate, 3
ἐάν: εἰ ἄν, if (+ subj.), 2
ἐμ-πίπτω: to fall upon, 1
ἔπ-ειτα: then, next, secondly, 4
εὔ-οδος, -ον: easy to pass, accessible 3
εὑρίσκω: to find, discover, devise, invent, 4
ἡμεῖς: we, 5
θαυμαστός, -ή, -όν: wonderful, marvelous, strange, 2
κακός, -ή, -όν: bad, base, cowardly, evil, 5
ὅλος, -η, -ον: whole, entire, complete, 5
ὅταν: ὅτε ἄν, whenever, 5
περιττεύω: to go beyond, outflank (gen) 1
περιττός, -η, -ον: surplus, reserve, excess, 1
πῃ: in some way, somehow, 2
προσ-άγω: to bring to, attach; advance, 3
τάττω: post, station, arrange, order, 6
χράομαι: use, employ, enjoy, indulge (dat) 6

1 **διασπασθήσεται**: 3s fut. pass.
τῇ μὲν...τῇ δὲ: *here...there*
2 **εὑρήσομεν**: 1p fut.
ποιήσει: *will cause*
3 **ὅταν...ὁρῶσιν**: *whenever (the soldiers)...*; general temporal clause, pres. subj. ὁράω
τεταγμένοι: pf. pass. pple τάττω
ταύτην: i.e. φάλαγγα ; obj. of ὁρῶσιν
διεσπασμένην: pf. pass. pple
4 **ἔπειτα**: *furthermore, next*
ἢν...προσάγωμεν...χρήσονται: *if...*; ἐάν, fut. more vivid (εἰ ἄν + subj., fut.)
ἐπὶ πολλῶν: *many deep*; 'in the case of many,' a phalanx with many men behind one another will not be wide in front
τεταγμένοι: pf. pass. pple τάττω
5 **ἡμῶν**: obj. of verb (gen. of comparison)
τοῖς περιττοῖς: *surplus (troops)*; dat. obj.
6 **ὅ τι ἂν βούλωνται**: *for whatever...*; the missing antecedent is inner acc. of the verb χρήσονται: 'make whatever (use)...'
ἐὰν...τεταγμένοι ὦμεν: periphrastic 1p pf. pass. subj. (pf. pass. pple + pres. subj. εἰμί) protasis in a mixed condition
ἐπὶ ὀλίγων: *a few deep*; 'in the case of...'
7 **ἂν εἴη...εἰ διακοπείη**: *would be..., if our phalanx should...*; fut. less vivid condition (εἰ opt., ἄν + opt.)
8 **ὑπο... ἐμπεσόντω**: *because of...*; gen. of cause and agent; supply 'us' as object; aor. pple ἐμπίπτω
καὶ...καὶ...: *both... and...*
εἰ...ἔσται,...ἐσται: an emotional fut. more vivid (εἰ fut., fut.), where a fut. replaces ἄν + subj. for heightened emotion
8 **τῇ ὅλῃ φάλαγγι**: *for...*; dat. of interest
ἔσται: *it will be*; impersonal

ὀρθίους τοὺς λόχους ποιησαμένους τοσοῦτον χωρίον κατα- 10
σχεῖν διαλιπόντας τοῖς λόχοις ὅσον ἔξω τοὺς ἐσχάτους λόχους
γενέσθαι τῶν πολεμίων κεράτων· καὶ οὕτως ἐσόμεθα τῆς
τε τῶν πολεμίων φάλαγγος ἔξω [οἱ ἔσχατοι λόχοι], καὶ
ὀρθίους ἄγοντες οἱ κράτιστοι ἡμῶν πρῶτοι προσίασιν, ᾗ τε
ἂν εὔοδον ᾖ, ταύτῃ ἕκαστος ἄξει [ὁ λόχος]. 13. καὶ εἴς τε τὸ 15
διαλεῖπον οὐ ῥᾴδιον ἔσται τοῖς πολεμίοις εἰσελθεῖν ἔνθεν
καὶ ἔνθεν λόχων ὄντων, διακόψαι τε οὐ ῥᾴδιον ἔσται λόχον
ὄρθιον προσιόντα. ἄν τέ τις πιέζηται τῶν λόχων, ὁ πλησίον

δια-κόπτω: to knock through, break in two, 2
δια-λείπω: to leave or set at intervals, 3
εἰσ-έρχομαι: to go to, approach; enter, 2
ἔξω: out of (+ gen.); adv. outside, 5
ἔσχατος, -η, -ον: extreme, last, furthest, 2
εὔ-οδος, -ον: easy to pass, accessible, 3
ἡμεῖς: we, 5
κατ-έχω: to hold fast, take possession of, 7
κέρας, -ατος, τό: horn, wing (of an army), 2
κράτιστος, -η, -ον: best; strongest, 7
οὔ-πω: not yet, 1
πιέζω: press, weigh down, squeeze, 1
πλησίος, -η, -ον: near, close to; neighbors, 5
ῥᾴδιος, -α, -ον: easy, ready, 3
τοσοῦτος, -αύτη, -οῦτο: so great, so much, so many, 3

10 **(ἡμᾶς) ὀρθίους ...κατασχεῖν**: *that (we)...*; add ἡμᾶς as acc. subject
ὀρθίους: *in columns*; i.e. single file lines
ποιησαμένους: *making (x) (y)*; governing a double acc.
11 **διαλιπόντας τοῖς λόχοις**: *leaving the units at intervals*; aor. dat. of compound verb
ὅσον...λόχους γενέσθαι: *so far as to...*; + acc. + inf. equiv. to a result clause; ὅσος can often mean 'enough for' or 'sufficient to' with an inf. (S2497)
12 **τῶν πολεμίων κεράτων**: gen. obj. of ἔξω
ἐσόμεθα: 1p fut. dep. εἰμί
τῆς...φάλαγγος: gen. object of ἔξω
[οἱ ἔσχατοι λόχοι]: Do not translate. The editor thinks this has been inserted later.
14 **ἡμῶν**: *of us (captains)*; partitive gen.
προσίασιν: 3p fut. προσέρχομαι
ᾗ...ταύτῃ: *in whichever way...in this way*; dat. of manner; ᾗ is a relative pronoun and ταύτῃ is the antecedent
15 **ἂν...ᾖ**: 3s pres. subj. εἰμί, general relative
ἄξει: fut.
τε...τε...τε...: *and...and...and...*; Xenophon unusually but repeatedly uses τε to connect sentences (D499, S2968)
εἴς τε τὸ διαλεῖπον: *into the interval*; i. e. the space between columns; neut. sg. pple
16 **ἔσται**: *it will be...*; fut. deponent εἰμί
τοῖς πολεμίοις: *for...*; dat. of interest
εἰσελθεῖν: aor. inf. εἰσέρχομαι
ἔνθεν καὶ ἔνθεν: *on one side and the other*
17 **λόχων ὄντων**: gen. abs.
διακόψαι: aor. inf. διακόπτω
λόχον: *each company/unit*; obj. of inf.
18 **ὄρθιον**: *in a column*
προσιόντα: acc. sg. pple προσέρχομαι
ἄν...πιέζηται: *if...*; ἐάν, pres. pass. subj. in a fut. more vivid condition
τῶν λόχων: partitive gen. with τις
ὁ πλησίον (λόχος): *the (company) nearby*; adverbial acc....

Xenophon recommends forming a checkboard pattern of units—with intervals inbetween—to confront the single phalanx of the enemy. The Romans used this formation with great success.

βοηθήσει. ἤν τε εἷς πῃ δυνηθῇ τῶν λόχων ἐπὶ τὸ ἄκρον
ἀναβῆναι, οὐδεὶς μηκέτι μείνῃ τῶν πολεμίων.' 14. ταῦτα ἔδοξε, 20
καὶ ἐποίουν ὀρθίους τοὺς λόχους. Ξενοφῶν δὲ ἀπιὼν ἐπὶ
τὸ εὐώνυμον ἀπὸ τοῦ δεξιοῦ ἔλεγε τοῖς στρατιώταις· 'ἄνδρες,
οὗτοί εἰσιν οὓς ὁρᾶτε μόνοι ἔτι ἡμῖν ἐμποδὼν τὸ μὴ ἤδη
εἶναι ἔνθα πάλαι σπεύδομεν· τούτους, ἤν πως δυνώμεθα,
καὶ ὠμοὺς δεῖ καταφαγεῖν. 25

15. ἐπεὶ δ' ἐν ταῖς χώραις ἕκαστοι ἐγένοντο καὶ τοὺς λόχους

βοηθέω: to come to aid, to assist, aid, 2
δεξιός, -ά, -όν: on the right hand or side, 5
ἐμποδὼν: in the way, in one's path, 1
ἔτι: still, besides, further, 7
εὐ-ώνυμος, -ον: of good name; left (side), 3
ἡμεῖς: we, 5
κατα-εσθίω: to eat up, devour, 1
μηκέτι: no longer, no more, 1
μόνος, -η, -ον: alone, only, solitary, 2
πάλαι: long ago, formerly, of old, 2
πῃ: in some way, somehow, 2
πως: somehow, in any way, 4
σπεύδω: to be eager, be urgent, 3
ὠμός, -ή, -όν: raw, uncooked, 1

19 **ἤν...δυνηθῇ**: *if...*; ἐάν, 3s aor. pass. dep. subj. in a mixed condition
τε: *and*; Xenophon throughout this passage employs τε to connect sentences (S2968)
εἷς...τῶν λόχων: nom. subj., partitive gen.
20 **ἀναβῆναι**: aor. inf. ἀναβαίνω
μηκετι μείνῃ: *Don't let ...*; or 'let...not...' a prohibitive subj. (μή + aor. subj.); 3s aor. subj. μένω
ἔδοξε: *seemed best*
21 **ὀρθίους**: *in columns*; i.e. single file
ἀπιὼν: nom. sg. pple ἀπέρχομαι ; Cheirisophus holds the right wing. Xenophon comes from a conference with Cheirisophus on the right and returns to his own troops on the left wing.
23 **οὗτοί**: i.e. the enemy
εἰσιν: 3p pres. εἰμί
οὓς: *(the ones) whom...*; relative
ἡμῖν: *for...*; dat. of interest
ἐμποδὼν τὸ μὴ ἤδη εἶναι: *in the way from (our) being now...*; 'lest being...' μή + inf. (or, as here, articular inf.) following verbs of hindering or their equivalent (S2740)
24 **ἔνθα**: *where...*; relative adv.
σπεύδομεν: *we have been hastening*; πάλαι + pres. is often equiv. to pf. progressive in English
ἤν...δυνώμεθα: *if...*; ἐάν + subj.
25 **καταφαγεῖν**: aor. inf. κατα-εσθίω ; i.e. utterly destroy the enemy.

ὀρθίους ἐποιήσαντο, ἐγένοντο μὲν λόχοι τῶν ὁπλιτῶν ἀμφὶ 1
τοὺς ὀγδοήκοντα, ὁ δὲ λόχος ἕκαστος σχεδὸν εἰς τοὺς ἑκατόν·
τοὺς δὲ πελταστὰς καὶ τοὺς τοξότας τριχῇ ἐποιήσαντο, τοὺς
μὲν τοῦ εὐωνύμου ἔξω, τοὺς δὲ τοῦ δεξιοῦ, τοὺς δὲ κατὰ
μέσον, σχεδὸν ἑξακοσίους ἑκάστους. 16. ἐκ τούτου παρηγ- 5
γύησαν οἱ στρατηγοὶ εὔχεσθαι· εὐξάμενοι δὲ καὶ παιανίσαντες ἐπορεύοντο. καὶ Χειρίσοφος μὲν καὶ Ξενοφῶν καὶ
οἱ σὺν αὐτοῖς πελτασταὶ τῆς τῶν πολεμίων φάλαγγος ἔξω
γενόμενοι ἐπορεύοντο· 17. οἱ δὲ πολέμιοι ὡς εἶδον αὐτούς, ἀντι-

---

ἀντι-παρα-θέω: run out alongside opposite, 1
δεξιός, -ά, -όν: on the right hand or side, 5
ἑκατόν: a hundred, 1
ἑξακόσιοι, -αι, -α: six hundred, 1
ἔξω: out of (+ gen.); adv. outside, 5
εὔχομαι: to pray, offer prayers, vow, 5
εὐ-ώνυμος, -ον: of good name; left (side), 3
μέσος, -η, -ον: middle, in the middle of, 5
ὀγδοήκοντα: eighty, 1
παιανίζω: to sing a paean, 4
παρ-εγγυάω: to pass on word or command 5
σχεδόν: nearly, almost, just about, 3
τοξότης, ὁ: an archer, bowman, 4
τριχῇ: in threes, in three parts, 1

1 **ὀρθίους**: *in columns*; i.e. single files
ἀμφὶ: *around*; + acc., in approximation
2 **εἰς**: *nearly*; 'up to,' in approximation
3 **τοὺς μὲν...τοὺς δὲ... τοὺς δὲ...**: *some...others...(still) others...*
4 **τοῦ δεξιοῦ (ἔξω)**
κατὰ: *in...*
5 **ἐκ τούτου**: *after this*; 'from this'
8 **τῆς...φάλαγγος**: object of ἔξω ; i.e. in a checkerboard pattern, the Greeks extended wider than the width of the enemy's phalanx
9 **ὡς**: *as, when*
εἶδον: aor. ὁράω
ἀντιπαραθέοντες: confronted with the Greek's extended frontline, the enemy stretched out their front line so that the troops on the ends would be beside (παρα) and opposite (ἀντί) the ends of the Greek troops

παραθέοντες οἱ μὲν ἐπὶ τὸ δεξιὸν οἱ δὲ ἐπὶ τὸ εὐώνυμον 10
διεσπάσθησαν, καὶ πολὺ τῆς αὑτῶν φάλαγγος ἐν τῷ μέσῳ
κενὸν ἐποίησαν. 18. οἱ δὲ κατὰ τὸ Ἀρκαδικὸν πελτασταί, ὧν
ἦρχεν Αἰσχίνης ὁ Ἀκαρνάν, νομίσαντες φεύγειν ἀνακραγόντες ἔθεον· καὶ οὗτοι πρῶτοι ἐπὶ τὸ ὄρος ἀναβαίνουσι·
συνεφείπετο δὲ αὐτοῖς καὶ τὸ Ἀρκαδικὸν ὁπλιτικόν, ὧν ἦρχε 15
Κλεάνωρ ὁ Ὀρχομένιος. 19. οἱ δὲ πολέμιοι, ὡς ἤρξαντο θεῖν,
οὐκέτι ἔστησαν, ἀλλὰ φυγῇ ἄλλος ἄλλῃ ἐτράπετο. οἱ δὲ
Ἕλληνες ἀναβάντες ἐστρατοπεδεύοντο ἐν πολλαῖς κώμαις

Αἰσχίνης, ὁ: Aeschines, 2
Ἀκαρνάν, Ἀκαρνᾶνος, ὁ: Acarnian, 1
ἀνα-κράζω: to cry out, shout, 3
Ἀρκαδικός, -ή, -όν: Arcadian, 2
δεξιός, -ά, -όν: on the right hand or side, 5
δια-σπάω: to pull apart, separate, 3
εὐ-ώνυμος, -ον: of good name; left (side), 3
ἵστημι: make stand, set up, stop, establish, 7
κενός, -ή, -όν: empty, 1
Κλεάνωρ, ὁ: Cleanor, 2
μέσος, -η, -ον: middle, in the middle of, 5
νομίζω: to believe, think, deem, 2
ὁπλιτικός, -ή, -όν: of a hoplite; infantry, 2
Ὀρχομένιος, -α, -ον: of Orchomenus, 1
οὐκ-έτι: no more, no longer, no further, 1
στρατοπεδεύω: to encamp, take a position, 4
συν-εφ-έπομαι: to follow after together, 1
τρέπω: to turn; rout, 2
φυγή, ἡ: flight, escape, exile, 3

10 ἀντιπαραθέοντες: see previous note
οἱ μὲν...οἱ δὲ...: *some...others...*; the enemy
ἐπὶ...: *to...*
11 διεσπάσθησαν: aor. pass.
πολὺ: *a majority*; neuter acc. sg.
(ἑ)αυτῶν: reflexive
12 ἐποίησεν: governing a double acc.
κατὰ τὸ Ἀρκαδικὸν: *in the Arcadian division*
ὧν: *whom...*; gen. obj. of ἄρχω
13 φεύγειν: *that (the enemy)...*; ind. disc., take τοὺς πολεμίους as acc. subject
14 ἔθεον: *began to...*; inchoative impf. θέω; the Arcadian peltasts are the subject
οὗτοι: *these*; i.e. the Arcadian peltasts
15 συνεφείπετο: impf.
αὐτοῖς: dat. of compound verb
καὶ: *also*
τὸ...ὁπλιτικόν: nom. subject
ὧν: *whom...*; see line 12
16 ὡς: *as, when*
ἤρξαντο: the peltasts are subject
17 ἔστησαν: aor. ἵστημι
φυγῇ: *in...*; dat. of manner
ἄλλος ἄλλῃ: *one in one direction, another in another direction*; dat. of manner; a common expression when junxtaposing two cases of ἄλλος
ἐτράπετο: aor. mid. τρέπω
18 ἀναβάντες: aor. pple ἀναβαίνω

καὶ τἀπιτήδεια πολλὰ ἐχούσαις. 20. *καὶ τὰ μὲν ἄλλα οὐδὲν ὅ τι καὶ ἐθαύμασαν· τὰ δὲ σμήνη πολλὰ ἦν αὐτόθι, καὶ τῶν* 20 *κηρίων ὅσοι ἔφαγον τῶν στρατιωτῶν πάντες ἄφρονές τε ἐγίγνοντο καὶ ἤμουν καὶ κάτω διεχώρει αὐτοῖς καὶ ὀρθὸς οὐδεὶς ἐδύνατο ἵστασθαι, ἀλλ' οἱ μὲν ὀλίγον ἐδηδοκότες σφόδρα μεθύουσιν ἐῴκεσαν, οἱ δὲ πολὺ μαινομένοις, οἱ δὲ καὶ ἀποθνήσκουσιν.* 21. *ἔκειντο δὲ οὕτω πολλοὶ ὥσπερ τροπῆς* 25 *γεγενημένης, καὶ πολλὴ ἦν ἀθυμία. τῇ δ' ὑστεραίᾳ ἀπέθανε μὲν οὐδείς, ἀμφὶ δὲ τὴν αὐτήν πως ὥραν ἀνεφρόνουν· τρίτῃ δὲ καὶ τετάρτῃ ἀνίσταντο ὥσπερ ἐκ φαρμακοποσίας.*

ἀ-θυμία ἡ: faintheartedness, discouragement 3
ἄ-φρων, -ονος: senseless, foolish, 1
ἀνα-φρονέω: to come to (their) senses, 1
αὐτό-θι: on the very spot or moment, 2
δια-χωρέω: run/pass through (as diarrhea), 1
ἐμέω: to vomit, throw up, 1
ἔοικα: to be like; seem like (dat) 1
ἐσθίω: to eat, 3
θαυμάζω: to wonder, marvel, be amazed at, 1
ἵστημι: make stand, set up, stop, establish, 7
κάτω: downwards, below, 4
κεῖμαι: to lie, lie down 2
κηρίον, -ου, τό: honeycomb, 1
μαίνομαι: to be mad, be driven made, crazy, 1
μεθύω: to be drunk with wine, 1
ὀρθός, -ή, -όν: straight, upright, right, 1
πως: somehow, in any way, 4
σμῆνος, -εος, τό: swarm of bees, beehive, 2
σφόδρα: very, very much, exceedingly, earnestly, 1
τέταρτος, -η, -ον: fourth, 1
τρίτος, -η, -ον: the third, 4
τροπή, ἡ: rout, turning, 1
ὑστεραῖος, -α, -ον: the next day; later, 5
φαρμακο-ποσία, ἡ: a drinking of medicine 1
ὥρα, ἡ: season, time, period of time, 3

19 τὰ (ἐ)πιτήδεια
ἐχούσαις: pple
τὰ μὲν ἄλλα: *in other respects*; acc. respect
οὐδὲν (ἐστί): *(there is)...*
20 ὅ τι: neuter sg. ὅστις
καὶ: *in fact, actually*; adverbial
σμήνη: σμήνε-α
21 τῶν κηρίων: partitive gen. obj. of ἔφαγον within the relative clause
ἔφαγον: aor. ἐσθίω
τῶν στρατιωτῶν: partitive with ὅσοι
21 ἤμουν: ἤμεον, 3p impf. ἐμέω
22 κάτω διεχώρει αὐτοῖς: *it was running down through them*; i.e. they had diarrhea; an impersonal construction
23 ὀλίγον: *a little*
ἐδηδοκότες: pf. act. pple ἐσθίω
24 σφόδρα μεθύουσιν: *to (those)...*; dat. pl. pple
ἐῴκεσαν: plpf. ἔοικα + dat.
οἱ δὲ πολὺ (ἐδηδοκότες): *but those...*;
μαινομένοις (ἐῴκεσαν): *to (those)...*; dat. pl. pple, obj. of missing ἐῴκεσαν
οἱ δὲ (πολὺ ἐδηδοκότες): *and still others...*
25 ἀποθνῄσκουσιν (ἐῴκεσαν): *to (those)...*; dat. pl. pple, obj. of missing ἐῴκεσαν
ἔκειντο: impf.
25 τροπῆς γεγενημένης: i.e. as if defeated and lying on the battlefield wounded and dead; gen. abs, pf. mid. γίγνομαι
26 τῇ ὑστεραίᾳ (ἡμέρᾳ): dat. of time when
ἀπέθανε: aor. ἀποθνῄσκω
27 τρίτῃ...τετάρτῃ (ἡμέρᾳ): time when

22. ἐντεῦθεν δ᾽ ἐπορεύθησαν δύο σταθμοὺς παρασάγγας ἑπτά, 1
καὶ ἦλθον ἐπὶ θάλατταν εἰς Τραπεζοῦντα πόλιν Ἑλληνίδα
οἰκουμένην ἐν τῷ Εὐξείνῳ Πόντῳ, Σινωπέων ἀποικίαν, ἐν
τῇ Κόλχων χώρᾳ. ἐνταῦθα ἔμειναν ἡμέρας ἀμφὶ τὰς τριάκοντα ἐν ταῖς τῶν Κόλχων κώμαις· 23. κἀντεῦθεν ὁρμώμενοι 5
ἐλῄζοντο τὴν Κολχίδα. ἀγορὰν δὲ παρεῖχον τῷ στρατοπέδῳ Τραπεζούντιοι, καὶ ἐδέξαντό τε τοὺς Ἕλληνας καὶ
ξένια ἔδοσαν βοῦς καὶ ἄλφιτα καὶ οἶνον. 24. συνδιεπράττοντο
δὲ καὶ ὑπὲρ τῶν πλησίον Κόλχων τῶν ἐν τῷ πεδίῳ μάλιστα

ἀγορά, ἡ: marketplace, exchange; assembly 2
ἄλφιτον, τό: barley-meal, 2
ἀπ-οικία, ἡ: colony, 1
δέχομαι: to receive, accept, 7
Ἑλληνίς, -ίδος, ἡ: Greek (fem. adj.), 1
ἑπτά: seven, 5
Εὔξείνος, ὁ: Black sea, Euxine, Hospitable 1
θάλαττα, ἡ: the sea, 7
Κολχίς, Κολχίδος, ἡ: Colchis, 1
λῄζομαι: to carry off as loot, plunder 1
μάλιστα: most of all; certainly, especially, 5
ξένια, τά: gifts of friendship or hospitality, 2
οἰκέω: to inhabit, dwell, live, 5
οἶνος, ὁ: wine, 5
ὁρμάω: to set in motion, set out, begin, 2
παρ-έχω: to provide, furnish, supply, 5
πλησίος, -η, -ον: near, close to; neighbors, 5
πόλις, ἡ: a city, 3
πόντος, ὁ: sea, 1
Σινωπεύς, -έως, ὁ: Sinopean, of Sinope, 1
συν-δια-πράττω: to negotiate with; help in accomplishing or transacting, 1
Τραπεζούντιος, -α, -ον: Trapezuntian, 1
Τραπεζοῦς, ὁ: Trapezus (city), 1
τριάκοντα: thirty, 4

1 **ἐπορεύθησαν**: 3p aor. pass. dep. πορεύομαι; translate in the active
σταθμοὺς...παρασάγγας: *for*...; acc. of extent
2 **ἦλθον**: aor. ἔρχομαι
3 **οἰκουμένην**: *inhabited*
ἀποικίαν: in apposition to πόλιν
4 **ἔμειναν**: aor. μένω
ἡμέρας: acc. of duration
ἀμφὶ: in approximation
5 **κα(ὶ) (ἐ)ντεῦθεν**
6 **ἐλῃζοντο**: impf. mid. λῄζομαι
τῷ στρατοπέδῳ: *for*...; dat. of interest
7 **ἐδέξαντο**: *welcomed*
8 **ξένια**: *as*...
ἔδοσαν: aor. δίδωμι
συνδιέπράττοντο (τοῖς Ἕλλησιν): *they helped in negotiating (with the Greeks)*...
ὑπὲρ: *on behalf of*...;
9 **πλησίον**: *nearby*; '(living) nearby' adv.
τῶν...οἰκούντων: in the attributive position modifying Κόλχων

οἰκούντων, καὶ ξένια καὶ παρ' ἐκείνων ἦλθον βόες. 25. *μετὰ* 10
δὲ τοῦτο τὴν θυσίαν ἣν ηὔξαντο παρεσκευάζοντο· ἦλθον δ'
αὐτοῖς ἱκανοὶ βόες ἀποθῦσαι τῷ Διὶ τῷ σωτῆρι καὶ τῷ
Ἡρακλεῖ ἡγεμόσυνα καὶ τοῖς ἄλλοις θεοῖς ἃ ηὔξαντο.
ἐποίησαν δὲ καὶ ἀγῶνα γυμνικὸν ἐν τῷ ὄρει ἔνθαπερ ἐσκή-
νουν. εἵλοντο δὲ Δρακόντιον Σπαρτιάτην, ὃς ἔφυγε παῖς 15
ὢν οἴκοθεν, παῖδα ἄκων κατακανὼν ξυήλῃ πατάξας, δρόμου
τ' ἐπιμεληθῆναι καὶ τοῦ ἀγῶνος προστατῆσαι. 26. *ἐπειδὴ δὲ*
ἡ θυσία ἐγένετο, τὰ δέρματα παρέδοσαν τῷ Δρακοντίῳ, καὶ

ἀγών, ὁ: contest, competition, 2
αἱρέω: seize, take; *mid.* choose, 3
ἄκων (ἀ-έκων), ἄκουσα, ἄκον: unwilling, 1
ἀπο-θύω: to offer up (in sacrifice), 1
γυμνικός, -ή, -όν: athletic, gymnastic, 1
δέρμα, -ατος, τό: the skin, hide, 2
Δρακόντιος, ὁ: Dracontius, 2
δρόμος, ὁ: run, running, flight; race course, 5
ἔνθα-περ: the very place where, there where 1
ἐπι-μέλ(ε)ομαι: to care for, look after (gen) 3
εὔχομαι: to pray, offer prayers, vow, 5
Ζεύς, ὁ: Zeus, 1
ἡγεμόσυνα, τό: offerings for safe conduct, 1
Ἡρακλέης, ὁ: Heracles, 1
θεός, ὁ: a god, divinity, 3
θυσία, ἡ: an offering, sacrifice, 2
ἱκανός, -ή, -όν: enough, sufficient; capable 4
κατα-καίνω: to kill, slay, 2
ξένια, τά: gifts of friendship or hospitality, 2
ξυήλη, ἡ: whittling knife (to make a javelin) 2
οἴκα-θεν: from home, 1
οἰκέω: to inhabit, dwell, live, 5
παρα-δίδωμι: to hand over, give over, 4
παρασκευάζω: to prepare, get ready, 4
πατάσσω: to strike; beat, knock, 1
προ-στατέω: be over, be in charge of (gen)1
σκηνέω: to encamp, bivouac, set up tents, 5
Σπαρτιάτης, ὁ: Spartan, 1
σωτήρ, ὁ: deliverer, preserver, 1

10 **οἰκούντων**: pple modifies Κόλχων
ξένια: *as...*
παρ(ὰ): *from...*; gen. of source
ἦλθον: aor. ἔρχομαι
11 **ἣν ηὔξαντο**: *which...*;
ἦλθον: i.e. through gifts
12 **αὐτοῖς**: *for...*; dat. of interest
ἀποθῦσαι: *to...*; aor. inf. of purpose
τῷ Διὶ: dat. sg. Ζεύς
13 **ἡγεμόσυνα**: acc. obj. of inf.
τοῖς θεοῖς: dat. ind. obj. parallel to τῷ Διὶ
ἃ: *(for the thing) which...;* '(in respect to the things) which,' missing antecedent is acc. of respect or simply acc. obj.
15 **εἵλοντο**: aor. middle αἱρέω (ἑλ-)
ἔφυγε: aor. φεύγω; i.e. he was banished and therefore 'was an exile'
16 **ὢν**: *(while)...*; circumstantial pple εἰμί, παῖς is predicate
παῖδα ἄκων κατακανὼν ξυήλῃ πατάξας: *because of...*; or 'by...;' the two aor. pples are causal in sense and explain why the Dracontius was exiled
ξηύλῃ: dat. of means
17 **δρόμου ἐπιμεληθῆναι**: *both to...and to...*; inf. of purpose, aor. pass. dep. inf.; i.e. to mark out and construct the racetrack
προστατῆσαι: another inf. of purpose; aor. inf. + gen.
18 **παρέδοσαν**: aor. παραδίδωμι

ἡγεῖσθαι ἐκέλευον ὅπου τὸν δρόμον πεποιηκὼς εἴη. ὁ δὲ
δείξας οὗπερ ἑστηκότες ἐτύγχανον 'οὗτος ὁ λόφος,' ἔφη, 20
'κάλλιστος τρέχειν ὅπου ἂν τις βούληται.' 'πῶς οὖν,' ἔφασαν,
'δυνήσονται παλαίειν ἐν σκληρῷ καὶ δασεῖ οὕτως;' ὁ δ' εἶπε·
'μᾶλλόν τι ἀνιάσεται ὁ καταπεσών.' 27. ἠγωνίζοντο δὲ παῖδες
μὲν στάδιον τῶν αἰχμαλώτων οἱ πλεῖστοι, δόλιχον δὲ Κρῆτες
πλείους ἢ ἑξήκοντα ἔθεον, πάλην δὲ καὶ πυγμὴν καὶ παγ- 25

ἀγωνίζομαι: to contend, compete, fight, 3
αἰχμ-άλωτος, -ον: taken by spear, captive, 4
ἀν-ιάω: to grieve, distress, 1
δασύς, -εῖα, -ύ: thick; thicket (bush/woods), 5
δείκνυμι: to show, indicate, point out, 4
δόλιχος, ὁ: long race (a dolicium), 1
δρόμος, ὁ: run, running, flight; race course, 5
ἑξήκοντα: sixty, 2
ἵστημι: make stand, set up, stop, establish, 7
κατα-πίπτω: to fall down, drop down, 1
Κρής, Κρητός, ὁ: a Cretan, 3
μᾶλλον: more, rather, 4
ὅπου: where, 5
οὗ-περ: the very place where, 1
παγ-κράτιον, τό: pancration, box-wrestling 1
παλαιός, -ά, -όν: old, aged, ancient, 2
πάλη, ἡ: wrestling, 1
πλεῖστος, -η, -ον: most, very many, 3
πυγμήν, ἡ: boxing, 1
πῶς: how? in what way?, 2
σκληρός, -ά, -όν: hard, harsh, severe, 1
τρέχω: to run, 3
τυγχάνω: chance upon, get; meet; happen, 5

19 **(αὐτὸν) ἡγεῖσθαι**: *(him) to lead the way*; i.e. Dracontius
ὅπου...πεποιηκὼς εἴη: *wherever...*; general relative clause in secondary seq. with periphrastic pf. act. opt. (pf. pple + pres. opt. εἰμί): translate as plpf.
ὁ δὲ: *and he*
20 **οὗπερ**: relative pronoun
ἑστηκότες ἐτύγχανον: *happened to...*; τυγχάνω + complementary pple, here pf. pple of ἵστημι, translate pple as an inf.
ἔφη: Dracontius is subject, φημί
21 **κάλλιστος (ἐστίν)**
τρέχειν: explanatory (epexegetical) inf. qualifying κάλλιστος
ὅπου ἂν...βούληται: *wherever...*; general relative clause. in primary seq. with ἄν + subj
ἔφασαν: participants and spectators, φημί
22 **δασεῖ**: *overgrown (ground)*; dat. sg.
εἶπε: aor. λέγω
23 **μᾶλλόν τι**: *somewhat more*;'more by some'a comparative adv. and adverbial acc. (acc. of extent in degree)
ὁ καταπεσών: *the one...*; aor. pple καταπίπτω
24 **στάδιον**: *a stadium race*; lit. 'a stade' (600 feet/~185 meters) but here an inner acc.: 'make a stade-contest'
τῶν αἰχμαλώτων οἱ πλεῖστοι: in apposition to παῖδες
24 **δόλιχον**: *a dolicium race*; equiv. to 12 stades (7200 feet/~2.2 km)
25 **πλεῖο(ν)ες**: nom. pl. comparative modifying Κρῆτες

κράτιον †ἕτεροι†, καὶ καλὴ θέα ἐγένετο· πολλοὶ γὰρ κατέ- 1
βησαν καὶ ἅτε θεωμένων τῶν ἑταίρων πολλὴ φιλονικία ἐγίγνετο. 28. ἔθεον δὲ καὶ ἵπποι καὶ ἔδει αὐτοὺς κατὰ τοῦ πρανοῦς
ἐλάσαντας ἐν τῇ θαλάττῃ ἀποστρέψαντας πάλιν πρὸς τὸν
βωμὸν ἄγειν. καὶ κάτω μὲν οἱ πολλοὶ ἐκαλινδοῦντο· ἄνω 5
δὲ πρὸς τὸ ἰσχυρῶς ὄρθιον μόλις βάδην ἐπορεύοντο οἱ
ἵπποι· ἔνθα πολλὴ κραυγὴ καὶ γέλως καὶ παρακέλευσις
ἐγίγνετο.

ἀπο-στρέφω: to turn back, turn away, 1
ἅτε: inasmuch as, since, seeing that (+ pple) 3
βάδην: step by step, gradually, 2
βωμός, ὁ: platform, stand; altar, 1
ἐλαύνω: to march, ride, drive, 2
ἑταῖρος, ὁ: comrade, companion, mate, 2
ἕτερος, -α, -ον: one of two, other, different, 4
θάλαττα, ἡ: the sea, 7
θέα, ἡ: sight, spectacle, 1
θεάομαι: to see, gaze at, watch, 2
ἰσχυρός, -ά, -όν: strong, powerful; severe, 7
καλινδέομαι: to roll over, 1
κάτω: downwards, below, 4
κραυγή, ἡ: shouting, crying, screaming, 3
μόλις (μόγις): with difficulty, hardly, 1
παρακέλευσις -εως ἡ: cheering, urging on, 1
πρανής, ές: headlong, head down, down hill 1
φιλο-νικία, ἡ: rivalry, 1

1 **†ἕτεροι†**: A obelus (†) indicates that the word or clause is plainly corrupt but the editor cannot see how to emend it. Omit in translation.
θέα: note the placement of the accent: θεά means 'spectacle,' while θέα means 'goddess'
κατέβησαν: *entered into contest*; aor. καταβάινω, an idiom for participating in the games
2 **ἅτε...ἑταίρων**: *inasmuch as...*; 'since...' ἅτε + pple (here, a gen. absolute) expresses cause from the narrator's point of view
3 **ἔδει**: impf. δεῖ
αὐτοὺς...ἄγειν: *that (the Greeks)...*; ind. disc. with missing. acc. subj.; αὐτοὺς, i.e. the horses, object of both ἐλάσαντας and ἄγειν
κατὰ τοῦ πρανοῦς: *headlong downhill*; 'down headlong'
4 **ἐλάσαντας**: aor. pple modifying the missing acc. subject of ἄγειν
5 **βωμὸν**: *stand*; marking the start of the race
ἄγειν: *bring, drive*
κάτω μὲν...ἄνω δὲ: *downhill...uphill...*; as the horses race down to the sea and back
ἐκαλινδοῦντο: i.e. fell down uncontrollably as they raced downhill
6 **πρὸς τὸ ἰσχυρῶς ὄρθιον**: *against the exceedingly steep (hill)*
7 **ἔνθα**: *then*

Greek Text

For Classroom Use

ΚΥΡΟΥ ΑΝΑΒΑΣΕΩΣ Δ

[ὅσα μὲν δὴ ἐν τῇ ἀναβάσει ἐγένετο μέχρι τῆς μάχης, 1
καὶ ὅσα μετὰ τὴν μάχην ἐν ταῖς σπονδαῖς ἃς βασιλεὺς καὶ
οἱ σὺν Κύρῳ ἀναβάντες Ἕλληνες ἐποιήσαντο, καὶ ὅσα παραβάντος τὰς σπονδὰς βασιλέως καὶ Τισσαφέρνους ἐπολεμήθη
πρὸς τοὺς Ἕλληνας ἐπακολουθοῦντος τοῦ Περσικοῦ στρατε- 5
ματος, ἐν τῷ πρόσθεν λόγῳ δεδήλωται. 2. ἐπεὶ δὲ ἀφίκοντο
ἔνθα ὁ μὲν Τίγρης ποταμὸς παντάπασιν ἄπορος ἦν διὰ τὸ
βάθος καὶ μέγεθος, πάροδος δὲ οὐκ ἦν, ἀλλὰ τὰ Καρδούχεια
ὄρη ἀπότομα ὑπὲρ αὐτοῦ τοῦ ποταμοῦ ἐκρέματο, ἐδόκει δὴ
τοῖς στρατηγοῖς διὰ τῶν ὀρέων πορευτέον εἶναι. 3. ἤκουον γὰρ 10
τῶν ἁλισκομένων ὅτι εἰ διέλθοιεν τὰ Καρδούχεια ὄρη, ἐν τῇ
Ἀρμενίᾳ τὰς πηγὰς τοῦ Τίγρητος ποταμοῦ, ἢν μὲν βούλωνται,
διαβήσονται, ἢν δὲ μὴ βούλωνται, περιίασι. καὶ τοῦ Εὐφράτου δὲ τὰς πηγὰς ἐλέγετο οὐ πρόσω τοῦ Τίγρητος εἶναι,
καὶ ἔστιν οὕτως ἔχον. 4. τὴν δ᾽ εἰς τοὺς Καρδούχους ἐμβολὴν 15
ὧδε ποιοῦνται, ἅμα μὲν λαθεῖν πειρώμενοι, ἅμα δὲ φθάσαι
πρὶν τοὺς πολεμίους καταλαβεῖν τὰ ἄκρα.]

5. ἡνίκα δ᾽ ἦν ἀμφὶ τὴν τελευταίαν φυλακὴν καὶ ἐλείπετο
τῆς νυκτὸς ὅσον σκοταίους διελθεῖν τὸ πεδίον, τηνικαῦτα
ἀναστάντες ἀπὸ παραγγέλσεως πορευόμενοι ἀφικνοῦνται ἅμα 20
τῇ ἡμέρᾳ πρὸς τὸ ὄρος. 6. ἔνθα δὴ Χειρίσοφος μὲν ἡγεῖτο
τοῦ στρατεύματος λαβὼν τὸ ἀμφ᾽ αὐτὸν καὶ τοὺς γυμνῆτας
πάντας, Ξενοφῶν δὲ σὺν τοῖς ὀπισθοφύλαξιν ὁπλίταις εἵπετο

οὐδένα ἔχων γυμνῆτα· οὐδεὶς γὰρ κίνδυνος ἐδόκει εἶναι μή 1
τις ἄνω πορευομένων ἐκ τοῦ ὄπισθεν ἐπίσποιτο. 7. καὶ ἐπὶ
μὲν τὸ ἄκρον ἀναβαίνει Χειρίσοφος πρίν τινας αἰσθέσθαι
τῶν πολεμίων· ἔπειτα δ᾽ ὑφηγεῖτο· ἐφείπετο δὲ ἀεὶ τὸ
ὑπερβάλλον τοῦ στρατεύματος εἰς τὰς κώμας τὰς ἐν τοῖς 5
ἄγκεσί τε καὶ μυχοῖς τῶν ὀρέων. 8. ἔνθα δὴ οἱ μὲν Καρδοῦχοι
ἐκλιπόντες τὰς οἰκίας ἔχοντες καὶ γυναῖκας καὶ παῖδας ἔφευγον
ἐπὶ τὰ ὄρη. τὰ δὲ ἐπιτήδεια πολλὰ ἦν λαμβάνειν, ἦσαν δὲ
καὶ χαλκώμασι παμπόλλοις κατεσκευασμέναι αἱ οἰκίαι, ὧν 9
οὐδὲν ἔφερον οἱ Ἕλληνες, οὐδὲ τοὺς ἀνθρώπους ἐδίωκον, 10
ὑποφειδόμενοι, εἴ πως ἐθελήσειαν οἱ Καρδοῦχοι διιέναι
αὐτοὺς ὡς διὰ φιλίας τῆς χώρας, ἐπείπερ βασιλεῖ πολέμιοι
ἦσαν· 9. τὰ μέντοι ἐπιτήδεια ὅτῳ τις ἐπιτυγχάνοι ἐλάμβανεν·
ἀνάγκη γὰρ ἦν. οἱ δὲ Καρδοῦχοι οὔτε καλούντων ὑπήκουον
οὔτε ἄλλο φιλικὸν οὐδὲν ἐποίουν. 10. ἐπεὶ δὲ οἱ τελευταῖοι τῶν 15
Ἑλλήνων κατέβαινον εἰς τὰς κώμας ἀπὸ τοῦ ἄκρου ἤδη
σκοταῖοι (διὰ γὰρ τὸ στενὴν εἶναι τὴν ὁδὸν ὅλην τὴν ἡμέραν
ἡ ἀνάβασις αὐτοῖς ἐγένετο καὶ κατάβασις), τότε δὴ συλλεγέντες τινὲς τῶν Καρδούχων τοῖς τελευταίοις ἐπετίθεντο,
καὶ ἀπέκτεινάν τινας καὶ λίθοις καὶ τοξεύμασι κατέτρωσαν, 20
ὀλίγοι ὄντες· ἐξ ἀπροσδοκήτου γὰρ αὐτοῖς ἐπέπεσε τὸ Ἑλληνικόν. 11. εἰ μέντοι τότε πλείους συνελέγησαν, ἐκινδύνευσεν ἂν
διαφθαρῆναι πολὺ τοῦ στρατεύματος. καὶ ταύτην μὲν τὴν
νύκτα οὕτως ἐν ταῖς κώμαις ηὐλίσθησαν· οἱ δὲ Καρδοῦχοι
πυρὰ πολλὰ ἔκαιον κύκλῳ ἐπὶ τῶν ὀρέων καὶ συνεώρων 25
ἀλλήλους. 12. ἅμα δὲ τῇ ἡμέρᾳ συνελθοῦσι τοῖς στρατηγοῖς
καὶ λοχαγοῖς τῶν Ἑλλήνων ἔδοξε τῶν τε ὑποζυγίων τὰ

ἀναγκαῖα καὶ δυνατώτατα ἔχοντας πορεύεσθαι, καταλιπόντας 1
τἆλλα, καὶ ὅσα ἦν νεωστὶ αἰχμάλωτα ἀνδράποδα ἐν τῇ
στρατιᾷ πάντα ἀφεῖναι. 13. σχολαίαν γὰρ ἐποίουν τὴν πορείαν
πολλὰ ὄντα τὰ ὑποζύγια καὶ τὰ αἰχμάλωτα, πολλοὶ δὲ οἱ ἐπὶ
τούτοις ὄντες ἀπόμαχοι ἦσαν, διπλάσιά τε ἐπιτήδεια ἔδει 5
πορίζεσθαι καὶ φέρεσθαι πολλῶν τῶν ἀνθρώπων ὄντων.
δόξαν δὲ ταῦτα ἐκήρυξαν οὕτω ποιεῖν.

14. ἐπεὶ δὲ ἀριστήσαντες ἐπορεύοντο, ὑποστήσαντες ἐν τῷ
στενῷ οἱ στρατηγοί, εἴ τι εὑρίσκοιεν τῶν εἰρημένων μὴ ἀφει- 9
μένον, ἀφῃροῦντο, οἱ δ᾽ ἐπείθοντο, πλὴν εἴ τις ἔκλεψεν, οἷον 10
ἢ παιδὸς ἐπιθυμήσας ἢ γυναικὸς τῶν εὐπρεπῶν. καὶ ταύτην
μὲν τὴν ἡμέραν οὕτως ἐπορεύθησαν, τὰ μέν τι μαχόμενοι τὰ
δὲ καὶ ἀναπαυόμενοι. 15. εἰς δὲ τὴν ὑστεραίαν γίγνεται χειμὼν
πολύς, ἀναγκαῖον δ᾽ ἦν πορεύεσθαι· οὐ γὰρ ἦν ἱκανὰ τἀπιτήδεια. καὶ ἡγεῖτο μὲν Χειρίσοφος, ὠπισθοφυλάκει δὲ 15
Ξενοφῶν. 16. καὶ οἱ πολέμιοι ἰσχυρῶς ἐπετίθεντο, καὶ στενῶν
ὄντων τῶν χωρίων ἐγγὺς προσιόντες ἐτόξευον καὶ ἐσφεν-
δόνων· ὥστε ἠναγκάζοντο οἱ Ἕλληνες ἐπιδιώκοντες καὶ πάλιν
ἀναχάζοντες σχολῇ πορεύεσθαι· καὶ θαμινὰ παρήγγελλεν ὁ
Ξενοφῶν ὑπομένειν, 17. ὅτε οἱ πολέμιοι ἰσχυρῶς ἐπικέοιντο. 20
ἐνταῦθα ὁ Χειρίσοφος ἄλλοτε μὲν ὅτε παρεγγυῷτο ὑπέμενε,
τότε δὲ οὐχ ὑπέμενεν, ἀλλ᾽ ἦγε ταχέως καὶ παρηγγύα ἕπεσθαι,
ὥστε δῆλον ἦν ὅτι πρᾶγμά τι εἴη· σχολὴ δ᾽ οὐκ ἦν ἰδεῖν
παρελθόντι τὸ αἴτιον τῆς σπουδῆς· ὥστε ἡ πορεία ὁμοία
φυγῇ ἐγίγνετο τοῖς ὀπισθοφύλαξι. 18. καὶ ἐνταῦθα ἀποθνῄσκει 25
ἀνὴρ ἀγαθὸς Λακωνικὸς Λεώνυμος τοξευθεὶς διὰ τῆς ἀσπίδος
καὶ τῆς σπολάδος εἰς τὰς πλευράς, καὶ Βασίας Ἀρκὰς

διαμπερὲς τὴν κεφαλήν. 19. ἐπεὶ δὲ ἀφίκοντο ἐπὶ σταθμόν, 1
εὐθὺς ὥσπερ εἶχεν ὁ Ξενοφῶν ἐλθὼν πρὸς τὸν Χειρίσοφον
ᾐτιᾶτο αὐτὸν ὅτι οὐχ ὑπέμενεν, ἀλλ᾽ ἠναγκάζοντο φεύγοντες
ἅμα μάχεσθαι. καὶ νῦν δύο καλώ τε καὶ ἀγαθὼ ἄνδρε
τέθνατον καὶ οὔτε ἀνελέσθαι οὔτε θάψαι ἐδυνάμεθα. 20. ἀποκρί- 5
νεται ὁ Χειρίσοφος· 'βλέψον,' ἔφη, 'πρὸς τὰ ὄρη καὶ ἰδὲ ὡς
ἄβατα πάντα ἐστί· μία δ᾽ αὕτη ὁδὸς ἣν ὁρᾷς ὀρθία, καὶ ἐπὶ
ταύτῃ ἀνθρώπων ὁρᾶν ἔξεστί σοι ὄχλον τοσοῦτον, οἳ κατειληφότες φυλάττουσι τὴν ἔκβασιν. 21. ταῦτ᾽ ἐγὼ ἔσπευδον καὶ 9
διὰ τοῦτό σε οὐχ ὑπέμενον, εἴ πως δυναίμην φθάσαι πρὶν 10
κατειλῆφθαι τὴν ὑπερβολήν· οἱ δ᾽ ἡγεμόνες οὓς ἔχομεν οὔ
φασιν εἶναι ἄλλην ὁδόν.' 22. ὁ δὲ Ξενοφῶν λέγει· 'ἀλλ᾽ ἐγὼ ἔχω
δύο ἄνδρας. ἐπεὶ γὰρ ἡμῖν πράγματα παρεῖχον, ἐνηδρεύ-
σαμεν, ὅπερ ἡμᾶς καὶ ἀναπνεῦσαι ἐποίησε, καὶ ἀπεκτείναμέν
τινας αὐτῶν, καὶ ζῶντας προυθυμήθημεν λαβεῖν αὐτοῦ τούτου 15
ἕνεκα ὅπως ἡγεμόσιν εἰδόσι τὴν χώραν χρησαίμεθα.

23. καὶ εὐθὺς ἀγαγόντες τοὺς ἀνθρώπους ἤλεγχον διαλαβόντες
εἴ τινα εἰδεῖεν ἄλλην ὁδὸν ἢ τὴν φανεράν. ὁ μὲν οὖν ἕτερος
οὐκ ἔφη μάλα πολλῶν φόβων προσαγομένων· ἐπεὶ δὲ οὐδὲν
ὠφέλιμον ἔλεγεν, ὁρῶντος τοῦ ἑτέρου κατεσφάγη. 24. ὁ δὲ 20
λοιπὸς ἔλεξεν ὅτι οὗτος μὲν οὐ φαίη διὰ ταῦτα εἰδέναι, ὅτι
αὐτῷ ἐτύγχανε θυγάτηρ ἐκεῖ παρ᾽ ἀνδρὶ ἐκδεδομένη· αὐτὸς
δ᾽ ἔφη ἡγήσεσθαι δυνατὴν καὶ ὑποζυγίοις πορεύεσθαι ὁδόν.
25. ἐρωτώμενος δ᾽ εἰ εἴη τι ἐν αὐτῇ δυσπάριτον χωρίον, ἔφη
εἶναι ἄκρον ὃ εἰ μή τις προκαταλήψοιτο, ἀδύνατον ἔσεσθαι 25

παρελθεῖν. 26. ἐνταῦθα δ' ἐδόκει συγκαλέσαντας λοχαγοὺς καὶ 1
πελταστὰς καὶ τῶν ὁπλιτῶν λέγειν τε τὰ παρόντα καὶ ἐρωτᾶν
εἴ τις αὐτῶν ἔστιν ὅστις ἀνὴρ ἀγαθὸς ἐθέλοι ἂν γενέσθαι καὶ
ὑποστὰς ἐθελοντὴς πορεύεσθαι. 27. ὑφίσταται τῶν μὲν ὁπλιτῶν
Ἀριστώνυμος Μεθυδριεὺς [Ἀρκὰς] καὶ Ἀγασίας Στυμφάλιος 5
[Ἀρκάς], ἀντιστασιάζων δὲ αὐτοῖς Καλλίμαχος Παρράσιος
[Ἀρκὰς καὶ οὗτος] ἔφη ἐθέλειν πορεύεσθαι προσλαβὼν
ἐθελοντὰς ἐκ παντὸς τοῦ στρατεύματος· 'ἐγὼ γάρ,' ἔφη,
'οἶδα ὅτι ἕψονται πολλοὶ τῶν νέων ἐμοῦ ἡγουμένου.' 28. ἐκ 9
τούτου ἐρωτῶσιν εἴ τις καὶ τῶν γυμνήτων ταξιάρχων ἐθέλοι 10
συμπορεύεσθαι. ὑφίσταται Ἀριστέας Χῖος, ὃς πολλαχοῦ
πολλοῦ ἄξιος τῇ στρατιᾷ εἰς τὰ τοιαῦτα ἐγένετο.

1. καὶ ἦν μὲν δείλη, οἱ δ' ἐκέλευον αὐτοὺς ἐμφαγόντας
πορεύεσθαι. καὶ τὸν ἡγεμόνα δήσαντες παραδιδόασιν αὐτοῖς,
καὶ συντίθενται τὴν μὲν νύκτα, ἢν λάβωσι τὸ ἄκρον, τὸ 15
χωρίον φυλάττειν, ἅμα δὲ τῇ ἡμέρᾳ τῇ σάλπιγγι σημαίνειν·
καὶ τοὺς μὲν ἄνω ὄντας ἰέναι ἐπὶ τοὺς κατέχοντας τὴν φανερὰν
ἔκβασιν, αὐτοὶ δὲ συμβοηθήσειν ἐκβαίνοντες ὡς ἂν δύνωνται
τάχιστα. 2. ταῦτα συνθέμενοι οἱ μὲν ἐπορεύοντο πλῆθος ὡς
δισχίλιοι· καὶ ὕδωρ πολὺ ἦν ἐξ οὐρανοῦ· Ξενοφῶν δὲ ἔχων 20
τοὺς ὀπισθοφύλακας ἡγεῖτο πρὸς τὴν φανερὰν ἔκβασιν, ὅπως
ταύτῃ τῇ ὁδῷ οἱ πολέμιοι προσέχοιεν τὸν νοῦν καὶ ὡς
μάλιστα λάθοιεν οἱ περιιόντες. 3. ἐπεὶ δὲ ἦσαν ἐπὶ χαράδρᾳ οἱ
ὀπισθοφύλακες ἣν ἔδει διαβάντας πρὸς τὸ ὄρθιον ἐκβαίνειν,
τηνικαῦτα ἐκύλινδον οἱ βάρβαροι ὁλοιτρόχους ἁμαξιαίους καὶ 25

μείζους καὶ ἐλάττους, οἳ φερόμενοι πρὸς τὰς πέτρας παίοντες 1
διεσφενδονῶντο· καὶ παντάπασιν οὐδὲ πελάσαι οἷόν τ' ἦν τῇ
εἰσόδῳ. 4. ἔνιοι δὲ τῶν λοχαγῶν, εἰ μὴ ταύτῃ δύναιντο, ἄλλῃ
ἐπειρῶντο· καὶ ταῦτα ἐποίουν μέχρι σκότος ἐγένετο· ἐπεὶ δὲ
ᾤοντο ἀφανεῖς εἶναι ἀπιόντες, τότε ἀπῆλθον ἐπὶ τὸ δεῖπνον· 5
ἐτύγχανον δὲ καὶ ἀνάριστοι ὄντες αὐτῶν οἱ ὀπισθοφυλακή-
σαντες. οἱ μέντοι πολέμιοι οὐδὲν ἐπαύσαντο δι' ὅλης τῆς
νυκτὸς κυλίνδοντες τοὺς λίθους· τεκμαίρεσθαι δ' ἦν τῷ ψόφῳ.
5. οἱ δ' ἔχοντες τὸν ἡγεμόνα κύκλῳ περιιόντες καταλαμβάνουσι 9
τοὺς φύλακας ἀμφὶ πῦρ καθημένους· καὶ τοὺς μὲν κατα- 10
καίνοντες τοὺς δὲ καταδιώξαντες αὐτοὶ ἐνταῦθ' ἔμενον ὡς τὸ
ἄκρον κατέχοντες. 6. οἱ δ' οὐ κατεῖχον, ἀλλὰ μαστὸς ἦν ὑπὲρ
αὐτῶν παρ' ὃν ἦν ἡ στενὴ αὕτη ὁδὸς ἐφ' ᾗ ἐκάθηντο οἱ
φύλακες. ἔφοδος μέντοι αὐτόθεν ἐπὶ τοὺς πολεμίους ἦν
οἳ ἐπὶ τῇ φανερᾷ ὁδῷ ἐκάθηντο. 7. καὶ τὴν μὲν νύκτα ἐνταῦθα 15
διήγαγον· ἐπεὶ δ' ἡμέρα ὑπέφαινεν, ἐπορεύοντο σιγῇ συντεταγμένοι ἐπὶ τοὺς πολεμίους· καὶ γὰρ ὁμίχλη ἐγένετο, ὥστ'
ἔλαθον ἐγγὺς προσελθόντες. ἐπεὶ δὲ εἶδον ἀλλήλους, ἥ τε
σάλπιγξ ἐφθέγξατο καὶ ἀλαλάξαντες ἵεντο ἐπὶ τοὺς ἀνθρώ-
πους· οἱ δὲ οὐκ ἐδέξαντο, ἀλλὰ λιπόντες τὴν ὁδὸν φεύγοντες 20
ὀλίγοι ἀπέθνῃσκον· εὔζωνοι γὰρ ἦσαν. 8. οἱ δὲ ἀμφὶ Χειρίσοφον ἀκούσαντες τῆς σάλπιγγος εὐθὺς ἵεντο ἄνω κατὰ τὴν
φανερὰν ὁδόν· ἄλλοι δὲ τῶν στρατηγῶν κατὰ ἀτριβεῖς ὁδοὺς
ἐπορεύοντο ᾗ ἔτυχον ἕκαστοι ὄντες, καὶ ἀναβάντες ὡς ἐδύναντο ἀνίμων ἀλλήλους τοῖς δόρασι. 9. καὶ οὗτοι πρῶτοι 25
συνέμειξαν τοῖς προκαταλαβοῦσι τὸ χωρίον. Ξενοφῶν δὲ

ἔχων τῶν ὀπισθοφυλάκων τοὺς ἡμίσεις ἐπορεύετο ᾗπερ οἱ 1
τὸν ἡγεμόνα ἔχοντες· εὐοδωτάτη γὰρ ἦν τοῖς ὑποζυγίοις·
τοὺς δὲ ἡμίσεις ὄπισθεν τῶν ὑποζυγίων ἔταξε. 10. πορευόμενοι
δ' ἐντυγχάνουσι λόφῳ ὑπὲρ τῆς ὁδοῦ κατειλημμένῳ ὑπὸ τῶν
πολεμίων, οὓς ἢ ἀποκόψαι ἦν ἀνάγκη ἢ διεζεῦχθαι ἀπὸ 5
τῶν ἄλλων Ἑλλήνων. καὶ αὐτοὶ μὲν ἂν ἐπορεύθησαν ᾗπερ
οἱ ἄλλοι, τὰ δὲ ὑποζύγια οὐκ ἦν ἄλλῃ ἢ ταύτῃ ἐκβῆναι.
11. ἔνθα δὴ παρακελευσάμενοι ἀλλήλοις προσβάλλουσι πρὸς
τὸν λόφον ὀρθίοις τοῖς λόχοις, οὐ κύκλῳ ἀλλὰ καταλιπόντες 9
ἄφοδον τοῖς πολεμίοις, εἰ βούλοιντο φεύγειν. 12. καὶ τέως 10
μὲν αὐτοὺς ἀναβαίνοντας ὅπῃ ἐδύναντο ἕκαστος οἱ βάρβαροι
ἐτόξευον καὶ ἔβαλλον, ἐγγὺς δ' οὐ προσίεντο, ἀλλὰ φυγῇ
λείπουσι τὸ χωρίον. καὶ τοῦτόν τε παρεληλύθεσαν οἱ
Ἕλληνες καὶ ἕτερον ὁρῶσιν ἔμπροσθεν λόφον κατεχόμενον
ἐπὶ τοῦτον αὖθις ἐδόκει πορεύεσθαι. 13. ἐννοήσας δ' ὁ Ξενοφῶν 15
μή, εἰ ἔρημον καταλίποι τὸν ἡλωκότα λόφον, [καὶ] πάλιν
λαβόντες οἱ πολέμιοι ἐπιθοῖντο τοῖς ὑποζυγίοις παριοῦσιν
(ἐπὶ πολὺ δ' ἦν τὰ ὑποζύγια ἅτε διὰ στενῆς τῆς ὁδοῦ
πορευόμενα), καταλείπει ἐπὶ τοῦ λόφου λοχαγούς, Κηφισόδωρον Κηφισοφῶντος Ἀθηναῖον καὶ Ἀμφικράτην Ἀμφιδήμου 20
Ἀθηναῖον καὶ Ἀρχαγόραν Ἀργεῖον φυγάδα, αὐτὸς δὲ σὺν
τοῖς λοιποῖς ἐπορεύετο ἐπὶ τὸν δεύτερον λόφον, καὶ τῷ αὐτῷ
τρόπῳ καὶ τοῦτον αἱροῦσιν. 14. ἔτι δ' αὐτοῖς τρίτος μαστὸς
λοιπὸς ἦν πολὺ ὀρθιώτατος ὁ ὑπὲρ τῆς ἐπὶ τῷ πυρὶ καταληφθείσης φυλακῆς τῆς νυκτὸς ὑπὸ τῶν ἐθελοντῶν. 15. ἐπεὶ δ' 25
ἐγγὺς ἐγένοντο οἱ Ἕλληνες, λείπουσιν οἱ βάρβαροι ἀμαχητὶ
τὸν μαστόν, ὥστε θαυμαστὸν πᾶσι γενέσθαι καὶ ὑπώπτευον

δείσαντας αὐτοὺς μὴ κυκλωθέντες πολιορκοῖντο ἀπολιπεῖν. 1
οἱ δ' ἄρα ἀπὸ τοῦ ἄκρου καθορῶντες τὰ ὄπισθεν γιγνόμενα
πάντες ἐπὶ τοὺς ὀπισθοφύλακας ἐχώρουν. 16. *καὶ Ξενοφῶν μὲν*
σὺν τοῖς νεωτάτοις ἀνέβαινεν ἐπὶ τὸ ἄκρον, τοὺς δὲ ἄλλους
ἐκέλευσεν ὑπάγειν, ὅπως οἱ τελευταῖοι λόχοι προσμείξειαν, 5
καὶ προελθόντας κατὰ τὴν ὁδὸν ἐν τῷ ὁμαλῷ θέσθαι τὰ ὅπλα
εἶπε. 17. *καὶ ἐν τούτῳ τῷ χρόνῳ ἦλθεν Ἀρχαγόρας ὁ Ἀργεῖος*
πεφευγὼς καὶ λέγει ὡς ἀπεκόπησαν ἀπὸ τοῦ λόφου καὶ
ὅτι τεθνᾶσι Κηφισόδωρος *καὶ Ἀμφικράτης καὶ ἄλλοι ὅσοι*
μὴ ἁλόμενοι κατὰ τῆς πέτρας πρὸς τοὺς ὀπισθοφύλακας 10
ἀφίκοντο. 18. *ταῦτα δὲ διαπραξάμενοι οἱ βάρβαροι ἧκον ἐπ'*
ἀντίπορον λόφον τῷ μαστῷ· καὶ ὁ Ξενοφῶν διελέγετο αὐτοῖς
δι' ἑρμηνέως περὶ σπονδῶν καὶ τοὺς νεκροὺς ἀπῄτει. 19. *οἱ δὲ*
ἔφασαν ἀποδώσειν ἐφ' ᾧ μὴ καίειν τὰς οἰκίας. συνωμολόγει
ταῦτα ὁ Ξενοφῶν. ἐν ᾧ δὲ τὸ μὲν ἄλλο στράτευμα παρῄει, 15
οἱ δὲ ταῦτα διελέγοντο, πάντες οἱ ἐκ τούτου τοῦ τόπου
συνερρύησαν· †ἐνταῦθα ἵσταντο οἱ πολέμιοι†. 20. *καὶ ἐπεὶ*
ἤρξαντο καταβαίνειν ἀπὸ τοῦ μαστοῦ πρὸς τοὺς ἄλλους
ἔνθα τὰ ὅπλα ἔκειντο, ἵεντο δὴ οἱ πολέμιοι πολλῷ πλήθει
καὶ θορύβῳ· καὶ ἐπεὶ ἐγένοντο ἐπὶ τῆς κορυφῆς τοῦ μαστοῦ 20
ἀφ' οὗ Ξενοφῶν κατέβαινεν, ἐκυλίνδουν πέτρους· καὶ ἑνὸς
μὲν κατέαξαν τὸ σκέλος, Ξενοφῶντα δὲ ὁ ὑπασπιστὴς
ἔχων τὴν ἀσπίδα ἀπέλιπεν· 21. Εὐρύλοχος δὲ Λουσιεὺς [Ἀρκὰς]
προσέδραμεν αὐτῷ ὁπλίτης, καὶ πρὸ ἀμφοῖν προβεβλημένος
ἀπεχώρει, καὶ οἱ ἄλλοι πρὸς τοὺς συντεταγμένους ἀπῆλθον. 25
22. *ἐκ δὲ τούτου πᾶν ὁμοῦ ἐγένετο τὸ Ἑλληνικόν, καὶ ἐσκήνησαν*
αὐτοῦ ἐν πολλαῖς καὶ καλαῖς οἰκίαις καὶ ἐπιτηδείοις δαψιλέσι·

καὶ γὰρ οἶνος πολὺς ἦν, ὥστε ἐν λάκκοις κονιατοῖς εἶχον. 1
23. Ξενοφῶν δὲ καὶ Χειρίσοφος διεπράξαντο ὥστε λαβόντες
τοὺς νεκροὺς ἀπέδοσαν τὸν ἡγεμόνα· καὶ πάντα ἐποίησαν
τοῖς ἀποθανοῦσιν ἐκ τῶν δυνατῶν ὥσπερ νομίζεται ἀνδράσιν
ἀγαθοῖς. 24. τῇ δὲ ὑστεραίᾳ ἄνευ ἡγεμόνος ἐπορεύοντο· μαχό- 5
μενοι δ᾽ οἱ πολέμιοι καὶ ὅπῃ εἴη στενὸν χωρίον προκατα-
λαμβάνοντες ἐκώλυον τὰς παρόδους. 25. ὁπότε μὲν οὖν τοὺς
πρώτους κωλύοιεν, Ξενοφῶν ὄπισθεν ἐκβαίνων πρὸς τὰ ὄρη
ἔλυε τὴν ἀπόφραξιν τῆς ὁδοῦ τοῖς πρώτοις ἀνωτέρω πειρώμενος γίγνεσθαι τῶν κωλυόντων, 26. ὁπότε δὲ τοῖς ὄπισθεν 10
ἐπιθοῖντο, Χειρίσοφος ἐκβαίνων καὶ πειρώμενος ἀνωτέρω
γίγνεσθαι τῶν κωλυόντων ἔλυε τὴν ἀπόφραξιν τῆς παρόδου
τοῖς ὄπισθεν· καὶ ἀεὶ οὕτως ἐβοήθουν ἀλλήλοις καὶ ἰσχυρῶς
ἀλλήλων ἐπεμέλοντο. 27. ἦν δὲ καὶ ὁπότε αὐτοῖς τοῖς ἀναβᾶσι
πολλὰ πράγματα παρεῖχον οἱ βάρβαροι πάλιν καταβαίνουσιν· 15
ἐλαφροὶ γὰρ ἦσαν ὥστε καὶ ἐγγύθεν φεύγοντες ἀποφεύγειν·
οὐδὲν γὰρ εἶχον ἄλλο ἢ τόξα καὶ σφενδόνας. 28. ἄριστοι δὲ καὶ
τοξόται ἦσαν· εἶχον δὲ τόξα ἐγγὺς τριπήχη, τὰ δὲ τοξεύματα πλέον ἢ διπήχη· εἷλκον δὲ τὰς νευρὰς ὁπότε τοξεύοιεν
πρὸς τὸ κάτω τοῦ τόξου τῷ ἀριστερῷ ποδὶ προσβαίνοντες. 20
τὰ δὲ τοξεύματα ἐχώρει διὰ τῶν ἀσπίδων καὶ διὰ τῶν
θωράκων. ἐχρῶντο δὲ αὐτοῖς οἱ Ἕλληνες, ἐπεὶ λάβοιεν,
ἀκοντίοις ἐναγκυλῶντες. ἐν τούτοις τοῖς χωρίοις οἱ Κρῆτες
χρησιμώτατοι ἐγένοντο. ἦρχε δὲ αὐτῶν Στρατοκλῆς Κρής.
1. ταύτην δ᾽ αὖ τὴν ἡμέραν ηὐλίσθησαν ἐν ταῖς κώμαις 25
ταῖς ὑπὲρ τοῦ πεδίου παρὰ τὸν Κεντρίτην ποταμόν, εὖρος ὡς
δίπλεθρον, ὃς ὁρίζει τὴν Ἀρμενίαν καὶ τὴν τῶν Καρδούχων

χώραν. καὶ οἱ Ἕλληνες ἐνταῦθα ἀνέπνευσαν ἄσμενοι ἰδόντες 1
πεδίον· ἀπεῖχε δὲ τῶν ὀρέων ὁ ποταμὸς ἓξ ἢ ἑπτὰ στάδια
τῶν Καρδούχων. 2. τότε μὲν οὖν ηὐλίσθησαν μάλα ἡδέως καὶ
τἀπιτήδεια ἔχοντες καὶ πολλὰ τῶν παρεληλυθότων πόνων
μνημονεύοντες. ἑπτὰ γὰρ ἡμέρας ὅσασπερ ἐπορεύθησαν διὰ 5
τῶν Καρδούχων πάσας μαχόμενοι διετέλεσαν, καὶ ἔπαθον
κακὰ ὅσα οὐδὲ τὰ σύμπαντα ὑπὸ βασιλέως καὶ Τισσαφέρνους.
ὡς οὖν ἀπηλλαγμένοι τούτων ἡδέως ἐκοιμήθησαν.

3. ἅμα δὲ τῇ ἡμέρᾳ ὁρῶσιν ἱππέας που πέραν τοῦ ποταμοῦ
ἐξωπλισμένους ὡς κωλύσοντας διαβαίνειν, πεζοὺς δ' ἐπὶ ταῖς 10
ὄχθαις παρατεταγμένους ἄνω τῶν ἱππέων ὡς κωλύσοντας
εἰς τὴν Ἀρμενίαν ἐκβαίνειν. 4. ἦσαν δ' οὗτοι Ὀρόντα καὶ
Ἀρτούχα Ἀρμένιοι καὶ Μάρδοι καὶ Χαλδαῖοι μισθοφόροι.
ἐλέγοντο δὲ οἱ Χαλδαῖοι ἐλεύθεροί τε καὶ ἄλκιμοι εἶναι·
ὅπλα δ' εἶχον γέρρα μακρὰ καὶ λόγχας. 5. αἱ δὲ ὄχθαι αὗται 15
ἐφ' ὧν παρατεταγμένοι οὗτοι ἦσαν τρία ἢ τέτταρα πλέθρα
ἀπὸ τοῦ ποταμοῦ ἀπεῖχον· ὁδὸς δὲ μία ὁρωμένη ἦν ἄγουσα
ἄνω ὥσπερ χειροποίητος· ταύτῃ ἐπειρῶντο διαβαίνειν οἱ
Ἕλληνες. 6. ἐπεὶ δὲ πειρωμένοις τό τε ὕδωρ ὑπὲρ τῶν μαστῶν
ἐφαίνετο, καὶ τραχὺς ἦν ὁ ποταμὸς μεγάλοις λίθοις καὶ 20
ὀλισθηροῖς, καὶ οὔτ' ἐν τῷ ὕδατι τὰ ὅπλα ἦν ἔχειν· εἰ δὲ
μή, ἥρπαζεν ὁ ποταμός· ἐπί τε τῆς κεφαλῆς τὰ ὅπλα εἴ τις
φέροι, γυμνοὶ ἐγίγνοντο πρὸς τὰ τοξεύματα καὶ τἆλλα βέλη,
ἀνεχώρησαν καὶ αὐτοῦ ἐστρατοπεδεύσαντο παρὰ τὸν ποταμόν.
7. ἔνθα δὲ αὐτοὶ τὴν πρόσθεν νύκτα ἦσαν ἐπὶ τοῦ ὄρους ἑώρων 25
τοὺς Καρδούχους πολλοὺς συνειλεγμένους ἐν τοῖς ὅπλοις.
ἐνταῦθα δὴ πολλὴ ἀθυμία ἦν τοῖς Ἕλλησιν, ὁρῶσι μὲν τοῦ
ποταμοῦ τὴν δυσπορίαν, ὁρῶσι δὲ τοὺς διαβαίνειν κωλύ-

σοντας, ὁρῶσι δὲ τοῖς διαβαίνουσιν ἐπικεισομένους τοὺς 1
Καρδούχους ὄπισθεν. 8. ταύτην μὲν οὖν τὴν ἡμέραν καὶ νύκτα
ἔμειναν ἐν πολλῇ ἀπορίᾳ ὄντες. Ξενοφῶν δὲ ὄναρ εἶδεν·
ἔδοξεν ἐν πέδαις δεδέσθαι, αὗται δὲ αὐτῷ αὐτόμαται περιρρυῆναι, ὥστε λυθῆναι καὶ διαβαίνειν ὁπόσον ἐβούλετο. ἐπεὶ 5
δὲ ὄρθρος ἦν, ἔρχεται πρὸς τὸν Χειρίσοφον καὶ λέγει ὅτι
ἐλπίδας ἔχει καλῶς ἔσεσθαι, καὶ διηγεῖται αὐτῷ τὸ ὄναρ.
9. ὁ δὲ ἥδετό τε καὶ ὡς τάχιστα ἕως ὑπέφαινεν ἐθύοντο πάντες
παρόντες οἱ στρατηγοί· καὶ τὰ ἱερὰ καλὰ ἦν εὐθὺς ἐπὶ τοῦ
πρώτου. καὶ ἀπιόντες ἀπὸ τῶν ἱερῶν οἱ στρατηγοὶ καὶ 10
λοχαγοὶ παρήγγελλον τῇ στρατιᾷ ἀριστοποιεῖσθαι. 10. καὶ ἀριστῶντι τῷ Ξενοφῶντι προσέτρεχον δύο νεανίσκω· ᾔδεσαν
γὰρ πάντες ὅτι ἐξείη αὐτῷ καὶ ἀριστῶντι καὶ δειπνοῦντι
προσελθεῖν καί, εἰ καθεύδοι, ἐπεγείραντα εἰπεῖν, εἴ τίς τι
ἔχοι τῶν πρὸς τὸν πόλεμον. 11. καὶ τότε ἔλεγον ὅτι τυγχά- 15
νοιεν φρύγανα συλλέγοντες ὡς ἐπὶ πῦρ, κἄπειτα κατίδοιεν
ἐν τῷ πέραν ἐν πέτραις καθηκούσαις ἐπ᾽ αὐτὸν τὸν ποταμὸν
γέροντά τε καὶ γυναῖκα καὶ παιδίσκας ὥσπερ μαρσίπους ἱμα-
τίων κατατιθεμένους ἐν πέτρᾳ ἀντρώδει. 12. ἰδοῦσι δὲ σφίσι
δόξαι ἀσφαλὲς εἶναι διαβῆναι· οὐδὲ γὰρ τοῖς πολεμίοις 20
ἱππεῦσι προσβατὸν εἶναι κατὰ τοῦτο. ἐκδύντες δ᾽ ἔφασαν
ἔχοντες τὰ ἐγχειρίδια γυμνοὶ ὡς νευσόμενοι διαβαίνειν·
πορευόμενοι δὲ πρόσθεν διαβῆναι πρὶν βρέξαι τὰ αἰδοῖα·
καὶ διαβάντες, λαβόντες τὰ ἱμάτια πάλιν ἥκειν. 13. εὐθὺς οὖν
Ξενοφῶν αὐτός τε ἔσπενδε καὶ τοῖς νεανίσκοις ἐγχεῖν ἐκέ- 25
λευε καὶ εὔχεσθαι τοῖς φήνασι θεοῖς τά τε ὀνείρατα καὶ τὸν
πόρον καὶ τὰ λοιπὰ ἀγαθὰ ἐπιτελέσαι. σπείσας δ᾽ εὐθὺς
ἦγε τοὺς νεανίσκους παρὰ τὸν Χειρίσοφον, καὶ διηγοῦνται

ταὐτά. ἀκούσας δὲ καὶ ὁ Χειρίσοφος σπονδὰς ἐποίει. 14. σπεί- 1
σαντες δὲ τοῖς μὲν ἄλλοις παρήγγελλον συσκευάζεσθαι,
αὐτοὶ δὲ συγκαλέσαντες τοὺς στρατηγοὺς ἐβουλεύοντο ὅπως
ἂν κάλλιστα διαβαῖεν καὶ τούς τε ἔμπροσθεν νικῷεν καὶ
ὑπὸ τῶν ὄπισθεν μηδὲν πάσχοιεν κακόν. 15. καὶ ἔδοξεν αὐτοῖς 5
Χειρίσοφον μὲν ἡγεῖσθαι καὶ διαβαίνειν ἔχοντα τὸ ἥμισυ
τοῦ στρατεύματος, τὸ δ' ἥμισυ ἔτι ὑπομένειν σὺν Ξενοφῶντι,
τὰ δὲ ὑποζύγια καὶ τὸν ὄχλον ἐν μέσῳ τούτων διαβαίνειν.
ἐπεὶ δὲ ταῦτα καλῶς εἶχεν, ἐπορεύοντο· 16. ἡγοῦντο δ' οἱ νεα-
νίσκοι ἐν ἀριστερᾷ ἔχοντες τὸν ποταμόν· ὁδὸς δὲ ἦν ἐπὶ 10
τὴν διάβασιν ὡς τέτταρες στάδιοι. 17. πορευομένων δ' αὐτῶν
ἀντιπαρῆσαν αἱ τάξεις τῶν ἱππέων. ἐπειδὴ δὲ ἦσαν κατὰ
τὴν διάβασιν καὶ τὰς ὄχθας τοῦ ποταμοῦ, ἔθεντο τὰ ὅπλα,
καὶ αὐτὸς πρῶτος Χειρίσοφος στεφανωσάμενος καὶ ἀποδὺς
ἐλάμβανε τὰ ὅπλα καὶ τοῖς ἄλλοις πᾶσι παρήγγελλε, καὶ 15
τοὺς λοχαγοὺς ἐκέλευεν ἄγειν τοὺς λόχους ὀρθίους, τοὺς μὲν
ἐν ἀριστερᾷ τοὺς δ' ἐν δεξιᾷ ἑαυτοῦ. καὶ οἱ μὲν μάντεις
ἐσφαγιάζοντο εἰς τὸν ποταμόν· 18. οἱ δὲ πολέμιοι ἐτόξευον καὶ
ἐσφενδόνων· ἀλλ' οὔπω ἐξικνοῦντο· 19. ἐπεὶ δὲ καλὰ ἦν τὰ
σφάγια, ἐπαιάνιζον πάντες οἱ στρατιῶται καὶ ἀνηλάλαζον, 20
συνωλόλυζον δὲ καὶ αἱ γυναῖκες ἅπασαι. πολλαὶ γὰρ ἦσαν
ἑταῖραι ἐν τῷ στρατεύματι. 20. καὶ Χειρίσοφος μὲν ἐνέβαινε
καὶ οἱ σὺν ἐκείνῳ· ὁ δὲ Ξενοφῶν τῶν ὀπισθοφυλάκων
λαβὼν τοὺς εὐζωνοτάτους ἔθει ἀνὰ κράτος πάλιν ἐπὶ τὸν
πόρον τὸν κατὰ τὴν ἔκβασιν τὴν εἰς τὰ τῶν Ἀρμενίων ὄρη, 25
προσποιούμενος ταύτῃ διαβὰς ἀποκλείσειν τοὺς παρὰ τὸν
ποταμὸν ἱππέας. 21. οἱ δὲ πολέμιοι ὁρῶντες μὲν τοὺς ἀμφὶ
Χειρίσοφον εὐπετῶς τὸ ὕδωρ περῶντας, ὁρῶντες δὲ τοὺς
ἀμφὶ Ξενοφῶντα θέοντας εἰς τοὔμπαλιν, δείσαντες μὴ

ἀποληφθείησαν φεύγουσιν ἀνὰ κράτος ὡς πρὸς τὴν τοῦ ποταμοῦ 1
ἄνω ἔκβασιν. ἐπεὶ δὲ κατὰ τὴν ὁδὸν ἐγένοντο, ἔτεινον ἄνω
πρὸς τὸ ὄρος. 22. Λύκιος δ' ὁ τὴν τάξιν ἔχων τῶν ἱππέων καὶ
Αἰσχίνης ὁ τὴν τάξιν τῶν πελταστῶν τῶν ἀμφὶ Χειρίσοφον
ἐπεὶ ἑώρων ἀνὰ κράτος φεύγοντας, εἵποντο· οἱ δὲ στρα- 5
τιῶται ἐβόων μὴ ἀπολείπεσθαι, ἀλλὰ συνεκβαίνειν ἐπὶ τὸ
ὄρος. 23. Χειρίσοφος δ' αὖ ἐπεὶ διέβη, τοὺς ἱππέας οὐκ ἐδίωκεν,
εὐθὺς δὲ κατὰ τὰς προσηκούσας ὄχθας ἐπὶ τὸν ποταμὸν
ἐξέβαινεν ἐπὶ τοὺς ἄνω πολεμίους. οἱ δὲ ἄνω, ὁρῶντες μὲν
τοὺς ἑαυτῶν ἱππέας φεύγοντας, ὁρῶντες δ' ὁπλίτας σφίσιν 10
ἐπιόντας, ἐκλείπουσι τὰ ὑπὲρ τοῦ ποταμοῦ ἄκρα. 24. Ξενοφῶν
δ' ἐπεὶ τὰ πέραν ἑώρα καλῶς γιγνόμενα, ἀπεχώρει τὴν
ταχίστην πρὸς τὸ διαβαῖνον στράτευμα· καὶ γὰρ οἱ Καρδοῦχοι φανεροὶ ἤδη ἦσαν εἰς τὸ πεδίον καταβαίνοντες ὡς
ἐπιθησόμενοι τοῖς τελευταίοις. 25. καὶ Χειρίσοφος μὲν τὰ ἄνω 15
κατεῖχε, Λύκιος δὲ σὺν ὀλίγοις ἐπιχειρήσας ἐπιδιῶξαι ἔλαβε
τῶν σκευοφόρων τὰ ὑπολειπόμενα καὶ μετὰ τούτων ἐσθῆτά
τε καλὴν καὶ ἐκπώματα. 26. καὶ τὰ σκευοφόρα τῶν Ἑλλήνων
καὶ ὁ ὄχλος ἀκμὴν διέβαινε, Ξενοφῶν δὲ στρέψας πρὸς τοὺς
Καρδούχους ἀντία τὰ ὅπλα ἔθετο, καὶ παρήγγειλε τοῖς 20
λοχαγοῖς κατ' ἐνωμοτίας ποιήσασθαι ἕκαστον τὸν ἑαυτοῦ
λόχον, παρ' ἀσπίδα παραγαγόντας τὴν ἐνωμοτίαν ἐπὶ φά-
λαγγος· καὶ τοὺς μὲν λοχαγοὺς καὶ τοὺς ἐνωμοτάρχους πρὸς
τῶν Καρδούχων ἰέναι, οὐραγοὺς δὲ καταστήσασθαι πρὸς τοῦ
ποταμοῦ. 27. οἱ δὲ Καρδοῦχοι ὡς ἑώρων τοὺς ὀπισθοφύλακας 25
τοῦ ὄχλου ψιλουμένους καὶ ὀλίγους ἤδη φαινομένους, θᾶττον
δὴ ἐπῇσαν ᾠδάς τινας ᾄδοντες. ὁ δὲ Χειρίσοφος, ἐπεὶ

τὰ παρ' αὐτῷ ἀσφαλῶς εἶχε, πέμπει παρὰ Ξενοφῶντα τοὺς 1
πελταστὰς καὶ σφενδονήτας καὶ τοξότας καὶ κελεύει ποιεῖν
ὅ τι ἂν παραγγέλλῃ. 28. ἰδὼν δ' αὐτοὺς διαβαίνοντας Ξενοφῶν
πέμψας ἄγγελον κελεύει αὐτοῦ μεῖναι ἐπὶ τοῦ ποταμοῦ μὴ
διαβάντας· ὅταν δ' ἄρξωνται αὐτοὶ διαβαίνειν, ἐναντίους 5
ἔνθεν καὶ ἔνθεν σφῶν ἐμβαίνειν ὡς διαβησομένους, διηγκυλωμένους τοὺς ἀκοντιστὰς καὶ ἐπιβεβλημένους τοὺς τοξότας·
μὴ πρόσω δὲ τοῦ ποταμοῦ προβαίνειν. 29. τοῖς δὲ παρ' ἑαυτῷ
παρήγγειλεν, ἐπειδὰν σφενδόνη ἐξικνῆται καὶ ἀσπὶς ψοφῇ,
παιανίσαντας θεῖν εἰς τοὺς πολεμίους, ἐπειδὰν δ' ἀναστρέ- 10
ψωσιν οἱ πολέμιοι καὶ ἐκ τοῦ ποταμοῦ ὁ σαλπικτὴς σημήνῃ
τὸ πολεμικόν, ἀναστρέψαντας ἐπὶ δόρυ ἡγεῖσθαι μὲν τοὺς
οὐραγούς, θεῖν δὲ πάντας καὶ διαβαίνειν ὅτι τάχιστα ᾗ
ἕκαστος τὴν τάξιν εἶχεν, ὡς μὴ ἐμποδίζειν ἀλλήλους· ὅτι
οὗτος ἄριστος ἔσοιτο ὃς ἂν πρῶτος ἐν τῷ πέραν γένηται. 15
30. οἱ δὲ Καρδοῦχοι ὁρῶντες ὀλίγους ἤδη τοὺς λοιπούς (πολλοὶ
γὰρ καὶ τῶν μένειν τεταγμένων ᾤχοντο ἐπιμελόμενοι οἱ μὲν
ὑποζυγίων, οἱ δὲ σκευῶν, οἱ δ' ἑταιρῶν), ἐνταῦθα δὴ ἐπέκειντο θρασέως καὶ ἤρχοντο σφενδονᾶν καὶ τοξεύειν. 31. οἱ
δὲ Ἕλληνες παιανίσαντες ὥρμησαν δρόμῳ ἐπ' αὐτούς· οἱ 20
δὲ οὐκ ἐδέξαντο· καὶ γὰρ ἦσαν ὡπλισμένοι ὡς μὲν ἐν τοῖς
ὄρεσιν ἱκανῶς πρὸς τὸ ἐπιδραμεῖν καὶ φεύγειν, πρὸς δὲ
τὸ εἰς χεῖρας δέχεσθαι οὐχ ἱκανῶς. 32. ἐν τούτῳ σημαίνει ὁ
σαλπικτής· καὶ οἱ μὲν πολέμιοι ἔφευγον πολὺ ἔτι θᾶττον,
οἱ δὲ Ἕλληνες τἀναντία στρέψαντες ἔφευγον διὰ τοῦ ποταμοῦ 25
ὅτι τάχιστα. 33. τῶν δὲ πολεμίων οἱ μέν τινες αἰσθόμενοι
πάλιν ἔδραμον ἐπὶ τὸν ποταμὸν καὶ τοξεύοντες ὀλίγους
ἔτρωσαν, οἱ δὲ πολλοὶ καὶ πέραν ὄντων τῶν Ἑλλήνων ἔτι

φανεροὶ ἦσαν φεύγοντες. 34. οἱ δὲ ὑπαντήσαντες ἀνδριζόμενοι 1
καὶ προσωτέρω τοῦ καιροῦ προϊόντες ὕστερον τῶν μετὰ Ξενοφῶντος διέβησαν πάλιν· καὶ ἐτρώθησάν τινες καὶ τούτων.
1. ἐπεὶ δὲ διέβησαν, συνταξάμενοι ἀμφὶ μέσον ἡμέρας
ἐπορεύθησαν διὰ τῆς Ἀρμενίας πεδίον ἅπαν καὶ λείους γη- 5
λόφους οὐ μεῖον ἢ πέντε παρασάγγας· οὐ γὰρ ἦσαν ἐγγὺς
τοῦ ποταμοῦ κῶμαι διὰ τοὺς πολέμους τοὺς πρὸς τοὺς Καρδούχους. 2. εἰς δὲ ἣν ἀφίκοντο κώμην μεγάλη τε ἦν καὶ
βασίλειον εἶχε τῷ σατράπῃ καὶ ἐπὶ ταῖς πλείσταις οἰκίαις
τύρσεις ἐπῆσαν· 3. ἐπιτήδεια δ' ἦν δαψιλῆ. ἐντεῦθεν δ' ἐπο- 10
ρεύθησαν σταθμοὺς δύο παρασάγγας δέκα μέχρι ὑπερῆλθον
τὰς πηγὰς τοῦ Τίγρητος ποταμοῦ. ἐντεῦθεν δ' ἐπορεύθησαν
σταθμοὺς τρεῖς παρασάγγας πεντεκαίδεκα ἐπὶ τὸν Τηλεβόαν
ποταμόν. οὗτος δ' ἦν καλὸς μέν, μέγας δ' οὔ· κῶμαι δὲ
πολλαὶ περὶ τὸν ποταμὸν ἦσαν. 4. ὁ δὲ τόπος οὗτος Ἀρμενία 15
ἐκαλεῖτο ἡ πρὸς ἑσπέραν. ὕπαρχος δ' ἦν αὐτῆς Τιρίβαζος,
ὁ καὶ βασιλεῖ φίλος γενόμενος, καὶ ὁπότε παρείη, οὐδεὶς
ἄλλος βασιλέα ἐπὶ τὸν ἵππον ἀνέβαλλεν. 5. οὗτος προσήλασεν ἱππέας ἔχων, καὶ προπέμψας ἑρμηνέα εἶπεν ὅτι βούλοιτο διαλεχθῆναι τοῖς ἄρχουσι. τοῖς δὲ στρατηγοῖς ἔδοξεν 20
ἀκοῦσαι· καὶ προσελθόντες εἰς ἐπήκοον ἠρώτων τί θέλει.
6. ὁ δὲ εἶπεν ὅτι σπείσασθαι βούλοιτο ἐφ' ᾧ μήτε αὐτὸς τοὺς
Ἕλληνας ἀδικεῖν μήτε ἐκείνους καίειν τὰς οἰκίας λαμβάνειν
τε τἀπιτήδεια ὅσων δέοιντο. ἔδοξε ταῦτα τοῖς στρατηγοῖς
καὶ ἐσπείσαντο ἐπὶ τούτοις. 25
7. ἐντεῦθεν δ' ἐπορεύθησαν σταθμοὺς τρεῖς διὰ πεδίου
παρασάγγας πεντεκαίδεκα· καὶ Τιρίβαζος παρηκολούθει ἔχων
τὴν ἑαυτοῦ δύναμιν ἀπέχων ὡς δέκα σταδίους· καὶ ἀφίκοντο
εἰς βασίλεια καὶ κώμας πέριξ πολλὰς πολλῶν τῶν ἐπιτηδείων μεστάς. 8. στρατοπεδευομένων δ' αὐτῶν γίγνεται τῆς 30

νυκτὸς χιὼν πολλή· καὶ ἕωθεν ἔδοξε διασκηνῆσαι τὰς τάξεις 1
καὶ τοὺς στρατηγοὺς κατὰ τὰς κώμας· οὐ γὰρ ἑώρων πολέ-
μιον οὐδένα καὶ ἀσφαλὲς ἐδόκει εἶναι διὰ τὸ πλῆθος τῆς
χιόνος. 9. ἐνταῦθα εἶχον τὰ ἐπιτήδεια ὅσα ἐστὶν ἀγαθά,
ἱερεῖα, σῖτον, οἴνους παλαιοὺς εὐώδεις, ἀσταφίδας, ὄσπρια 5
παντοδαπά. τῶν δὲ ἀποσκεδαννυμένων τινὲς ἀπὸ τοῦ στρα-
τοπέδου ἔλεγον ὅτι κατίδοιεν νύκτωρ πολλὰ πυρὰ φαίνοντα.
10. ἐδόκει δὴ τοῖς στρατηγοῖς οὐκ ἀσφαλὲς εἶναι διασκηνοῦν,
ἀλλὰ συναγαγεῖν τὸ στράτευμα πάλιν. ἐντεῦθεν συνῆλθον·
καὶ γὰρ ἐδόκει διαιθριάζειν. 11. νυκτερευόντων δ' αὐτῶν 10
ἐνταῦθα ἐπιπίπτει χιὼν ἄπλετος, ὥστε ἀπέκρυψε καὶ τὰ
ὅπλα καὶ τοὺς ἀνθρώπους κατακειμένους· καὶ τὰ ὑποζύγια
συνεπόδισεν ἡ χιών· καὶ πολὺς ὄκνος ἦν ἀνίστασθαι· κατακειμένων γὰρ ἀλεεινὸν ἦν ἡ χιὼν ἐπιπεπτωκυῖα ὅτῳ μὴ
παραρρυείη. 12. ἐπεὶ δὲ Ξενοφῶν ἐτόλμησε γυμνὸς ἀναστὰς 15
σχίζειν ξύλα, τάχ' ἀναστάς τις καὶ ἄλλος ἐκείνου ἀφελόμενος ἔσχιζεν. ἐκ δὲ τούτου καὶ ἄλλοι ἀναστάντες πῦρ
ἔκαιον καὶ ἐχρίοντο· 13. πολὺ γὰρ ἐνταῦθα ηὑρίσκετο χρῖμα, ᾧ
ἐχρῶντο ἀντ' ἐλαίου, σύειον καὶ σησάμινον καὶ ἀμυγδάλινον
ἐκ τῶν πικρῶν καὶ τερμίνθινον. ἐκ δὲ τῶν αὐτῶν τούτων 20
καὶ μύρον ηὑρίσκετο.

14. μετὰ ταῦτα ἐδόκει πάλιν διασκηνητέον εἶναι [τὰς κώμας]
εἰς στέγας. ἔνθα δὴ οἱ στρατιῶται σὺν πολλῇ κραυγῇ
καὶ ἡδονῇ ᾖσαν ἐπὶ τὰς στέγας καὶ τὰ ἐπιτήδεια· ὅσοι δὲ

ὅτε τὸ πρότερον ἀπῇσαν τὰς οἰκίας ἐνέπρησαν ὑπὸ ἀτασθα- 1
λίας, δίκην ἐδίδοσαν κακῶς σκηνοῦντες. 15. ἐντεῦθεν ἔπεμψαν
νυκτὸς Δημοκράτην Τημνίτην ἄνδρας δόντες ἐπὶ τὰ ὄρη ἔνθα
ἔφασαν οἱ ἀποσκεδαννύμενοι καθορᾶν τὰ πυρά· οὗτος γὰρ
ἐδόκει καὶ πρότερον πολλὰ ἤδη ἀληθεῦσαι τοιαῦτα, τὰ ὄντα τε 5
ὡς ὄντα καὶ τὰ μὴ ὄντα ὡς οὐκ ὄντα. 16. πορευθεὶς δὲ τὰ μὲν
πυρὰ οὐκ ἔφη ἰδεῖν, ἄνδρα δὲ συλλαβὼν ἧκεν ἄγων ἔχοντα
τόξον Περσικὸν καὶ φαρέτραν καὶ σάγαριν οἵανπερ καὶ <αἱ>
Ἀμαζόνες ἔχουσιν. 17. ἐρωτώμενος δὲ ποδαπὸς εἴη, Πέρσης
μὲν ἔφη εἶναι, πορεύεσθαι δ' ἀπὸ τοῦ Τιριβάζου στρατο- 10
πέδου, ὅπως ἐπιτήδεια λάβοι. οἱ δὲ ἠρώτων αὐτὸν τὸ
στράτευμα ὁπόσον τε εἴη καὶ ἐπὶ τίνι συνειλεγμένον. 18. ὁ δὲ
εἶπεν ὅτι Τιρίβαζος εἴη ἔχων τήν τε ἑαυτοῦ δύναμιν καὶ
μισθοφόρους Χάλυβας καὶ Ταόχους· παρεσκευάσθαι δὲ αὐτὸν
ἔφη ὡς ἐπὶ τῇ ὑπερβολῇ τοῦ ὄρους ἐν τοῖς στενοῖς ᾗπερ 15
μοναχῇ εἴη πορεία, ἐνταῦθα ἐπιθησόμενον τοῖς Ἕλλησιν.
19. ἀκούσασι τοῖς στρατηγοῖς ταῦτα ἔδοξε τὸ στράτευμα συν-
αγαγεῖν· καὶ εὐθὺς φύλακας καταλιπόντες καὶ στρατηγὸν ἐπὶ
τοῖς μένουσι Σοφαίνετον Στυμφάλιον ἐπορεύοντο ἔχοντες
ἡγεμόνα τὸν ἁλόντα ἄνθρωπον. 20. ἐπειδὴ δὲ ὑπερέβαλλον τὰ 20
ὄρη, οἱ πελτασταὶ προϊόντες καὶ κατιδόντες τὸ στρατόπεδον
οὐκ ἔμειναν τοὺς ὁπλίτας, ἀλλ' ἀνακραγόντες ἔθεον ἐπὶ τὸ
στρατόπεδον. 21. οἱ δὲ βάρβαροι ἀκούσαντες τὸν θόρυβον οὐχ
ὑπέμειναν, ἀλλ' ἔφευγον· ὅμως δὲ καὶ ἀπέθανόν τινες τῶν
βαρβάρων καὶ ἵπποι ἥλωσαν εἰς εἴκοσι καὶ ἡ σκηνὴ ἡ Τιρι- 25
βάζου ἑάλω καὶ ἐν αὐτῇ κλῖναι ἀργυρόποδες καὶ ἐκπώματα
καὶ οἱ ἀρτοκόποι καὶ οἱ οἰνοχόοι φάσκοντες εἶναι. 22. ἐπειδὴ

δὲ ἐπύθοντο ταῦτα οἱ τῶν ὁπλιτῶν στρατηγοί, ἐδόκει αὐτοῖς 1
ἀπιέναι τὴν ταχίστην ἐπὶ τὸ στρατόπεδον, μή τις ἐπίθεσις
γένοιτο τοῖς καταλελειμμένοις. καὶ εὐθὺς ἀνακαλεσάμενοι
τῇ σάλπιγγι ἀπῇσαν, καὶ ἀφίκοντο αὐθημερὸν ἐπὶ τὸ στρατόπεδον. 5

1. τῇ δ' ὑστεραίᾳ ἐδόκει πορευτέον εἶναι ὅπῃ δύναιντο
τάχιστα πρὶν ἢ συλλεγῆναι τὸ στράτευμα πάλιν καὶ καταλαβεῖν τὰ στενά. συσκευασάμενοι δ' εὐθὺς ἐπορεύοντο διὰ
χιόνος πολλῆς ἡγεμόνας ἔχοντες πολλούς· καὶ αὐθημερὸν
ὑπερβαλόντες τὸ ἄκρον ἐφ' ᾧ ἔμελλεν ἐπιτίθεσθαι Τιρίβαζος 10
κατεστρατοπεδεύσαντο. 2. ἐντεῦθεν δ' ἐπορεύθησαν σταθμοὺς
ἐρήμους τρεῖς παρασάγγας πεντεκαίδεκα ἐπὶ τὸν Εὐφράτην
ποταμόν, καὶ διέβαινον αὐτὸν βρεχόμενοι πρὸς τὸν ὀμφαλόν.
3. ἐλέγοντο δ' οὐδὲ πηγαὶ πρόσω εἶναι. ἐντεῦθεν ἐπορεύοντο
διὰ χιόνος πολλῆς καὶ πεδίου σταθμοὺς τρεῖς παρασάγγας 15
†πεντεκαίδεκα†. ὁ δὲ τρίτος ἐγένετο χαλεπὸς καὶ ἄνεμος
βορρᾶς ἐναντίος ἔπνει παντάπασιν ἀποκαίων πάντα καὶ
πηγνὺς τοὺς ἀνθρώπους. 4. ἔνθα δὴ τῶν μάντεών τις εἶπε
σφαγιάσασθαι τῷ ἀνέμῳ, καὶ σφαγιάζεται· καὶ πᾶσι δὴ
περιφανῶς ἔδοξεν λῆξαι τὸ χαλεπὸν τοῦ πνεύματος. ἦν δὲ 20
τῆς χιόνος τὸ βάθος ὀργυιά· ὥστε καὶ τῶν ὑποζυγίων καὶ
τῶν ἀνδραπόδων πολλὰ ἀπώλετο καὶ τῶν στρατιωτῶν ὡς
τριάκοντα. 5. διεγένοντο δὲ τὴν νύκτα πῦρ καίοντες· ξύλα δ'
ἦν ἐν τῷ σταθμῷ πολλά· οἱ δὲ ὀψὲ προσιόντες ξύλα οὐκ
εἶχον. οἱ οὖν πάλαι ἥκοντες καὶ τὸ πῦρ καίοντες οὐ προσ- 25

ίεσαν πρὸς τὸ πῦρ τοὺς ὀψίζοντας, εἰ μὴ μεταδοῖεν αὐτοῖς 1
πυροὺς ἢ ἄλλο [τι] εἴ τι ἔχοιεν βρωτόν. 6. ἔνθα δὴ μετεδίδοσαν ἀλλήλοις ὧν εἶχον ἕκαστοι. ἔνθα δὲ τὸ πῦρ ἐκαίετο,
διατηκομένης τῆς χιόνος βόθροι ἐγένοντο μεγάλοι ἔστε ἐπὶ
τὸ δάπεδον· οὗ δὴ παρῆν μετρεῖν τὸ βάθος τῆς χιόνος. 5
7. ἐντεῦθεν δὲ τὴν ἐπιοῦσαν ἡμέραν ὅλην ἐπορεύοντο διὰ
χιόνος, καὶ πολλοὶ τῶν ἀνθρώπων ἐβουλιμίασαν. Ξενοφῶν δ'
ὀπισθοφυλακῶν καὶ καταλαμβάνων τοὺς πίπτοντας τῶν ἀνθρώπων ἠγνόει ὅ τι τὸ πάθος εἴη. 8. ἐπειδὴ δὲ εἶπέ τις αὐτῷ
τῶν ἐμπείρων ὅτι σαφῶς βουλιμιῶσι κἄν τι φάγωσιν ἀνα- 10
στήσονται, περιιὼν περὶ τὰ ὑποζύγια, εἴ πού τι ὁρῴη βρωτόν,
διεδίδου καὶ διέπεμπε διδόντας τοὺς δυναμένους περιτρέχειν
τοῖς βουλιμιῶσιν. 9. ἐπειδὴ δέ τι ἐμφάγοιεν, ἀνίσταντο καὶ
ἐπορεύοντο. πορευομένων δὲ Χειρίσοφος μὲν ἀμφὶ κνέφας
πρὸς κώμην ἀφικνεῖται, καὶ ὑδροφορούσας ἐκ τῆς κώμης 15
πρὸς τῇ κρήνῃ γυναῖκας καὶ κόρας καταλαμβάνει ἔμπροσθεν
τοῦ ἐρύματος. 10. αὗται ἠρώτων αὐτοὺς τίνες εἶεν. ὁ δ' ἑρμη-
νεὺς εἶπε Περσιστὶ ὅτι παρὰ βασιλέως πορεύονται πρὸς τὸν
σατράπην. αἱ δὲ ἀπεκρίναντο ὅτι οὐκ ἐνταῦθα εἴη, ἀλλ'
ἀπέχει ὅσον παρασάγγην. οἱ δ', ἐπεὶ ὀψὲ ἦν, πρὸς τὸν 20
κώμαρχον συνεισέρχονται εἰς τὸ ἔρυμα σὺν ταῖς ὑδροφόροις.
11. Χειρίσοφος μὲν οὖν καὶ ὅσοι ἐδυνήθησαν τοῦ στρατεύματος
ἐνταῦθα ἐστρατοπεδεύσαντο, τῶν δ' ἄλλων στρατιωτῶν οἱ
μὴ δυνάμενοι διατελέσαι τὴν ὁδὸν ἐνυκτέρευσαν ἄσιτοι καὶ
ἄνευ πυρός· καὶ ἐνταῦθά τινες ἀπώλοντο τῶν στρατιωτῶν. 25
12. ἐφείποντο δὲ τῶν πολεμίων συνειλεγμένοι τινὲς καὶ τὰ μὴ
δυνάμενα τῶν ὑποζυγίων ἥρπαζον καὶ ἀλλήλοις ἐμάχοντο
περὶ αὐτῶν. ἐλείποντο δὲ τῶν στρατιωτῶν οἵ τε διεφθαρ-

μένοι ὑπὸ τῆς χιόνος τοὺς ὀφθαλμοὺς οἵ τε ὑπὸ τοῦ ψύχους 1
τοὺς δακτύλους τῶν ποδῶν ἀποσεσηπότες. 13. ἦν δὲ τοῖς μὲν
ὀφθαλμοῖς ἐπικούρημα τῆς χιόνος εἴ τις μέλαν τι ἔχων πρὸ
τῶν ὀφθαλμῶν ἐπορεύετο, τῶν δὲ ποδῶν εἴ τις κινοῖτο καὶ
μηδέποτε ἡσυχίαν ἔχοι καὶ εἰς τὴν νύκτα ὑπολύοιτο· 14. ὅσοι δὲ 5
ὑποδεδεμένοι ἐκοιμῶντο, εἰσεδύοντο εἰς τοὺς πόδας οἱ ἱμάντες
καὶ τὰ ὑποδήματα περιεπήγνυντο· καὶ γὰρ ἦσαν, ἐπειδὴ
ἐπέλιπε τὰ ἀρχαῖα ὑποδήματα, καρβάτιναι πεποιημέναι ἐκ
τῶν νεοδάρτων βοῶν. 15. διὰ τὰς τοιαύτας οὖν ἀνάγκας ὑπελεί-
ποντό τινες τῶν στρατιωτῶν· καὶ ἰδόντες μέλαν τι χωρίον 10
διὰ τὸ ἐκλελοιπέναι αὐτόθι τὴν χιόνα, εἴκαζον τετηκέναι· καὶ
ἐτετήκει διὰ κρήνην τινὰ ἣ πλησίον ἦν ἀτμίζουσα ἐν νάπῃ.
ἐνταῦθ' ἐκτραπόμενοι ἐκάθηντο καὶ οὐκ ἔφασαν πορεύεσθαι.
16. ὁ δὲ Ξενοφῶν ἔχων ὀπισθοφύλακας ὡς ᾔσθετο, ἐδεῖτο αὐτῶν
πάσῃ τέχνῃ καὶ μηχανῇ μὴ ἀπολείπεσθαι, λέγων ὅτι ἕπονται 15
πολλοὶ πολέμιοι συνειλεγμένοι, καὶ τελευτῶν ἐχαλέπαινεν.
οἱ δὲ σφάττειν ἐκέλευον· οὐ γὰρ ἂν δύνασθαι πορευθῆναι.
17. ἐνταῦθα ἔδοξε κράτιστον εἶναι τοὺς ἑπομένους πολεμίους
φοβῆσαι, εἴ τις δύναιτο, μὴ ἐπίοιεν τοῖς κάμνουσι. καὶ ἦν
μὲν σκότος ἤδη, οἱ δὲ προσῇσαν πολλῷ θορύβῳ ἀμφὶ ὧν 20
εἶχον διαφερόμενοι. 18. ἔνθα δὴ οἱ ὀπισθοφύλακες, ἅτε ὑγιαίνοντες, ἐξαναστάντες ἔδραμον εἰς τοὺς πολεμίους· οἱ δὲ
κάμνοντες ἀνακραγόντες ὅσον ἐδύναντο μέγιστον τὰς ἀσπίδας
πρὸς τὰ δόρατα ἔκρουσαν. οἱ δὲ πολέμιοι δείσαντες ἧκαν
ἑαυτοὺς κατὰ τῆς χιόνος εἰς τὴν νάπην, καὶ οὐδεὶς ἔτι οὐ- 25
δαμοῦ ἐφθέγξατο. 19. καὶ Ξενοφῶν μὲν καὶ οἱ σὺν αὐτῷ
εἰπόντες τοῖς ἀσθενοῦσιν ὅτι τῇ ὑστεραίᾳ ἥξουσί τινες
ἐπ' αὐτούς, πορευόμενοι πρὶν τέτταρα στάδια διελθεῖν ἐν-

τυγχάνουσιν ἐν τῇ ὁδῷ ἀναπαυομένοις ἐπὶ τῆς χιόνος τοῖς 1
στρατιώταις ἐγκεκαλυμμένοις, καὶ οὐδὲ φυλακὴ οὐδεμία
καθειστήκει· καὶ ἀνίστασαν αὐτούς. οἱ δ᾽ ἔλεγον ὅτι οἱ
ἔμπροσθεν οὐχ ὑποχωροῖεν. 20. ὁ δὲ παριὼν καὶ παραπέμπων
τῶν πελταστῶν τοὺς ἰσχυροτάτους ἐκέλευε σκέψασθαι τί 5
εἴη τὸ κωλῦον. οἱ δὲ ἀπήγγελλον ὅτι ὅλον οὕτως ἀνα-
παύοιτο τὸ στράτευμα. 21. ἐνταῦθα καὶ οἱ περὶ Ξενοφῶντα
ηὐλίσθησαν αὐτοῦ ἄνευ πυρὸς καὶ ἄδειπνοι, φυλακὰς οἵας
ἐδύναντο καταστησάμενοι. ἐπεὶ δὲ πρὸς ἡμέραν ἦν, ὁ μὲν
Ξενοφῶν πέμψας πρὸς τοὺς ἀσθενοῦντας τοὺς νεωτάτους 10
ἀναστήσαντας ἐκέλευεν ἀναγκάζειν προϊέναι. 22. ἐν δὲ τούτῳ
Χειρίσοφος πέμπει τῶν ἐκ τῆς κώμης σκεψομένους πῶς
ἔχοιεν οἱ τελευταῖοι. οἱ δὲ ἄσμενοι ἰδόντες τοὺς μὲν
ἀσθενοῦντας τούτοις παρέδοσαν κομίζειν ἐπὶ τὸ στρατόπεδον, αὐτοὶ δὲ ἐπορεύοντο, καὶ πρὶν εἴκοσι στάδια διεληλυ- 15
θέναι ἦσαν πρὸς τῇ κώμῃ ἔνθα Χειρίσοφος ηὐλίζετο. 23. ἐπεὶ
δὲ συνεγένοντο ἀλλήλοις, ἔδοξε κατὰ τὰς κώμας ἀσφαλὲς
εἶναι τὰς τάξεις σκηνοῦν. καὶ Χειρίσοφος μὲν αὐτοῦ ἔμενεν,
οἱ δὲ ἄλλοι διαλαχόντες ἃς ἑώρων κώμας ἐπορεύοντο ἕκαστοι
τοὺς ἑαυτῶν ἔχοντες. 24. ἔνθα δὴ Πολυκράτης Ἀθηναῖος λοχα- 20
γὸς ἐκέλευσεν ἀφιέναι ἑαυτόν· καὶ λαβὼν τοὺς εὐζώνους,
θέων ἐπὶ τὴν κώμην ἣν εἰλήχει Ξενοφῶν καταλαμβάνει
πάντας ἔνδον τοὺς κωμήτας καὶ τὸν κώμαρχον, καὶ πώλους
εἰς δασμὸν βασιλεῖ τρεφομένους ἑπτακαίδεκα, καὶ τὴν
θυγατέρα τοῦ κωμάρχου ἐνάτην ἡμέραν γεγαμημένην· ὁ δ᾽ 25
ἀνὴρ αὐτῆς λαγῶς ᾤχετο θηράσων καὶ οὐχ ἥλω ἐν τῇ
κώμῃ. 25. αἱ δ᾽ οἰκίαι ἦσαν κατάγειοι, τὸ μὲν στόμα ὥσπερ

φρέατος, κάτω δ' εὐρεῖαι· αἱ δὲ εἴσοδοι τοῖς μὲν ὑποζυγίοις 1
ὀρυκταί, οἱ δὲ ἄνθρωποι κατέβαινον ἐπὶ κλίμακος. ἐν δὲ
ταῖς οἰκίαις ἦσαν αἶγες, οἶες, βόες, ὄρνιθες, καὶ τὰ ἔκγονα
τούτων· τὰ δὲ κτήνη πάντα χιλῷ ἔνδον ἐτρέφοντο. 26. ἦσαν
δὲ καὶ πυροὶ καὶ κριθαὶ καὶ ὄσπρια καὶ οἶνος κρίθινος ἐν 5
κρατῆρσιν. ἐνῆσαν δὲ καὶ αὐταὶ αἱ κριθαὶ ἰσοχειλεῖς, καὶ
κάλαμοι ἐνέκειντο, οἱ μὲν μείζους οἱ δὲ ἐλάττους, γόνατα
οὐκ ἔχοντες· 27. τούτους ἔδει ὁπότε τις διψῴη λαβόντα εἰς τὸ
στόμα μύζειν. καὶ πάνυ ἄκρατος ἦν, εἰ μή τις ὕδωρ ἐπι-
χέοι· καὶ πάνυ ἡδὺ συμμαθόντι τὸ πῶμα ἦν. 28. ὁ δὲ Ξενοφῶν 10
τὸν ἄρχοντα τῆς κώμης ταύτης σύνδειπνον ἐποιήσατο καὶ
θαρρεῖν αὐτὸν ἐκέλευε λέγων ὅτι οὔτε τῶν τέκνων στερήσοιτο τήν τε οἰκίαν αὐτοῦ ἀντεμπλήσαντες τῶν ἐπιτηδείων
ἀπίασιν, ἢν ἀγαθόν τι τῷ στρατεύματι ἐξηγησάμενος φαί-
νηται ἔστ' ἂν ἐν ἄλλῳ ἔθνει γένωνται. 29. ὁ δὲ ταῦτα ὑπισχνεῖτο, 15
καὶ φιλοφρονούμενος οἶνον ἔφρασεν ἔνθα ἦν κατορωρυγμένος.
ταύτην μὲν τὴν νύκτα διασκηνήσαντες οὕτως ἐκοιμήθησαν
ἐν πᾶσιν ἀφθόνοις πάντες οἱ στρατιῶται, ἐν φυλακῇ ἔχοντες
τὸν κώμαρχον καὶ τὰ τέκνα αὐτοῦ ὁμοῦ ἐν ὀφθαλμοῖς. 30. τῇ
δ' ἐπιούσῃ ἡμέρᾳ Ξενοφῶν λαβὼν τὸν κώμαρχον πρὸς Χειρί- 20
σοφον ἐπορεύετο· ὅπου δὲ παρίοι κώμην, ἐτρέπετο πρὸς τοὺς
ἐν ταῖς κώμαις καὶ κατελάμβανε πανταχοῦ εὐωχουμένους καὶ
εὐθυμουμένους, καὶ οὐδαμόθεν ἀφίεσαν πρὶν παραθεῖναι αὐτοῖς ἄριστον· 31. οὐκ ἦν δ' ὅπου οὐ παρετίθεσαν ἐπὶ τὴν αὐτὴν
τράπεζαν κρέα ἄρνεια, ἐρίφεια, χοίρεια, μόσχεια, ὀρνίθεια, 25
σὺν πολλοῖς ἄρτοις τοῖς μὲν πυρίνοις τοῖς δὲ κριθίνοις.
32. ὁπότε δέ τις φιλοφρονούμενός τῳ βούλοιτο προπιεῖν, εἷλκεν

ἐπὶ τὸν κρατῆρα, ἔνθεν ἐπικύψαντα ἔδει ῥοφοῦντα πίνειν 1
ὥσπερ βοῦν. καὶ τῷ κωμάρχῳ ἐδίδοσαν λαμβάνειν ὅ τι
βούλοιτο. ὁ δὲ ἄλλο μὲν οὐδὲν ἐδέχετο, ὅπου δέ τινα τῶν
συγγενῶν ἴδοι, πρὸς ἑαυτὸν ἀεὶ ἐλάμβανεν. 33. ἐπεὶ δ' ἦλθον
πρὸς Χειρίσοφον, κατελάμβανον κἀκείνους σκηνοῦντας ἐστε- 5
φανωμένους τοῦ ξηροῦ χιλοῦ στεφάνοις, καὶ διακονοῦντας
Ἀρμενίους παῖδας σὺν ταῖς βαρβαρικαῖς στολαῖς· τοῖς παισὶν ἐδείκνυσαν ὥσπερ ἐνεοῖς ὅ τι δέοι ποιεῖν. 34. ἐπεὶ δ' ἀλλήλους ἐφιλοφρονήσαντο Χειρίσοφος καὶ Ξενοφῶν, κοινῇ δὴ
ἀνηρώτων τὸν κώμαρχον διὰ τοῦ Περσίζοντος ἑρμηνέως τίς 10
εἴη ἡ χώρα. ὁ δ' ἔλεγεν ὅτι Ἀρμενία. καὶ πάλιν ἠρώτων
τίνι οἱ ἵπποι τρέφονται. ὁ δ' ἔλεγεν ὅτι βασιλεῖ δασμός·
τὴν δὲ πλησίον χώραν ἔφη εἶναι Χάλυβας, καὶ τὴν ὁδὸν
ἔφραζεν ᾗ εἴη. 35. καὶ αὐτὸν τότε μὲν ᾤχετο ἄγων ὁ Ξενοφῶν
πρὸς τοὺς ἑαυτοῦ οἰκέτας, καὶ ἵππον ὃν εἰλήφει παλαίτερον 15
δίδωσι τῷ κωμάρχῳ ἀναθρέψαντι καταθῦσαι, ὅτι ἤκουεν
αὐτὸν ἱερὸν εἶναι τοῦ Ἡλίου, δεδιὼς μὴ ἀποθάνῃ· ἐκεκάκωτο γὰρ ὑπὸ τῆς πορείας· αὐτὸς δὲ τῶν πώλων λαμβάνει,
καὶ τῶν ἄλλων στρατηγῶν καὶ λοχαγῶν ἔδωκεν ἑκάστῳ
πῶλον. 36. ἦσαν δ' οἱ ταύτῃ ἵπποι μείονες μὲν τῶν Περσικῶν, 20
θυμοειδέστεροι δὲ πολύ. ἐνταῦθα δὴ καὶ διδάσκει ὁ κώμαρχος περὶ τοὺς πόδας τῶν ἵππων καὶ τῶν ὑποζυγίων σακία
περιειλεῖν, ὅταν διὰ τῆς χιόνος ἄγωσιν· ἄνευ γὰρ τῶν σακίων
κατεδύοντο μέχρι τῆς γαστρός.

1. ἐπεὶ δ' ἡμέρα ἦν ὀγδόη, τὸν μὲν ἡγεμόνα παραδίδωσι 25
Χειρισόφῳ, τοὺς δὲ οἰκέτας καταλείπει τῷ κωμάρχῳ, πλὴν
τοῦ υἱοῦ τοῦ ἄρτι ἡβάσκοντος· τοῦτον δὲ Πλεισθένει Ἀμφιπολίτῃ δίδωσι φυλάττειν, ὅπως εἰ καλῶς ἡγήσοιτο, ἔχων

καὶ τοῦτον ἀπίοι. καὶ εἰς τὴν οἰκίαν αὐτοῦ εἰσεφόρησαν ὡς 1
ἐδύναντο πλεῖστα, καὶ ἀναζεύξαντες ἐπορεύοντο. 2. ἡγεῖτο δ'
αὐτοῖς ὁ κώμαρχος λελυμένος διὰ χιόνος· καὶ ἤδη τε ἦν ἐν
τῷ τρίτῳ σταθμῷ, καὶ Χειρίσοφος αὐτῷ ἐχαλεπάνθη ὅτι οὐκ
εἰς κώμας ἤγαγεν. ὁ δ' ἔλεγεν ὅτι οὐκ εἶεν ἐν τῷ τόπῳ 5
τούτῳ. 3. ὁ δὲ Χειρίσοφος αὐτὸν ἔπαισεν, ἔδησε δ' οὔ. ἐκ
δὲ τούτου ἐκεῖνος τῆς νυκτὸς ἀποδρὰς ᾤχετο καταλιπὼν τὸν
υἱόν. τοῦτό γε δὴ Χειρισόφῳ καὶ Ξενοφῶντι μόνον διάφορον ἐν τῇ πορείᾳ ἐγένετο, ἡ τοῦ ἡγεμόνος κάκωσις καὶ
ἀμέλεια. Πλεισθένης δὲ ἠράσθη τοῦ παιδὸς καὶ οἴκαδε 10
κομίσας πιστοτάτῳ ἐχρῆτο. 4. μετὰ τοῦτο ἐπορεύθησαν ἑπτὰ
σταθμοὺς ἀνὰ πέντε παρασάγγας τῆς ἡμέρας παρὰ τὸν Φᾶσιν
ποταμόν, εὖρος πλεθριαῖον. 5. ἐντεῦθεν ἐπορεύθησαν σταθμοὺς δύο παρασάγγας δέκα· ἐπὶ δὲ τῇ εἰς τὸ πεδίον ὑπερβολῇ ἀπήντησαν αὐτοῖς Χάλυβες καὶ Τάοχοι καὶ Φασιανοί. 15
6. Χειρίσοφος δ' ἐπεὶ κατεῖδε τοὺς πολεμίους ἐπὶ τῇ ὑπερβολῇ,
ἐπαύσατο πορευόμενος, ἀπέχων εἰς τριάκοντα σταδίους, ἵνα
μὴ κατὰ κέρας ἄγων πλησιάσῃ τοῖς πολεμίοις· παρήγγειλε
δὲ καὶ τοῖς ἄλλοις παράγειν τοὺς λόχους, ὅπως ἐπὶ φάλαγγος
γένοιτο τὸ στράτευμα. 7. ἐπεὶ δὲ ἦλθον οἱ ὀπισθοφύλακες, 20
συνεκάλεσε στρατηγοὺς καὶ λοχαγούς, καὶ ἔλεξεν ὧδε. 'οἱ
μὲν πολέμιοι, ὡς ὁρᾶτε, κατέχουσι τὰς ὑπερβολὰς τοῦ ὄρους·
ὥρα δὲ βουλεύεσθαι ὅπως ὡς κάλλιστα ἀγωνιούμεθα. 8. ἐμοὶ
μὲν οὖν δοκεῖ παραγγεῖλαι μὲν ἀριστοποιεῖσθαι τοῖς στρατιώταις, ἡμᾶς δὲ βουλεύεσθαι εἴτε τήμερον εἴτε αὔριον δοκεῖ 25
ὑπερβάλλειν τὸ ὄρος.' 9. 'ἐμοὶ δέ γε,' ἔφη ὁ Κλεάνωρ, 'δοκεῖ,
ἐπὰν τάχιστα ἀριστήσωμεν, ἐξοπλισαμένους ὡς κράτιστα

ἰέναι ἐπὶ τοὺς ἄνδρας. εἰ γὰρ διατρίψομεν τὴν τήμερον 1
ἡμέραν, οἵ τε νῦν ἡμᾶς ὁρῶντες πολέμιοι θαρραλεώτεροι
ἔσονται καὶ ἄλλους εἰκὸς τούτων θαρρούντων πλείους προσγενέσθαι.' 10. μετὰ τοῦτον Ξενοφῶν εἶπεν· 'ἐγὼ δ' οὕτω
γιγνώσκω. εἰ μὲν ἀνάγκη ἐστὶ μάχεσθαι, τοῦτο δεῖ παρα- 5
σκευάσασθαι, ὅπως ὡς κράτιστα μαχούμεθα· εἰ δὲ βουλόμεθα
ὡς ῥᾷστα ὑπερβάλλειν, τοῦτό μοι δοκεῖ σκεπτέον εἶναι, ὅπως
ὡς ἐλάχιστα μὲν τραύματα λάβωμεν, ὡς ἐλάχιστα δὲ
σώματα ἀνδρῶν ἀποβάλωμεν. 11. τὸ μὲν οὖν ὄρος ἐστὶ τὸ
ὁρώμενον πλέον ἢ ἐφ' ἑξήκοντα στάδια, ἄνδρες δ' οὐδαμοῦ 10
φυλάττοντες ἡμᾶς φανεροί εἰσιν ἀλλ' ἢ κατ' αὐτὴν τὴν ὁδόν·
πολὺ οὖν κρεῖττον τοῦ ἐρήμου ὄρους καὶ κλέψαι τι πειρᾶσθαι
λαθόντας καὶ ἁρπάσαι φθάσαντας, εἰ δυναίμεθα, μᾶλλον ἢ
πρὸς ἰσχυρὰ χωρία καὶ ἀνθρώπους παρεσκευασμένους μάχεσθαι. 12. πολὺ γὰρ ῥᾷον ὄρθιον ἀμαχεὶ ἰέναι ἢ ὁμαλὲς ἔνθεν 15
καὶ ἔνθεν πολεμίων ὄντων, καὶ νύκτωρ ἀμαχεὶ μᾶλλον ἂν τὰ
πρὸ ποδῶν ὁρῴη τις ἢ μεθ' ἡμέραν μαχόμενος, καὶ ἡ τραχεῖα
τοῖς ποσὶν ἀμαχεὶ ἰοῦσιν εὐμενεστέρα ἢ ἡ ὁμαλὴ τὰς κεφαλὰς
βαλλομένοις. 13. καὶ κλέψαι δ' οὐκ ἀδύνατόν μοι δοκεῖ εἶναι,
ἐξὸν μὲν νυκτὸς ἰέναι, ὡς μὴ ὁρᾶσθαι, ἐξὸν δ' ἀπελθεῖν 20
τοσοῦτον ὡς μὴ αἴσθησιν παρέχειν. δοκοῦμεν δ' ἄν μοι
ταύτῃ προσποιούμενοι προσβάλλειν ἐρημοτέρῳ ἂν τῷ ὄρει
χρῆσθαι· μένοιεν γὰρ ἂν αὐτοῦ μᾶλλον ἁθρόοι οἱ πολέμιοι.
14. ἀτὰρ τί ἐγὼ περὶ κλοπῆς συμβάλλομαι; ὑμᾶς γὰρ ἔγωγε, ὦ
Χειρίσοφε, ἀκούω τοὺς Λακεδαιμονίους ὅσοι ἐστὲ τῶν ὁμοίων 25
εὐθὺς ἐκ παίδων κλέπτειν μελετᾶν, καὶ οὐκ αἰσχρὸν εἶναι

ἀλλὰ καλὸν κλέπτειν ὅσα μὴ κωλύει νόμος. 15. ὅπως δὲ ὡς κράτιστα κλέπτητε καὶ πειρᾶσθε λανθάνειν, νόμιμον ἄρα ὑμῖν ἐστιν, ἐὰν ληφθῆτε κλέπτοντες, μαστιγοῦσθαι. νῦν οὖν μάλα σοι καιρός ἐστιν ἐπιδείξασθαι τὴν παιδείαν, καὶ φυλάξασθαι μὴ ληφθῶμεν κλέπτοντες τοῦ ὄρους, ὡς μὴ πληγὰς λάβωμεν.' 16. 'ἀλλὰ μέντοι,' ἔφη ὁ Χειρίσοφος, 'κἀγὼ ὑμᾶς τοὺς Ἀθηναίους ἀκούω δεινοὺς εἶναι κλέπτειν τὰ δημόσια, καὶ μάλα ὄντος δεινοῦ κινδύνου τῷ κλέπτοντι, καὶ τοὺς κρατίστους μέντοι μάλιστα, εἴπερ ὑμῖν οἱ κράτιστοι ἄρχειν ἀξιοῦνται· ὥστε ὥρα καὶ σοὶ ἐπιδείκνυσθαι τὴν παιδείαν.' 17. 'ἐγὼ μὲν τοίνυν,' ἔφη ὁ Ξενοφῶν, 'ἕτοιμός εἰμι τοὺς ὀπισθοφύλακας ἔχων, ἐπειδὰν δειπνήσωμεν, ἰέναι καταληψόμενος τὸ ὄρος. ἔχω δὲ καὶ ἡγεμόνας· οἱ γὰρ γυμνῆτες τῶν ἑπομένων ἡμῖν κλωπῶν ἔλαβόν τινας ἐνεδρεύσαντες· τούτων καὶ πυνθάνομαι ὅτι οὐκ ἄβατόν ἐστι τὸ ὄρος, ἀλλὰ νέμεται αἰξὶ καὶ βουσίν· ὥστε ἐάνπερ ἅπαξ λάβωμέν τι τοῦ ὄρους, βατὰ καὶ τοῖς ὑποζυγίοις ἔσται. 18. ἐλπίζω δὲ οὐδὲ τοὺς πολεμίους μενεῖν ἔτι, ἐπειδὰν ἴδωσιν ἡμᾶς ἐν τῷ ὁμοίῳ ἐπὶ τῶν ἄκρων· οὐδὲ γὰρ νῦν ἐθέλουσι καταβαίνειν εἰς τὸ ἴσον ἡμῖν.' 19. ὁ δὲ Χειρίσοφος εἶπε· 'καὶ τί δεῖ σὲ ἰέναι καὶ λιπεῖν τὴν ὀπισθοφυλακίαν; ἀλλὰ ἄλλους πέμψον, ἂν μή τινες ἐθέλοντες ἀγαθοὶ φαίνωνται.' 20. ἐκ τούτου Ἀριστώνυμος Μεθυδριεὺς ἔρχεται ὁπλίτας ἔχων καὶ Ἀριστέας ὁ Χῖος γυμνῆτας καὶ Νικόμαχος Οἰταῖος γυμνῆτας· καὶ σύνθημα ἐποιήσαντο, ὁπότε ἔχοιεν τὰ ἄκρα, πυρὰ καίειν πολλά. 21. ταῦτα συνθέμενοι ἠρίστων· ἐκ δὲ τοῦ ἀρίστου προήγαγεν ὁ Χειρίσοφος

τὸ στράτευμα πᾶν ὡς δέκα σταδίους πρὸς τοὺς πολεμίους, 1
ὅπως ὡς μάλιστα δοκοίη ταύτῃ προσάξειν.

22. ἐπειδὴ δὲ ἐδείπνησαν καὶ νὺξ ἐγένετο, οἱ μὲν ταχθέντες
ᾤχοντο, καὶ καταλαμβάνουσι τὸ ὄρος, οἱ δὲ ἄλλοι αὐτοῦ
ἀνεπαύοντο. οἱ δὲ πολέμιοι ἐπεὶ ᾔσθοντο τὸ ὄρος ἐχόμενον, 5
ἐγρηγόρεσαν καὶ ἔκαιον πυρὰ πολλὰ διὰ νυκτός. 23. ἐπειδὴ δὲ
ἡμέρα ἐγένετο Χειρίσοφος μὲν θυσάμενος ἦγε κατὰ τὴν
ὁδόν, οἱ δὲ τὸ ὄρος καταλαβόντες κατὰ τὰ ἄκρα ἐπῇσαν.
24. τῶν δὲ πολεμίων τὸ μὲν πολὺ ἔμενεν ἐπὶ τῇ ὑπερβολῇ τοῦ
ὄρους, μέρος δ᾽ αὐτῶν ἀπήντα τοῖς κατὰ τὰ ἄκρα. πρὶν δὲ 10
ὁμοῦ εἶναι τοὺς πολλοὺς ἀλλήλοις, συμμιγνύασιν οἱ κατὰ
τὰ ἄκρα, καὶ νικῶσιν οἱ Ἕλληνες καὶ διώκουσιν. 25. ἐν τούτῳ
δὲ καὶ οἱ ἐκ τοῦ πεδίου οἱ μὲν πελτασταὶ τῶν Ἑλλήνων
δρόμῳ ἔθεον πρὸς τοὺς παρατεταγμένους, Χειρίσοφος δὲ
βάδην ταχὺ ἐφείπετο σὺν τοῖς ὁπλίταις. 26. οἱ δὲ πολέμιοι οἱ 15
ἐπὶ τῇ ὁδῷ ἐπειδὴ τὸ ἄνω ἑώρων ἡττώμενον, φεύγουσι· καὶ
ἀπέθανον μὲν οὐ πολλοὶ αὐτῶν, γέρρα δὲ πάμπολλα ἐλήφθη·
ἃ οἱ Ἕλληνες ταῖς μαχαίραις κόπτοντες ἀχρεῖα ἐποίουν.
27. ὡς δ᾽ ἀνέβησαν, θύσαντες καὶ τρόπαιον στησάμενοι κατέβησαν εἰς τὸ πεδίον, καὶ εἰς κώμας πολλῶν καὶ ἀγαθῶν 20
γεμούσας ἦλθον.

1. ἐκ δὲ τούτων ἐπορεύθησαν εἰς Ταόχους σταθμοὺς πέντε
παρασάγγας τριάκοντα· καὶ τὰ ἐπιτήδεια ἐπέλειπε· χωρία
γὰρ ᾤκουν ἰσχυρὰ οἱ Τάοχοι, ἐν οἷς καὶ τὰ ἐπιτήδεια ἅπαντα
εἶχον ἀνακεκομισμένοι. 2. ἐπεὶ δ᾽ ἀφίκοντο πρὸς χωρίον ὃ 25
πόλιν μὲν οὐκ εἶχεν οὐδ᾽ οἰκίας, συνεληλυθότες δ᾽ ἦσαν
αὐτόσε καὶ ἄνδρες καὶ γυναῖκες καὶ κτήνη πολλά, Χειρί-

σοφος μὲν οὖν πρὸς τοῦτο προσέβαλλεν εὐθὺς ἥκων· ἐπειδὴ 1
δὲ ἡ πρώτη τάξις ἀπέκαμνεν, ἄλλη προσῄει καὶ αὖθις ἄλλη·
οὐ γὰρ ἦν ἁθρόοις περιστῆναι, ἀλλ' ἀπότομον ἦν κύκλῳ.
3. ἐπειδὴ δὲ Ξενοφῶν ἦλθε σὺν τοῖς ὀπισθοφύλαξι καὶ πελτα-
σταῖς καὶ ὁπλίταις, ἐνταῦθα δὴ λέγει Χειρίσοφος· 'εἰς καλὸν 5
ἥκετε· τὸ γὰρ χωρίον αἱρετέον· τῇ γὰρ στρατιᾷ οὐκ ἔστι τὰ
ἐπιτήδεια, εἰ μὴ ληψόμεθα τὸ χωρίον. 4. ἐνταῦθα δὴ κοινῇ ἐβου-
λεύοντο· καὶ τοῦ Ξενοφῶντος ἐρωτῶντος τί τὸ κωλῦον εἴη
εἰσελθεῖν, εἶπεν ὁ Χειρίσοφος· 'μία αὕτη πάροδός ἐστιν ἣν
ὁρᾷς· ὅταν δέ τις ταύτῃ πειρᾶται παριέναι, κυλίνδουσι λίθους 10
ὑπὲρ ταύτης τῆς ὑπερεχούσης πέτρας· ὃς δ' ἂν καταληφθῇ,
οὕτω διατίθεται.' ἅμα δ' ἔδειξε συντετριμμένους ἀνθρώπους
καὶ σκέλη καὶ πλευράς. 5. 'ἣν δὲ τοὺς λίθους ἀναλώσωσιν,'
ἔφη ὁ Ξενοφῶν, 'ἄλλο τι ἢ οὐδὲν κωλύει παριέναι; οὐ γὰρ
δὴ ἐκ τοῦ ἐναντίου ὁρῶμεν εἰ μὴ ὀλίγους τούτους ἀνθρώπους, 15
καὶ τούτων δύο ἢ τρεῖς ὡπλισμένους. 6. τὸ δὲ χωρίον, ὡς καὶ
σὺ ὁρᾷς, σχεδὸν τρία ἡμίπλεθρά ἐστιν ὃ δεῖ βαλλομένους
διελθεῖν· τούτου δὲ ὅσον πλέθρον δασὺ πίτυσι διαλειπούσαις
μεγάλαις, ἀνθ' ὧν ἑστηκότες ἄνδρες τί ἂν πάσχοιεν ἢ ὑπὸ
τῶν φερομένων λίθων ἢ ὑπὸ τῶν κυλινδομένων; τὸ λοιπὸν 20
οὖν γίγνεται ὡς ἡμίπλεθρον, ὃ δεῖ ὅταν λωφήσωσιν οἱ λίθοι
παραδραμεῖν.' 7. 'ἀλλὰ εὐθύς,' ἔφη ὁ Χειρίσοφος, 'ἐπειδὰν
ἀρξώμεθα εἰς τὸ δασὺ προσιέναι, φέρονται οἱ λίθοι πολλοί.'
'αὐτὸ ἄν,' ἔφη, 'τὸ δέον εἴη· θᾶττον γὰρ ἀναλώσουσι τοὺς
λίθους. ἀλλὰ πορευώμεθα ἔνθεν ἡμῖν μικρόν τι παραδραμεῖν 25
ἔσται, ἢν δυνώμεθα, καὶ ἀπελθεῖν ῥᾴδιον, ἢν βουλώμεθα.'

8. ἐντεῦθεν ἐπορεύοντο Χειρίσοφος καὶ Ξενοφῶν καὶ Καλ- 1
λίμαχος Παρράσιος λοχαγός· τούτου γὰρ ἡ ἡγεμονία ἦν
τῶν ὀπισθοφυλάκων λοχαγῶν ἐκείνῃ τῇ ἡμέρᾳ· οἱ δὲ ἄλλοι
λοχαγοὶ ἔμενον ἐν τῷ ἀσφαλεῖ. μετὰ τοῦτο οὖν ἀπῆλθον
ὑπὸ τὰ δένδρα ἄνθρωποι ὡς ἑβδομήκοντα, οὐχ ἁθρόοι ἀλλὰ 5
καθ' ἕνα, ἕκαστος φυλαττόμενος ὡς ἐδύνατο. 9. Ἀγασίας δὲ
ὁ Στυμφάλιος καὶ Ἀριστώνυμος Μεθυδριεὺς καὶ οὗτοι τῶν
ὀπισθοφυλάκων λοχαγοὶ ὄντες, καὶ ἄλλοι δέ, ἐφέστασαν
ἔξω τῶν δένδρων· οὐ γὰρ ἦν ἀσφαλῶς ἐν τοῖς δένδροις
ἑστάναι πλέον ἢ τὸν ἕνα λόχον. 10. ἔνθα δὴ Καλλίμαχος 10
μηχανᾶταί τι· προύτρεχεν ἀπὸ τοῦ δένδρου ὑφ' ᾧ ἦν αὐτὸς
δύο ἢ τρία βήματα· ἐπειδὴ δὲ οἱ λίθοι φέροιντο, ἀνέχαζεν
εὐπετῶς· ἐφ' ἑκάστης δὲ τῆς προδρομῆς πλέον ἢ δέκα ἅμαξαι
πετρῶν ἀνηλίσκοντο. 11. ὁ δὲ Ἀγασίας ὡς ὁρᾷ τὸν Καλλίμαχον ἃ ἐποίει τὸ στράτευμα πᾶν θεώμενον, δείσας μὴ οὐ 15
πρῶτος παραδράμῃ εἰς τὸ χωρίον, οὐδὲ τὸν Ἀριστώνυμον
πλησίον ὄντα παρακαλέσας οὐδὲ Εὐρύλοχον τὸν Λουσιέα,
ἑταίρους ὄντας, οὐδὲ ἄλλον οὐδένα χωρεῖ αὐτός, καὶ παρέρ-
χεται πάντας. 12. ὁ δὲ Καλλίμαχος ὡς ὁρᾷ αὐτὸν παριόντα,
ἐπιλαμβάνεται αὐτοῦ τῆς ἴτυος· ἐν δὲ τούτῳ παραθεῖ αὐτοὺς 20
Ἀριστώνυμος Μεθυδριεύς, καὶ μετὰ τοῦτον Εὐρύλοχος Λου-
σιεύς· πάντες γὰρ οὗτοι ἀντεποιοῦντο ἀρετῆς καὶ διηγωνίζοντο πρὸς ἀλλήλους· καὶ οὕτως ἐρίζοντες αἱροῦσι τὸ χωρίον.
ὡς γὰρ ἅπαξ εἰσέδραμον, οὐδεὶς πέτρος ἄνωθεν ἠνέχθη.
13. ἐνταῦθα δὴ δεινὸν ἦν θέαμα. αἱ γὰρ γυναῖκες ῥίπτουσαι 25

τὰ παιδία εἶτα ἑαυτὰς ἐπικατερρίπτουν, καὶ οἱ ἄνδρες ὡσαύ- 1
τως. ἐνταῦθα δὴ καὶ Αἰνείας Στυμφάλιος λοχαγὸς ἰδών τινα
θέοντα ὡς ῥίψοντα ἑαυτὸν στολὴν ἔχοντα καλὴν ἐπιλαμβάνεται ὡς κωλύσων· 14. ὁ δὲ αὐτὸν ἐπισπᾶται, καὶ ἀμφότεροι
ᾤχοντο κατὰ τῶν πετρῶν φερόμενοι καὶ ἀπέθανον. ἐντεῦθεν 5
ἄνθρωποι μὲν πάνυ ὀλίγοι ἐλήφθησαν, βόες δὲ καὶ ὄνοι
πολλοὶ καὶ πρόβατα.

15. ἐντεῦθεν ἐπορεύθησαν διὰ Χαλύβων σταθμοὺς ἑπτὰ
παρασάγγας πεντήκοντα. οὗτοι ἦσαν ὧν διῆλθον ἀλκιμώτατοι, καὶ εἰς χεῖρας ᾖσαν. εἶχον δὲ θώρακας λινοῦς μέχρι 10
τοῦ ἤτρου, ἀντὶ δὲ τῶν πτερύγων σπάρτα πυκνὰ ἐστραμμένα.
16. εἶχον δὲ καὶ κνημῖδας καὶ κράνη καὶ παρὰ τὴν ζώνην μαχαίριον
ὅσον ξυήλην Λακωνικήν, ᾧ ἔσφαττον ὧν κρατεῖν δύναιντο,
καὶ ἀποτεμόντες ἂν τὰς κεφαλὰς ἔχοντες ἐπορεύοντο, καὶ
ᾖδον καὶ ἐχόρευον ὁπότε οἱ πολέμιοι αὐτοὺς ὄψεσθαι ἔμελ- 15
λον. εἶχον δὲ καὶ δόρυ ὡς πεντεκαίδεκα πήχεων μίαν
λόγχην ἔχον. 17. οὗτοι ἐνέμενον ἐν τοῖς πολίσμασιν· ἐπεὶ δὲ
παρέλθοιεν οἱ Ἕλληνες, εἵποντο ἀεὶ μαχούμενοι. ᾤκουν
δὲ ἐν τοῖς ὀχυροῖς, καὶ τὰ ἐπιτήδεια ἐν τούτοις ἀνακεκομισμένοι ἦσαν· ὥστε μηδὲν λαμβάνειν αὐτόθεν τοὺς Ἕλληνας, 20
ἀλλὰ διετράφησαν τοῖς κτήνεσιν ἃ ἐκ τῶν Ταόχων ἔλαβον.
18. ἐκ τούτων οἱ Ἕλληνες ἀφίκοντο ἐπὶ Ἅρπασον ποταμόν,
εὖρος τεττάρων πλέθρων. ἐντεῦθεν ἐπορεύθησαν διὰ Σκυθηνῶν σταθμοὺς τέτταρας παρασάγγας εἴκοσι διὰ πεδίου
εἰς κώμας· ἐν αἷς ἔμειναν ἡμέρας τρεῖς καὶ ἐπεσιτίσαντο. 25
19. ἐντεῦθεν διῆλθον σταθμοὺς τέτταρας παρασάγγας εἴκοσι

πρὸς πόλιν μεγάλην καὶ εὐδαίμονα καὶ οἰκουμένην ἣ ἐκαλεῖτο 1
Γυμνιάς. *ἐκ ταύτης †τῆς χώρας† ὁ ἄρχων τοῖς Ἕλλησιν ἡγεμόνα πέμπει, ὅπως διὰ τῆς ἑαυτῶν πολεμίας χώρας ἄγοι αὐτούς.* 20. *ἐλθὼν δ' ἐκεῖνος λέγει ὅτι ἄξει αὐτοὺς πέντε ἡμερῶν εἰς χωρίον ὅθεν ὄψονται θάλατταν· εἰ δὲ μή, τεθνάναι* 5
ἐπηγγείλατο. καὶ ἡγούμενος ἐπειδὴ ἐνέβαλλεν εἰς τὴν ἑαυτοῦ πολεμίαν, παρεκελεύετο αἴθειν καὶ φθείρειν τὴν χώραν· ᾧ καὶ δῆλον ἐγένετο ὅτι τούτου ἕνεκα ἔλθοι, οὐ τῆς τῶν Ἑλλήνων εὐνοίας. 21. *καὶ ἀφικνοῦνται ἐπὶ τὸ ὄρος τῇ πέμπτῃ ἡμέρᾳ· ὄνομα δὲ τῷ ὄρει ἦν Θήχης. ἐπεὶ δὲ οἱ* 10
πρῶτοι ἐγένοντο ἐπὶ τοῦ ὄρους καὶ κατεῖδον τὴν θάλατταν, κραυγὴ πολλὴ ἐγένετο. 22. *ἀκούσας δὲ ὁ Ξενοφῶν καὶ οἱ ὀπισθοφύλακες ᾠήθησαν ἔμπροσθεν ἄλλους ἐπιτίθεσθαι πολεμίους· εἵποντο γὰρ ὄπισθεν ἐκ τῆς καιομένης χώρας, καὶ αὐτῶν οἱ ὀπισθοφύλακες ἀπέκτεινάν τέ τινας καὶ ἐζώγρησαν* 15
ἐνέδραν ποιησάμενοι, καὶ γέρρα ἔλαβον δασειῶν βοῶν ὠμοβόεια ἀμφὶ τὰ εἴκοσιν. 23. *ἐπειδὴ δὲ βοὴ πλείων τε ἐγίγνετο καὶ ἐγγύτερον καὶ οἱ ἀεὶ ἐπιόντες ἔθεον δρόμῳ ἐπὶ τοὺς ἀεὶ βοῶντας καὶ πολλῷ μείζων ἐγίγνετο ἡ βοὴ ὅσῳ δὴ πλείους ἐγίγνοντο,* 24. *ἐδόκει δὴ μεῖζόν τι εἶναι τῷ Ξενοφῶντι, καὶ* 20
ἀναβὰς ἐφ' ἵππον καὶ Λύκιον καὶ τοὺς ἱππέας ἀναλαβὼν παρεβοήθει· καὶ τάχα δὴ ἀκούουσι βοώντων τῶν στρατιωτῶν 'θάλαττα θάλαττα' καὶ παρεγγυώντων. ἔνθα δὴ ἔθεον πάντες καὶ οἱ ὀπισθοφύλακες, καὶ τὰ ὑποζύγια ἠλαύνετο καὶ οἱ

ἵπποι. 25. ἐπεὶ δὲ ἀφίκοντο πάντες ἐπὶ τὸ ἄκρον, ἐνταῦθα δὴ 1
περιέβαλλον ἀλλήλους καὶ στρατηγοὺς καὶ λοχαγοὺς δα-
κρύοντες. καὶ ἐξαπίνης ὅτου δὴ παρεγγυήσαντος οἱ στρατιῶται φέρουσι λίθους καὶ ποιοῦσι κολωνὸν μέγαν. 26. ἐνταῦθα
ἀνετίθεσαν δερμάτων πλῆθος ὠμοβοείων καὶ βακτηρίας καὶ 5
τὰ αἰχμάλωτα γέρρα, καὶ ὁ ἡγεμὼν αὐτός τε κατέτεμνε τὰ
γέρρα καὶ τοῖς ἄλλοις διεκελεύετο. 27. μετὰ ταῦτα τὸν ἡγεμόνα
οἱ Ἕλληνες ἀποπέμπουσι δῶρα δόντες ἀπὸ κοινοῦ ἵππον καὶ
φιάλην ἀργυρᾶν καὶ σκευὴν Περσικὴν καὶ δαρεικοὺς δέκα·
ᾔτει δὲ μάλιστα τοὺς δακτυλίους, καὶ ἔλαβε πολλοὺς παρὰ 10
τῶν στρατιωτῶν. κώμην δὲ δείξας αὐτοῖς οὗ σκηνήσουσι
καὶ τὴν ὁδὸν ἣν πορεύσονται εἰς Μάκρωνας, ἐπεὶ ἑσπέρα
ἐγένετο, ᾤχετο τῆς νυκτὸς ἀπιών.

1. ἐντεῦθεν δ᾽ ἐπορεύθησαν οἱ Ἕλληνες διὰ Μακρώνων
σταθμοὺς τρεῖς παρασάγγας δέκα. τῇ πρώτῃ δὲ ἡμέρᾳ 15
ἀφίκοντο ἐπὶ τὸν ποταμὸν ὃς ὥριζε τὴν τῶν Μακρώνων καὶ
τὴν τῶν Σκυθηνῶν. 2. εἶχον δ᾽ ὑπὲρ δεξιῶν χωρίον οἷον
χαλεπώτατον καὶ ἐξ ἀριστερᾶς ἄλλον ποταμόν, εἰς ὃν ἐνέβαλλεν ὁ ὁρίζων, δι᾽ οὗ ἔδει διαβῆναι. ἦν δὲ οὗτος δασὺς
δένδρεσι παχέσι μὲν οὔ, πυκνοῖς δέ. ταῦτ᾽ ἐπεὶ προσῆλθον 20
οἱ Ἕλληνες ἔκοπτον, σπεύδοντες ἐκ τοῦ χωρίου ὡς τάχιστα
ἐξελθεῖν. 3. οἱ δὲ Μάκρωνες ἔχοντες γέρρα καὶ λόγχας καὶ
τριχίνους χιτῶνας κατ᾽ ἀντιπέραν τῆς διαβάσεως παρατεταγμένοι ἦσαν καὶ ἀλλήλοις διεκελεύοντο καὶ λίθους εἰς τὸν
ποταμὸν ἔρριπτον· ἐξικνοῦντο γὰρ οὒ οὐδ᾽ ἔβλαπτον οὐδέν. 25

4. ἔνθα δὴ προσέρχεται Ξενοφῶντι τῶν πελταστῶν ἀνὴρ

Ἀθήνησι φάσκων δεδουλευκέναι, λέγων ὅτι γιγνώσκοι τὴν 1
φωνὴν τῶν ἀνθρώπων. 'καὶ οἶμαι,' ἔφη, 'ἐμὴν ταύτην πατρίδα
εἶναι· καὶ εἰ μή τι κωλύει, ἐθέλω αὐτοῖς διαλεχθῆναι.'
5. 'ἀλλ' οὐδὲν κωλύει,' ἔφη, 'ἀλλὰ διαλέγου καὶ μάθε πρῶτον
τίνες εἰσίν.' οἱ δ' εἶπον ἐρωτήσαντος ὅτι 'Μάκρωνες.' 'ἐρώτα 5
τοίνυν,' ἔφη, 'αὐτοὺς τί ἀντιτετάχαται καὶ χρῄζουσιν ἡμῖν
πολέμιοι εἶναι.' 6. οἱ δ' ἀπεκρίναντο ὅτι 'καὶ ὑμεῖς ἐπὶ τὴν
ἡμετέραν χώραν ἔρχεσθε.' λέγειν ἐκέλευον οἱ στρατηγοὶ
ὅτι 'οὐ κακῶς γε ποιήσοντες, ἀλλὰ βασιλεῖ πολεμήσαντες
ἀπερχόμεθα εἰς τὴν Ἑλλάδα, καὶ ἐπὶ θάλατταν βουλόμεθα 10
ἀφικέσθαι.' 7. ἠρώτων ἐκεῖνοι εἰ δοῖεν ἂν τούτων τὰ πιστά.
οἱ δ' ἔφασαν καὶ δοῦναι καὶ λαβεῖν ἐθέλειν. ἐντεῦθεν
διδόασιν οἱ Μάκρωνες βαρβαρικὴν λόγχην τοῖς Ἕλλησιν,
οἱ δὲ Ἕλληνες ἐκείνοις Ἑλληνικήν· ταῦτα γὰρ ἔφασαν
πιστὰ εἶναι· θεοὺς δ' ἐπεμαρτύραντο ἀμφότεροι. 15

8. μετὰ δὲ τὰ πιστὰ εὐθὺς οἱ Μάκρωνες τὰ δένδρα συνεξέ-
κοπτον τήν τε ὁδὸν ὡδοποίουν ὡς διαβιβάσοντες ἐν μέσοις
ἀναμεμιγμένοι τοῖς Ἕλλησι, καὶ ἀγορὰν οἵαν ἐδύναντο
παρεῖχον, καὶ παρήγαγον ἐν τρισὶν ἡμέραις ἕως ἐπὶ τὰ
Κόλχων ὅρια κατέστησαν τοὺς Ἕλληνας. 9. ἐνταῦθα ἦν ὄρος 20
μέγα, προσβατὸν δέ· καὶ ἐπὶ τούτου οἱ Κόλχοι παρατεταγμένοι ἦσαν. καὶ τὸ μὲν πρῶτον οἱ Ἕλληνες ἀντιπαρετάξαντο φάλαγγα, ὡς οὕτως ἄξοντες πρὸς τὸ ὄρος· ἔπειτα δὲ
ἔδοξε τοῖς στρατηγοῖς βουλεύσασθαι συλλεγεῖσιν ὅπως ὡς
κάλλιστα ἀγωνιοῦνται. 10. ἔλεξεν οὖν Ξενοφῶν ὅτι δοκοίη 25
παύσαντας τὴν φάλαγγα λόχους ὀρθίους ποιῆσαι· 'ἡ μὲν γὰρ

φάλαγξ διασπασθήσεται εὐθύς· τῇ μὲν γὰρ ἄνοδον τῇ δὲ 1
εὔοδον εὑρήσομεν τὸ ὄρος· καὶ εὐθὺς τοῦτο ἀθυμίαν ποιήσει
ὅταν τεταγμένοι εἰς φάλαγγα ταύτην διεσπασμένην ὁρῶσιν.
11. ἔπειτα ἢν μὲν ἐπὶ πολλῶν τεταγμένοι προσάγωμεν, περιτ-
τεύσουσιν ἡμῶν οἱ πολέμιοι καὶ τοῖς περιττοῖς χρήσονται 5
ὅ τι ἂν βούλωνται· ἐὰν δὲ ἐπ' ὀλίγων τεταγμένοι ὦμεν,
οὐδὲν ἂν εἴη θαυμαστὸν εἰ διακοπείη ἡμῶν ἡ φάλαγξ ὑπὸ
ἁθρόων καὶ βελῶν καὶ ἀνθρώπων πολλῶν ἐμπεσόντων· εἰ δέ
πῃ τοῦτο ἔσται, τῇ ὅλῃ φάλαγγι κακὸν ἔσται. 12. ἀλλά μοι δοκεῖ
ὀρθίους τοὺς λόχους ποιησαμένους τοσοῦτον χωρίον κατα- 10
σχεῖν διαλιπόντας τοῖς λόχοις ὅσον ἔξω τοὺς ἐσχάτους λόχους
γενέσθαι τῶν πολεμίων κεράτων· καὶ οὕτως ἐσόμεθα τῆς
τε τῶν πολεμίων φάλαγγος ἔξω [οἱ ἔσχατοι λόχοι], καὶ
ὀρθίους ἄγοντες οἱ κράτιστοι ἡμῶν πρῶτοι προσίασιν, ᾗ τε
ἂν εὔοδον ᾖ, ταύτῃ ἕκαστος ἄξει [ὁ λόχος]. 13. καὶ εἴς τε τὸ 15
διαλεῖπον οὐ ῥᾴδιον ἔσται τοῖς πολεμίοις εἰσελθεῖν ἔνθεν
καὶ ἔνθεν λόχων ὄντων, διακόψαι τε οὐ ῥᾴδιον ἔσται λόχον
ὄρθιον προσιόντα. ἄν τέ τις πιέζηται τῶν λόχων, ὁ πλησίον
βοηθήσει. ἤν τε εἷς πῃ δυνηθῇ τῶν λόχων ἐπὶ τὸ ἄκρον
ἀναβῆναι, οὐδεὶς μηκέτι μείνῃ τῶν πολεμίων.' 14. ταῦτα ἔδοξε, 20
καὶ ἐποίουν ὀρθίους τοὺς λόχους. Ξενοφῶν δὲ ἀπιὼν ἐπὶ
τὸ εὐώνυμον ἀπὸ τοῦ δεξιοῦ ἔλεγε τοῖς στρατιώταις· 'ἄνδρες,
οὗτοί εἰσιν οὓς ὁρᾶτε μόνοι ἔτι ἡμῖν ἐμποδὼν τὸ μὴ ἤδη
εἶναι ἔνθα πάλαι σπεύδομεν· τούτους, ἤν πως δυνώμεθα,
καὶ ὠμοὺς δεῖ καταφαγεῖν. 25

15. ἐπεὶ δ' ἐν ταῖς χώραις ἕκαστοι ἐγένοντο καὶ τοὺς λόχους

ὀρθίους ἐποιήσαντο, ἐγένοντο μὲν λόχοι τῶν ὁπλιτῶν ἀμφὶ 1
τοὺς ὀγδοήκοντα, ὁ δὲ λόχος ἕκαστος σχεδὸν εἰς τοὺς ἑκατόν·
τοὺς δὲ πελταστὰς καὶ τοὺς τοξότας τριχῇ ἐποιήσαντο, τοὺς
μὲν τοῦ εὐωνύμου ἔξω, τοὺς δὲ τοῦ δεξιοῦ, τοὺς δὲ κατὰ
μέσον, σχεδὸν ἑξακοσίους ἑκάστους. 16. ἐκ τούτου παρηγ- 5
γύησαν οἱ στρατηγοὶ εὔχεσθαι· εὐξάμενοι δὲ καὶ παιανίσαντες ἐπορεύοντο. καὶ Χειρίσοφος μὲν καὶ Ξενοφῶν καὶ
οἱ σὺν αὐτοῖς πελτασταὶ τῆς τῶν πολεμίων φάλαγγος ἔξω
γενόμενοι ἐπορεύοντο· 17. οἱ δὲ πολέμιοι ὡς εἶδον αὐτούς, ἀντιπαραθέοντες οἱ μὲν ἐπὶ τὸ δεξιὸν οἱ δὲ ἐπὶ τὸ εὐώνυμον 10
διεσπάσθησαν, καὶ πολὺ τῆς αὐτῶν φάλαγγος ἐν τῷ μέσῳ
κενὸν ἐποίησαν. 18. οἱ δὲ κατὰ τὸ Ἀρκαδικὸν πελτασταί, ὧν
ἦρχεν Αἰσχίνης ὁ Ἀκαρνάν, νομίσαντες φεύγειν ἀνακραγόντες ἔθεον· καὶ οὗτοι πρῶτοι ἐπὶ τὸ ὄρος ἀναβαίνουσι·
συνεφείπετο δὲ αὐτοῖς καὶ τὸ Ἀρκαδικὸν ὁπλιτικόν, ὧν ἦρχε 15
Κλεάνωρ ὁ Ὀρχομένιος. 19. οἱ δὲ πολέμιοι, ὡς ἤρξαντο θεῖν,
οὐκέτι ἔστησαν, ἀλλὰ φυγῇ ἄλλος ἄλλῃ ἐτράπετο. οἱ δὲ
Ἕλληνες ἀναβάντες ἐστρατοπεδεύοντο ἐν πολλαῖς κώμαις
καὶ τἀπιτήδεια πολλὰ ἐχούσαις. 20. καὶ τὰ μὲν ἄλλα οὐδὲν
ὅ τι καὶ ἐθαύμασαν· τὰ δὲ σμήνη πολλὰ ἦν αὐτόθι, καὶ τῶν 20
κηρίων ὅσοι ἔφαγον τῶν στρατιωτῶν πάντες ἄφρονές τε
ἐγίγνοντο καὶ ἤμουν καὶ κάτω διεχώρει αὐτοῖς καὶ ὀρθὸς
οὐδεὶς ἐδύνατο ἵστασθαι, ἀλλ᾽ οἱ μὲν ὀλίγον ἐδηδοκότες
σφόδρα μεθύουσιν ἐῴκεσαν, οἱ δὲ πολὺ μαινομένοις, οἱ δὲ
καὶ ἀποθνήσκουσιν. 21. ἔκειντο δὲ οὕτω πολλοὶ ὥσπερ τροπῆς 25
γεγενημένης, καὶ πολλὴ ἦν ἀθυμία. τῇ δ᾽ ὑστεραίᾳ ἀπέθανε
μὲν οὐδείς, ἀμφὶ δὲ τὴν αὐτήν πως ὥραν ἀνεφρόνουν· τρίτῃ
δὲ καὶ τετάρτῃ ἀνίσταντο ὥσπερ ἐκ φαρμακοποσίας.

22. ἐντεῦθεν δ' ἐπορεύθησαν δύο σταθμοὺς παρασάγγας ἑπτά, 1
καὶ ἦλθον ἐπὶ θάλατταν εἰς Τραπεζοῦντα πόλιν Ἑλληνίδα
οἰκουμένην ἐν τῷ Εὐξείνῳ Πόντῳ, Σινωπέων ἀποικίαν, ἐν
τῇ Κόλχων χώρᾳ. ἐνταῦθα ἔμειναν ἡμέρας ἀμφὶ τὰς τριάκοντα ἐν ταῖς τῶν Κόλχων κώμαις· 23. κἀντεῦθεν ὁρμώμενοι 5
ἐλῄζοντο τὴν Κολχίδα. ἀγορὰν δὲ παρεῖχον τῷ στρατοπέδῳ Τραπεζούντιοι, καὶ ἐδέξαντό τε τοὺς Ἕλληνας καὶ
ξένια ἔδοσαν βοῦς καὶ ἄλφιτα καὶ οἶνον. 24. συνδιεπράττοντο
δὲ καὶ ὑπὲρ τῶν πλησίον Κόλχων τῶν ἐν τῷ πεδίῳ μάλιστα
οἰκούντων, καὶ ξένια καὶ παρ' ἐκείνων ἦλθον βόες. 25. μετὰ 10
δὲ τοῦτο τὴν θυσίαν ἣν ηὔξαντο παρεσκευάζοντο· ἦλθον δ'
αὐτοῖς ἱκανοὶ βόες ἀποθῦσαι τῷ Διὶ τῷ σωτῆρι καὶ τῷ
Ἡρακλεῖ ἡγεμόσυνα καὶ τοῖς ἄλλοις θεοῖς ἃ ηὔξαντο.
ἐποίησαν δὲ καὶ ἀγῶνα γυμνικὸν ἐν τῷ ὄρει ἔνθαπερ ἐσκή-
νουν. εἵλοντο δὲ Δρακόντιον Σπαρτιάτην, ὃς ἔφυγε παῖς 15
ὢν οἴκοθεν, παῖδα ἄκων κατακανὼν ξυήλῃ πατάξας, δρόμου
τ' ἐπιμεληθῆναι καὶ τοῦ ἀγῶνος προστατῆσαι. 26. ἐπειδὴ δὲ
ἡ θυσία ἐγένετο, τὰ δέρματα παρέδοσαν τῷ Δρακοντίῳ, καὶ
ἡγεῖσθαι ἐκέλευον ὅπου τὸν δρόμον πεποιηκὼς εἴη. ὁ δὲ
δείξας οὗπερ ἑστηκότες ἐτύγχανον 'οὗτος ὁ λόφος,' ἔφη, 20
'κάλλιστος τρέχειν ὅπου ἄν τις βούληται.' 'πῶς οὖν,' ἔφασαν,
'δυνήσονται παλαίειν ἐν σκληρῷ καὶ δασεῖ οὕτως;' ὁ δ' εἶπε·
'μᾶλλόν τι ἀνιάσεται ὁ καταπεσών.' 27. ἠγωνίζοντο δὲ παῖδες
μὲν στάδιον τῶν αἰχμαλώτων οἱ πλεῖστοι, δόλιχον δὲ Κρῆτες
πλείους ἢ ἑξήκοντα ἔθεον, πάλην δὲ καὶ πυγμὴν καὶ παγ- 25

κράτιον †ἕτεροι†, καὶ καλὴ θέα ἐγένετο· πολλοὶ γὰρ κατέ- 1
βησαν καὶ ἅτε θεωμένων τῶν ἑταίρων πολλὴ φιλονικία ἐγίγνετο. 28. ἔθεον δὲ καὶ ἵπποι καὶ ἔδει αὐτοὺς κατὰ τοῦ πρανοῦς
ἐλάσαντας ἐν τῇ θαλάττῃ ἀποστρέψαντας πάλιν πρὸς τὸν
βωμὸν ἄγειν. καὶ κάτω μὲν οἱ πολλοὶ ἐκαλινδοῦντο· ἄνω 5
δὲ πρὸς τὸ ἰσχυρῶς ὄρθιον μόλις βάδην ἐπορεύοντο οἱ
ἵπποι· ἔνθα πολλὴ κραυγὴ καὶ γέλως καὶ παρακέλευσις
ἐγίγνετο.

Glossary

Declensions

ἡ κρήνη, τῆς κρήνης - spring		ὁ ἀγρός, τοῦ ἀργοῦ - field		ὁ παῖς, τοῦ παιδός - child	
Nom. ἡ κρήνη	αἱ κρῆναι	ὁ ἀγρός	οἱ ἀγροί	ὁ παῖς	οἱ παῖδ-ες
Gen. τῆς κρήνης	τῶν κρηνῶν	τοῦ ἀγροῦ	τῶν ἀγρῶν	τοῦ παιδ-ός	τῶν παίδ-ων
Dat. τῇ κρήνῃ	ταῖς κρήναις	τῷ ἀγρῷ	τοῖς ἀγροῖς	τῷ παιδ-ί	τοῖς παι-σί(ν)
Acc. τὴν κρήνην	τὰς κρήνᾱς	τὸν ἀγρόν	τοὺς ἀγρούς	τὸν παῖδ-α	τοὺς παῖδ-ας
Voc. ὦ κρήνη	ὦ κρῆναι	ὦ ἀγρέ	ὦ ἀγροί		

Personal Pronouns

Nom.	ἐγώ	I	ἡμεῖς	we
Gen.	ἐμοῦ μου	my	ἡμῶν	our
Dat.	ἐμοί μοι	to me	ἡμῖν	to us
Acc.	ἐμέ	me	ἡμᾶς	us
Nom.	σύ	you	ὑμεῖς	you
Gen.	σοῦ σου	your	ὑμῶν	your
Dat.	σοί σοι	to you	ὑμῖν	to you
Acc.	σέ	you	ὑμᾶς	you

Nom.	αὐτός	(himself)	αὐτή	(herself)	αὐτό	(itself)
Gen.	αὐτοῦ	his	αὐτῆς	her	αὐτοῦ	its
Dat.	αὐτῷ	to him	αὐτῇ	to her	αὐτῷ	to it
Acc.	αὐτόν	him	αὐτήν	her	αὐτό	it
Nom.	αὐτοί	(themselves)	αὐταί	(themselves)	αὐτά	(themselves)
Gen.	αὐτῶν	their	αὐτῶν	their	αὐτῶν	their
Dat.	αὐτοῖς	to them	αὐταῖς	to them	αὐτοῖς	to them
Acc.	αὐτούς	them	αὐτᾱ́ς	them	αὐτά	them

Relative Pronoun – who, which, that

	m.	f.	n.	m.	f.	n.
Nom.	ὅς	ἥ	ὅ	οἵ	αἵ	ἅ
Gen.	οὗ	ἧς	οὗ	ὧν	ὧν	ὧν
Dat.	ᾧ	ᾗ	ᾧ	οἷς	αἷς	οἷς
Acc.	ὅν	ἥν	ὅ	οὕς	ἅς	ἅ

Indefinite Relative Pronoun – whoever, anyone who; whatever, anything which

Nom.	ὅστις	ἥτις	ὅτι (ὅ τι)
Gen.	οὗτινος (ὅτου)	ἧστινος	οὗτινος (ὅτου)
Dat.	ᾧτινι (ὅτῳ)	ᾗτινι	ᾧτινι (ὅτῳ)
Acc.	ὅντινα	ἥντινα	ὅτι (ὅ τι)
Nom.	οἵτινες	αἵτινες	ἅτινα
Gen.	ὧντινων (ὅτων)	ὧντινων	ὧντινων (ὅτων)
Dat.	οἷστισιν (ὅτοις)	αἷστισιν	οἷστισιν (ὅτοις)
Acc.	οὕστινας	ἅστινας	ἅτινα

Correlative Adverbs

Interrogative	Indefinite	Demonstrative	Relative	Indefinite Relative
ποῦ *where?*	που *somewhere (I suppose)*	ἐνθάδε *here* ἐκεῖ [5] *there*	οὗ *where*	ὅπου *where(ver)*
ποῖ *to where?*	ποι *to somewhere*	δεῦρο *to here* ἐκείσε *to there*	οἷ *to where*	ὅποι *to where(ver)*
πόθεν *from where?*	ποθεν *from anywhere*	ἐνθένδε *from here* (ἐ)κεῖθεν *from there*	ὅθεν *from where*	ὁπόθεν *from where(ver)*
πότε *when?*	ποτέ *at some time ever, then*	τότε *at that time, then*	ὅτε *when* ὅταν	ὅπότε *when(ever)*
πῇ *which way?*	πή *some way*	τῇ τῇδε ταύτῃ *in this way*	ᾗ *in which way*	ὅπῃ *in which way*
πῶς *how?*	πως *somehow*	ὧδε , οὕτως *thus, so in this way*	ὡς *how, as* ὥσπερ *as if, just as*	ὅπως *how(ever)* **ὁπωσοῦν** *howsoever*

Correlative Pronouns

Interrogative	Indefinite	Demonstrative	Relative	Indefinite Relative
τίς, τί *who, what?*	τις, τι *someone/thing anyone/thing*	ὅδε οὗτος *this* (ἐ)κεῖνος *there*	ὅς, ἥ, ὅ *who, which*	ὅστις, ἥτις, ὅ τι *anyone who, whoever* **ὅστισ-οῦν** *whosoever, what-*
πότερος *which of two?*	ποτερος *one of two*	ἕτερος *one (of two)*	ὁπότερος *which of two*	ὁπότερος *whichever of two* ὁπότεροσ-οῦν[1] *whichsoever of two*
πόσος *how much?*	ποσός *of some amount*	τοσόσδε *so much/many* τοσοῦτος [5] *so much/many*	ὅσος *as much/ many as* ὅσοσπερ [1]	ὁπόσος *of whatever size/ number*
ποῖος *of what sort?*	ποιός *of some sort*	τοιόσδε *such, this sort* τοιοῦτος *such*	οἷος *of which sort, such as, as* οἷοσπερ	ὁποῖος *of whatever sort*
πηλίκος *how old/large?*	πηλικος *of some age, size*	τηλικόσδε τηλικοῦτος *of such an age, size*	ἡλίκος *of which age, size*	ὁπηλίκος *of whatever age/ size*

λύω, λύσω, ἔλυσα, λέλυκα, λέλυμαι, ἐλύθην: loosen, ransom

	PRESENT		FUTURE		
	Active	Middle/Pass.	Active	Middle	Passive
Primary Indicative	λύω λύεις λύει λύομεν λύετε λύουσι(ν)	λύομαι λύε(σ)αι λύεται λυόμεθα λύεσθε λύονται	λύσω λύσεις λύσει λύσομεν λύσετε λύσουσι(ν)	λύσομαι λύσε(σ)αι λύσεται λυσόμεθα λύσεσθε λύσονται	λυθήσομαι λυθήσε(σ)αι λυθήσεται λυθησόμεθα λυθήσεσθε λυθήσονται
Secondary Indicative	ἔλυον ἔλυες ἔλυε(ν) ἐλύομεν ἐλύετε ἔλυον	ἐλυόμην ἐλύε(σ)ο ἐλύετο ἐλυόμεθα ἐλύεσθε ἐλύοντο			
Subjunctive	λύω λύῃς λύῃ λύωμεν λύητε λύωσι(ν)	λύωμαι λύῃ λύηται λυώμεθα λύησθε λύωνται			
Optative	λύοιμι λύοις λύοι λύοιμεν λύοιτε λύοιεν	λυοίμην λύοιο λύοιτο λυοίμεθα λύοισθε λύοιντο	λύσοιμι λύσοις λύσοι λύσοιμεν λύσοιτε λύσοιεν	λυσοίμην λύσοιο λύσοιτο λυσοίμεθα λύσοισθε λύσοιντο	λυθησοίμην λυθήσοιο λυθήσοιτο λυθησοίμεθα λυθήσοισθε λυθήσοιντο
Imp	λῦε λύετε	λύε(σ)ο λύεσθε			
Pple	λύων, λύουσα, λύον	λυόμενος, λυομένη, λυόμενον	λύσων, λύσουσα, λύσον	λυσόμενος, λυσομένη, λυσόμενον	λυθησόμενος, λυθησομένη, λυθησόμενον
Inf.	λύειν	λύεσθαι	λύσειν	λύσεσθαι	λυθήσεσθαι

2nd sg. mid/pass -σ is often dropped except in pf. and plpf. tenses: ε(σ)αι → ῃ,ει ε(σ)ο → ου

AORIST			**PERFECT**		
Active	Middle	Passive	Active	Middle/Passive	
			λέλυκα λέλυκας λέλυκε λελύκαμεν λελύκατε λελύκασι(ν)	λέλυμαι λέλυσαι λέλυται λελύμεθα λελύσθε λελύνται	**Primary Indicative**
ἔλυσα ἔλυσας ἔλυε(ν) ἐλύσαμεν ἐλύσατε ἔλυσαν	ἐλυσάμην ἐλύσα(σ)ο ἐλύσατο ἐλυσάμεθα ἐλύσασθε ἐλύσαντο	ἐλύθην ἐλύθης ἐλύθη ἐλύθημεν ἐλύθητε ἐλύθησαν	ἐλελύκη ἐλελύκης ἐλελύκει ἐλελύκεμεν ἐλελύκετε ἐλελύκεσαν	ἐλελύμην ἐλέλυσο ἐλέλυτο ἐλελύμεθα ἐλελύσθε ἐλέλυντο	**Secondary Indicative**
λύσω λύσῃς λύσῃ λύσωμεν λύσητε λύσωσι(ν)	λυσώμαι λύσῃ λύσηται λυσώμεθα λύσησθε λύσωνται	λυθῶ λυθῇς λυθῇ λυθῶμεν λυθῆτε λυθῶσι(ν)	λελύκω λελύκῃς λελύκῃ λελύκωμεν λελύκητε λελύκωσι(ν)	λελυμένος ὦ —— ᾖς —— ᾖ —— ὦμεν —— ἦτε —— ὦσιν	**Subjunctive**
λύσαιμι λύσαις λύσαι λύσαιμεν λύσαιτε λύσαιεν	λυσαίμην λύσαιο λύσαιτο λυσαίμεθα λύσαισθε λύσαιντο	λυθείην λυθείης λυθείη λυθεῖμεν λυθεῖτε λυθεῖεν	λελύκοιμι λελύκοις λελύκοι λελύκοιμεν λελύκοιτε λελύκοιεν	λελυμένος εἴην —— εἴης —— εἴη —— εἴημεν —— εἴητε —— εἴησαν	**Optative**
λῦσον λῦσατε	λῦσαι λῦσασθε	λύθητι λύθητε		λέλυσο λέλυσθε	**Imp**
λῦσᾱς, λῦσᾱσα, λῦσαν	λυσάμενος, λυσαμένη, λυσάμενον	λύθείς, λυθεῖσα, λυθέν	λελυκώς, λελυκυῖα λελυκός	λελυμένος, λελυμένη λελυμένον	**Pple**
λῦσαι	λῦσασθαι	λυθῆναι	λελυκέναι	λελύσθαι	**Inf.**

Adapted from a handout by Dr. Helma Dik (http://classics.uchicago.edu/faculty/dik/niftygreek)

δίδωμι, δώσω, ἔδωκα, δέδωκα, δέδομαι, ἐδόθην: give

	Present	Imperfect	Aorist
Active	δίδωμι δίδομεν δίδως δίδοτε δίδωσιν διδόᾱσιν	ἐδίδουν ἐδίδομεν ἐδίδους ἐδίδοτε ἐδίδου ἐδίδοσαν	ἔδωκα ἔδομεν ἔδωκας ἔδοτε ἔδωκεν ἔδοσαν
Imp	δίδου δίδοτε		δός δότε
Pple	διδούς, διδοῦσα, διδόν διδόντος, -ούσης, -όντος		δούς, δοῦσα, δόν δόντος, δούσης, δόντος
Inf.	διδόναι		δοῦναι, δόμεναι
Middle	δίδομαι διδόμεθα δίδοσαι δίδοσθε δίδοται δίδονται	ἐδιδόμην ἐδιδόμεθα ἐδίδοσο ἐδίδοσθε ἐδίδοτο ἐδίδοντο	ἐδόμην ἐδόμεθα ἔδου ἔδοσθε ἔδοτο ἔδοντο
Imp	δίδου δίδοσθε		δοῦ δόσθε
Pple	διδόμενος, η, ον		δόμενος, η, ον
Inf.	δίδοσθαι		δόσθαι

τίθημι, θήσω, ἔθηκα, τέθηκα, τέθειμαι, ἐτέθην: put, place; make

	Present	Imperfect	Aorist
Active	τίθημι τίθεμεν τίθης τίθετε τίθησιν τιθέᾱσιν	ἐτίθην ἐτίθεμεν ἐτίθεις ἐτίθετε ἐτίθει ἐτίθεσαν	ἔθηκα ἔθεμεν ἔθηκας ἔθετε ἔθηκεν ἔθεσαν
Imp	τίθει τίθετε		θές θέτε
Pple	τιθείς, τιθεῖσα, τιθέν τιθέντος, -εῖσης, -έντος		θείς, θεῖσα, θέν θέντος, θεῖσα, θέντος
Inf.	τιθέναι		θεῖναι
Middle	τίθεμαι τιθέμεθα τίθεσαι τίθεσθε τίθεται τίθενται	ἐτιθέμην ἐτιθέμεθα ἐτίθεσο ἐτίθεσθε ἐτίθετο ἐτίθεντο	ἐθέμην ἐθέμεθα ἔθου ἔθεσθε ἔθετο ἔθεντο
Imp	τίθεσο τίθεσθε		θοῦ θέσθε
Pple	τιθέμενος, η, ον		θέμενος, η, ον
Inf.	τίθεσθαι		θέσθαι

ἵημι, ἥσω, ἧκα, εἷκα, εἷμαι, εἵθην: send, release, let go

	Present	Imperfect	Aorist
Active	ἵημι ἵεμεν ἵης ἵετε ἵησιν ἱᾶσι	ἵην ἵεμεν ἵεις ἵετε ἵει ἵεσαν	ἧκα εἷμεν ἧκας εἷτε ἧκεν εἷσαν
Imp	ἵει ἵετε		ἕς ἕτε
Pple	ἱείς, ἱεῖσα, ἱέν ἵεντος, ἱείσης, ἵεντος		εἵς, εἷσα, ἕν ἕντος, εἵσης, ἕντος
Inf.	ἱέναι, epic ἱέμεναι		εἷναι
Middle	ἵεμαι ἱέμεθα ἵεσαι ἵεσθε ἵεται ἵενται	ἱέμην ἱέμεθα ἵεσο ἵεσθε ἵετο ἵεντο	εἵμην εἵμεθα εἷσο εἷσθε εἷτο εἷντο
Imp	ἵεσο ἵεσθε		οὗ ἕσθε
Pple	ἱέμενος, η, ον		ἕμενος, η, ον
Inf.	ἵεσθαι		ἕσθαι

ἵστημι, στήσω, ἔστην, ἕστηκα, ἕσταμαι, ἐστάθην: stand, stop

	Present	1st Aorist (transitive)	Aorist (intransitive)
Active	ἵστημι ἵσταμεν ἵστης ἵστατε ἵστησιν ἱστᾶσιν	ἔστησα ἐστήσαμεν ἔστησας ἐστήσατε ἔστησε ἔστησαν	ἔστην ἔστημεν ἔστης ἔστητε ἔστη ἔστ(ησ)αν
Imp	ἵστη ἵστατε	στῆσον στήσατε	στῆθι στῆτε
Pple	ἱστάς, ἱστᾶσα, ἱστάν ἱστάντος, ἱστᾶσα, ἱστάντος	στήσας, ᾶσα, άν	στάς, στᾶσα, στάν στάντος στάσης στάντος
Inf.	ἱστάναι	στῆσαι	στῆναι, στήμεναι
Middle	ἵσταμαι ἱστάμεθα ἵστασαι ἵστασθε ἵσταται ἱστανται		ἐστησάμην ἐστησάμεθα ἐστήσω ἐστήσασθε ἐστήσατο ἐστήσαντο
Imp	ἵστασο ἵστασθε		στῆσαι στήσασθε
Pple	ἱστάμενος, η, ον		στησάμενος, η, ον
Inf.	ἵστασθαι		στήσασθαι

οἶδα: to know (pf. with pres. sense)

	Perfect	Pluperfect	
Active	οἶδα ἴσμεν οἶσθα ἴστε οἶδε ἴσᾱσι	ᾔδη ᾖσμεν ᾔδησθα ᾖστε ᾔδει ᾖσαν	
Imp	ἴσθι ἴστε		
Pple	εἰδώς, εἰδυῖα, εἰδός εἰδότος, εἰδυίᾱς, εἰδότος		
Inf.	εἰδέναι		
subj/opt	εἰδῶ εἰδῶμεν εἰδῇς εἰδῆτε εἰδῇ εἰδῶσι	εἰδείην εἰδεῖμεν εἰδείης εἰδεῖτε εἰδείη εἰδεῖεν	

εἰμί (to be)

	Present	Imperfect	
Active	εἰμί ἐσμέν εἶ ἐστέ ἐστίν εἰσίν	ἦ, ἦν ἦμεν ἦσθα ἦτε ἦν ἦσαν	
Imp	ἴσθι ἔστε		
Pple	ὤν, οὖσα, ὄν ὄντος, οὔσης, ὄντος		
Inf.	εἶναι		
subj/opt	ὦ ὦμεν ᾖς ἦτε ᾖ ὦσιν	εἴην εἶμεν εἴης εἶτε εἴη εἶεν	

εἶμι (to go; pres. indicate used as the fut. of ἔρχομαι)

	Present	Imperfect	
Active	εἶμι ἴμεν εἶ ἴτε εἶσι ἴᾱσιν	ᾖα ᾖμεν ᾔεισθα ᾖτε ᾔειν ᾖσαν	
Imp	ἴθι ἴτε		
Pple	ἰών, ἰοῦσα, ἰόν ἰόντος, ἰούσης, ἰόντος		
Inf.	ἰέναι		
subj/opt	ἴω ἴωμεν ἴῃς ἴητε ἴῃ ἴωσιν	ἴοιμι ἴοιμεν ἴοις ἴοιτε ἴοι ἴοιεν	

Xenophon's *Anabasis* Book IV: Alphabetized Core Vocabulary List

The following is an alphabetized list of all words that occur eight or more times in Xenophon's *Anabasis* Book IV. This list complements a running vocabulary list of the same words in the introduction. The number of occurrences, indicated at the end of the dictionary entry, were tabulated by the author.

ἀγαθός, -ή, -όν: good, brave, capable, 9
ἄγω, ἄξω, ἤγαγον, ἦχα, ἦγμαι, ἤχθην: to lead, bring, carry, convey, 17
ἀκούω, ἀκούσομαι, ἤκουσα, ἀκήκοα, ἠκούσθην: to hear, listen to, 11
ἄκρος, -η, -ον: topmost; heights, highpoints, 17
ἀλλά: but, yet, 66
ἀλλήλος, -α, -ον: one another, 15
ἄλλος, -η, -ο: other, one...another, 8
ἅμα: at the same time; as soon as, at, along with (+ dat.), 8
ἀμφί: on both sides, 14
ἄν: modal adv., 25
ἀν-ίστημι, -στήσω, -έστησα, -έστηκα, -έσταμαι,,: to make stand up, raise; rise, 10
ἀνα-βαίνω, -βήσομαι, -έβην, -βέβηκα: to go up, climb, mount, 10
ἀνήρ, ἀνδρός, ὁ: a man, 16
ἄνθρωπος, ὁ: human being, person, 18
ἄνω: up, above, 12
ἀπ-έρχομαι: to go away, depart, 15
ἀπό: from, away from. (+ gen.), 14
ἀπο-θνήσκω, ἀποθανοῦμαι, ἀπέθανον, τέθνηκα,,: to die off, perish, 9
ἄρχω, ἄρξω, ἦρξα, ἦρχα, ἦργμαι, ἤρχθην: to begin; to rule, be leader of, 12
αὖ: again, once more; further, moreover, 8
αὐτός, -ή, -ό: -self; he, she, it; the same, 110
ἀπ-ικνέομαι, ἀφίξομαι, ἀφικόμην, --, ἀφῖγμαι, --: to come, arrive, 14
βασιλεύς, ὁ: a king, chief, 10
βούλομαι, βουλήσομαι,,, βεβούλημαι, ἐβουλήθην: to wish, be willing, desire, 13
βοῦς, ὁ, ἡ: ox, bull, cow; cattle, 9
γάρ: for, since, 55
γίγνομαι, γενήσομαι, ἐγενόμην, γέγονα: to come to be, become, be born, 48
δέ: but, and, on the other hand, 377
δεῖ: it is necessary, must, ought (+ inf.), 13
δή: indeed, surely, really, certainly, just, 34
διά: through (+gen) on account of (+ acc), 34
δια-βαίνω, -βήσομαι, -έβην, -βέβηκα: to walk or pass over; cross 27
δίδωμι, δώσω, ἔδωκα, δέδωκα, δέδομαι, ἐδόθην: to give, offer, grant, provide, 12
δοκέω, δόξω, ἔδοξα, δέδογμαι: to seem (good), think, imagine, 34
δύναμαι, δυνήσομαι,,, δεδύνημαι, ἐδυνήθην: to be able, can, be capable, 25
δύο: two, 8
ἑαυτοῦ, -ῆς, -οῦ: himself, her-, it-, thems-, 15

ἐγώ: I, 14
ἐθέλω (θέλω), ἐθελήσω, ἠθέλησα, ἠθέληκα: to be willing, wish, desire, 8
εἰ: if, whether, 37
εἶδον: aor. of ὁράω
εἰμί: to be, exist, 200
εἶπον: aor. of λέγω
εἰς (ἐς): into, to, in regard to (+ acc.), 48
εἷς, μία, ἕν: one, single, alone, 8
ἐκ, ἐξ: out of, from (+ gen.), 30
ἕκαστος, -η, -ον: each, every one, 13
ἐκεῖνος, -η, -ον: that, those, 10
Ἕλλην, Ἕλληνος, ὁ: Greek, 37
ἐν: in, on, among. (+ dat.), 70
ἔνθα: here, there, where, 20
ἔνθεν: from there, on one side; from where, 8
ἐνταῦθα: here, hither, there, thither, then, 28
ἐντεῦθεν: from here, from there, 18
ἐπεί: when, after, since, because, 41
ἐπειδή: when, since, after, 15
ἐπί: near (gen.), to, toward (acc.); near, at, 49
ἐπιτήδειος, -η, -ον: necessities; provisions, 18
ἕπομαι, ἕψομαι, ἑσπόμην: to follow, accompany, escort, 9
ἔρχομαι, εἶμι, ἦλθον, ἐληλυθα: to come or go, 23
ἐρωτάω, ἐρωτήσω, ἠρόμην: to ask, inquire, question, 11
εὐθύς: right away, straight, directly, at once 16
ἔχω, ἕξω, ἔσχον, ἔσχηκα: have, possess; be able; be disposed, 64
ἤ: or (either...or); than, 27
ἡγεμών, ὁ: leader, commander, guide, 15
ἡγέομαι, ἡγήσομαι, ἡγησάμην,, ἥγημαι, ἡγήθην: to lead; consider, believe (dat) 12
ἤδη: already, now, at this time, 8
ἡμέρα, ἡ: day, 36
ἤν: if ever, ἐάν, 10
θέω: to run, 14
ἱππεύς, ὁ: a horseman, cavalry, 10
ἵππος, ὁ: a horse, 11
καίω: to kindle, light, 10
καλός, -ή, -όν: beautiful, fair, noble, fine, 18
Καρδοῦχοι, οἱ: Carduchians, 17
κατά: according to, over (acc); down, against (gen), 25
κατα-βαίνω, -βήσομαι, -έβην, -βέβηκα:: to step, come down, 9
κατα-λαμβάνω, -λήψομαι, -έλαβον,,, -ελήφθην: to seize, lay hold of, find, 16
κατα-λείπω: to leave behind, abandon, 8
κελεύω, κελεύσω, ἐκέλευσα, κεκέλευκα, κεκέλευσμαι, ἐκελεύσθην: to bid, order, command, 13
κλέπτω, κλέψω, ἔκλεψα: to steal; do or seize secretly, 9
κωλύω, κωλύσω, ἐκώλυσα: to hinder or prevent, 14

κώμ-αρχος, ὁ: leader of a town, 11
κώμη, ἡ: town, country town, 27
λαμβάνω, λήψομαι, ἔλαβον,,, ἐλήφθην: to take, receive, catch, grasp, 35
λέγω, λέξω (ἐρέω), ἔλεξα (εἶπον), εἴλοχα, ἐλέγην: to say, speak; gather, 39
λίθος, ὁ: a stone, 12
λόφος, ὁ: hill, 9
λοχαγός, ὁ: captain, 17
λόχος, ὁ: ambush; company, unit of men, 20
μάχομαι, μαχοῦμαι, ἐμαχεσάμην: to fight, contend, quarrel, dispute 10
μέγας, μεγάλη, μέγα: big, great, important, 8
μέν: on the one hand, 94
μένω, μενῶ, ἔμεινα, μεμένηκα: to stay, remain, 14
μετά: with (+ gen.); after (+ acc.), 12
νύξ, νυκτος, ἡ: a night, 18
Ξενοφῶν, -ῶντος, ὁ: Xenophon, 50
ὁ, ἡ, τό: the, 1135
ὁδός, ἡ: road, way, path, journey, 26
οἰκία, ἡ: house, dwelling, building, 12
ὀλίγος -η, -ον: few, little, small, 10
ὅμοιος, -η, -ον: resembling, similar to (dat) 21
ὄπισθεν: (from) behind; in the future; (+ gen.), 9
ὀπισθο-φύλαξ, -ακος, ὁ: rear-guard, 19
ὁπλίτης, -ου ὁ: hoplite, armed soldier, 11
ὅπλον, τό: a tool, implement; arms, 10
ὁπότε: when, by what time, 9
ὅπως: how, in what way; so that, 14
ὁράω, ὄψομαι, εἶδον, ἑώρακα, ὤφθην: to see, look, behold, 50
ὄρθιος, -α, -ον: steep, straight up, sheer, 13
ὄρος, -εος, τό: a mountain, hill, 39
ὅς, ἥ, ὅ: who, which, that, 63
ὅσος, -η, -ον: as many as; all who or which 21
ὅτι: that; because, 38
οὐ, οὐκ, οὐχ: not, 57
οὐδέ: and not, but not, nor, not even, 13
οὐδ-είς, οὐδε-μία, οὐδ-έν: no one, nothing, 22
οὖν: and so, then; at all events, 18
οὗτος, αὕτη, τοῦτο: this, these, 121
οὕτως: in this way, thus, so, 14
παῖς, παιδός, ὁ, ἡ: child, boy, girl; slave, 9
πάλιν: again, once more; back, backwards, 12
παρασάγγης, ὁ: parasang (5.7 or 5.3 km), 15
παρ-έρχομαι, -ειμι, -ηλθον, -εληλυθα: to go past, pass, enter, 13
πᾶς, πᾶσα, πᾶν: every, all, the whole, 28
πεδίον, τό: plain, 12
πελταστής, ὁ: light troop (with light shield) 11

περί: around, about, concerning, 7
πέτρα, ἡ: a rock, a ledge, 9
πλείων, -οντος: more, greater, 9
ποιέω, ποιήσω, ἐποίησα, πεποίηκα, πεποίημαι, ἐποιήθην: to do, make, create, 29
πολέμιος, -α, -ον: hostile; *subst.* enemy, 54
πολύς, πολλή, πολύ: much, many, 71
πορεύομαι, πορεύσομαι, ἐπορευσάμην,,, ἐπορεύθην: to travel, journey, march, 62
ποταμός, ὁ: river, stream 35
πρίν: until, before, 9
πρός: to (acc.), near, in addition to (dat.), 51
προσ-έρχομαι, -ειμι, -ηλθον, -εληλυθα: to come or go to, approach, 10
πρῶτος, -η, -ον: first, earliest, 14
πῦρ, πυρός,τό: fire, 10
στάδιον, τό: a stade, (pl. at times στάδιοι), 9
σταθμός, ὁ: stage (~5 parasangs, distance covered in one day's journey), 16
στενός, -ή, -όν: narrow, 8
στράτευμα, τό: army, expedition, 19
στρατηγός, ὁ: general, 20
στρατιώτης, -ου, ὁ: soldier, 16
στρατόπεδον τό: camp, encampment; army 8
σύ: you, 15
σύν: along with, with, together (+ gen.), 15
ταχύς, -εῖα, -ύ: quick, swift, hastily, 11
τις, τι: anyone, anything, someone, something, 45
τίς, τί: who? which?, 36
τρεῖς, τρία: three, 11
ὑπέρ: above, on behalf of (gen.); over, beyond (acc.), 10
ὑπό: by, because of, from (gen) under (dat) 13
ὑπο-ζύγιον, τό: a yoke-animal, ox, 18
φάλαξ, φάλαγγος, ὁ: phalanx, 11
φανερός, -ά, -όν: visible, manifest, evident, 8
φέρω, οἴσω, ἤνεγκον, ἐνήνοχα, ἐνήνεγμαι, ἠνέχθην: to carry, bring, convey; fly, 9
φεύγω, φεύξομαι, ἔφυγον, πέφευγα,,: to flee, escape; defend in court, 17
φημί, φήσω, ἔφησα, (εἴρηκα, εἴρημαι, ἐρρήθην): to say, claim, assert, 28
Χειρίσοφος, ὁ: Cheirisophus, 45
χιών, -όνος, ἡ: snow, 18
χώρα, ἡ: land, region, country, 12
χωρίον, τό: place, spot, region, 20
ὡς: as, thus, so, that; when, since, 59
ὥσπερ: as, just as, as if, 9
ὥστε: so that, that, so as to, 14